The Thinking Reader

by Ciera Harris

The Thinking Reader
Cultivating Critical Thinkers in the Classroom

Ciera Harris

Copyright © 2025 Ciera Harris. All rights, including for text and data mining, AI training, and similar technologies, are reserved.

Published by John Wiley & Sons, Inc., Hoboken, New Jersey.
Published simultaneously in Canada.

No part of this publication may be reproduced, stored in a retrieval system, or transmitted in any form or by any means, electronic, mechanical, photocopying, recording, scanning, or otherwise, except as permitted under Section 107 or 108 of the 1976 United States Copyright Act, without either the prior written permission of the Publisher, or authorization through payment of the appropriate per-copy fee to the Copyright Clearance Center, Inc., 222 Rosewood Drive, Danvers, MA 01923, (978) 750-8400, fax (978) 750-4470, or on the web at www.copyright.com. Requests to the Publisher for permission should be addressed to the Permissions Department, John Wiley & Sons, Inc., 111 River Street, Hoboken, NJ 07030, (201) 748-6011, fax (201) 748-6008, or online at http://www.wiley.com/go/permission.

Trademarks: Wiley and the Wiley logo are trademarks or registered trademarks of John Wiley & Sons, Inc. and/or its affiliates in the United States and other countries and may not be used without written permission. All other trademarks are the property of their respective owners. John Wiley & Sons, Inc. is not associated with any product or vendor mentioned in this book.

Limit of Liability/Disclaimer of Warranty: While the publisher and author have used their best efforts in preparing this book, they make no representations or warranties with respect to the accuracy or completeness of the contents of this book and specifically disclaim any implied warranties of merchantability or fitness for a particular purpose. No warranty may be created or extended by sales representatives or written sales materials. The advice and strategies contained herein may not be suitable for your situation. You should consult with a professional where appropriate. Further, readers should be aware that websites listed in this work may have changed or disappeared between when this work was written and when it is read. Neither the publisher nor author shall be liable for any loss of profit or any other commercial damages, including but not limited to special, incidental, consequential, or other damages.

For general information on our other products and services or for technical support, please contact our Customer Care Department within the United States at (800) 762-2974, outside the United States at (317) 572-3993 or fax (317) 572-4002.

Wiley also publishes its books in a variety of electronic formats. Some content that appears in print may not be available in electronic formats. For more information about Wiley products, visit our website at www.wiley.com.

Library of Congress Cataloging-in-Publication Data:

ISBN: 978-1-394-27617-2
ISBN: 978-1-394-27618-9 (ebk)
ISBN: 978-1-394-27619-6 (ebk)

Cover Design: Wiley
Cover Image: © cienpies/Getty Images
Author Photo: Victoria Hunt Photography

To my family, whose love fuels me, and to the hardworking teachers around the globe—you are the heart of every child's story.

CONTENTS

Acknowledgments — ix
About the Author — xi
Introduction — xiii

Chapter 1 What Reading Really Is — 1
Chapter 2 Setting Up for Success — 39
Chapter 3 The Reader's Blueprint — 67
Chapter 4 Reading and the Brain — 95
Chapter 5 Schema: The Power of Perspective — 131
Chapter 6 Curiosity: The Motivation Maximizer — 165
Chapter 7 Metacognition: Inquiry and Independence — 193
Chapter 8 Metacognitive Strategies for Success — 227
Chapter 9 Talking (Meaningfully) About Texts — 277

Chapter 10	Fostering Critical Thinking in the Classroom	327
Chapter 11	Building Persistence and Cultivating the Reader's Mindset	373
Closing		409
Index		419

ACKNOWLEDGMENTS

To my incredible husband, Matt, there are no words that can truly capture the depth of my gratitude. From the moment I dreamed of stepping beyond the classroom to pursue a bigger vision, you never hesitated—it was an unwavering "yes" from you, even when the road seemed uncertain. Your love, encouragement, and belief in me have been my constant source of strength.

Thank you for your faith in me when I needed it most, for pushing me when I doubted myself, and for standing by my side through every triumph and challenge. This journey has been made possible because of your endless support, and I am extremely grateful to have you as my partner in both life and dreams. I love you beyond words.

To my amazing friend and colleague, Katie, your positivity, creativity, and unwavering support have been a true gift throughout this journey. I couldn't have written this book without your help. Thank you for being by my side every step of the way.

To my best friend, Renee—your brilliance as an educator is only matched by your incredible friendship. Helping me launch my first-ever workshop set me on the path to this book, and I couldn't have done it without you. Thank you for being there from the very beginning and for believing in me every step of the way.

To the amazing teachers who have been by my side, using and believing in the resources, approaches, and philosophies I teach—your support and encouragement have meant more to me than you will ever know. Your daily emails, feedback, and words of thanks remind me that together, we are making a real difference in the world of literacy. Thank you for believing in me and for all that you do.

ABOUT THE AUTHOR

Ciera Harris is a seasoned educator with more than 15 years of experience in literacy instruction and the author of *The Thinking Reader*, an educational textbook that equips educators with evidence-based strategies to foster critical thinking and deepen reading comprehension in young learners. She brings a wealth of expertise and passion to her role as a presenter and literacy advocate. With a background encompassing 10 years of elementary teaching and 2 years as a K-4 instructional coach, she possesses a deep understanding of the complexities of literacy development in young learners. Currently pursuing her doctoral degree in literacy at St. John's University, Ciera is dedicated to advancing her knowledge and expertise in the field.

Ciera's teaching philosophy is rooted in the belief that fostering a love of reading begins with equipping students to think critically and independently, empowering them to become lifelong learners. Based in Indiana, she is committed to supporting educators worldwide in creating impactful literacy experiences. She has impacted hundreds of thousands of teachers around the world through her multimedia platforms, including *The Literacy Lounge* podcast, her website (cieraharristeaching.com), blog, YouTube channel, and private professional development sessions. Additionally, she offers an exclusive membership called *The Building Comprehension Hub*, where educators can access practical tools to support reading comprehension in the classroom.

Ciera has presented at conferences across the country, including the SDE National Educators Conference in Las Vegas and multiple statewide conferences. She has a particular passion for bringing literacy strategies to underserved communities, having worked with educators both nationally and internationally to close literacy gaps and foster reading equity.

With her doctorate in progress, Ciera plans to continue her research on literacy interventions and expand her resources for educators around the globe. Beyond her professional pursuits, she is a devoted wife and mother of three, residing in Indiana with her family and two beloved dogs. In her leisure time, she indulges her passion for collecting earrings and unwinds by cheering on Notre Dame football. Ciera's unique blend of academic rigor, practical experience, and personal warmth makes her a dynamic and inspiring presenter in the field of literacy instruction.

INTRODUCTION

This book differs from others you might have encountered in your teaching journey. Countless resources are already available if you're looking for intervention strategies to deploy immediately in your classroom or if you're seeking small group activities designed to support fluency and identify needs in struggling readers. But that's not what this book offers. You're here because you and I both sense that something crucial is missing in our approach to teaching reading. Despite our best efforts, incorporating the latest research, and diligently following the science of reading research, it still feels like we're missing a vital piece of the puzzle.

You're here because you believe, as I do, that reading encompasses more than the five literacy components. You want more for your students than just basic literacy skills. You're here because you aspire to cultivate the very best readers your students can be, and together, that's precisely what we will achieve. This book is different because it doesn't just aim to improve reading skills; it seeks to transform how students think about reading and engage with texts.

In this book, I will not merely touch upon the five essential components of literacy—phonemic awareness, phonics, fluency, vocabulary, and comprehension. Instead, I integrate these components into a broader framework designed to build what I call the *Thinking Reader*. A Thinking Reader is cognitively aware of their thinking processes as they read. They don't just decode words; they interact with the text, ask questions, make connections, and reflect on their understanding.

A Thinking Reader identifies as a reader, regardless of their proficiency level. They embrace challenges and persevere through complex texts, employing critical thinking strategies to extract meaning and insights. This transformation from a passive reader to an active, engaged thinker sets this book apart.

We are going to build thinkers, not just readers. I explore strategies that foster deep, reflective, and analytical thinking. I delve into practices that encourage students to see themselves as capable, confident readers who can tackle any text. This book will guide you through creating an environment where students are not just learning to read but are reading to learn, grow, and think critically.

So, if this resonates with you and if you're ready to push your students beyond the basics and into the realm of thoughtful, engaged reading, then you're in the right place. This journey won't be easy, but it will be gratifying. Together, we will reshape how our students view reading and help them become the best thinkers and readers they can be. Welcome to a new way of teaching reading.

Meet Ciera!

When picking up this book, you probably looked at the name and had no idea who I was, so let's fix that! Hi! I'm Ciera Harris, an educational consultant passionate about literacy. My journey in education began at Ball State University in Muncie, Indiana, where I earned both my undergraduate and master's degrees in Elementary Education. I am currently a doctoral candidate at St. John's University, specializing in Literacy. While I could tell you the familiar tale of always knowing I wanted to be a teacher, I prefer to focus on the unique path that led me here. Yes, I love teaching, but my journey has shown me that my true passion lies in working with teachers and helping them inspire a love for reading in their students.

As I started my career in teaching, I quickly realized that I was as enthusiastic about collaborating with my colleagues as I was about teaching my students. I became known as the "literacy geek" who eagerly anticipated planning days when everyone gathered in my classroom to prepare their lessons. This passion extended to mentoring, and I eagerly accepted the mentor-teacher role, where I could share my insights and strategies with others. My enthusiasm for teaching naturally evolved from focusing on children to concentrating on teachers, guiding them to become more effective literacy educators.

After years of teaching in the elementary classroom, I transitioned to an instructional specialist for a K-4 building. While I loved supporting teachers across all grades, I found the scope of the role to be challenging. This realization led me to start my own educational consulting business, Ciera Harris Teaching. Through my business, I have had the privilege of connecting with hundreds of thousands of teachers from across the country and worldwide, all sharing my passion for literacy and my commitment to fostering growth in young readers.

Through Ciera Harris Teaching, I support teachers with online articles, my podcast "The Literacy Lounge," my YouTube channel, social media platforms, and my exclusive membership club, The Building Comprehension Hub. These platforms have allowed me to reach and assist countless educators, sharing strategies and insights beyond the basics of literacy instruction. My experiences as an educator, instructional specialist, and consultant have revealed the profound complexities of literacy and the transformative power of reading. This book is the culmination of everything I've learned and shared with thousands of teachers, offering a deeper understanding of literacy that you will experience as you turn these pages.

Curricula Aren't Enough

As a teacher in the classroom, I experienced the same frustrations and challenges that many of you face. I went through the motions, trying every educational fad—pre-/post-tests, digital literacy, balanced literacy. You name it, we tried it. Yet, despite our best efforts, the results remained the same year after year. We ended up with students on, above, and below levels, neatly fitting into the desired bell curve. But this isn't good enough. The system might be content with these outcomes, but as teachers, we know there's more to literacy and reading than just fitting students into predetermined categories.

Teachers want more than just a checklist of standards to teach. We understand that literacy and reading are about more than meeting benchmarks; they are about life, awareness, and personality. Unfortunately, our current curricula and programs often fail to reflect this understanding. While states across the country claim to value critical thinking and complex reading skills, they still mandate the same old standards, expecting us to teach them in a rote, mechanical way. This approach won't produce the type of readers we aspire to nurture.

A genuinely complex reader who can think, analyze, evaluate, and infer won't emerge from a curriculum that treats literacy as a series of boxes to tick. Developing such a reader requires nurturing curiosity, fostering critical thinking, and encouraging students to ask questions and explore. This type of reader is a one-of-a-kind thinker who sees beyond the text and connects with the world around them. They don't just read; they engage with the material on a deeper level, drawing insights and making connections that go beyond the surface.

> We are going to build thinkers, not just readers.

As educators, we strive to create these Thinking Readers. We want our students to become individuals who are cognitively aware of their reading processes, can engage with texts thoughtfully, and see themselves as capable and confident readers. This goes beyond merely teaching standards; it's about building a culture of curiosity and critical thinking in our classrooms. We aim to inspire our students to become lifelong learners who can navigate complex texts and draw meaningful conclusions.

Together, we can build these Thinking Readers. This book guides you through strategies and practices that move beyond traditional literacy instruction, focusing on developing students' critical thinking and comprehension skills. And don't worry, it is research based! I explore methods to encourage students to think deeply, ask questions, and make connections. By the end of this journey, you will have the tools to transform your students into readers who are not only proficient but also passionate and insightful. Let's embark on this path together and create a new generation of thinkers and readers.

> "I felt overwhelmed, confused and defeated. Now that I understand, have strategies, plans, and understanding, I now feel more confident and motivated to stay on track and keep teaching reading comprehension a priority."
>
> -Kris McRae, 3rd Grade, Walsh Elementary School, Illinois

The Structure of This Book: Building the Thinking Reader

This book is structured around five essential steps to building a Thinking Reader, each designed to guide you through transforming your students into critical thinkers who engage deeply with texts. The image represents these steps:

- Foundations of Reading
- Cognitive Science of a Reader
- Cultivating Metacognitive Thinkers
- Communication and Critical Thinking
- Building Resilience and Persistence

Each step is crucial in creating readers who do more than decode words—they think, analyze, and connect with what they read.

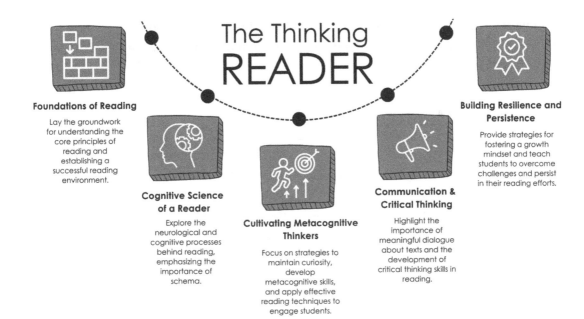

Foundations of Reading

The first step, Foundations of Reading, lays the groundwork for understanding the core principles of reading. This section focuses on establishing a thriving reading environment where the essential literacy components are taught and integrated into a cohesive framework. Here, you learn how to set the stage for effective reading instruction by creating a classroom atmosphere that fosters a love for reading and encourages students to see reading as an essential part of their lives. This foundational knowledge is crucial because it prepares students for the more advanced skills they will develop in the subsequent steps.

Cognitive Science of a Reader

Next, I delve into the Cognitive Science of a Reader. This section explores the neurological and cognitive processes behind reading, emphasizing the importance of schema and how the brain processes and comprehends text. Understanding these cognitive processes is vital for teachers, as it allows you to tailor your instruction to align with how students naturally learn and process information. By applying insights from cognitive science, you can help students develop more effective reading strategies that enhance their comprehension and retention of material.

Cultivating Metacognitive Thinkers

The third step, Cultivating Metacognitive Thinkers, focuses on strategies to maintain curiosity and develop metacognitive skills. *Metacognition*—thinking about one's thinking—is crucial to critical reading. This section provides techniques to help students become aware of their thought processes as they read, enabling them to monitor their comprehension, identify areas of confusion, and apply strategies to improve their understanding. By cultivating these skills, you empower students to take control of their learning and become more independent, reflective readers.

Communication and Critical Thinking

The fourth step, Communication and Critical Thinking, highlights the importance of meaningful dialogue about texts and developing critical thinking skills in reading. This section encourages teachers to create opportunities for students to discuss their reading, share their insights, and engage in debates and discussions. By fostering a classroom culture where open communication and critical analysis are valued, you can help students develop the ability to think deeply about texts, ask probing questions, and connect their reading to broader themes and ideas. This step is essential for building readers who can engage with complex texts and think critically about what they read.

Building Resilience and Persistence

The final step, Building Resilience and Persistence, provides strategies for fostering a growth mindset and teaching students to overcome challenges and persist in their reading efforts. Reading complex texts can be difficult and frustrating for students, but by building resilience and persistence, you can help them develop the grit and determination needed to tackle challenging material. This section offers practical techniques for encouraging students to persevere through difficulties, view mistakes as learning opportunities, and maintain a positive attitude toward reading. By instilling these qualities, you prepare students to become lifelong readers who are not deterred by obstacles but instead view them as opportunities for growth.

> "I realized the importance of connecting with my students as thinkers and learning who they are as readers before diving into curriculum. So many times in the past year I tried implementing thinking strategies but failed. My students didn't understand the connection and I was failing to explain the purpose behind readers being thinkers. The problem was trying to get them thinking while also teaching them new curricular content. I realized you can't do both consecutively. Students need to be taught the foundational skills of thinking first before they can use the strategies effectively in content."
>
> -Courtney R. Sidener, 4th Grade, Bookcliff Christian School, Colorado

Bringing It All Together

Throughout these five steps, the overarching goal is to build readers who can think critically. Each component plays a vital role in this transformation. By laying a solid foundation in reading, you can ensure that students have the essential skills and environment they need to succeed. Understanding the cognitive science behind reading allows you to align your teaching with how students naturally learn, enhancing their comprehension and retention. Cultivating metacognitive thinkers empowers students to be aware of their thought processes, enabling them to become independent and reflective readers.

Encouraging communication and critical thinking fosters a classroom culture where students feel comfortable discussing and analyzing texts, developing their ability to think deeply and make connections. Building resilience and persistence equips students with the grit and determination needed to tackle challenging material, viewing difficulties as opportunities for growth rather than obstacles. These components collectively create a comprehensive framework for literacy instruction that goes beyond basic skills, aiming to develop well-rounded, thoughtful readers.

By following this structured approach, you will be equipped to guide your students on their journey to becoming Thinking Readers. This book is designed to be more than just a collection of strategies; it is a comprehensive guide to transforming how we teach reading and how our students experience it. Each of the five components—Foundations of Reading, Cognitive Science of a Reader, Cultivating Metacognitive Thinkers, Communication and Critical Thinking, and Building Resilience and Persistence—works together to build a new generation of readers who are not only proficient in literacy but also thoughtful, reflective, and engaged thinkers.

Together, we embark on this journey to create readers who do more than decode words. They will engage deeply with texts, think critically about what they read, and connect their reading to the world around them. This transformation is at the heart of the Thinking Reader, and it is the ultimate goal of this book. Let's take this journey together and impact our students' lives by building readers who think, analyze, and grow with every text they encounter.

How to Use This Book

This book provides a clear and structured path that will set you and your students on a journey to becoming enlightened and critical thinkers and readers if followed at the beginning of the year. The first step is to read through this book entirely to make the most out of it. Understanding the big picture and how each component fits together is essential before diving into the individual lessons.

As you read, you'll notice that each chapter concludes with three carefully designed lesson plans. These lesson plans are versatile, suitable for any grade level, and require no prior reading, making them ideal for the beginning of the school year. They are hands-on and engaging, designed to prepare your students for the journey ahead and to ignite their passion for reading. By starting with these lessons, you can create an interactive and stimulating learning environment that sets the stage for developing critical reading skills.

After you have read the entire book, it's time to create a strategic plan tailored to your students' needs. Reflect on which lessons will benefit your students the most and in what order. While the lessons are best followed in the sequence presented in the book, they are flexible and can be adapted to meet the specific needs of your classroom. Inside the book, you'll find images of the lesson plans and a brief overview of each lesson, providing a visual guide to help you plan effectively.

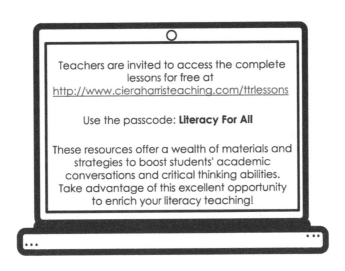

Teachers are invited to access the complete lessons for free at
http://www.cieraharristeaching.com/ttrlessons

Use the passcode: **Literacy For All**

These resources offer a wealth of materials and strategies to boost students' academic conversations and critical thinking abilities. Take advantage of this excellent opportunity to enrich your literacy teaching!

These resources will be invaluable year after year, helping you establish a strong foundation for building amazing readers. As you revisit this book annually, you'll find that these lessons continue to work effectively and grow richer with each implementation. This book is designed to be a lasting resource, evolving with your teaching practice and continually enhancing your students' reading experiences.

By following the steps outlined in this book and utilizing the lesson plans provided, you'll be well on your way to creating a classroom of Thinking Readers—students who are engaged, thoughtful, and passionate about reading. Together, let's embark on this journey and make a lasting impact on our students' lives.

> "One of my win moments is after I taught several weeks of these lessons, one student in her journal wrote about her new schema from a book she read and how she used metacognition, visualization and synthesizing as she read. She actually used these terms!"
>
> -Mindy Carroll, 3rd Grade, Aspen Elementary School, Utah

Benefits of Reading this Book

Benefits for the teacher:

- **Understand what a reader truly is:** Develop a deep understanding that a genuine reader actively thinks, engages with, and questions the text.

- **Equip and encourage use of metacognition:** Equip and encourage teachers to understand and use metacognitive strategies to support their students in becoming active, thoughtful readers.

- **Foster a reader's mindset:** Help teachers foster a reader's mindset in their students, promoting resilience, perseverance, and a passion for continuous improvement in reading.

- **Integrate cognitive science:** Enable teachers to incorporate principles from cognitive science into their reading instruction, enhancing students' understanding and retention of material.

- **Create an intentional learning environment:** Support teachers in creating a learning environment that is intentional about planning for and supporting critical thinking at all student ability levels.

Benefits for the students:

- **Develop critical thinking skills:** Cultivate students' ability to think critically about texts, analyze content, make inferences, and draw meaningful connections.

- **Enhance metacognitive awareness:** Increase students' awareness of their thought processes while reading, enabling them to monitor and improve their comprehension and learning strategies.

- **Foster a love for reading:** Inspire a genuine passion for reading by engaging students with hands-on, interactive lessons that make reading an enjoyable and enriching experience.

- **Build resilience and persistence:** Encourage students to develop resilience and persistence in their reading efforts, helping them overcome challenges and view difficulties as opportunities for growth.

- **Create lifelong learners:** Nurture students to become lifelong learners who are curious, reflective, and capable of independent thought, equipped with the skills to engage deeply with texts throughout their lives.

By focusing on these goals, this book aims to transform how teachers approach literacy instruction and how students experience reading, ultimately creating a more dynamic and thoughtful learning environment.

A Quick Note from Ciera

As you embark on this journey with me, I encourage you always to do what's best for your students. There is no such thing as a perfect curriculum, and research can often contradict itself. The key is to get to know your students, understand their unique needs, and tailor your approach to support, challenge, and inspire them. Love them, encourage them, and create an environment where they feel valued and capable.

Remember, in the end, your students will grow and blossom into the exceptional individuals they were always meant to be. Your dedication, flexibility, and passion for teaching will make all the difference in their lives. Thank you for being an incredible teacher and for committing to this journey of building Thinking Readers together.

CHAPTER 1

WHAT READING REALLY IS

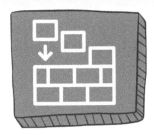

Foundations of Reading

Lay the groundwork for understanding the core principles of reading and establishing a successful reading environment.

Reading is a deeply personal journey intertwined with our identity and experiences. It goes beyond the mechanics of fluency, decoding, and morphology, encompassing a rich tapestry of thoughts, emotions, and reflections. True reading is an immersive experience, an interplay between the text and the reader's mind. As educators, our goal is not merely to produce students who can read words accurately but to cultivate individuals who think critically, connect deeply, and reflect meaningfully on what they read. This chapter is a call to action for teachers to build a classroom culture that celebrates and nurtures these profound aspects of reading.

The essence of reading lies in the unique relationship each student forms with a text. While foundational skills like phonics and vocabulary are essential, they are just the starting point. Reading must be seen as an active process where students engage with the material, draw upon their experiences, and construct new understandings. Teachers play a crucial role in this process by fostering an environment where students feel confident and motivated to explore texts beyond their surface meanings. Doing so, teachers help students become readers and thinkers who approach texts with curiosity and insight.

> True reading is an immersive experience, an interplay between the text and the reader's mind.

Creating a culture of reading in the classroom starts with recognizing and valuing each student's reading journey. It is vital to encourage students to see themselves as readers, regardless of their current skill level. This belief forms the foundation for developing strong, independent readers.

Teachers must emphasize that reading is an act of thinking, where comprehension involves connecting with the text, visualizing, questioning, and applying it to one's life. This holistic approach to reading empowers students to see the relevance of their reading and inspires a lifelong love of learning.

This chapter explores strategies and techniques to help you, as an educator, inspire and develop critical thinkers through reading. By integrating thoughtful questioning, modeling deep comprehension, and fostering reflective discussions, you can transform your classroom into a vibrant community of readers. Together, let's embark on this journey to redefine what it means to be a reader and elevate the role of reading in our students' lives.

Chapter 1 Objectives

The readers will learn that reading is not merely decoding words but involves active thinking, making connections, and comprehending the text on a deeper level.

The readers will gain the ability to distinguish between merely recalling information from a text (consumption) and making meaningful connections and understanding (comprehension).

The readers will learn methods to help students see themselves as capable readers, regardless of their decoding skills, by emphasizing the importance of thinking and personal connections in the reading process.

Reading Is Thinking

We as teachers must refrain from asking our students to come into our classrooms understanding what reading is. And yes, even if you are a 5th or 6th-grade teacher, that is still an assumption we should not make. I know if you ask your students, "What is reading?," they would probably say, "It's when you open a book and read the words." That's the answer that we're going to get. But is that reading? Is being a strong reader all about being a master decoder? Or does it mean we have the best fluency or strongest vocabulary? These are all literacy factors and have an impact, but in the end, none matters unless one key factor is present. "Sounding out or decoding words is part of the reading puzzle, but falls short of real reading. If children don't understand what they read, they're not really reading. If they don't unlock meaning as they read, the words are boring babble and they will never read well or enjoy reading."[1] At the beginning of the year, we have to make sure that we are spending time explaining to all of our students what reading really means.

One of the biggest roadblocks to student success in reading is confidence and belief in themselves. Many students do not see themselves as readers—whether that is because they are still struggling to decode or they simply don't enjoy reading for pleasure. Teachers must ensure that all students see themselves as readers before we can ever reach them all. Teachers need to ensure that students know from the beginning of the year that reading is a personal experience. They need to know that reading is all about who they are as students, as people, and what they bring to the table. If we can explain this and help them understand that they are a reader right now, at this very moment, and what they know in their brain and what they've done in their life makes them a reader, then we can help them understand that they are a reader right now. What you know in your brain and what you've done in your life make you a reader.

Explaining this to students will increase their confidence. It will give them the self-esteem boost they need to tackle the year successfully. It will set them off on the right path during that year and help build them up as readers. By focusing on "What Is Reading" at the beginning of the year, you're helping to set that purpose for the year. You're helping to

---

[1] Zimmermann, S. and Hutchins, C. (2003). *7 Keys to Comprehension: How to Help Your Kids Read It and Get It!* Three Rivers Press.

build strong and independent readers. It's something that teachers need to take time to discuss and explain. You need to show your students that everyone can be a reader.

> "Reading and comprehension are two different concepts. Some children can read but don't understand what they just read. It is our job to help them break down the walls of comprehension."
>
> -Christina Mcnally, 3rd Grade, Roosevelt Wilson Elementary, Texas

Here is where I might lose some of you, and that's okay. I promise to try and win you over as you keep reading. To be a reader, it does not matter if a student struggles with fluency. It does not matter if they can't decode words. It doesn't matter if they don't know a single sight word. Students can still be readers. How? Because reading is thinking. And I think this is one of the biggest and least spoken-about pieces of literacy. It's not JUST about the words. Reading is thinking. It's inside our brains. It's combining all of our knowledge and understanding from that text with what the author has given us and thinking about what you just read.

Even readers who can't read the words themselves but are being read to can do the thinking part, which is the most critical part. I always love to say that your struggling readers can be your most exceptional thinkers. Don't disregard the fact that kids struggle to read the words. That's only part one. We must ensure that we teach our students from day one that reading is all about thinking. It's not JUST about the words. "Real comprehension has to do with thinking, learning, and expanding a reader's knowledge and horizons. It has to do with building on past knowledge, mastering new information, connecting with the minds of those you've never met."[2]

> "I now see comprehension as important as decoding."
>
> -Jennifer Rothstein, 3rd Grade, Jewish Academy of Fine Arts, Maryland

It's okay if students struggle with the words. Teachers can help with that, but that's not the most essential part. The most important part is thinking while you read the words. Teaching students this concept from day one will help set all of your struggling readers, exceptional

---

[2] Zimmermann, S. and Hutchins, C. (2003). *7 Keys to Comprehension: How to Help Your Kids Read It and Get It!* Three Rivers Press.

readers, and everybody in between on the right path. It's okay if students struggle at reading words. That will come with time. But they can think. They can think, connect to that text, visualize the text that the teacher is reading to them, ask questions about that text, and do all these strategies to better their comprehension, and that is what makes them a reader.

When you teach that to your students, especially your struggling and striving readers, you know they will have a confidence boost they won't get from anything else. They're going to see that they already have what they need. It's not something they will learn in two or three years down the road. They've already got it. They can think. Now, when I teach this year, we will improve our thinking. It will be a huge stepping stone toward literacy that your students already have. So when they see that they are a reader already, and we will make them better readers, who wouldn't want to hear that message?

 Reflect: What is reading?

Five Components of Literacy

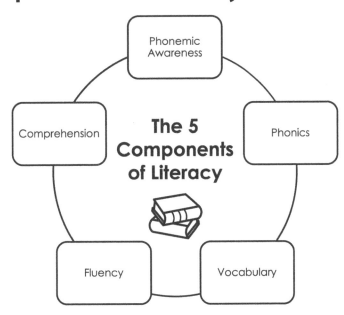

In the pursuit of literacy, the ultimate goal is for all students to comprehend texts on a deeper level. While each literacy component is crucial, comprehension and thinking are paramount to achieving this objective. A comprehensive understanding of a text requires more than just the ability to read words; it necessitates the ability to think critically about what is being read. Therefore, while all literacy components are necessary, the emphasis on comprehension and thinking is vital to genuinely developing proficient readers. The following sections quickly review the five essential components of literacy.

Component 1: Phonemic Awareness

Phonemic awareness is the most foundational literacy skill. It involves recognizing that individual sounds, or phonemes, construct words, making it an auditory skill that predicts reading abilities. This skill is typically introduced in preschool and continues to be essential throughout the school years. It lays the groundwork for understanding how sounds form words, setting students up for success in their future reading endeavors. Students may need more advanced literacy skills with a solid foundation in phonemic awareness.

Component 2: Phonics

While often confused with phonemic awareness, phonics is distinctly different. Phonemic awareness is about sounds; phonics involves the systematic relationship between letters (graphemes) and sounds (phonemes). This relationship is critical for decoding words essential for reading, spelling, and writing. Phonics instruction enables students to understand how letters combine to form words, making it a crucial step in developing reading proficiency.

Component 3: Fluency

Fluency refers to the ability to read text accurately, quickly, and with proper expression. It transforms reading from a mechanical process into an enjoyable and meaningful activity.

Fluency acts as a bridge within the five components, connecting the ability to decode words with the ability to read smoothly and effortlessly. In analyzing the association between fluency and comprehension, an article by Frankel et al. argued that speed and accuracy of word reading tie fluency to word identification, and prosody ties fluency to comprehension.[3] When students achieve fluency, they can focus on understanding the text rather than decoding each word, making reading a more engaging experience.

Component 4: Vocabulary

Vocabulary encompasses the words a person knows and uses in listening, reading, and writing. It builds on background knowledge, schema, and life experiences. A robust vocabulary is essential for understanding texts, as it equips students with the words they need to comprehend diverse materials. Expanding students' vocabulary enhances their ability to engage with and understand the content they encounter, thus supporting overall comprehension.

Component 5: Comprehension

Comprehension is the pinnacle of reading—the ability to understand and interpret the meaning of a text. This skill is the overall objective of reading. Students with solid comprehension can derive meaning from texts and apply this understanding to their lives. Comprehension is the culmination of all the other literacy components; it combines phonemic awareness, phonics, fluency, and vocabulary into a cohesive ability to understand and engage with texts.

---

[3] Frankel, K.K., Becker, B.L.C., Rowe, M.W., and Pearson, P.D. (2016). "What Is Reading?" to what is literacy? *The Journal of Education* 196 (3): 7–17. Sage Publications, Inc. https://www.jstor.org/stable/10.2307/26612624.

Despite the importance of the five literacy components, many teachers find that their students still struggle with comprehension. A study published in *Reading Psychology* discusses the persistent difficulties students face with reading comprehension, even when foundational literacy components like phonemic awareness, phonics, and fluency are taught. The study emphasizes that while these foundational components are crucial, many students, especially struggling readers, continue to have challenges in understanding text, suggesting that more targeted interventions are needed to improve comprehension outcomes.[4] Additionally, another study published in *Reading and Writing* analyzed reading interventions for upper elementary students and found that while interventions focused on fluency and word recognition can improve certain aspects of reading, comprehension often remains a challenge, especially when students lack the ability to connect prior knowledge to new material.[5]

This often happens because the critical element of thinking is missing from instruction. Teaching students to think as they read is essential for deep understanding. Students need to foster critical thinking to decode and read texts fluently, but they will not fully grasp the meaning or implications of what they read. Thus, while the five literacy components are foundational, integrating thinking into literacy instruction is crucial for developing proper comprehension skills. The following table shows how each literacy component supports the overall goals of deeper comprehension.

---

[4] Magableh, I.S.I. and Abdullah, A. (2021). The impact of differentiated instruction on students' reading comprehension attainment in mixed-ability classrooms. *Interchange* 52: 255–272. https://doi.org/10.1007/s10780-021-09427-3.

[5] Jefferson, R.E., Grant, C.E., and Sander, J.B. (2016). Effects of Tier 1 differentiation and reading intervention on reading fluency, comprehension, and high stakes measures. *Reading Psychology* 38 (1): 970124.

Component	Description	Support for Comprehension
Phonemic Awareness	Recognition and manipulation of individual sounds (phonemes) that construct words	Lays the foundation for decoding, crucial for reading words correctly
Phonics	Systematic relationship between letters (graphemes) and sounds (phonemes)	Decoding ability allows readers to recognize words accurately
Fluency	Ability to read text accurately, quickly, and with proper expression	Fluent reading frees cognitive resources for understanding text
Vocabulary	The bank of words a person knows and uses in listening, reading, and writing	Rich vocabulary enhances understanding of complex texts
Comprehension	Ability to understand and interpret the meaning of a text	Combines all components to enable understanding and interpretation of texts, fostering critical thinking

Explanation

The previous table highlights how each component contributes to achieving the ultimate goal of reading comprehension.

- **Phonemic Awareness** is foundational. It ensures that students can recognize and manipulate sounds, which is essential for decoding words.
- **Phonics** builds on this by teaching the relationship between letters and sounds, which is crucial for accurate word recognition.
- **Fluency** allows for smooth and expressive reading, freeing cognitive resources to focus on understanding the text.

- **Vocabulary** is essential for comprehension, providing the necessary words to understand and engage with diverse texts.
- **Comprehension** is the culmination of these components, enabling students to understand, interpret, and think critically about texts.

While the first four components of literacy—phonemic awareness, phonics, fluency, and vocabulary—are essential building blocks, they alone do not guarantee the ultimate goal of reading comprehension. It is possible for students to be proficient in each of these areas yet still struggle with understanding texts, especially as the complexity of reading material increases with age. Gaps in any of the early components can hinder comprehension, but even without those gaps, students may still find themselves unable to engage deeply with the material. This is because comprehension is not just the sum of these parts; it requires higher-order thinking skills, such as making connections, drawing inferences, and synthesizing information. For true comprehension to occur, students must not only be proficient in the foundational skills but also be guided to think critically about the content they are reading. This challenge becomes particularly evident as students advance in their education, where content complexity demands more than just surface-level understanding.

Despite our accumulated knowledge about the vital components of literacy, significant challenges remain in ensuring all students achieve reading proficiency. For example, research highlights that many students experience stagnation in their reading progress around third or fourth grade, a critical period for literacy development. Alarmingly, recent estimates reveal that 64% of fourth graders, including nearly 80% of Black and Hispanic students, are performing at or below proficient levels on standardized reading assessments. This data underscores the persistent gaps in literacy education, particularly for marginalized groups, despite advancements in our understanding of reading comprehension processes.[6]

---

[6] Dore, R.A., Amendum, S.J., Golinkoff, R.M., and Hirsh-Pasek, K. (2018). Theory of mind: a hidden factor in reading comprehension? *Educational Psychology Review* 30 (3): 1067–1089. Springer Nature. https://www.jstor.org/stable/44956427.

Reading Consumption vs. Reading Comprehension

I'm going to start with a scenario. I like getting teachers to put themselves in their students' shoes to gain some empathy for what they are going through as new readers. Teachers tend to forget because they're going through the motions. Sometimes, they just forget what being a 10-year-old in a classroom is like. I want you to put yourself in a situation they see themselves in daily. I want you to pretend that you open a book and read yourself 5 to 10 medical terms.

Medical Condition	Explanation
Polyarteritis Nodosa	Polyarteritis nodosa is a rare autoimmune malady characterized by inflammation affecting medium-sized arteries, resulting in the development of nodular lesions within arterial walls. The etiology remains enigmatic but is thought to implicate aberrant immune responses against vascular structures.
Wegener's Granulomatosis (Granulomatosis with Polyangiitis)	Wegener's granulomatosis is an infrequent autoimmune ailment marked by small-to-medium vessel inflammation (vasculitis) impacting various organs, notably the respiratory system, kidneys, and upper airways.
Hemophagocytic Lymphohistiocytosis (HLH)	Hemophagocytic lymphohistiocytosis is a perilous hyperinflammatory syndrome characterized by uncontrolled proliferation and activation of immune cells, resulting in systemic tissue damage and multi-organ dysfunction.
Pulmonary Arterial Hypertension (PAH)	PAH may arise idiopathically or in association with connective tissue disorders, congenital cardiac anomalies, or exposure to specific toxins or medications. Clinical manifestations include dyspnea, fatigue, anginal chest discomfort, syncope, and hemodynamic instability.
Acute Intermittent Porphyria (AIP)	Acute intermittent porphyria is a rare inherited metabolic disorder characterized by deficiencies in enzymes involved in heme biosynthesis, leading to the accumulation of porphyrin precursors in the body.

These are big, fancy words. You're able to read them out loud. You can decode them. You can verbally say them. And as your "teacher," I ask you to read them. After you read them,

I will ask you about the terms: "What were the terms you read? What did you remember?" And because you're a strong reader, and you place them, you can easily repeat them. Maybe not all of them. Perhaps you can't remember all 10, but a good majority, you'll be able to remember.

What is this testing? Is this testing your ability to comprehend or consume the information? When information is regurgitated, is that comprehension? So that's the big question right now. I want you to understand what comprehension is, proper. Can you repeat what you read, or is it something more?

Reflect: What is comprehension?

Unfortunately, teachers often confuse reading *consumption* with reading *comprehension*. How are they different? Which one might your students be doing when they read? Let's discuss the difference.

We know that we consume oxygen and food. Consumption involves things that we take in. Reading consumption is when a student can remember facts and details from a text. So when you remember those medical facts and repeat them back, you just consume and regurgitate the information. "When students view reading as an opportunity to construct new knowledge, they use higher order thinking more frequently than students who believe that the goal of reading is to establish only a literal understanding of text to give back to the teacher."[7]

I wish I could think of a better word for regurgitate because I know it's a yucky word, but it's the first word that comes to mind! It's just that rote recitation of information back to you. I see a detail, and I'm reciting it back. I know a number, and I'm reciting it back. No connection was truly made, and there needed to be a deeper understanding of the text.

---

[7] Afflerbach, P., Cho, B., Kim, J., and Crassas, M. (2013). Reading: what else matters besides strategies and skills? *The Reading Teacher* 404–448.

Let's go back to the list of medical terms. If I asked you what those medical terms meant, as teachers, you might understand a few of the terms, but many of them, you probably don't know much more other than how to pronounce the word. There was no connection there. There wasn't any deep understanding of the medical terms.

So when students are consuming, that's what's happening. They're reading the text.

They're able to decode. Their fluency is good, and they can tell you lots of information about that text. But the big missing piece is no connection or deep understanding. The students are only consuming the info instead of comprehending it.

Reading Comprehension is when a student can recall details from a text AND make meaning of them. The first part of the definition is the same as reading consumption, but a second part has been added. This means the information has been taken in and then processed for meaning. It means the reader is not just taking it in and spitting it out. They're taking it in and figuring out what this means to them. There are two levels of comprehension. The first is making meaning, and the second is taking it outside the text and applying that meaning to the reader's life. In that second part, connections have been made to that text, and the information of the text has been used in the reader's life.

Proper deep critical comprehension means that you have taken the information from the text and put it in your brain. You are able to dissect, analyze, and evaluate it to make meaning. Then, you take that meaning and determine if you can make any connections to it to make it a more profound understanding in your brain.

Do you truly understand what this character is going through? Do you know the significance of this event? Have you been able to make a connection? And then, have you applied this understanding to your life somehow? Has it changed your way of thinking? Has it changed a viewpoint or an opinion? Has it impacted different things you think about in the world, or has it made you reflect on specific situations you've lived through?

Unfortunately, I see a lot of consumption in the classroom. Everyone, from teachers to students, administrators, and even those going higher into the Department of Education and curriculum designers, has a skewed definition of comprehension.

As teachers, we want our students to refrain from consuming and regurgitating information. We want them to break it down, evaluate, analyze, apply, make connections, and ask questions. We want them to think deeply about this text, think critically, and figure out what it means to them.

 Reflect: What is the difference between consumption and comprehension?

Making Meaning

The latter part of the definition of comprehension is what differentiates consumption from comprehension. It consists of two words: making meaning. Let's break down what that means.

Making meaning is where students can apply the information from the text to their own lives. If they can't connect the text to their lives somehow, it does not have meaning. So, meaning comes from understanding, and understanding comes from experience.

If you have researched the Science of Reading, you know that schema, or background knowledge, is one of the most important things a student brings to the table to comprehend. "As he or she reads, the skilled reader gains access to and integrates relevant knowledge to create a mental model of the text. The informed educator recognizes the importance of background knowledge and designs instruction to activate it, assess it, build it, and facilitate students' connections to it."[8]

Much of a student's ability to read comes from their schema. That is much of the comprehension puzzle, which doesn't come from the text. It comes from the student's

---

[8] Hennessy, N.L. (2020). *The Reading Comprehension Blueprint: Helping Students Make Meaning from Text*. Paul H. Brookes Publishing Co.

ability to THINK and use metacognition to access their brains and use what they already know. A student's experiences, life, the events they've participated in, relationships, the places they've traveled, and everything about them make up one-third of their ability to read and comprehend a text. "Each reader is unique in that he or she possesses certain traits or characteristics that are distinctly applied with each text and situation."[9] So, if you think backward about that definition of comprehension, it all makes sense now. As a reader, you might be able to read and understand the details. But are you also making meaning of them and connecting them to your schema and background knowledge? Are you understanding and relating to the text due to your background knowledge? And then, are you making meaning and connecting it to your own life?

Definition: schema

A mental framework that a student uses to understand and organize information. This includes their prior knowledge, experiences, beliefs, and skills. In reading, a student's schema helps them make sense of new texts by connecting what they already know with what they are learning, enhancing comprehension and retention.

Schema definition from The Reading Teacher: "The process of connecting known information to new information takes place through a series of networkable connections known as schema."[10]

Let's examine an example of the difference between reading comprehension and reading consumption. In this example, we'll have Student A and Student B. Let's pretend you, as the teacher, have just read the text and are asking the class a question.

---

[9] Pardo, L. (2004). What every teacher needs to know about comprehension. *The Reading Teacher* 66 (8): 272–280.

[10] Ibid.

Sarah's Search

Once upon a time in a small town, there was a girl named Sarah who loved animals more than anything else in the world. She spent her afternoons volunteering at the local animal shelter, helping to feed and care for the animals. One sunny Saturday, as Sarah was walking home from the shelter, she noticed a flyer on a telephone pole. It showed a picture of a dog named Max with the words "MISSING SERVICE DOG" in big, bold letters. The flyer explained that Max was a service dog for Mrs. Thompson, a woman known for her kindness and cheerfulness, often seen with Max by her side.

Sarah felt a pang of concern and decided right then that she would do everything she could to find Max and bring him home.

For the next few days, Sarah searched everywhere. She asked her friends, neighbors, and even strangers if they had seen Max. She posted on social media and handed out flyers at the local park. Just when she was starting to lose hope, she heard a faint barking sound coming from an abandoned house at the edge of town. Following the sound, Sarah cautiously entered the old building and found Max, trapped and scared but otherwise unharmed.

Overjoyed, Sarah carefully led Max out and rushed to Mrs. Thompson's house. When Mrs. Thompson opened the door and saw Max, she burst into tears of relief and happiness. She thanked Sarah over and over, explaining how much Max meant to her.

Teacher: Why were Sarah's actions so significant?

Student A: They were substantial because she could find the missing dog.

Let's analyze this answer: Honestly, that was the correct answer. She found the dog, which was a big deal and a significant event in the story. But is this a reading comprehension answer or a reading consumption answer?

Teacher: Why were Sarah's actions so significant?

Student B: They were substantial because since she could find the dog, she could reintroduce it to its owner, who is physically disabled, and without the dog, she couldn't get around. She was lost, figuratively speaking.

Let's delve deeper into this response: It's clear that the student has comprehended the text. They provided a correct answer and explained the reasoning behind it. For instance, she inferred that the character was lost without her dog, a service animal. If Student B hadn't possessed the schema or background knowledge about physical disabilities and the crucial role of service dogs, she wouldn't have been able to make that inference.

Consider a student with no schema regarding service dogs and no awareness or exposure to people with disabilities, particularly physical disabilities or blindness, where service dogs are essential for mobility. Such a student likely wouldn't grasp the significance of the scenario. They might simply think, "Well, she's happy now that she got her dog back," without understanding the more profound implications. This example highlights the two levels of comprehension rooted in a student's schema. What they bring to the text significantly influences their ability to achieve deep critical comprehension.

In this case, Student A consumed the text while Student B genuinely comprehended it. However, Student A might also have comprehended the text; they just needed to provide more information to demonstrate it. As a teacher, if I received Student A's response, I would engage with them further to extract more details. My goal would be to determine whether they are merely consuming the text or truly comprehending it. To do this, I would ask follow-up questions such as:

"She found the missing dog, but why is that important? What impact did that have on the story? Is that a significant event? Why?"

These questions are designed to probe deeper and assess whether the student is comprehending or simply consuming the text.

 Reflect: How can you tell when a student is consuming a text vs. comprehending it? What should you be listening for?

Promoting Comprehension Over Consumption

It all boils down to one crucial aspect: asking the right kinds of questions and expecting more detailed, thoughtful answers. This is fundamentally about the relationship between questions and answers.

Basic questions simply won't suffice. Asking questions like, "Who are the characters?" may be necessary in kindergarten or first grade, but beyond that level, especially in second grade and above, teachers need to move beyond these simplistic inquiries.

For instance, questions such as, "Who was the character's best friend?" or "Why didn't they get along?" are examples of basic, regurgitation questions. These are one-sided, closed questions that do not encourage deeper thinking. We need to eliminate such questions from our repertoire. Our time is too valuable to be spent on questions with only one correct answer that leave no room for making inferences, critical thinking, or analysis.

Instead, we should focus on asking questions that challenge students to think critically and engage more deeply with the text. This approach will help develop their ability to analyze, infer, and understand complex concepts, leading to a richer and more meaningful learning experience.

	Open Question	**Closed Question**
Definition	Open questions are broad and do not have a single correct answer. They encourage students to think critically, analyze information, and express their thoughts and opinions.	Closed questions typically have a specific correct answer, often a yes/no or factual response. They focus on verifying understanding or recalling specific details from the text.
Purpose	Encourages deeper analysis, interpretation, and synthesis of information from the text.	Tests comprehension of explicit information and helps assess whether students have understood specific details or concepts.
Effectiveness	Promotes higher-order thinking skills, encourages creativity, and allows for diverse responses from students.	Useful for assessing basic comprehension skills, factual recall, and verifying understanding of specific information in the text.

Reflecting on the teacher's question about Sarah and her dog, it's evident there was only one correct answer. While it could have been phrased differently, arriving at the answer required inferencing, schema, and critical thinking. Closed questions, when used, must be profound and necessitate a thoughtful process to answer. Alternatively, open-ended questions, which allow for multiple correct answers, encourage deeper student engagement.

Open-ended questions require students to invest time and engage in conversations to arrive at their answers. This process pushes them to evaluate their prior knowledge and analyze the information gathered from the text to formulate a comprehensive response. This method of questioning fosters a richer understanding and a more meaningful connection to the material. We will discuss open-ended questions more deeply later in the book.

So, how can you help your students by providing these more in-depth answers? Here are some strategies:

How do you support your students in providing these more in-depth answers?

- Use tiered questions (like the ones suggested for Student A above) to extract more from the student's answer. Tiered questions help your students think deeper, look for ways to connect, and access schema. They also allow your students to see your expectations for how you want questions to be answered.

- Reflect on how you're modeling answering questions for your students. We should constantly model reading aloud and thinking aloud for our students. In that think-aloud, we should ask ourselves questions and answer them. Within our answers, students will see the depth of the question and the extension of the answer that's needed. You're setting the bar high and keeping it there, supporting your students along the way.

If you only model basic one-answer, one-word, or phrase answers to questions about a text, then that's all they'll think is acceptable. You are also NOT modeling that reading is thinking. That's what students think is needed to answer questions they are being asked. But if you're modeling going into detail, using evidence, and making inferences, then your students will pick up on what is expected of them when they answer a question.

Open-Ended Questions
to ask with any text!

- What do you think the author's message is in this text?
- How do you relate to the characters in the story? Can you connect their experiences to your own life?
- Why do you think the author chose to write this story from the perspective of [a specific character]?
- What emotions did you feel while reading this text? How did the author create those emotions?
- Can you predict what might happen next in the story? What clues from the text support your prediction?
- What questions do you still have about the text? What would you like to learn more about?
- How does the setting of the story influence the events that occur? Can you imagine the story taking place in a different setting?
- What do you think the author wants readers to learn or understand from reading this text?
- Are there any parts of the story that you found confusing or unclear? What strategies could you use to clarify your understanding?
- How does the author use descriptive language to create vivid images in your mind?
- Can you identify any themes or recurring ideas in the text? How are they developed throughout the story?
- If you could change the ending of the story, what would you change and why?
- What lessons or morals can be learned from the experiences of the characters?
- How does the author build suspense or tension in the story? What effect does it have on the reader?
- How do you think the story might be different if it were told from a different character's perspective?

Quick Tip: Prepare your questions in advance. You need to know your text and control where you want the text conversation to go. Do this by prepping your open-ended questions in advance!

Reading Strategies vs. Reading Skills

I address reading strategies later in this book, but it is crucial to understand the significant impact that reading strategies have on a child's ability to comprehend compared to reading skills. Research supports the concept that reading strategies make a substantial difference in comprehension. "In teaching comprehension strategies, we focus on how readers can actually get better at reading rather than simply on how they answer questions and retell. Although it remains critically important to focus on content, we now know that teaching children to approach and learn content strategically makes it more likely that they'll understand, retain, and reapply the information."[11]

This highlights the importance of strategies over skills. While reading skills such as decoding and fluency are foundational, they only sometimes ensure deep comprehension. Conversely, strategies equip students with tools to actively engage with the text, think critically, and make connections. Strategies such as predicting, questioning, clarifying, and summarizing enable students to navigate complex texts and enhance their understanding.

Focusing on strategies also helps students become more independent readers. They learn to monitor their comprehension and employ different techniques when encountering difficulties. This strategic approach to reading fosters a deeper and more meaningful interaction with the text, leading to better retention and the ability to apply knowledge in various contexts.

By emphasizing reading strategies, you prepare your students to become more proficient and thoughtful readers, capable of understanding and analyzing a wide range of texts. This approach ultimately leads to improved comprehension and a lifelong love of reading.

---

[11] Keene, E.O. and Zimmerman, S. (2013). Years later, comprehension strategies still at work. *The Reading Teacher* 66 (8): 601–606.

	Reading Skills	**Reading Strategies**
Definition	Reading skills are the fundamental abilities or competencies that enable individuals to decode, understand, and interpret written language.	Reading strategies are deliberate, goal-directed techniques or approaches that readers use to comprehend text, extract meaning, and engage with written material effectively.
Purpose	Reading skills provide the necessary building blocks for proficient reading. Decoding skills enable readers to translate written symbols into sounds, while fluency allows for smooth and expressive reading.	Reading strategies help readers actively engage with text, enhance comprehension, and navigate challenges encountered during reading. They empower readers to construct meaning from text by employing cognitive, metacognitive, and affective processes.

Strategies are metacognitive concepts such as visualization, asking questions, synthesizing, and determining importance. These strategies are more impactful than other skills because they actively engage the reader within the strategy itself. They rely on what the reader brings to the text and what the reader is doing in their mind. For instance, readers can only make connections by combining their background knowledge with information from the text. Similarly, visualization requires readers to merge their internal knowledge with the rhetoric from the passage. I talk more about metacognition and metacognitive strategies later in the book.

I refer to reading strategies as "Student-Centric." This means they keep the reader at the center of their focus, emphasizing the reader's thoughts while engaging with the text. Focusing significantly on reading strategies is essential if we want our students to be active participants in the reading process.

Remember, reading is THINKING. It is all about the dynamic interaction between the reader and the author. This process involves asking questions, visualizing the story, using background knowledge, and monitoring one's thoughts through metacognition. Active reading, which improves comprehension, requires active thinking where students simultaneously monitor the text and their cognitive processes.

A student could be the most fluent reader, with excellent decoding skills and a strong vocabulary foundation; however, proper comprehension will only occur by engaging in the reading process and actively thinking about the text. Reading strategies are essential for fostering this level of active involvement and ensuring that students not only read but truly understand and connect with the material.

Reading Skills	Reading Strategies
Main Idea Author's Purpose Cause & Effect Compare & Contrast Fact & Opinion Genre Plot Point Of View Sequencing Theme Story Elements	Making Predictions Asking Questions Summarizing Visualizing Making Connections Monitoring Comprehension Inferring Evaluating

On the other side is the traditional approach to teaching reading comprehension: reading skills. Reading skills are what I call "Text-Centric," meaning they prioritize the content within the text as the most crucial element. These skills do not include or involve the reader in any meaningful capacity.

For example, consider teaching the skill of identifying the main idea. This is a one-sided approach focused solely on the text. While understanding the main idea is important, it doesn't fully engage the reader or encourage them to think critically about what they are reading. True reading comprehension involves more than just extracting information; it requires the reader to be actively engaged and to connect with the text on a deeper level.

To achieve this, you must shift your focus from solely teaching reading skills to emphasizing reading strategies. Reading strategies are designed to make the reader actively participate in the reading process. These strategies involve the reader's thoughts, background knowledge, and cognitive processes, creating a more prosperous and dynamic interaction with the text.

For instance, while identifying the main idea is essential, you should also teach your students to ask questions about the text, make predictions, visualize scenes, and synthesize information. These strategies help students become more engaged and thoughtful readers, allowing them to better understand and retain information.

While reading skills are essential, to foster true reading comprehension and create active readers, you must prioritize reading strategies. These strategies ensure that the reader is not just passively receiving information but actively engaging with the text, thinking critically, and making meaningful connections. The following table shows a quick example of how you can take a simple reading skill, such as the main idea, and ensure that you take them further to encourage deeper comprehension and more critical thinking.

Traditional Text-Based Skill	Deeper, Reader-Involved Skill	Metacognitive Approach
Objective: Identify the main idea of a passage.	**Objective**: Understand the main idea and relate it to personal knowledge and experiences.	**Objective**: Reflect on the process of identifying the main idea and how it enhances understanding.
Activity: Read the passage and find the main idea.	**Activity**: Read the passage, find the main idea, and connect it to your own experiences or other texts.	**Activity**: Read the passage, identify the main idea, connect it to prior knowledge, and reflect on how this process aids comprehension.
Questions: "What is the main idea of this passage?"	**Questions**: "What is the main idea of this passage? How does this idea relate to something you already know?"	**Questions**: "What is the main idea of this passage? How did you figure it out? How does connecting this idea to your own experiences or knowledge help you understand the text better?"
Example Exercise: "Read the passage and write down the main idea."	**Example Exercise**: "Read the passage, write down the main idea, and then write a paragraph on how this idea connects to something you have experienced or learned before."	**Example Exercise**: "Read the passage, write down the main idea, explain how you identified it, and reflect on how this process helped you understand the text. Also, write about how this main idea connects to your prior knowledge or experiences."
Assessment: Correct identification of the main idea.	**Assessment**: Correct identification of the main idea and a clear connection to personal knowledge or other texts.	**Assessment**: Correct identification of the main idea, a clear explanation of the identification process, and a reflective connection to personal knowledge or experiences.

This table demonstrates how to move from a simple, text-based skill of identifying the main idea to a more profound, more involved critical thinking skill. This approach engages students more comprehensively and encourages them to reflect on their thinking processes, enhancing their overall comprehension and metacognitive abilities.

Skills vs. Strategies

Reading Skills	Reading Strategies
- Reading skills are typically associated with abilities required to answer comprehension questions - Skills are more automatic - Reading skills are usually assessed by a type of question after reading - Skills are very repetitive, involved practice and feedback - Actions associated with reading skills are automatic and routine - Students use a reading skill without even knowing it - Reading skills are practiced within the same manner across multiple situations	- Students are actively thinking about the ideas in the text if they are going to understand - Strategies are not about answers, but about actions readers take to remember the text - Students use reading strategies intentionally to meet a specific goal - Strategies are not learned by repetition, but from teacher think-alouds or modeling - Needs to be based on a complex text so students aren't pretending to practice - Strategies can become skills over time - Strategies are effortful, deliberate, and active involvement

As I said, I discuss reading strategies later in this book, but I wanted to lay down this groundwork because when I discussed the overarching question, "What is Reading?," I must include reading strategies.

Promoting active involvement in the text is crucial for developing readers who are not merely decoding words but are engaged thinkers. Active reading encourages students to interact with the text on a deeper level, fostering critical thinking and comprehension. By teaching students to use metacognitive strategies, such as questioning, visualizing, and summarizing, you help them become more aware of their thought processes and how they can be used to enhance understanding. This approach transforms reading from a passive activity into an active and dynamic process, where students are continually interacting with and reflecting on the text.

Building Thinking Readers means cultivating individuals who recognize that their brains must be engaged in the reading process. These readers understand that reading involves a give-and-take relationship between themselves and the author. They use strategies when necessary, realizing that comprehension is not automatic but requires active participation and mental effort. By promoting this mindset, you are helping students develop the skills and habits needed for lifelong learning and intellectual engagement. A Thinking Reader is not just a person who reads words on a page but someone who actively constructs meaning, makes connections, and thinks critically about what they read.

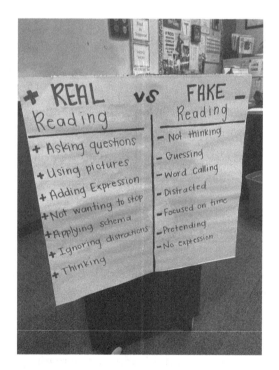

What a Thinking Reader Is and Isn't

Aspect	Active Reading	Non-active Reading
Metacognitive Skills	The reader actively monitors comprehension and adjusts strategies as needed.	The reader reads through text without self-monitoring or adjustments.
Critical Thinking	The reader engages deeply, questioning and evaluating the content.	The reader accepts information without deeper analysis or questioning.
Connecting to Prior Knowledge	The reader relates new information to existing knowledge and experiences.	The reader processes information in isolation, without making connections.
Asking Questions	The reader formulates questions to explore and understand the text more deeply.	The reader focuses solely on the text, not considering broader questions.
Visualizing	The reader creates mental images to enhance understanding and memory.	The reader reads the text without forming any mental images.
Summarizing	The reader periodically summarizes key points to reinforce understanding.	The reader moves on without summarizing or reviewing key information.
Making Prediction	The reader anticipates future events or outcomes in the text, staying engaged.	The reader does not think ahead or make predictions about the text.
Reflecting	The reader considers the implications and personal relevance of the text.	The reader finishes the text without reflecting on its meaning or relevance.
Using Fix-Up Strategies	The reader employs strategies like rereading or looking up words to overcome difficulties.	The reader ignores confusion and continues reading without clarification.
Engaging in Discussions	The reader discusses the text with peers, gaining diverse insights and perspectives.	The reader reads alone without discussing or sharing insights.

Reading Is Me, Reading Is Thinking, Reading Is Power

Reading is a multifaceted journey that intertwines personal identity, critical thinking, and the boundless power of discovery. At its core, reading is deeply personal—*Reading Is Me*—as it reflects our unique experiences and perspectives, turning every story into a reflection of who we are. But reading is also an intellectual endeavor—*Reading Is Thinking*—requiring us to engage deeply with texts, analyze ideas, and draw meaningful connections. This active engagement transforms words into understanding and fosters critical thinking. Ultimately, *Reading Is Power*, offering a gateway to knowledge and the tools to explore the world, satisfy curiosity, and grow as lifelong learners. Together, these elements demonstrate that reading is not just a skill but a dynamic process of personal growth, intellectual exploration, and empowerment.

Reading Is Me

Reading is a deeply personal experience, reflecting who we are as individuals. Every reader brings their own schema, or background knowledge, to a text, which shapes their interpretation and understanding. This means that no two readers will have the same experience with a book, as their personal histories, emotions, and perspectives color their reading. For instance, a story about a family might resonate differently with someone who has a large, close-knit family compared to someone who has grown up in foster care. These unique experiences and perspectives make reading a highly individualized activity.

When students recognize that reading is an extension of themselves, they begin to see it as a reflection of their identity rather than just a school assignment. They start to understand that their personal experiences and knowledge contribute to their reading experience, making it richer and more meaningful. This realization can be incredibly empowering for students, as it validates their individual perspectives and encourages them to engage more deeply with texts. It transforms reading from a chore into a personal journey of discovery and self-reflection.

Reading Is Thinking

Reading is fundamentally an act of thinking, and this cognitive engagement is what makes comprehension possible. Beyond decoding letters and words, reading requires the brain to make connections, analyze information, and draw conclusions. At its core, comprehension involves processing the ideas within a text, relating them to prior knowledge, and constructing meaning. This intricate thinking process transforms reading from a mechanical skill into an intellectual exercise, allowing readers to engage deeply with ideas, infer meaning beyond the surface, and critically evaluate what they read. Without active thinking, words remain static on the page, and true understanding is never achieved.

Thinking is the most powerful aspect of comprehension because it bridges the gap between words and understanding. Comprehension thrives on the reader's ability to question, predict, synthesize, and evaluate as they navigate through a text. This active engagement not only enhances understanding but also fosters empathy, creativity, and critical thinking skills. By thinking through what they read, students can uncover layers of meaning, grasp complex concepts, and apply knowledge to their own lives. It is this active cognitive involvement that empowers readers to move beyond memorization and into meaningful learning.

Ultimately, teaching students to think as they read is one of the most impactful strategies educators can employ. When we help students become intentional thinkers, we equip them with the tools to approach any text with curiosity and confidence. This approach not only strengthens their comprehension but also cultivates lifelong skills that extend far beyond the classroom, allowing them to navigate and make sense of the increasingly complex world around them.

Reading Is Power

Reading is the key to unlocking the secrets of the universe. It holds immense power because it is a gateway to knowledge and understanding. Everything we want to know about the world around us can be found in books, waiting to be discovered. By reading, we can explore different cultures, learn about historical events, delve into scientific theories, and much more. This vast reservoir of information empowers students, giving them the tools to understand and navigate the world.

To help your students realize the power of reading, you need to create a learning environment that sparks their curiosity and encourages exploration. Curiosity is a driving force behind the power of reading. When students are curious, they are motivated to read and explore new topics. As educators, we can cultivate this curiosity by introducing students to a wide range of reading materials and encouraging them to ask questions and seek answers. By creating an environment where curiosity is valued and nurtured, you can help your students see reading as an exciting and rewarding activity.

Provoking curiosity in students involves providing them with diverse and engaging reading materials that cater to their interests and challenge their thinking. This involves asking thought-provoking questions, providing intriguing experiences, and making reading an integral part of their learning journey. It also means fostering a classroom culture where questioning and exploration are encouraged. When students see how reading can answer their questions and expand their horizons, they begin to appreciate its true value. They understand that reading is not just a means to an end but a powerful tool for lifelong learning and personal growth.

Building a Reading Identity

By emphasizing that reading is a personal and powerful experience, you can help students develop a reading identity. This identity is crucial for fostering a love of reading and a commitment to lifelong learning. When students see themselves as readers, they are more likely to engage with texts, seek out new reading materials, and continue reading outside the classroom. This self-perception is essential for their academic success and personal development.

Teachers play a pivotal role in helping students build their reading identities. By validating their experiences, encouraging their curiosity, and showing them the power of reading, teachers can inspire them to become passionate, confident readers. This involves creating a classroom culture that celebrates reading and provides opportunities for students to explore and reflect on their reading experiences. It also means modeling a love of reading and demonstrating how reading can enrich our lives.

Reading is much more than a mechanical skill; it is a deeply personal and powerful experience. By helping students see that reading is thinking, reading is me, and reading is power, teachers can transform their approach to reading and inspire a lifelong love of learning. Through thoughtful engagement, personal connection, and the recognition of reading's immense power, they can develop strong, critical readers who are not only academically successful but also equipped to navigate and understand the world around them. Let us commit to fostering this transformative understanding of reading in our classrooms, ensuring that every student sees reading as an essential and enriching part of their identity and learning journey.

Closing

As I conclude this chapter, it's essential to reflect on the transformative power of fostering a culture of reading in our classrooms. When students begin to see themselves as readers, they embark on a journey that transcends the mechanics of fluency and decoding. They start to understand that reading is a dynamic process of thinking, connecting, and engaging with the world. By nurturing this perspective, we empower our students to become thoughtful, independent readers who can navigate texts with confidence and curiosity.

Reading holds immense power in shaping critical thinkers and lifelong learners. When we emphasize that reading is about thinking deeply, questioning, and making personal connections, we equip our students with the tools to explore and understand complex ideas. This shift in perspective helps students realize that their experiences and reflections are valuable components of the reading process. By fostering this mindset, we create an environment where students feel motivated to engage with texts and see reading as a meaningful, enriching activity.

> "Many children enter school knowing they are able to learn and to enjoy learning. For many reasons, they come up against a lot of hurdles and lose that confidence they had at the eager age of five years. The lessons you teach show me how to help those students to regain their positive self image as a student who is capable of great strides in learning."
>
> -Ann Stern, Grades K-4, Cuba Elementary School, New Mexico

In developing strong, critical readers, we lay the foundation for academic success and personal growth. Our students will not only excel in their studies but also become informed, empathetic individuals capable of making thoughtful contributions to society. As educators, we have the privilege and responsibility to guide our students on this path, helping them discover the joy and power of reading. Let us continue to inspire and support our students in becoming the readers and thinkers they are destined to be.

Consider these questions as you ponder this issue more and try the following lessons.

End of Chapter Reflection Questions:

- How do reading strategies take comprehension to the highest level?
- How do we effectively model the difference between reading words and reading with your mind (thinking)?
- Why is it important to get buy-in at the start of the year?

Lessons to Try

As mentioned in the Introduction, you can access all these lessons for free by visiting `http://www.cieraharristeaching.com/ttrlessons` and using the passcode: `literacy for all`. This resource provides comprehensive materials and strategies designed to enhance students' academic conversations and critical thinking skills. Don't miss out on this valuable tool to support your literacy instruction!

"Reading Is Me" Lesson

The lesson plan "Reading Is Me!" is designed to help students identify as readers and reflect on their reading habits and attitudes. The lesson begins with a "stand up/sit down" activity where students respond to questions about their reading experiences, fostering self-awareness and group discussion about the diverse nature of reading preferences. This interactive activity sets the stage for students to understand that being a reader is a personal journey and that everyone's experiences and tastes in reading materials are unique.

The core of the lesson involves reading the story "Miss Brooks Loves Books (And I Don't)" and engaging in a discussion using targeted questions. This story provides a relatable context for students who may feel disconnected from reading, showing them that it's normal to not enjoy every book and that finding the right book can be transformative. The discussion questions encourage students to think critically about their reading experiences, understand the character's journey, and relate it to their own lives. This part of the lesson emphasizes the importance of perseverance in finding books that resonate with individual interests and highlights the diverse nature of reading journeys.

The lesson concludes with a creative activity where students define what it means to be a reader and create personal and classroom posters affirming their identities as readers. This visual and tangible affirmation reinforces the idea that everyone can be a reader, regardless of their past experiences or current preferences. By displaying these posters, teachers can create an inclusive and supportive reading environment.

Quick Tip Encourage students to share their personal reading journeys and preferences openly, fostering a classroom culture where all types of reading are valued. This can help students feel more comfortable and motivated to explore different genres and types of books, ultimately enhancing their reading experiences and confidence.

"Reading Is Thinking" Lesson

This lesson plan aims to redefine the concept of reading for elementary students by contrasting "fake reading" with "real reading." The lesson begins with a teacher reading a short text without demonstrating any thinking or comprehension, followed by a discussion on whether this constitutes reading. Students are encouraged to explore and express their definitions of reading. Through guided questions and activities, they discover that reading involves active engagement, thinking, and interaction with the text. The lesson incorporates a T-Chart activity to distinguish between "fake" and "real" reading behaviors, and students practice these behaviors in pairs.

The importance of this lesson lies in its focus on developing critical thinking and comprehension skills. By highlighting that reading is not merely decoding words but involves understanding, questioning, and connecting ideas, students learn to become more thoughtful and engaged readers. This approach helps to combat the issue of "fake reading," where students may appear to be reading but are not truly comprehending the material. By instilling these habits early, students are better equipped to handle more complex texts in the future and develop a lifelong love for reading.

Teaching this lesson provides numerous benefits. It fosters an environment where students feel comfortable discussing their thoughts and questions about a text, promoting deeper understanding and retention. Additionally, the collaborative activities enhance social and communication skills as students work together to identify and practice real reading behaviors. Teachers can also use this lesson as a foundation for building more advanced reading strategies throughout the year.

Quick Tip When teaching this lesson, use a variety of texts that are engaging and relevant to your students' interests. This will help to capture their attention and make the concept of real reading more relatable and enjoyable.

"Reading Is Power" Lesson

The "Reading Is Power" lesson plan is designed to illustrate the essential role of reading in empowering individuals through a hands-on activity. In this lesson, students are initially tasked with building a catapult without any instructions, which is expected to be challenging and frustrating. This experience serves as a metaphor for the lack of power that comes with not having access to information. After this initial attempt, students are provided with written instructions and given another opportunity to build the catapult. This time, with the aid of reading, they are expected to achieve greater success and efficiency. The lesson is structured to lead students to the realization that reading provides access to crucial knowledge and skills that are otherwise inaccessible.

The importance of this lesson lies in its clear demonstration of how reading can transform difficult tasks into manageable ones by providing necessary information and guidance. By comparing the two attempts at building the catapult, students experience firsthand the difference that reading can make in understanding and performing tasks. This lesson not only emphasizes the practical benefits of reading but also encourages students to appreciate reading as a powerful tool that can enhance their abilities and broaden their horizons. It aligns with essential questions such as the power of reading over those who do not read and how reading can be a source of knowledge, exploration, and personal growth.

Teaching this lesson offers numerous benefits. It actively engages students in a collaborative and reflective process, fostering critical thinking and problem-solving skills. By making the connection between reading and practical success, students are likely to develop a deeper appreciation for reading and be motivated to improve their literacy skills.

Moreover, the lesson incorporates differentiated instruction to cater to various reading levels, ensuring that all students can participate meaningfully.

Quick Tip

Ensure to facilitate reflective discussions after each part of the activity, encouraging students to share their insights and connect the lesson to broader real-life contexts. This will help reinforce the understanding that reading is not just a classroom activity but a vital skill for navigating and succeeding in the world.

CHAPTER 2

SETTING UP FOR SUCCESS

Foundations of Reading

Lay the groundwork for understanding the core principles of reading and establishing a successful reading environment.

Many teachers, including myself, are eager to dive straight into the curriculum and establish a routine. As a Type A personality, I thrive on routines and schedules. As a classroom teacher, I was always ready to start following the curriculum map as soon as the first week of school ended. I wanted to jump right into teaching and get things moving.

However, I've learned that this approach doesn't create successful readers. It's crucial to spend time at the beginning of the year laying a solid foundation, getting to know your students as readers, and preparing your environment to support their reading journey. As discussed in Chapter 1, you cannot assume your students know what reading truly entails when they enter your classroom. Taking the time to establish these foundations before jumping into the curriculum will significantly impact your students' overall success.

This chapter explores the importance of dedicating time at the start of the year to build a strong foundation for reading. It covers strategies for understanding your students as readers and creating an environment that supports their growth. By prioritizing these steps, you will set your students up for long-term success in their reading journey.

Chapter 2 Objectives

 The readers will learn why dedicating time at the beginning of the school year to build relationships with students is essential for fostering a successful reading environment.

 The readers will gain knowledge on how to match books to students' interests, likes, dislikes, and cultural backgrounds to enhance their engagement and love for reading.

 The readers will discover how student motivation and providing choices in reading materials can significantly affect their reading stamina and comprehension.

 The readers will learn about additional factors such as genre, text structure, culture, memory, discussion, and access to instruction that can influence a student's reading comprehension and strategies to address them.

Getting to Know Your Readers

The most crucial task for a teacher at the beginning of the year is to get to know each and every one of their students. We all recognize the importance of relationships; we cannot effectively teach someone we don't truly understand. But it goes even beyond that. Understanding your students as readers can significantly enhance your reading instruction, leading to greater academic gains throughout the year. It's essential to know your students not only as learners but as individuals, understanding their cultures, habits, likes, and dislikes. The more time you invest in getting to know them at the beginning of the year, the more success you'll see as the year progresses. This foundational effort sets the stage for a year filled with meaningful connections, engaged learning, and academic achievement.

Why Is This Important?

- **Matching books:** Students' engagement in the books they read can help them fall in love with reading. When you get to know your readers more and find out their likes, dislikes, wants, dreams, memories, and pastimes, you can better help students find the right book. When students are early readers (grades K-3), they don't yet know the possibilities that are out there for reading. Teachers must help and guide them and match books to make the magic happen.

- **Finding texts:** When you pick books to read aloud or find texts to use for lessons, it's essential to really consider what texts you pick. Your students' engagement level and access to the schema are directly correlated with their ability to comprehend the text you chose. So, by knowing your readers on a deeper level, you can better select texts for small groups, mini-lessons, or even classroom read-alouds that match your students.

- **Understand schema:** Schema is the most essential tool that students bring to the table. Their ability to access and use their schema can directly impact their level of comprehension. So, when teachers get to know students better, they know what is and is not in the student's schema and can provide texts that match the students' schema to help make reading lessons and experiences more concrete and connected. I talk more about schema later in Chapter 5.

Relationships matter. We know that. But what do we actually need to do? What steps should we take to build them? While "Get to Know You" games and team-building activities are great, we must delve deeper. We need to understand our students at their core. What motivates them? What brings them joy? What makes them sad or upset? What experiences have shaped them? This information is crucial in understanding what drives them as readers.

> The more time you invest in getting to know them at the beginning of the year, the more success you'll see as the year progresses.

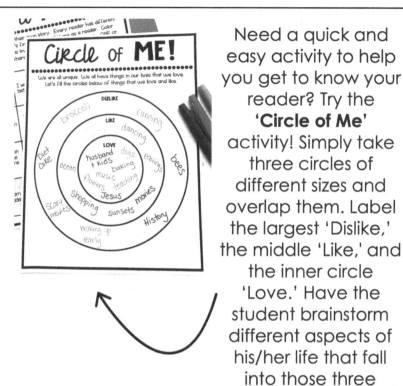

Need a quick and easy activity to help you get to know your reader? Try the **'Circle of Me'** activity! Simply take three circles of different sizes and overlap them. Label the largest 'Dislike,' the middle 'Like,' and the inner circle 'Love.' Have the student brainstorm different aspects of his/her life that fall into those three categories. Use this information to help you get to know and guide your reader!

Take a moment to reflect on yourself as a reader. What motivates you to read? It's shaped by who you are at this point in your life—your interests, preferred genres, likes and dislikes, and your life experiences. All these factors influence the books you choose. If you don't take the time to understand these aspects about your students, you won't be able to guide them to reach their full potential by the end of the year.

42   The Thinking Reader

TIPS FOR BUILDING RELATIONSHIPS WITH YOUR STUDENTS

- **Create opportunities for one-on-one interaction:** Schedule individual check-ins with students to discuss their progress, goals, and any concerns they may have. This shows that you value their individual needs and perspectives.
- **Share personal anecdotes:** Share personal experiences with your students to help them see you as a relatable human being, not just an authority figure. Don't be afraid to be vulnerable!
- **Incorporate student interests:** Incorporate students' interests and preferences into your lesson plans whenever possible. This shows that you value their input and makes learning more engaging.
- **Provide positive reinforcement:** Offer praise and encouragement to students for their efforts, achievements, and improvements. Positive reinforcement can boost students' confidence and motivation.
- **Create a collaborative classroom culture:** Foster a sense of collaboration and teamwork among students by incorporating group activities, discussions, and projects into your lessons.
- **Respect students' opinions:** Respect students' opinions, even if they differ from your own. Encourage open dialogue and critical thinking in the classroom.
- **Be available:** Make yourself available to students outside of class time for extra help, questions, or just to talk. This shows that you are accessible and supportive.
- **Show empathy:** Show empathy towards students' challenges and struggles by acknowledging their feelings and offering support and understanding.
- **Celebrate achievements:** Celebrate students' achievements, both big and small, to acknowledge their hard work and accomplishments.
- **Encourage autonomy:** Provide opportunities for students to make choices and take ownership of their learning. Empowering students can help build confidence and independence.
- **Follow up:** Follow up on conversations, concerns, or goals discussed with students to show that you are invested in their progress and well-being.
- **Be consistent:** Maintain consistency in your interactions, expectations, and discipline to build trust and stability in the classroom environment.

Reflect: How do you currently get to know your students? What might you do differently after reading this chapter?

Setting Up for Success

Factors That Impact Comprehension Success

Current research shows that students need to master five main factors of literacy in order to succeed in reading: phonemic awareness, phonics, fluency, vocabulary, and comprehension. As stated in Chapter 1, all of the components of literacy can be present and strong, but comprehension can still be a struggle for many. At the beginning of the year, as you get to know your students, it's essential to know and recognize other factors that can potentially affect a student's reading and comprehension outside of the five literacy components.

Factors That Can Impact Comprehension
➤ Schema and Background Knowledge
➤ Motivation
➤ Voice and Choice
➤ Genre

Schema and Background Knowledge

Research shows[1] that the best tool a reader brings to a text is their schema. "A reader's comprehension depends on her ability to relate the information that she gets from the text with her pre-existing background knowledge."[2] What a student already knows and understands about a topic when reading drastically impacts their comprehension. One of the first things that happens in our brains when reading is in the frontal lobe, which registers the level of interest and connection we have to what we are reading. That instant connection can make our brains turn on or turn off.

Students need to understand the power behind their schema and learn how to use it to their advantage when reading. "The implications of the theory for reading in general are

---

[1] Pardo, L. (2004). What every teacher needs to know about comprehension. *The Reading Teacher* 272–280.

[2] Gilakjani, A.P. and Ahmadi, S.M. (2011). The relationship between L2 reading comprehension and schema theory: a matter of text familiarity. *International Journal of Information and Education Technology* 142–149. https://doi.org/10.7763/ijiet.2011.v1.24.

that the more schematic knowledge a reader brings to a reading passage the better he or she is able to make predictions and inferences about a text and the better he or she is able to comprehend it."[3] As teachers, we also need to consider this tremendously when picking mentor texts, articles, and activities for our students. We need to prioritize giving students things to read that they DO have schema on to help them progress their reading comprehension.

Motivation

"Motivation is one of the most essential factors that has a direct impact on the development of reading comprehension, but the teachers need to know that the students are motivated differently. They should make the classroom as an enjoyable space to motivate them and increase their confidence, spontaneity, autonomy, and self-stimulation. Teachers need to pay attention to students' interests and their requirements."[4] As I mentioned, one of the first things that happens inside the brain when we read is the brain recognizing whether we have schema and interest in the topic we are reading. The more interest we have, the more our brain will stay focused and motivated, and the better our memories will recall information. It's a scientific fact. "When students read on the topic of reported interest to them, whether working animals or robotics, they employed a greater number and range of comprehension processes. This tells us that if our goal is to stretch students' comprehension muscles, we should provide them with texts of interest."[5] So, a student's motivation level is scientifically directly correlated with their ability to comprehend a text.

---

[3] Tierney, R., and Pearson, D. (1986). Reading Education Report Center for the Study of reading; Bolt, Beranek, and Newman, Inc., 46. Schema theory and implications for teaching reading: A conversation. https://eric.ed.gov/?id=ED281140.

[4] Mohseni Takaloo, N. and Ahmadi, M. (2017). The effect of learners' motivation on their reading comprehension skill: a literature review. *International Journal of Research in English Education* 4 (1): 286–314. https://doi.org/10.1080/02702711.2016.1235648.

[5] Duke, N.K., Pearson, P.D., Strachan, S.L., and Billman, A.K. (2011). Essential elements of fostering and teaching reading comprehension. In: *What Research Has to Say About Reading Instruction*, 4e, 286–314.

To keep students motivated, we need to allow them to choose what they read. We must do what we can to match the right book with the right reader. I love how in the book *From Striving to Thriving*, by Stephanie Harvey and Annie Ward, they say, "Change the book, change the reader,"[6] and it's SO TRUE! If we can get the students matched with the right book based on their interests, likes, and wants, then we won't need to teach them stamina. They will automatically have it!

Voice and Choice

Let me ask you this: Are there people right now selecting the books you read? Is someone finding articles and placing them in front of you? Or are they choosing books they think might interest you? No, that doesn't happen. We love reading as adults because we get to choose what we want to read. This should also be the case in our classrooms. Allow students to have a voice in selecting the texts they read. "When students can choose their reading materials, they are more likely to read. Choice is key to motivation and academic independence."[7]

Quick Tip

But what if you're trying to teach a specific skill? Here's one of the best tips you can take away from today: When selecting books and articles for your lessons, take the time to find multiple options for your students. If you're teaching a lesson on identifying the main idea and details in nonfiction articles, why not provide three to four different choices? It doesn't matter what they read as long as everyone is working toward the same goal. If offering choices increases their motivation, engagement, and overall comprehension, then it's worth the extra few minutes to find those articles.

---

[6] Harvey, S. and Ward, H. (2021). *From Striving to Thriving: How to Grow Confident, Capable Readers*. Scholastic.

[7] Schunk, D.H., Meece, J.L., and Pintrich, P.R. (2013). *Motivation in Education: Theory, Research, and Applications*, 4e. Pearson.

Genre

A book is a book is a book. That is true and not true at the same time. Books may all look alike on the outside, but on the inside, they are all structured and written in unique ways. That's why there are genres; classifications of the types of books that we read. If a student doesn't have exposure to a specific genre they are reading, it can impact their comprehension. This is one of the reasons why students typically struggle with nonfiction. Growing up, their parents usually read fiction out loud to them. So, when they get to school and begin to read nonfiction, they struggle. They are used to characters, plots, and the typical fictional text structure, and then we throw them into a new genre. Of course, they are going to lack comprehension!

It's very important to expose students to as many genres as possible and to take the time to teach the characteristics of each genre. This allows students to pick up on the specific differences between the genres and identify them as they read.

Setting Up for Success

Text Structure

A typical fictional text follows a conventional structure, characterized by standard story elements and a clear plot diagram. This familiar format helps students navigate the narrative with relative ease. However, when authors deviate from this norm by incorporating techniques such as flashbacks, prequels, or instances where characters break the fourth wall to address the reader directly, it can significantly disrupt the reader's comprehension. These unconventional text structures, although enriching the narrative complexity, can challenge students by creating confusion and making it difficult to follow the storyline. Such structural nuances demand higher cognitive engagement, which might hinder some readers' ability to grasp the unfolding events and the overall message of the text. Consequently, understanding these elements is crucial for fostering students' ability to analyze and appreciate diverse narrative techniques.

Definition: text structure

Text structure refers to the way a written work is organized and presented. It includes how information is arranged within a text, helping readers to understand the flow of ideas. Common text structures include narrative (story-like), chronological (in time order), compare and contrast, cause and effect, and problem and solution. Understanding text structure helps readers follow the author's message more clearly and improves comprehension, especially when reading nonfiction or informational texts.

Culture

Figurative language, slang, and multiple-meaning words are all deeply intertwined with language and culture. These elements are embedded in the books teachers read in the classroom. Students from diverse cultural backgrounds may not pick up on these linguistic and cultural cues, making it challenging for them to fully grasp the story. Even within the same country, regional phrases and expressions can vary widely, potentially confusing students who are unfamiliar with them. These language diversities can hinder students' comprehension and engagement with the text.

Furthermore, the cultural relevance of a story plays a significant role in students' understanding. For example, American students reading about a young girl celebrating her quinceañera—a cultural tradition marking a girl's 15th birthday—may find the concept confusing if they are not familiar with it. This highlights the importance of identifying the language and cultural components within a book and providing students with the necessary support and scaffolding.

Instead of leaving students to decipher these elements on their own, educators should offer context and explanations. This approach helps bridge cultural gaps and ensures that all students can engage with and comprehend the material effectively. By acknowledging and addressing these linguistic and cultural differences, you can create a more inclusive and supportive learning environment where every student has the opportunity to succeed.

Memory

Memory and age are closely linked, influencing how much we can reasonably expect students to retain and comprehend. Younger students generally have shorter attention spans and less developed memory capacities, so they are often asked to remember less complex information. Conversely, older students with more mature cognitive abilities can handle greater amounts of information and more intricate texts.

It's essential to consider these developmental differences when assigning reading materials. A student who struggles with longer texts may have memory challenges. Memory is a critical aspect of brain development, and it matures at different rates depending on age and individual growth. If a student finds even simpler texts challenging to remember and recall details from, it might be beneficial to incorporate memory-boosting activities into their routine.

Engaging students in memory exercises throughout the week can help strengthen their memory skills. Activities such as mnemonic devices, memory games, and repetition techniques can be effective in enhancing their ability to retain and recall information. By tailoring reading assignments to match their developmental stage and incorporating targeted memory activities, you can support students in overcoming these challenges and improving their reading comprehension skills.

Discussion

Proper comprehension is not a one-way street; it involves multiple perspectives beyond just those of the reader and the author to truly delve into the text. Too often, we expect students to navigate this complex process alone, but comprehension thrives in a collaborative environment. As adults, we naturally engage in discussions about what we read, sharing insights, asking questions, and seeking alternative viewpoints. This social aspect of reading enhances our understanding and deepens our engagement with the material.

The same holds true for students. Their comprehension significantly improves when they are given opportunities to discuss the text with their peers. Engaging in conversations about what they read allows them to articulate their thoughts, clarify misunderstandings, and gain new insights from others' perspectives. This interactive process not only reinforces their understanding but also encourages critical thinking and deeper analysis.

The availability and ability of students to discuss a text can directly impact their comprehension. Structured classroom discussions, reading groups, and peer-to-peer interactions provide valuable platforms for this exchange. Encouraging students to verbalize their thoughts and questions helps solidify their understanding and makes the reading experience more enriching and enjoyable. By fostering a collaborative reading environment, you can support students in developing stronger comprehension skills and a more profound appreciation for the texts they encounter.

I talk more about encouraging discussion and collaboration in Chapter 9.

Access to Instruction

A reader needs access to a teacher who not only understands reading but also knows how to effectively teach it. A skilled teacher models the cognitive processes involved in reading, offering students a glimpse into the mental strategies and thought patterns that proficient readers use. This insider's perspective is invaluable, as it demystifies the reading process and helps students understand how to navigate texts and comprehend their content.

When students are taught by a teacher who lacks a deep understanding of reading instruction, they may struggle to develop the necessary skills for effective reading and comprehension. This gap in teaching expertise can lead to significant challenges for students as they attempt to decode and make sense of texts on their own.

To address this issue, it is crucial for teachers to continually advance their knowledge of reading instruction and comprehension strategies beyond their undergraduate education. Ongoing professional development is essential to stay current with the latest research, methodologies, and best practices in the field of literacy education. Reading newly published professional development books is an excellent way for teachers to enhance their understanding and refine their teaching techniques.

By investing in your own education, you can better support your students, providing them with the tools and guidance needed to become confident and competent readers. Continuous learning empowers teachers to create more effective and engaging reading experiences, ultimately leading to improved literacy outcomes for their students.

> "This opened my eyes to how important it is to set the groundwork for what reading is and excite my students to want to develop their skills and spark curiosity. I feel more confident as a reading teacher!"
>
> -Amanda Ventling, 2nd Grade, St. John the Baptist School, Ohio

Give Them Access

As mentioned, getting to know your students fuels you with knowledge to help book match for your students. When you know your students, you can provide the books that you know (or hope) they will enjoy reading. But to do this, you need books! Providing ample access to books is one of the most important keys to their success for the year. "It is widely accepted that effective and engaged comprehenders tend to read more than their struggling counterparts. Particularly, the volume of experiences students have interacting with texts both in and out of the classroom significantly correlates with their overall reading success which suggests that effective comprehension instruction should provide students with ample opportunities to engage with texts."[8]

Your library is the heartbeat of your classroom. It is the area where students get to explore their own interests. Additionally, it is where students get to relax and see how exciting books are. Honestly, this is the most critical area of the classroom. Therefore, you must spend time analyzing your classroom library. It is crucial to ensure that books are appropriate for students while showing them how magical books are. "In addition to volume as an influencing factor, the quality and range of books to which students are exposed (e.g., electronic texts, leveled books, student/teacher published work) has a strong relationship with students' reading comprehension."

Your emphasis on your library can indirectly impact students' attitudes toward reading. If you are not excited about it, your students will likely not be. Similarly, if you do not show pride in your library or want to spend time in it, neither will your students. Honestly, teachers have a significant impact on student opinions toward reading. You need to show students how amazing it is when you get time to pick out a book, sit down, and explore the pages.

Quick Tip

Classroom libraries are hard to build. Teachers should not have to spend their own money on books for the classroom. However, having a solid classroom library is essential. If students do not have choices to meet their different interests, they will think books do not apply to what they like. This is absolutely not the case! There are books out there for every interest, hobby, and topic! So, search garage sales, library sales, Facebook group donations, and Scholastic book clubs for sales. These are great options for buying lots of books at reasonable prices.

---

[8] Duke, N.K., Pearson, P.D., Strachan, S.L., and Billman, A.K. (2011). Essential elements of fostering and teaching reading comprehension. In: *What Research Has to Say About Reading Instruction*, 286–314.

Sadly, some teachers are unable to create their own library. This may be a school policy or due to a limited budget. However, this should not stop students from reading books. Instead, the school library needs to become your best friend. You MUST make it a priority to take students to the library. They need ample opportunities to go throughout the week to find books. This time will prove to them how excellent books are.

Does having lots of books mean a strong classroom library? Not necessarily! There are other aspects you want to consider when building and analyzing your classroom library. "It is not enough to have shelves full of books; the collection needs to be carefully curated, weeded, and updated regularly in order to ensure it has books to entice every reader in the room. Just as produce managers remove bruised peaches and limp lettuce from the aisles, we need to review our collections regularly, adding recently published gems, replacing worn-out favorites, and eventually removing books that don't circulate."[9]

Old Versus New

It's essential to maintain a balance between new and older published books in your classroom library. This balance ensures a diverse range of topics, writing styles, and illustrations, providing students with a wealth of choices. Newer books often reflect contemporary themes and modern language, while older books can offer timeless stories and classic perspectives. By including both, you cater to varied interests and expose students to a broader literary landscape.

Variety of Genres

Every student has unique interests, but many might have only explored fiction and nonfiction books. Introducing a variety of genres—such as poetry, historical fiction, and graphic novels—can open up new worlds for them. Students who think they prefer fiction

---

[9] Harvey, S. and Ward, H. (2021). *From Striving to Thriving: How to Grow Confident, Capable Readers*. Scholastic.

or nonfiction may discover a newfound love for other genres once given the opportunity to explore them.

Exposing young readers to a wide range of genres is crucial for their overall literary development. It not only broadens their understanding of what literature can offer, but it also helps them discover different ways that stories and information can be presented. For example, a student who has never read poetry might find themselves captivated by the rhythm and imagery of language, while another might be drawn to the compelling way graphic novels combine visual storytelling with text. Each genre offers unique experiences, from the emotional depth of historical fiction to the creativity and structure of science fiction or fantasy.

Furthermore, introducing students to various genres can increase the likelihood of them finding something they truly enjoy, which can enhance their motivation to read. When students are given the freedom to explore a wide literary landscape, they can find books that resonate with their individual preferences, making reading a more enjoyable and engaging activity. This sense of discovery fosters lifelong readers who see literature as a diverse and enriching source of knowledge and pleasure, rather than a one-size-fits-all experience. By encouraging genre exploration, educators can cultivate a more inclusive and dynamic reading environment that speaks to every student's unique tastes and interests.

Organization

Effective organization is crucial for a well-functioning classroom library. Students should be able to quickly locate the books they are interested in, enhancing their reading experience and encouraging independent exploration. Organize your library by genre, topic, author, and series. This method not only helps students easily find the books they want to read but also simplifies the process of putting books away. An organized library is an inviting space that fosters a love of reading and makes the vast array of choices more accessible to all students.

By implementing these strategies—balancing old and new books, offering a variety of genres, and maintaining an organized library—you create a dynamic and engaging reading environment that supports diverse learning styles and preferences.

Representation of All Students

Do you have representation of ALL of your students in your classroom? If not, now is the time to update with more diversity. Your library needs to reflect the population of your students. In other words, the books must represent ALL students. "Building a classroom library while infusing multicultural content and multiple perspectives into the learning environment is an important job for teachers. Students need to have direct access to meaningful and relevant texts, and the classroom library is the optimal location."[10]

---

[10] Howlett, K.M. and Young, H.D. (2019). Building a classroom library based on multicultural principles: a checklist for future K-6 teachers. *Multicultural Education* 26: 40–46.

It is helpful to use the analyzing chart when performing a quick audit. This is a great way to ensure you have the needed representation. "Even though the number of children of color in the U.S. continues to rise, the number of books published by or about people of color has stayed the same or decreased. It is ultimately up to each educator to take action, make a commitment to seeking the necessary high-quality texts, and prioritize the value of building and continually growing a rich MC (multi-cultural) classroom library. It must be a top priority for our students not only to see themselves reflected in the classroom and school libraries but also to receive the educational equity that is the promise of our nation."[11]

While analyzing your classroom library, you can eliminate unwanted books to make room for new ones. You may donate ones you no longer want or set them aside to rotate them throughout the years. Either way, students must find books that reflect who they are.

Showcasing Select Books

How do you highlight special books throughout the year? How do you get students excited about your library and draw them in? Showcasing special books is a fantastic way to generate enthusiasm and engagement among students. Consider creating a designated spot in your classroom where you can feature books related to upcoming holidays, special days, or thematic events. This dynamic display will capture students' interest and curiosity, making them eager to explore new options.

If you don't already have a showcase area, now is the perfect time to set one up! Regularly updating this spot with fresh, relevant selections keeps the library experience lively and engaging. Whether it's books about seasonal holidays, historical events, or themed weeks, students will look forward to discovering what's new and exciting in the spotlight.

The classroom library is one of the most impactful areas of the classroom. It serves as a hub where students can learn more about themselves, their community, and the world around them. By thoughtfully curating and highlighting special books, you provide students with opportunities to connect with diverse perspectives and ideas. This not only broadens their understanding but also fosters a sense of inclusion and curiosity.

---

[11] Howlett, K.M. and Young, H.D. (2019). Building a classroom library based on multicultural principles: a checklist for future K-6 teachers. *Multicultural Education* 26: 40–46.

Moreover, an engaging classroom library is a powerful tool for motivating students to become independent readers. By regularly introducing them to new and exciting books, you can inspire a lifelong love of reading. Highlighting their progress and celebrating their reading milestones further reinforces their growth and confidence.

Let Them Read!

The final piece of the puzzle—let your students read! You've taken time to get to know them, and you've used that information to find the perfect book. Now it's time to let them read! As the years have gone by, the amount of time students actually get to read during the day has significantly decreased. One third of children ages 6–17 say their class has a designated time during the school day to read a book of choice independently, but only 17% do this every or almost every day.[12] There is a direct correlation between the volume of reading a student experiences and their success and ability to read and learn.

While we are laying a successful foundation at the beginning of the year, make sure to include perfecting your independent reading routine. Independent reading is one of the most important parts of your daily routine. Without it, students don't have the time or ability to actually put into practice what they are being taught to do. How do you perfect a craft without having time to practice? However, implementing independent reading is much more than finding time in your schedule. The next section is about perfecting independent reading time and how you can make it work for you and your students.

Independent Reading Priorities

First and foremost, independent reading must be made a priority. This means it should NEVER be canceled. And yes, I mean never! Too often, unexpected events arise: a special guest comes to speak, a ceremony takes place in the gym, or another subject, like math or

---

[12] Harvey, S. and Ward, H. (2021). *From Striving to Thriving: How to Grow Confident, Capable Readers*. Scholastic.

writing, runs overtime. As a result, independent reading time gets cut. This must not happen. "An unhurried daily block of independent reading should be the centerpiece of our reading curriculum."[13]

Canceling independent reading sends a detrimental message that reading for enjoyment is easily dismissible and less important than other activities. It implies that other parts of the school day take precedence over independent reading time. Allowing interruptions to encroach upon this critical period inadvertently devalues the practice of reading for pleasure and personal growth.

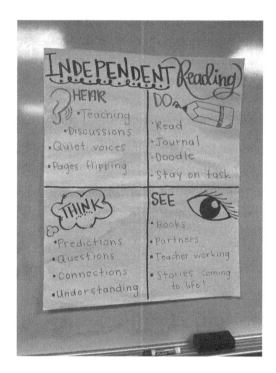

We must convey that, no matter what happens in our day, our reading time is sacred and will not be disrupted for any reason. Independent reading time should be seen as a

---

[13] Harvey, S. and Ward, H. (2021). *From Striving to Thriving: How to Grow Confident, Capable Readers*. Scholastic.

non-negotiable part of our schedule, much like lunch or recess. It is essential for fostering a love of reading and building lifelong readers.

During independent reading, students immerse themselves in books that capture their interests and imaginations. This uninterrupted time allows them to explore different worlds, learn new concepts, and develop their reading skills at their own pace. It is a time for everyone to enjoy, cherish, and love.

Furthermore, by consistently honoring this time, you model the importance of reading to your students. You demonstrate that reading is not just an academic task but a valuable and enjoyable activity that deserves its own dedicated time. This commitment helps to instill a sense of importance and respect for reading in your students, encouraging them to see it as an integral part of their daily lives.

Making independent reading a steadfast priority in your classroom sends a powerful message to your students. It tells them that reading is important, valued, and irreplaceable. By protecting this time from interruptions, you foster a culture that celebrates and prioritizes reading, ultimately contributing to your students' academic success and personal development.

Reading Stamina Is NOT a Thing

Yes, I said it. You have been tricked! Reading stamina is a facade to teach students that they have to love every book that is put into their hands. I completely understand teaching attention stamina in younger grades. This is needed. But reading stamina, not so much. "The more we focus on engagement, the less we need to focus on grit and stamina."[14]

Why? Because with the RIGHT book in the RIGHT reader's hands, reading stamina isn't a problem. You won't need to teach the student to focus and keep their attention for 21 minutes to fill in the chart. The stamina will come naturally. It will come from a place of want. So, if a student is unable to hold their stamina, it most likely isn't the student—it's

---

[14] Harvey, S. and Ward, H. (2021). *From Striving to Thriving: How to Grow Confident, Capable Readers*. Scholastic.

the book. Be relentless about changing the book to help find the right book for the right reader. This is so important!

Ways to Make Independent Reading Work

Consider these tips to help make independent reading work:

- **Every choice is a good choice.** Let the readers read what they WANT! It doesn't matter if it is a cookbook, graphic novel, a how-to book, or a wordless picture book. Reading is reading. To take away or limit students' choices is quite possibly hindering their love of reading.
- **Teach real vs. fake reading.** Your students need to know what reading is. We cannot assume, even in higher grades, that students know what "reading" is. Teach them what real reading is and what fake reading is. Have these conversations at the beginning of the year and quite often throughout the year to ensure your students know your expectations.
- **Teach reading voices.** Reading voices are a fantastic way of explaining "thinking" to students. Just like we do, students hear voices in their heads when they read. This voice falls into one of three categories. #1—Distracting Voice. This voice is distracting us from our reading and our thinking. #2—Interacting Voice. This voice is the voice we hear when we read the words, captions, and text in the book. And #3—Reacting Voice. This voice is what we think about the text voice. It's the voice we hear when we stop, ask questions, clarify our thinking, etc. Teaching these three voices can help distinguish which type of "thinking" students should be experiencing when reading.
- **Get rid of recording sheets and logs.** Yes, this, too, can hinder your students' love of reading. What's the purpose? Accountability? There are better ways to hold our students accountable for the books they read (see the next section for more)! So, instead of reading for enjoyment, they are now reading to fill in boxes and make a quota. Get RID of those logs!
- **Create a flexible seating option.** This doesn't mean you need to buy flexible seating furniture. It just means allowing students to be comfortable when reading. Let them find a cozy spot on the floor, or let them sit how they want in the chair! Comfort is super important to engagement when reading!

- **Make it fun!** Implement things such as book talks to help motivate and encourage your readers to read new and fun material in your library! See https://cieraharristeaching.com/2021/05/book-talks-in-the-elementary-classroom.html/.

Ways to Hold Students Accountable During Independent Reading

I know we all feel like we have to make sure everyone is doing what they are told. It's not fair that one student is reading and another isn't. But there are right and wrong ways to go about this. Things like taking tests on Accelerated Reader and filling out reading logs are not the right way. These all put a completely negative emphasis on WHY students are reading the book. It shows the students that they are reading to take a test and fill out boxes. Instead, we want to put into place ways that keep reading for the love of reading at the core but still hold students accountable. Here are some ideas.

- **Implement "status of the class."** This is a fun routine that only takes a few minutes of the day. Basically, you give each student 15–20 seconds to update you and the class on what they are reading. If they are reading a picture book, tell the class about it. And if they are reading a chapter book, tell the class where they are and what's going on. If students know that this is a daily expectation that you are GOING to ask of them, then they will do the reading!
- **Ask questions that focus on the reader.** This means that you need to have conversations with students and ask what they are getting out of the books they are reading. What are their responses to the books they have read? What are their thoughts? How did the book change their thinking? How did the book impact them? If you HAVE to do a daily log of some sort—these are the questions to be asking! They help to show the reader that THEY are at the heart of reading.
- **Use daily independent reading time as a time to conference with students.** If you're giving your students 10–15+ minutes a day to read, then this time is perfect for meeting 1:1 with your students to just listen to them read and talk about the book with NO agenda! At this time, each day, you can get to everyone in your class at least once per week, if not more. Use fun bookmarks to help set goals and communicate them with your students!

Independent reading time is such a valuable time of the day. But making it WORK takes thinking, action, and intentionality behind it. Take time to reflect on how you can make your independent reading time even better!

Closing

It doesn't matter what program you use in your classroom. It doesn't matter if you do Accelerated Reader® or don't do Accelerated Reader®, or if you use Wonders™ or Engage New York™. It does not matter. What matters is the time you take at the beginning of the year to lay a solid groundwork for your readers and get to know them and what barriers might be in their way to achieve true comprehension.

This means it's going to take time. It means you can't get into your routine for a few weeks after school starts. And yes, this means finding some busy work for your students to do while you get to know your readers. It means these ideas and lessons are sometimes more important than the mandated curriculum and assessments you have to give.

It's a lot, but it's worth it. You will see your students be involved as readers rather than reading just being what they do in reading class. If I could tell you, here's the key to ensuring all of your kids love to read at the end of the year or sooner, would you take that key? This is the key. The ideas and concepts in this chapter are the key. By doing all of this, you are setting the purpose of a strong foundation in everything you do throughout the rest of the year, not just in reading class but in math, science, and history.

You are setting the foundation for growth—internal growth, knowledge growth, human growth, and empathy growth. Every moment spent understanding your students' needs, recognizing their strengths, and addressing their challenges contributes to their overall development. This foundation extends beyond academics, fostering a love for learning and an ability to think critically and empathetically about the world around them.

Remember, the work you put in now will resonate throughout the year. Your dedication will be evident in your students' engagement and their evolving ability to comprehend and connect with what they read. It's not just about meeting standards or completing a curriculum; it's about cultivating a classroom environment where each student feels valued and capable of achieving their best.

So, take the time, make the effort, and trust the process. The benefits will ripple out, touching every aspect of your students' educational journey and their personal growth. You are not just teaching them to read; you are nurturing thinkers, learners, and compassionate individuals. This is the real key to their success and fulfillment.

Consider these questions as you ponder this issue more and try the following lessons.

End of Chapter Reflection Questions:

- What role does prior experience play in learning to read?

- What role does the classroom library play in teaching reading?

- Why is it essential to know your readers before jumping into curriculum (laying the solid groundwork)?

- Why can't I just rely on my assessment data to inform my reading instruction?

Lessons to Try

I have created three engaging and hands-on activities that I just know your students will enjoy participating in while at the same time, you'll benefit from by gathering data about your readers! Remember, you can access these lesson in full by heading to `www.cieraharristeaching.com/ttrlessons` and using the passcode: `literacy for all`.

"Building the Library" Lesson

The lesson plan "Building the Library" emphasizes the critical role of the classroom library in fostering a love for reading and supporting literacy development. The primary objective is to ensure that students understand the organization and expectations of the classroom library, helping them navigate and utilize it effectively throughout the year. This lesson aims to create an inviting and accessible library environment where students can find books that match their reading levels and interests. By emphasizing respect for the materials and proper handling of books, the lesson instills a sense of responsibility and care in students.

The importance of this lesson lies in its potential to set a strong foundation for students' reading habits and literacy skills. A well-organized and diverse library can significantly enhance students' engagement with reading, providing them with a wide range of genres and perspectives. The lesson encourages teachers to conduct a thorough assessment of their library's diversity, ensuring that it reflects the demographics and interests of their students. By introducing students to the library's organization and modeling how to select appropriate books, teachers help students develop critical skills for independent reading and comprehension.

Teaching this lesson offers several benefits, including fostering a positive reading culture in the classroom and promoting inclusivity through diverse book selections. It equips students with the skills to independently choose books that match their reading abilities, encouraging a lifelong love of reading. Additionally, the lesson's focus on modeling and practicing proper book handling and selection procedures helps students develop a sense of ownership and respect for the library. This foundation is essential for creating a supportive and enriching learning environment.

Quick Tip

When introducing the classroom library, show genuine enthusiasm and passion for reading. This enthusiasm can be contagious and inspire students to explore the library with excitement and curiosity. Make the introduction interactive by involving students in discussions about their favorite genres and interests, and encourage them to share their thoughts and recommendations. This interactive approach can make the library a dynamic and integral part of your classroom.

"Initial Reading Conferences" Lesson

The lesson plan outlines a comprehensive approach to conducting initial reading conferences with students at the beginning of the school year. The plan is divided into two primary components: the library conference and the goal-setting conference. The library conference is designed to help teachers understand students' reading preferences and habits by engaging them in one-on-one discussions about books. This conference involves exploring the classroom library, discussing various genres and book types, and helping students choose a "just right" book using the five-finger rule. The goal-setting conference focuses on assessing students' reading abilities and setting personalized reading goals. This includes listening to students read, identifying areas for improvement, and establishing clear objectives to enhance their reading skills.

The importance of this lesson lies in its ability to tailor reading experiences to individual students, thereby fostering a love for reading and improving literacy outcomes. By conducting these conferences, teachers can gain valuable insights into each student's interests, strengths, and areas needing support. This personalized approach not only helps in selecting books that engage and motivate students but also in setting achievable reading goals that cater to their specific needs. Additionally, discussing the initial reading curve helps students understand the challenges they might face when starting a new book, providing them with strategies to overcome these hurdles and stay engaged.

The benefits of teaching this lesson extend beyond improving reading skills. It builds a strong foundation for a positive teacher-student relationship, as the one-on-one interactions demonstrate the teacher's interest in each student's success. This individualized attention can boost students' confidence and foster a supportive learning environment. Furthermore, the goal-setting conference promotes critical thinking and self-reflection, encouraging students to take ownership of their learning. By setting and working toward personal reading goals, students develop a growth mindset and become more proactive in their literacy journey.

Quick Tip During the library conference, make sure to ask open-ended questions and listen actively to the students' responses. This will not only help you gather useful information but also make the students feel valued and understood. Encourage them to express their preferences and thoughts freely, creating a trusting and collaborative atmosphere.

"Independent Reading" Lesson

This lesson plan on independent reading is designed to instill a lifelong love of reading in students by explaining the expectations and procedures for independent reading. The lesson emphasizes the importance of independent reading as a daily activity, showcasing it as an opportunity for students to enjoy personal time, explore diverse literature, and develop their reading identities. The lesson plan includes a comprehensive guide to help teachers establish a positive and productive independent reading environment. It encourages teachers to create an anchor chart with students, outlining expectations and permissible activities during reading time, which helps students understand and internalize the benefits of reading independently.

One of the key benefits of teaching this lesson is that it promotes student engagement and motivation by transforming reading from a mandatory task to a cherished personal activity. By helping students see independent reading as a time to connect with characters, explore new worlds, and reflect on their own experiences, teachers can foster a deeper interest in reading. Additionally, the lesson aids in developing critical reading skills, such as comprehension and problem-solving, as students engage with a variety of texts. The lesson also underscores the significance of building a diverse and inclusive classroom library, enabling students to find books that resonate with their personal interests and experiences.

 Quick Tip Consistently use positive language and involve students in creating the anchor chart for independent reading expectations. Regularly revisit these expectations and hold individual reading conferences to maintain student enthusiasm and track progress. This approach helps students feel ownership and stay motivated throughout the year.

CHAPTER 3
THE READER'S BLUEPRINT

Foundations of Reading

Lay the groundwork for understanding the core principles of reading and establishing a successful reading environment.

This chapter delves into the critical importance of understanding each student's unique reading journey. The metaphor of students as architects and teachers as builders is emphasized, illustrating the necessity of comprehending individual reading blueprints to construct effective literacy instruction. By exploring the key components of a reader's blueprint, teachers will learn to gather meaningful data through observations and conversations.

The chapter begins by recognizing the significance of individual reading blueprints. Each student approaches reading in a unique way, shaped by their personal experiences, interests, and abilities. Understanding these distinctive blueprints is essential for tailoring instruction that meets each student's specific needs.

Next, the chapter guides you in gathering meaningful data. Effective observation and conversation techniques are essential for collecting valuable information about students' reading habits, preferences, and challenges. This data is crucial for designing personalized reading experiences that resonate with each student.

Finally, practical strategies for personalized instruction are provided. You'll discover how to apply the gathered data to create a supportive and personalized learning environment. These strategies will help you address the diverse needs of your students, ensuring that each one receives the guidance and support they need to thrive. Through these objectives, teachers will be equipped to foster a love of reading and enhance the literacy skills of each student.

Chapter 3 Objectives

The readers will learn how to view each student as having a unique reading blueprint that includes critical personal information. This understanding will help teachers tailor their literacy instruction to meet the individual needs of their students.

The readers will learn about the six essential components of a reader's blueprint: mental processing, overall reading skills, engagement and motivation, maturity and sensitivity, prior knowledge and experiences, and culture. This knowledge will enable them to gather and utilize specific information about each student.

The readers will discover effective methods for collecting detailed information about their students' reading habits, preferences, and challenges. This includes continuous observations, conversations, and specific activities designed to provide meaningful insights into each student's reading blueprint.

The readers will learn practical ways to use the information gathered from students' reading blueprints to enhance their literacy instruction. This includes building a classroom library that reflects students' interests, creating personalized reading goals, incorporating student interests into lessons, and fostering a culturally responsive classroom environment.

A Reader's Blueprint

Architects take a lot of time designing, styling, and creating a masterful blueprint for a house. The blueprint includes different essentials and necessary components the builders need to know about and see to build the building. Without the blueprint from the architect, the builders would be lost. In the world of literacy, the students are the architects, and the teachers are the builders. Each reader comes to us with their unique blueprint. It includes vital information that's personal to them that we, as teachers, need to know about to build them into the best readers they can be. At the beginning of the year, you must ensure that you are doing everything you can to understand your reader's blueprint.

You probably already do this at the beginning of each year. It's called "getting to know your students." It's perhaps your most important job during the first six weeks of school. You get to know your students and build relationships to create a supportive and meaningful learning environment. "There is no substitute for getting to know students well. When we do that, students trust us, feel comfortable and cared for, and want to work hard. It also helps us be better reading teachers."[1] You might play team-building games or partner activities for the students to learn about each other, and that's fantastic. But my question is, what are you doing to know and understand your students as readers?

In the past, teachers have used a variety of activities to help them get to know their readers. One of the most popular is the interest survey. Unfortunately, there are some issues with these. First, what are we learning about our students by giving these surveys? And second, how often are you, as their teacher, honestly sitting and looking at that data? I have been guilty of this in the past! I've been that teacher who knows I need to get to know my students, so I plan this fantastic interest survey I found on Teachers Pay Teachers and use it as one of the activities during the first week of school. Once collected, I'd give them a quick glance, and they turn into a pile on my desk because, let's be honest, it's the beginning of the year and there are piles everywhere! I'm trying to quickly get into a routine with my students and get started with the curriculum. But this is where we go wrong.

---

[1] Serravalo, J. (2018). *Understanding Texts & Readers: Responsive Comprehension Instruction with Leveled Texts*. Heinemann.

Definition: Reader's Blueprint

The unique set of information about each student's reading abilities and needs. Just like a blueprint helps builders construct a house, a reader's blueprint helps teachers understand each student's reading skills, interests, and background.

> One book can completely change the trajectory of a reader. That one book can make a reader who is unmotivated, unengaged, and uninterested in reading, go from that to wanting to read.

We have to get to know our kids on a much deeper level. We need to ensure that the activities we plan are not just time fillers but actually give us the information we need to secure meaningful learning in the future. This information could lead us to that one book that, when we present it to a student, could unlock a love of reading. One book is all it takes! As Stephanie Harvey and Annie Ward say in their amazing book, *From Striving to Thriving Readers:* "Change the book, change the reader."[2] One book can completely change the trajectory of a reader. That one book can make a reader who is unmotivated, unengaged, and uninterested in reading, go from that to wanting to read. That power right there simply comes from us knowing our readers inside and out.

Reflect: Think about your current practices for understanding your students as readers. What strategies do you use to uncover the individual reading blueprints of your students at the beginning of the school year? How might you improve or change these strategies to gain deeper insights into their reading preferences, strengths, and areas for growth?

---

[2] Harvey, S. and Ward, H. (2021). *From Striving to Thriving: How to Grow Confident, Capable Readers*. Scholastic.

What's Included in a Reader's Blueprint?

As you know from Chapter 1, reading is a deeply personal and individualized process. Each student brings a unique set of experiences, preferences, and challenges to their reading journey. For educators, it is crucial to support their students by understanding who they are as readers. This understanding goes beyond surface-level observations; it requires a thorough exploration of each student's reading blueprint.

Every student possesses a distinct reading blueprint that encompasses vital information about their reading habits, interests, strengths, and areas needing improvement. This blueprint serves as a road map, guiding us in tailoring our instructional approaches to meet each student's unique needs. By delving into these blueprints, we can gather critical data that allows us to create personalized and meaningful lesson plans, select books that resonate with our students, and provide targeted support that aligns with their individual reading pathways.

Understanding a student's reading blueprint is not a one-time task but an ongoing process. It involves continuous observation, dialogue, and reflection to keep up with their evolving needs and interests. This dynamic approach ensures that our teaching remains responsive and effective, fostering a learning environment where each student feels seen, understood, and motivated to grow as a reader.

Incorporating this deeper level of understanding into our teaching practices can transform our approach to literacy instruction. It enables us to unlock each student's potential by connecting with their personal reading journey, ultimately leading to a more engaged, motivated, and successful reader.

What can be included in a reader's blueprint?
- ✓ Mental Processing
- ✓ Overall Reading Skills
- ✓ Engagement & Motivation
- ✓ Maturity & Sensitivity
- ✓ Prior Knowledge & Experiences
- ✓ Cultural Background
- ✓ Reading Habits
- ✓ Learning Style
- ✓ Vocabulary
- ✓ Support Systems
- ✓ Challenges & Barriers
- ✓ Goals & Aspirations

The following sections break down the reader's blueprint into six components—mental processing, overall reading skills, engagement and motivation, maturity and sensitivity, prior knowledge and experiences, and culture.

Mental Processing

There is a lot that goes into understanding the mental processing of students! Essentially, you want to examine if the reader has the short-term working memory to understand the material. Additionally, you want to see if they have the critical and analytical skills needed to comprehend the text. However, it is vital to remember that the ability to process varies each day. Students may have an all-time high in the morning and an all-time low after recess. Or, they may struggle when hungry or going through something challenging at home. Since every student is different, mental processing varies for everyone.

Mental processing encompasses a range of cognitive functions, including attention, memory, problem-solving, and reasoning. Teachers need to be aware of these factors when designing and delivering lessons. For example, some students may excel in processing visual information but struggle with auditory instructions. It is also important to note the impact of cognitive load; too much information presented at once can overwhelm a student's working memory, leading to frustration and disengagement. A study from *Frontiers in Psychology* highlights how mental processes like attention, memory, problem-solving, and reasoning are deeply interconnected, influencing learning outcomes. These cognitive functions play a critical role in how students process and retain information in educational settings. Teachers need to design lessons that consider these mental processes to enhance learning effectiveness. For example, attention and memory are crucial for students to stay focused on relevant material and recall information later, while problem-solving and reasoning help them apply knowledge to new contexts.

This research suggests that incorporating strategies that engage these cognitive functions—such as interactive problem-solving tasks, memory aids, and attention-focusing techniques—can significantly improve lesson delivery and student comprehension.[3] Understanding individual differences in mental processing can help teachers provide more effective and personalized instruction, enhancing learning outcomes.

To understand your student's mental processing a little better, here are some questions you could ask or reflect upon when observing the student:

- Can you explain how you approached solving this problem?
- What strategies do you use to remember key information from the lesson?
- How do you feel your concentration changes throughout the day?

---

[3] Hafeez, C., Amin, H., Saad, M., and Malik, A. (2017). The Influences of emotion on learning and memory. *Frontiers in Psychology* 8.

Overall Reading Skills

It is vital to analyze how skillful the reader is at crucial comprehension skills. This includes inferring, predicting, and visualizing. By understanding the levels of each student, you can provide important scaffolds to help them succeed.

Overall reading skills encompass a variety of sub-skills that contribute to comprehension. These include decoding, fluency, vocabulary knowledge, and the ability to make connections within and between texts. Assessing these skills helps identify specific areas where a student may need additional support. For instance, a student might be able to decode words accurately but struggle with fluency, affecting their overall comprehension. Tailoring instruction to address these needs, such as through guided reading sessions or targeted vocabulary exercises, can significantly improve reading proficiency.

Engagement and Motivation

When learning about your readers, it is important to see if the text and task are engaging. For instance, if the topic of the text is spiders, and a student hates spiders, their mind will focus on their fear. So, the topic itself can change the course of a student's ability to comprehend at their best ability. Additionally, students benefit from having motivation beyond answering simple comprehension questions. They will feel motivated to do their best if they have a purpose and excitement.

Engagement and motivation are critical factors in reading comprehension. "Many of their reading difficulties stem from their lack of interest in reading, as much as anything else."[4]

Intrinsically motivated students who find personal relevance and interest in the material are more likely to invest effort and persist in challenging tasks. *Extrinsic motivators,* such as rewards or grades, can also play a role but may not sustain long-term interest. Teachers can enhance engagement by incorporating student interests into reading selections and providing varied, interactive tasks that connect to real-world experiences. Establishing a purpose for reading, such as solving a mystery or participating in a group discussion, can

---

[4] Harvey, S. and Ward, H. (2021). *From Striving to Thriving: How to Grow Confident, Capable Readers*. Scholastic.

further motivate students. "Motivation can influence the interest, purpose, emotion, or persistence with which a reader engages with text. More motivated readers are likely to apply more strategies and work harder at building meaning. Less motivated readers are not as likely to work as hard, and the meaning they create will not be as powerful as if they were highly motivated."[5]

To understand your students' engagement or motivation when interacting with them at the beginning of the year, here are a few questions you could ask or reflect upon:

- What do you find most interesting about this topic?
- How does this reading relate to your own experiences or interests?
- What motivates you to read and understand this text?

"Talented teachers know that there is more to successful reading than accurate and efficient strategy and skill use. The best strategy and skill teaching will be unsuccessful when students are unmotivated and unengaged or when they don't believe that they can succeed. Conceptualizing reading as a blend of cognition and affect should help inform curriculum and instruction that attends to all aspects of students' reading development."[6]

It's crucial to recognize that reading is not just a mechanical process but a deeply human one. When students are enthusiastic about what they read, their comprehension and retention improve significantly. Therefore, fostering a love for reading by connecting it to students' interests and experiences is essential.

Additionally, creating a supportive and encouraging classroom environment can make a substantial difference. Teachers should focus on building students' confidence in their reading abilities. This can be achieved through positive reinforcement, setting achievable goals, and celebrating progress, no matter how small. When students believe in their capacity to succeed, they are more likely to engage with the material and persist through challenges.

---

[5] Pardo, L.S. (2004). What every teacher needs to know about comprehension. *The Reading Teacher* 66 (6).

[6] Afflerbach, P., Cho, B., Kim, J., and Crassas, M. (2013). Reading: what else matters besides strategies and skills? *The Reading Teacher* 66 (6): 440–448.

Incorporating social aspects into reading can enhance engagement. Group discussions, peer reading sessions, and collaborative projects can make reading a more interactive and enjoyable experience. These activities not only improve comprehension but also allow students to learn from each other, share perspectives, and develop critical thinking skills.

Maturity and Sensitivity

This is a big one! Does the material contain themes or details beyond student understanding? Likewise, is it suitable for the reader at that age? You cannot just consider the Lexile level. This only measures the quantifiable data. It does not measure anything when it comes to the complexity, maturity, or sensitivity of the text. It is essential to look at the actual situations in the text to make sure it is appropriate for students.

Assessing the maturity and sensitivity of reading material involves considering students' developmental stage and emotional readiness. Texts with complex themes, such as death, war, or social issues, require careful handling to ensure they are presented in an age-appropriate and culturally sensitive way. Teachers need to be mindful of their students' backgrounds and experiences, as these can influence how content is received and understood. Discussions around sensitive topics should be facilitated with care, providing a safe space for students to express their thoughts and emotions.

Prior Knowledge and Experiences

A student's background knowledge is the one thing a teacher can count on a student to bring to the table. That's it. You cannot rely on your students coming in this school year with anything else. Prior skills? Nope. Understanding a main idea? Nope. They have their background knowledge, and that is it.

Prior knowledge and experience play a crucial role in reading comprehension. "Prior knowledge has been defined broadly within education as the knowledge, skills, or abilities the student brings to the learning process. It is basically a general collection of facts, concepts, and experiences. Acquisition of this knowledge begins early based on varied personal, academic, and cultural encounters. Depending on these experiences, individuals connect bits of information to build a fund of knowledge and a foundation for future learning. This foundation is essential for learning and purposefully developing a breadth and depth of background knowledge."[7] When students can connect new information to what they already know, they are better able to understand and retain the material. This connection-building process helps anchor new learning in a meaningful context. Teachers can facilitate this by activating prior knowledge before introducing new concepts, using techniques such as brainstorming, KWL charts (What I Know, What I Want to Know, What I Learned), and discussions. It's also important to recognize and value the diverse experiences students bring to the classroom, which can enrich the learning experience for everyone.

---

[7] Hennessy, N.L. (2021). *The Reading Comprehension Blueprint: Helping Students Make Meaning from Text*. Paul H. Brookes Publishing Co.

Culture

This connects to background knowledge in many ways. A reader's culture can significantly interfere with a student's ability to comprehend a text or a book. This is due to the impact of language, context, perspectives, and familiarity with other cultural references. Students may need help understanding important values in America if they are from China. Similarly, there may be confusion behind symbolism, cultural empathy, and themes based on culture. Teachers need to make sure to consider the entire reader when building comprehension.

Cultural background influences how students interpret and engage with texts. Language nuances, cultural references, and differing worldviews can affect comprehension and connection to the material. Comprehension is affected by a reader's culture, based on the degree to which it matches with the writer's culture or the culture espoused in the text.[8] Teachers should strive to include diverse perspectives in their reading selections and create an inclusive environment where all cultural backgrounds are respected and valued. Providing context and background information about cultural elements in a text can help bridge understanding. Additionally, encouraging students to share their cultural experiences can enrich classroom discussions and foster a deeper appreciation for diversity.

From these six pillars, you should be able to gather specific information that is crucial for understanding your students as readers. You should be able to deduce what types of books they might be interested in reading and the ones they most definitely won't want to read. You should know what motivates them, what scares them, what hurdles are in their way, and what support they will need in the upcoming months as you work with them to build their literacy knowledge.

---

[8] Pardo, L. (2004). What every teacher needs to know about comprehension. *The Reading Teacher* 58 (3): 272–280.

Gathering Data for a Reader's Blueprint

Now that you know what a reader's blueprint is and why it's essential, you're probably wondering how to gather all of this information. As mentioned, simply giving an interest survey and glancing at it doesn't provide the substance and depth you need from each student. One of the best and easiest ways to collect blueprint data is through observations and conversations.

Continuous observations and conversations are crucial to gaining deeper insights into each student's reading habits, preferences, and challenges This ongoing process helps teachers build a more comprehensive and accurate reading blueprint for their students. Observations can provide real-time data on how students interact with texts in various ways, revealing much about their reading behaviors, preferences, and difficulties that might not be evidenced through surveys or standardized assessments alone.

"We can't stress enough how much we learn about kids' reading and thinking by simply listening closely to what they say. If we listen, most of them will talk. Some strivers yearn for more informal conversations about their thoughts, wonderings, and interests. Others are more reticent, so we search for multiple ways into conversations."[9] This quote underscores the importance of creating a supportive environment where all students feel comfortable sharing their thoughts. Listening to students' verbal expressions of their reading experiences can uncover unique insights that formal assessments might miss.

"The most powerful way to reach a striving reader is to spend five or ten minutes engaging with him." This dedicated time allows teachers to connect on a personal level, understanding the specific hurdles and interests of each student. These brief yet focused

---

[9] Harvey, S. and Ward, H. (2021). *From Striving to Thriving: How to Grow Confident, Capable Readers*. Scholastic.

interactions can significantly impact a student's reading journey, fostering a deeper connection and a tailored approach to support their growth. By incorporating continuous observations and dedicated conversations, teachers can develop a nuanced understanding of each student's reading needs and effectively guide them toward becoming more proficient and enthusiastic readers.

We Can Observe...	
Book Selection	Watch how students choose books. Do they gravitate toward certain genres, authors, or types of books like graphic novels or chapter books?
Reading Behavior	Note their engagement level. Are they deeply engrossed, or do they frequently lose focus? Do they seem to enjoy reading or approach it with reluctance?
Reading Strategies	Pay attention to the strategies they use while reading. Do they re-read difficult sections, make notes, or use context clues to understand new words?
Peer Interactions	Observe how they discuss books with peers. Are they enthusiastic, or do they avoid book-related conversations? Do they recommend books to others?
Responses to Challenges	How do they handle difficult texts? Do they persevere, seek help, or give up easily?

Along the same lines as observing your students while they are interacting with texts, you can also simply have a conversation with them. Talk about books! Ask the students questions about the books on their desks or why they like a particular bin of books best from the library. Conversations, both formal and informal, can provide deeper insights into students' thoughts and feelings about reading. These conversations can uncover their interests, motivations, and any frustrations they might be experiencing or have experienced in the past.

> **Reflective Questions Teachers Can Ask During Book Conversations:**
> - What kinds of books do you enjoy most and why?
> - Can you tell me about a book that significantly impacted you?
> - How do you choose which book to read next?
> - What do you find most challenging about reading?
> - How has your reading taste changed over time?
> - How does your mood affect the type of book you choose to read?
> - What do you think makes a book a 'good read'?
> - How do you feel when you finish a book?
> - Do you prefer reading alone or with others? Why?
> - How do you balance reading with other activities in your life?
> - What motivates you to keep reading a book even if it's challenging?
> - How do you think reading has influenced your thinking or perspective on certain topics?
> - What role does reading play in your daily routine?
> - How do you decide when to abandon a book you're not enjoying?
> - What benefits do you think reading brings to your life?
> - How do you share your reading experiences with others?
> - What kinds of reading environments do you find most enjoyable?

In Chapter 2, I introduced a lesson encouraging you to conduct an initial reading conference with each of your students. This serves as an excellent example of how conversations with your students can provide valuable insights into their individual learning profiles. However, if you don't have time for one-on-one conferences, that's perfectly fine! Engaging students in casual conversations about their current reads, favorite books, or what they enjoy reading outside of school can be equally impactful. These chats can occur during transitions, recess, or even silent reading time.

Another effective strategy is to hold group discussions. Facilitate conversations where students share their thoughts on books they've read, which promotes peer learning and reveals how they articulate their understandings. This approach allows you to reach multiple students simultaneously.

If you prefer activities over discussions, don't worry! At the end of the chapter, you'll find a variety of engaging activities for you and your students to enjoy.

> **Quick Tip:** Don't forget about the parents! They have a wealth of information they can provide you regarding understanding your students as readers. Think about chatting with them at the beginning of the year to unlock even more information about your students!

Time to Act

Gathering all this information from your students requires effort, no doubt. But as discussed, understanding your readers is crucial to providing the best literacy instruction possible. So, if you're investing time in collecting this information, it's wise to have a clear plan for using it effectively.

In Chapter 2, I emphasized the importance of creating a robust library that students can access throughout the year. Limited book access is a significant barrier to reading. Now that you have insights into your students' preferences, you can build and organize a library that caters to their interests.

Here are six steps to ensure you create a classroom library tailored to your students' reading profiles:

1. **Create a diverse genre selection of books.** Your students have now told you what books they like and don't like. You might find that you don't have enough of a particular genre that they want and too much of a genre they don't like. Take some time to fix this! Include a balance of fiction and nonfiction texts to cater to your students' different reading preferences. Also, ensure that various types of books, such as graphic novels, comics, poetry, and plays, are included. These can be particularly engaging for reluctant readers and can help in building literacy skills through visual storytelling.
2. **Ensure that your library has diverse authors, perspectives, and characters.** We get a new batch of students every year, and with the populations of our towns and cities changing rapidly, the demographics of our classrooms change every year. Now that you know your students, ensure that the books in your library reflect the

demographics of the class. This helps students see themselves reflected in the stories they read and introduces them to different perspectives. And even if your classroom reflects a more homogenous population, having a diverse collection of books allows students to see and understand that there are people out there different from them.

3. **Include varied reading levels.** At this point, you may or may not have completed your beginning-of-the-year reading assessments. But because you took the time to observe your students interacting with texts and converse with them about their reading habits, you probably have a good idea of where they land concerning their reading levels. Now that you know this, use this information to ensure the library reflects this information. Stock books at various reading levels to cater to all of your students, including those who may struggle with reading and those who need more advanced material. A great addition to your library would be Hi-Lo books. These are high-interest, low-reading books and they can be particularly useful for older students who are still developing their reading skills.

4. **Have some fun and create some thematic book collections in your library!** You can organize books into bins or sections based on themes or topics your students expressed interest in. One of my personal favorite things to do was to create a seasonal display each month with brand-new books based on current seasonal themes, current events, or different cultural holidays.

5. **Make sure you have a way to have continuous student input in your growing library.** Regularly ask students for their feedback on what books they'd like to see. This can be done through surveys or even a suggestion box. Students may find new book series while out with their families or shopping at the bookstore and can have excellent suggestions to provide you. Encourage students to request these specific books when they see them!

6. **Create engaging displays and book talks.** Now that you have loads of information about your students' book interests, creating a time in your schedule for weekly book talks can be very motivating. You could try things such as "First Chapter Friday" (you read the first chapter of a book each Friday and then place it back on the shelf). You could even create a multimedia book trailer to spark interest in new books being added to the library or old classics you want to reveal.

But it doesn't stop at the library. Remember, you are getting to know your readers' blueprints so you can ensure systematic and supportive literacy instruction. In order to do this, you must be intentional on taking the information and creating small changes or additions to your instruction that reflect the data. It's not going to be some amazing and groundbreaking idea I provide you. They are simple ideas that have a powerful impact on your instruction and more importantly on your students' learning.

So how do you use the reader's blueprint information to support your teaching? The following image shows eight unique ideas on how to take action on the information you worked so hard on gathering.

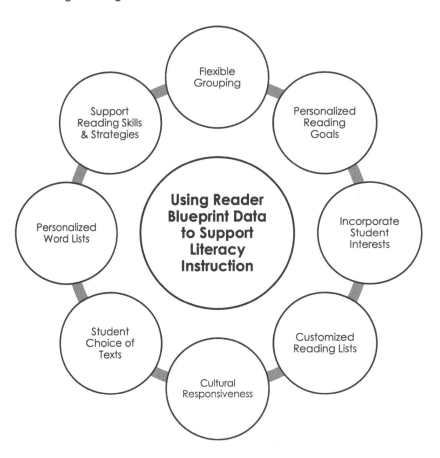

- **Flexible grouping:** By understanding students' reading levels, interests, and learning staples through their blueprints, teachers can create flexible groups for differentiated instruction. "When children have similar decoding needs, it is expedient and useful to group them for targeted instruction. Striving readers in particular benefit from that kind of short-term, small group instruction. But we believe that instruction should be temporary, needs-based, and flexible. If children remain in the same group for an inordinate amount of time, that is not guided reading. These fixed, long-term groups more closely resemble ability group reading, which leads to labeling and more labeling. In other words, it's hazardous to a striving reader's health. Research and support of ability group reading is sparse to non-existent. However, needs-based, small group reading is a powerful way to move kids forward."[10] Groups can be formed based on similar reading abilities, like we normally do, or we can take it a step further and group based on shared interests, cultural backgrounds, past experiences, and much more. This approach allows teachers to tailor instruction to meet the specific needs of each group, whether focusing on comprehension, vocabulary, or any of the other literacy components. Flexible grouping ensures that all students receive targeted support and opportunities for growth, fostering a supportive learning environment conductive to literacy success.
- **Personalized reading goals:** Teachers can use the information gathered from students' blueprints to collaboratively set personalized reading goals with each student. These goals could focus on areas such as improving fluency, expanding vocabulary, or exploring different genres based on individual interests and preferences. The goals could even be non-academic such as a goal for simply learning to love reading. Personalized goals empower students to take ownership of their reading progress and provide a clear road map for both teachers and students to monitor and celebrate achievements. By aligning goals with students' strengths and challenges identified in their blueprints, teachers can effectively scaffold instruction and provide meaningful feedback to support ongoing literacy development.

---

[10] Harvey, S. and Ward, H. (2021). *From Striving to Thriving: How to Grow Confident, Capable Readers*. Scholastic.

Ideas for Beginning of Year Goals Based on Blueprint Data:

- Improve oral reading fluency
- Expand vocabulary
- Exploring different genres of books
- Learn to love reading
- Read a variety of books by different authors
- Increase comprehension through summarizing
- Participate in reading discussions or book clubs
- Identify and use context clues to understand new words
- Read books at different difficulty levels to challenge myself
- Track reading progress by maintaining a reading journal
- Retell stories in my own words
- Make connections between the book and personal experiences
- Explore non-fiction books to learn about new topics
- Engage in creative activities related to reading, such as drawing scenes or writing new endings
- Develop critical thinking by asking questions and making predictions while reading

- **Incorporate student interests:** Utilizing insights from students' blueprints, teachers can incorporate topics and themes that align with students' interests into literacy instruction. Engaged reading is linked to every positive outcome imaginable—including a longer life! It's important to make sure that what children are reading is compelling to them. This can be best determined in reader-to-reader, heart-to-heart conferences, rather than by posing traditional comprehension questions.[11] Whether through book selections, project-based learning activities, or thematic units, integrating student interests enhances engagement and motivation. Students are more likely to actively participate in reading groups and related tasks when the content resonates with their personal interests and experiences. This approach not only supports literacy success but also cultivates a lifelong love of reading by connecting classroom learning to students' lives outside of school.

- **Customized reading lists:** Based on students' reading preferences and abilities outlined in their blueprints, teachers can curate customized reading lists tailored to

---

[11] Harvey, S. and Ward, H. (2021). *From Striving to Thriving: How to Grow Confident, Capable Readers*. Scholastic.

individual students. These lists may include a variety of genres, formats, and difficulty levels to cater to diverse reading preferences and support skill development. Customized reading lists empower students to explore new genres while providing opportunities for independent reading that align with their current reading abilities and interests. This personalized approach encourages self-directed learning and promotes continuous growth in literacy skills.

- **Cultural responsiveness:** Teachers can promote cultural responsiveness by selecting texts and instructional materials that reflect students' cultural backgrounds and identities identified in their blueprints.[12] Strong school culture supported students' development in understanding in that students gained a deeper understanding of content as well as learned the value of listening to each other's perspectives. Integrating diverse perspectives and voices into literacy instruction fosters inclusivity and respect for cultural diversity within the classroom. Through discussions and activities that acknowledge and validate students' cultural experiences, teachers create a supportive learning environment where all students feel valued and understood. Cultural responsiveness enhances students' comprehension and critical thinking skills by connecting learning to their lived experiences and broadening their perspectives through literature. "Culturally responsive teachers validate every student's culture, bridging gaps between school and home through diversified instructional strategies and multicultural curricula."[13]

- **Student choice of texts:** Using information from students' blueprints, teachers can offer opportunities for student choice in selecting reading materials. Allowing students to choose texts based on their interests, reading preferences, and comfort levels promotes autonomy and engagement in literacy activities. Student choice fosters a sense of ownership over learning and encourages exploration of diverse genres and topics. By honoring students' choices, teachers empower them to develop a deeper connection with reading and build confidence as independent readers. This approach supports literacy success by promoting intrinsic motivation and cultivating a positive reading identity among students.

---

[12] Aronson, B. and Laughter, J. (2016). The theory and practice of culturally relevant education. *Review of Educational Research* 86 (1): 163–206.

[13] Ibid.

> **Quick Tip:** When selecting a text to read for a lesson, choose two different texts and give your students the opportunity to pick which text they'd prefer to read. This takes little effort but allows students to use their blueprint and pick a text they relate to more.

- **Personalized word lists:** Teachers can create personalized word lists tailored to students' vocabulary needs identified in their blueprints. These lists may include high-frequency words, content-specific vocabulary, or words identified through assessments or observations. Personalized word lists support vocabulary development by targeting areas of growth and providing opportunities for students to practice and apply new words in context. By integrating vocabulary instruction that is responsive to students' individual needs, teachers enhance comprehension and fluency while promoting academic language proficiency across content areas.

- **Support reading skills and strategies:** Leveraging insights from students' blueprints, teachers can design targeted instruction to support specific reading skills and strategies. Whether focusing on comprehension, fluency, decoding, or critical analysis skills, teachers can tailor instructional approaches based on students' strengths and areas for growth. For example, knowing your students on a deeper level allows you to support them when needing to make connections with a text. It also allows you to know when certain students might need more support developing their schema on a topic more than other students will. This personalized approach ensures that students receive the support and scaffolding needed to develop proficiency in essential reading skills, ultimately promoting literacy success.

By implementing these strategies informed by students' individual blueprints, teachers create a dynamic and inclusive learning environment where every student can thrive in literacy. These approaches not only address students' unique needs and interests but also foster a love of reading, critical thinking skills, and lifelong learning habits essential for academic and personal success.

Closing

In concluding this chapter, I reaffirm the critical importance of understanding each student's unique reading journey. Just as architects meticulously design blueprints to guide builders, teachers must comprehend their students' individual reading blueprints to construct effective and personalized literacy instruction. This metaphor underscores the need for teachers to gather and utilize meaningful data from observations and conversations, creating a supportive and tailored learning environment that fosters a love of reading and enhances literacy skills.

By delving into the key components of a reader's blueprint, teachers can gain insights into students' mental processing, overall reading skills, engagement and motivation, maturity and sensitivity, prior knowledge and experiences, and cultural backgrounds. These components are integral to understanding the whole reader and tailoring instruction to meet their specific needs. This comprehensive approach ensures that students are not only seen and understood but also supported in ways that resonate with their personal reading journeys.

> "The ways to get to know my students as readers is important. I am guilty of giving out a reading inventory and never looking at it. Using the reading conferences you provided helped me to better understand my students as readers and how to direct my instruction for them based on their likes and dislikes."
>
> -Kristin Pulido, 5th Grade, St. Joseph Catholic School, South Carolina

It is essential to move beyond surface-level activities and surveys that provide limited insights. Instead, teachers should engage in continuous observations and meaningful conversations with students to gather in-depth information. This dynamic and ongoing process allows teachers to stay attuned to the evolving needs and interests of their students, ensuring that instruction remains responsive and effective. Through this deeper understanding, teachers can unlock each student's potential, transforming them into engaged, motivated, and successful readers.

As educators, our ultimate goal is to cultivate a lifelong love of reading in our students. By understanding and responding to their unique blueprints, we can create a classroom environment that not only improves literacy skills but also inspires a passion for reading. This holistic approach to literacy instruction will undoubtedly lead to more meaningful and impactful learning experiences, empowering students to become confident, capable readers who are prepared for academic success and beyond.

In closing, remember that every student's reading journey is unique and deserves careful consideration. By embracing the concept of the reader's blueprint, you commit to understanding and supporting your students in their individual paths to literacy. Through thoughtful and personalized instruction, you can help each student achieve their full potential and instill a lifelong love of reading that will enrich their lives for years to come.

Consider these questions as you ponder this issue more and try the following lessons.

End of Chapter Reflection Questions:

How can a single book change the trajectory of a reader?

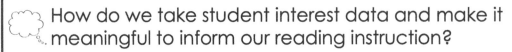
How do we take student interest data and make it meaningful to inform our reading instruction?

Why it is important to expose students to a variety of genres at the beginning of the year?

Lessons to Try

Remember, you can access these lessons in full by heading to `www.cieraharristeaching.com/ttrlessons` and using the passcode: `literacy for all`.

"Creating a Book Stack" Lesson

The "Creating a Book Stack" lesson is designed to help students explore their identities as readers by selecting and analyzing a personal collection of books. The objective of this lesson is for students to articulate who they are as readers by curating a book stack that reflects their interests, preferences, and reading habits. This activity not only allows teachers to gain insight into their students' reading choices but also helps students understand and express their own reading identities.

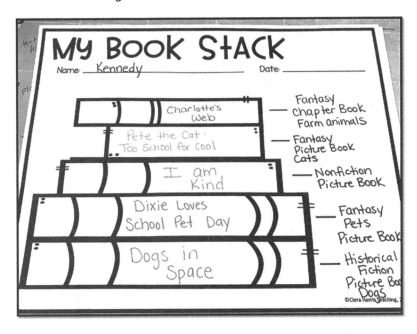

This lesson supports a child's literacy development by providing teachers with valuable insights into their students' reading preferences. By examining the book stacks, teachers can identify genres, topics, and book types that each student gravitates toward. This information allows teachers to tailor their instruction to better engage and motivate each reader. For instance, a student with a book stack full of fantasy novels may benefit from being introduced to a new fantasy series or books with similar themes. Similarly, if a student shows an interest in nonfiction books about animals, the teacher can incorporate related texts into lessons and reading activities. Understanding these preferences helps teachers create a more personalized and effective literacy experience for each student, fostering a love for reading and improving overall literacy skills.

The Reader's Blueprint

Quick Tip: Have your own book stack prepared in advance. By sharing your personal book choices and discussing what these books reveal about you as a reader, you can model the analytical process and set a clear example for students. This demonstration helps students understand how to approach their book stack creation and analysis, making the lesson more effective and engaging.

"Identity Map" Lesson

The objective of this lesson is for students to create an identity map to express and explore different aspects of their identity. This activity not only allows students to reflect on who they are but also provides teachers with valuable insights into their students' backgrounds, interests, and experiences. Understanding these facets of students' identities helps educators tailor their literacy instruction to better meet each student's needs, fostering a more inclusive and supportive learning environment.

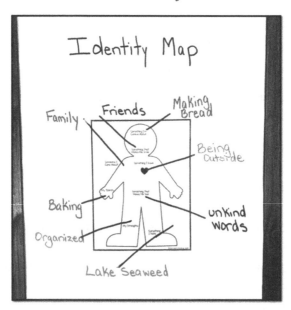

Example of 'Identity Map'

92 The Thinking Reader

By integrating personal identity exploration with literacy, this lesson supports overall literacy development in several ways. First, it encourages students to make connections between their personal experiences and the texts they read, enhancing comprehension and engagement. Second, it helps students see themselves as part of the learning process, which can increase motivation and a sense of ownership over their reading journey. Lastly, by sharing their identity maps, students practice communication skills and build a sense of community within the classroom, which is essential for collaborative learning and effective literacy instruction.

Quick Tip: Prior to the lesson, create your own identity map to model the process for your students. This not only provides a clear example for them to follow but also helps build a trusting relationship as you share parts of your identity. Encourage students to share their maps in small groups or pairs to foster deeper connections. Collect and review the identity maps to gather data that can guide your instructional decisions throughout the year. This personalized approach will help you understand your students better and support their literacy growth in a meaningful way.

"What Would You Choose?" Lesson

The objective of the "What Would You Choose?" lesson is to help students identify the genres and topics they enjoy reading about. This lesson is designed to replace the traditional interest survey, which often resulted in stacks of unused paperwork. Instead, it actively engages students by having them interact with "genre advertisements," giving them a hands-on experience to discover new genres and topics of interest. This approach not only makes the activity more dynamic but also provides valuable insights to teachers about their students' preferences.

By getting students up and moving around the classroom, this lesson gives them a brief overview of various genres, sparking their interest in learning about new books and expanding their reading horizons. This method is more effective than the passive interest surveys of the past, as it encourages students to physically explore and react to different genres.

The Reader's Blueprint

The information gathered from this activity helps teachers tailor their read-aloud selections and classroom library collections to better match their students' interests, thereby promoting a more engaging and personalized literacy experience throughout the year.

Don't forget to allocate time at the end of the lesson for a class discussion. After the students have explored the genres and marked their preferences, gather them together to share their thoughts. Discuss which genres they are most excited about, any new genres they discovered, and why they made their choices. This conversation not only reinforces their learning but also provides you with deeper insights into their interests, which can help in planning future lessons and stocking your classroom library.

CHAPTER 4

READING AND THE BRAIN

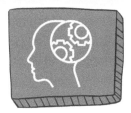

Cognitive Science of a Reader

Explore the neurological and cognitive processes behind reading, emphasizing the importance of schema.

This chapter delves into why integrating brain education into your literacy block is essential. Understanding how the brain works can have a profound impact on your students' reading experiences and overall academic success. This chapter explores five key benefits of incorporating brain education:

- **Fostering personal empathy.** Understanding the brain's role in emotions and social interactions helps students develop greater empathy, making them more attuned to their own feelings and those of others, and fostering a supportive classroom environment.
- **Enhancing cognitive awareness.** Knowledge about how the brain processes information increases students' self-awareness, allowing them to recognize their learning styles and cognitive strengths, which leads to more personalized and effective learning strategies.

- **Improving academic performance.** By integrating brain education, students can better understand how to optimize their study habits and reading techniques, leading to improved focus, retention, and comprehension and directly enhancing their academic performance.
- **Strengthening communication skills.** Additionally, understanding the neurological basis of language and communication enables students to develop stronger speaking and listening skills, helping them articulate their thoughts and engage in meaningful conversations.
- **Promoting lifelong learning.** Ultimately, this knowledge promotes lifelong learning by instilling a deeper understanding of how their incredible brains function.

I also break down the essentials of what you need to teach about the brain, focusing on two main areas: the brain's lobes and the intricate workings of neurons and dendrites. By the end of this chapter, you'll have practical strategies and activities to integrate this knowledge into your daily instruction, helping your students become more self-aware, resilient, and effective readers. Join me as I unravel the science behind reading so you can empower your students to take charge of their learning journey with a deeper understanding of their brains.

Chapter 4 Objectives

The readers will understand the structure and function of the brain's four lobes (frontal, parietal, temporal, and occipital) and their roles in reading and language processing.

The readers will develop an awareness of how neurons and dendrites function, including how neural pathways are strengthened through practice, enhancing learning and reading comprehension.

The readers will explore how understanding brain functions can foster personal empathy and cognitive awareness, helping them recognize and manage reading challenges.

The readers will identify how teaching about the brain can improve communication skills, metacognition, and overall academic performance by making students more aware of their cognitive processes.

The readers will apply brain-based strategies to promote lifelong learning skills in students, using insights about the brain to encourage curiosity, resilience, and a growth mindset.

Why the Brain?

The beginning of the school year is always crazy. It doesn't matter if you're new to teaching or a veteran, the to-do list is a mile long and growing. Your new set of students walk into your classroom and you're trying to learn their names, build relationships, take beginning-of-the-year assessments, and more. What if I tell you that you need to add something to that list?

When it comes to establishing your literacy block and routine, there are always stepping-stones you need to have in place before really jumping in. Teaching about the brain needs to be one of those stepping-stones. You might think this is crazy and will overload your back-to-school to-do list, but I assure you that the benefits outweigh the downsides.

Think about it. Teaching about the brain at the beginning of the year is a really smart thing to do. I break down the benefits of teaching about the brain in the following sections so I can win you over.

Creates Personal Empathy

This is probably the biggest benefit I've witnessed from students—when they understand how their brain works when they read and what's actually happening inside their mind. When they see this process, they very quickly realize that it's a hard, long, and complex process that they will learn to master. But along the way there will be bumps in the road. Because they see this as something that's complex and needs practice, the students realize these difficulties are normal and can be overcome with practice. Cognitive control and working memory play crucial roles in reading comprehension. Students who understand these processes can develop strategies to overcome challenges, realizing that difficulties in reading are part of a complex but conquerable process. Awareness of how their brain functions during reading helps students accept that setbacks are normal and motivates them to practice, ultimately improving their skills.[1] On top of that, the students also become

---

[1] Patael, S., Farris, E., and Black, J. (2018). Brain basis of cognitive resilience: prefrontal cortex predicts better reading comprehension in relation to decoding. *Plos One* https://doi.org/10.1371/journal.pone.0198791.

more empathetic toward themselves when they struggle as well as when they see others struggling. They become more patient with the process and are more likely to ask for help when they know that learning to read is a gradual process and not an instant talent.

Enhances Cognitive Awareness

You will learn later in Chapter 7 that metacognition is an integral part of the reading process. But in order for metacognition to take place, students need to learn to become more aware of what's happening inside their brains. This starts with teaching them about the brain and what reading looks like on the inside. When you teach this, students become aware of their own thought processes while reading. When students are more aware, they can then make better decisions on which strategies to use to tackle their reading difficulties.

A study published in the *Journal of Education and Educational Development* shows that students who develop metacognitive awareness, meaning they understand their thought processes during reading, can significantly improve their academic performance. This awareness helps them identify which reading strategies work best to tackle their challenges, such as decoding or comprehension issues. When students are taught about their cognitive processes, they are better equipped to adjust their reading strategies, making them more effective learners.[2]

Having this cognitive awareness also can help students use techniques to improve memory retention and lead to better focus during reading tasks. Overall, it puts the student in the driver's seat. They are witnessing their own learning in real time, making their own decisions, knowing when difficulties arise, and becoming a leader in their learning journey.

Definition: metacognition The awareness and understanding that readers have about their own thinking processes while they read. It involves thinking about how you comprehend and engage with the text

---

[2] Nath, P. (2021). The effect of planned instruction on metacognitive awareness of reading strategies. *Language Education and Acquisition Research Network* 14 (2).

Improves Academic Performance

When you teach your students about their brains and how they work, they become more invested, understanding, and aware of their reading progress. This of course then leads to advancement in academic performance. Students now have an awareness of how their brains process texts, and this leads to improved understanding of the text itself. The students are then also able to develop more effective study techniques. And as reading comprehension improves, so do performance metrics in various subject areas. The benefits go beyond literacy!

Strengthens Communication Skills

As teachers, we know that literacy expands outside of the "walls" of the reading block. So do the benefits of teaching our students about their brains. When students understand how their brain works when it comes to reading a text, they also understand the value in other literacy components such as their developing vocabulary and even writing skills. Beyond that, we see benefits in students' active listening and conversation skills, articulation of thoughts and ideas, and even better development of clear and coherent writing skills.

Promotes Lifelong Learning Skills

Our goal as teachers is always the betterment of our students beyond our four walls. When we stop and put our students in the driver's seat of their own learning, the possibilities are endless. This, in fact, starts with teaching our students about their brains and how they work. Understanding the brain sparks interest for our students in learning how other body systems work. They become more curious about the world around them, and curiosity is a reader's best friend. Knowledge about the learning process encourages self-directed learning and, over time, builds perseverance and resilience in learning for our students.

Reflect: How can understanding and teaching the science of how the brain works enhance my students' reading skills, empathy, cognitive development, and overall academic success in my classroom?

What Do You Need to Teach?

You're probably thinking, I teach elementary-age students. How should I teach them about brain science and relate it to reading? That's the teachers' typical reaction when I share this idea with them. I assure you it's not as complicated and scary as it sounds. I break down understanding the brain into two main sections—"Understanding the Lobes" and "Neurons and Dendrites." Once you know the basics of these two areas, you'll see how well it all connects and be ready to try it!

Let's Start with Something Simple. What Is the Brain?

The brain is the control center of our bodies, responsible for everything we think, feel, and do. It's made up of billions of nerve cells called *neurons* (you will learn more about them later), which communicate with each other through electrical and chemical signals. The brain is divided into different parts, called *lobes*, each with specialized functions.

Our students already know that the brain is essential to their life. But we are going to take it a step further. There are four main parts of the brain. When we read, different brain parts work together to help us understand and make sense of the text. The following sections break down what each of the four lobes of the brain does in terms of literacy.

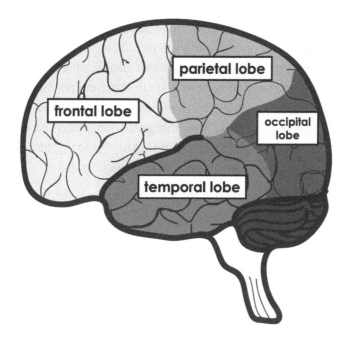

Frontal Lobe

- **Speaking and language production:** This lobe helps us form words and sentences when we read aloud or think about what we read.
- **Decoding words:** It plays a role in breaking down words into sounds (phonemes), which is crucial for decoding and sounding out words.
- **Comprehension and understanding:** It helps us understand the meaning of the text and connect it with our existing knowledge.

The frontal lobe is a key player in reading and language processing. It helps us form words and sentences, whether reading aloud or processing information silently, and is integral to decoding words. This decoding involves breaking words into their individual sounds (phonemes), a critical skill for accurately sounding out and understanding new words. Additionally, the frontal lobe supports comprehension by helping us interpret the meaning of text and connect it to what we already know.

As research highlights, "Reading was shown to require activation across a greater number of cortical areas than listening including the right temporal and right inferior frontal lobes, possibly suggesting that children require this additional activation to handle the more difficult semantic structures of written texts in meaning construction (Yeatman, Ben-Shachar, Glover, & Feldman, 2010)."[3] This indicates that reading is a complex process demanding more cognitive effort than listening, particularly because written texts often involve more challenging structures. Understanding and constructing meaning from these texts is the ultimate goal of developing strong reading skills!

As you discuss the frontal lobe with your students, ask them reflective questions such as: What would happen if my brain were injured and the frontal lobe was affected? How might that impact my ability to read?

Parietal Lobe

- **Decoding and phonological processing:** This lobe helps in processing the sounds of words, which is essential for decoding and recognizing words.
- **Spelling:** It's involved in understanding how letters combine to form words and helps with spelling.

The parietal lobe plays a critical role in decoding and phonological processing, essential steps for reading and recognizing words. This region of the brain helps process the sounds of words, enabling readers to decode and recognize them. Additionally, it is involved in spelling by helping individuals understand how letters combine to form words. By linking spoken and written language, the parietal lobe assigns meaning to what we read, making it a crucial part of the reading process. "There are some very consistent patterns of correlation in the neuroimaging studies of decoding that are available. Word processing appears to correlate with left-hemisphere activity. There is more neural activation in the left temporoparietal and occipitotemporal areas as reading skill increases."[4]

---

[3] Hruby, G.G. and Goswami, U. (2011). Neuroscience and reading: Aa review for reading education researchers. *Reading Research Quarterly* 46 (2): 156–172.

[4] Ibid.

For instance, when you hear the words "fan" and "van," your temporal lobe helps discriminate the sounds. However, the parietal lobe allows you to understand the meaning behind these words. It connects the sounds you hear to your knowledge of what a fan and a van are, providing context and comprehension. This integration of auditory and visual information in the parietal lobe is essential for compelling reading and language understanding.

Temporal Lobe

- **Vocabulary and word recognition:** This area helps us store and recall words and their meanings, which is crucial for vocabulary.
- **Understanding speech:** It helps understand spoken language, which is connected to reading comprehension as we often read silently as if we're hearing the words in our heads.

The temporal lobe plays a pivotal role in the brain's processing and understanding of language. This region helps store and recall words and their meanings, making it crucial for building vocabulary. "There is extensive activation bilaterally (i.e., in both hemispheres) in brain areas related to audition, vision, spatial and cross-modal processing, and spoken-language areas (e.g., posterior superior temporal cortex, occipitotemporal cortex, temporal and parietal areas, frontal cortex)."[5] As children learn to read, they rely on the temporal lobe to recognize and understand words, facilitating the transition from decoding individual letters and sounds to fluent reading. This brain area is also essential for understanding spoken language, directly connecting to reading comprehension. When we read silently, we often "hear" the words in our heads, a process that heavily involves the temporal lobe's functions.

The temporal lobe is also key to verbal memory, which is crucial in an educational setting. Remembering what a teacher says during a lesson depends significantly on this part of the brain. Phonological awareness, the ability to recognize and discriminate between sounds, also resides in the temporal lobe. For instance, distinguishing between the words "fan" and "van" involves detecting subtle differences in their initial sounds. This skill is

---

[5] Hruby, G.G. and Goswami, U. (2011). Neuroscience and reading: a review for reading education researchers. *Reading Research Quarterly* 46 (2): 156–172.

developed in the temporal lobe, enabling children to process and understand spoken words accurately and quickly. Thus, the temporal lobe's role in phonological awareness underpins many aspects of language learning and reading proficiency.

Teaching elementary students about how their brain works, particularly the functions of the temporal lobe, can enhance their understanding of reading and language. By knowing that their brain stores vocabulary and helps them recognize words, children can become more aware of the cognitive processes involved in reading. Understanding the brain's role in phonological awareness can motivate students to engage in activities that strengthen this skill, such as rhyming games and sound manipulation exercises. This awareness can foster a more profound interest in reading and language, ultimately supporting their academic growth.

Occipital Lobe

- **Visual processing:** This lobe helps us see and recognize letters and words on a page. It processes the visual information and sends it to other brain parts for further understanding.

The occipital lobe, located at the back of the brain, is crucial for visual processing. The occipital lobe helps us see and recognize letters and words on a page when we read. This part of the brain contains the primary visual cortex, which processes visual information received from our eyes. The primary visual cortex identifies shapes, colors, and movements, allowing us to distinguish and interpret the letters and words we see. "The left occipitotemporal cortex is involved in object recognition and is an area of interest in research on decoding, because it has been suggested to house a word form area. This area is in essence a part of the visual cortex specialized for recognizing print."[6] Once this information is processed, it is sent to other brain parts for further understanding and integration.

In addition to essential visual recognition, the occipital lobe works in concert with other brain regions to comprehend the meaning of the text. For instance, the information

---

[6] Hruby, G.G. and Goswami, U. (2011). Neuroscience and reading: a review for reading education researchers. *Reading Research Quarterly* 46 (2): 156–172.

processed in the occipital lobe is sent to the temporal lobe, associated with language and semantic understanding. This collaboration enables us to recognize letters and words and understand their context and meaning. Understanding the role of the occipital lobe in visual processing underscores the complexity of reading and highlights the brain's remarkable ability to coordinate multiple functions to facilitate comprehension.

How the Lobes Work Together

Reflect: How can understanding the specific functions of each brain lobe enhance your teaching strategies in literacy, and what practical steps can you take to integrate this knowledge into your daily reading instruction?

In simple terms, when we read, our brain is like a team where each player has a specific role. The frontal lobe helps us speak and understand the text, the parietal lobe decodes sounds and helps with spelling, the temporal lobe manages our vocabulary and understanding of words, and the occipital lobe helps us see and recognize the words on the page. Together, they allow us to read, understand, and enjoy books!

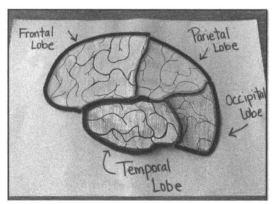

Completed brain diagram from Chapter 4 lessons

Put it all together now! When you're practicing and explaining the brain lobes with your students, try this quick activity:

Reading and the Brain

Engage the students in a fun and educational activity to demonstrate how different parts of the brain work together when they read. Begin by writing a simple sentence on the board, such as "The cat sat on the mat." Explain that you will walk them through the process of reading this sentence and show them which parts of their brain are involved.

First, ask the students to close their eyes. When they open them, point to the back of your head and explain that the occipital lobe is responsible for recognizing the letters they see. Next, read the first word aloud and point to the sides of your head where the temporal lobes are located, explaining that these lobes help process the sounds of the letters.

Continue reading the sentence fluently, and point to your forehead to illustrate that the frontal lobe is helping them read the sentence smoothly. Finally, after reading the sentence, discuss its meaning and point to the top of your head, highlighting that the parietal lobe helps them understand the sentence.

Repeat this process with two or three additional simple sentences, encouraging students to point to the corresponding parts of their brain as they read and understand each sentence. This exercise helps them visualize how their brain works during reading, emphasizing the coordination between the occipital, temporal, frontal, and parietal lobes. By the end, students will better appreciate the complex yet fascinating way their brains help them read and comprehend text.

Neurons and Dendrites

Diagram of a Neuron

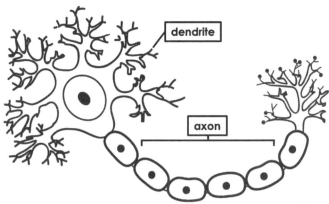

Our brains are filled with billions of neurons, which are the fundamental brain and nervous system units responsible for receiving sensory input, sending motor commands, and transforming and relaying electrical signals. Neurons are the building blocks of our brain mass and play a critical role in processing and comprehending information.

Each neuron comprises several parts: the cell body (or soma), dendrites, the nucleus, and the axon. The cell body contains the nucleus, which acts as the control center of the neuron, storing genetic information and managing cell activities.

- **Dendrites: Information Receivers.** Dendrites are branch-like extensions that protrude from the cell body. These structures are crucial because they receive other neurons' signals (or information). Think of dendrites as the antennas of the neuron, picking up messages from the surrounding neurons and transmitting them to the cell body.
- **Axons: Information Transmitters.** From the cell body extends a long, thin structure called the axon. The axon functions like a telephone wire, transmitting electrical impulses from the cell body and toward other neurons, muscles, or glands. At the end of the axon are terminal branches that connect to the dendrites of other neurons, forming a network through which information is relayed throughout the brain.

When we learn something new, neurons communicate by sending electrical signals through a process known as "firing." This firing starts when a neuron receives a signal through its dendrites. The signal travels through the cell body and down the axon to the terminal branches, which pass the signal to the next neuron's dendrites. This transfer of information from one neuron to another allows us to process and retain new information.

Neuron Part	Description	Function
Cell Body (soma)	Contains the nucleus	Acts as the control center of the neuron, storing genetic information and managing cell activities
Nucleus	Located within the cell body	Stores genetic information and controls cell activities
Dendrites	Branch-like extensions from the cell body	Receive signals from other neurons and transmit them to the cell body
Axon	Long, thin structure extending from the cell body	Transmits electrical impulses from the cell body to other neurons, muscles, or glands
Terminal Branches	Located at the end of the axon	Connect to the dendrites of other neurons, allowing information to be relayed throughout the brain

For example, imagine you are learning to ride a bike for the first time. Initially, the signals your neurons send are weak because the neural pathways for this skill still need to be well established. Your brain is figuring out the new task, so the signals are slower and less efficient. However, with practice, these neural pathways strengthen. The more you practice riding a bike, the faster and stronger the signals become, making the task easier and more automatic. Repeated practice and exposure are critical for learning and mastering new skills.

Neurons and their dendrites play a vital role in learning and comprehending new information. The neurons firing and forming connections is fundamental to building and reinforcing the neural pathways that support learning and memory. "For reading to occur, there must be sonic-speed automaticity for neuronal networks at the local level (such as within the visual cortex), which, in turn, allows for equally rapid connections across entire

Students making models of neurons and dendrites with craft supplies.
Image credit: Carmen Folse

structural expanses of the brain (e.g., connecting visual regions to language regions)."[7] Understanding this process can help us appreciate the importance of practice and repetition in achieving mastery and improving comprehension.

 Reflect: What importance do you see teaching about neurons and dendrites having on your students' literacy success in the classroom?

---

[7] Wolf, M. (2018). The science and poetry in learning (and teaching) to read. *Phi Delta Kappan* 100 (4): 13–17. https://doi.org/10.1177/0031721718815667.

From this, we see that there's a fascinating brain-based reason why we often struggle when we first attempt something new. Whether tackling long division, reading complex non-fiction articles, or mastering any new skill, our brain undergoes a remarkable process of adaptation and growth. When we encounter a new challenge, such as learning to read complex texts or solving advanced math problems, our neurons are firing and forming new connections. This process isn't instantaneous; it requires time and repetition. Research from UC San Francisco demonstrates the importance of *neuroplasticity*. This process, in which neurons in the brain form new synapses, is critical for learning and memory. The study found that consistent practice over time allows neurons to strengthen these connections, leading to more efficient learning. This is further supported by research showing that myelin formation, which insulates nerve fibers, helps stabilize these new connections and enhances long-term learning. The brain's ability to adapt through repeated practice highlights that mastering complex tasks takes time and ongoing effort, as the neural pathways need to strengthen through continuous activation. This reinforces the idea that learning is not instantaneous but rather a gradual process of building neural connections.[8] Our brain's response might initially feel slow and uncertain because the neural pathways associated with the task are still weak.

Dendrites, those crucial branches of neurons responsible for receiving information, actually grow and form new connections through practice. Each time we engage with challenging material or tasks, our dendrites become more adept at receiving and transmitting signals. This physical growth in our brains directly results from our efforts to learn and master new skills.

When students initially experience frustration or difficulty, it's important to understand that this struggle is part of the learning process. It's a sign that their brains are actively adapting and growing. By persevering through these challenges, students strengthen their neural pathways and develop resilience and persistence, essential qualities for lifelong learning.

Instead of being discouraged by initial difficulties, students should be encouraged to view them as opportunities for growth. Each struggle represents a chance to build upon existing knowledge and expand cognitive capabilities. Through continued effort and practice, what once seemed difficult can become more manageable and eventually second nature.

---

[8] Farley, P. (2020). UCSF Long-term learning requires new nerve insulation. https://www.ucsf.edu/news/2020/02/416621/long-term-learning-requires-new-nerve-insulation.

In essence, every challenge we face, especially at the beginning stages of learning, is a chance to physically grow our brain. By nurturing our dendrites, firing up our neurons, and persisting through initial struggles, we lay the foundation for mastering new skills and understanding complex concepts. This understanding not only empowers students but also reinforces the importance of perseverance and continuous learning in achieving academic success and personal growth.

Each time we engage with challenging material or tasks, our dendrites become more adept at receiving and transmitting signals.

Quick Tip

You've heard of growth mindset? Growth mindset is the belief that abilities and intelligence can be developed through effort, learning, and perseverance. If you incorporate growth mindset into your classroom, take it a step further and include lessons on neurons and dendrites!

A peer-reviewed study published in *Brain Sciences* provides strong support for the claim that teaching students about how their brain works can enhance their learning and literacy skills. The research emphasizes that understanding neuroplasticity—the brain's ability to form new connections as a result of learning—empowers students to approach their learning more effectively. When students are taught about brain structures and functions, such as how different lobes of the brain contribute to speech, comprehension, and visual recognition, they are better equipped to use metacognitive strategies. This awareness allows them to adjust their learning processes, which directly benefits their literacy and overall academic performance.

The study further notes that neuroscience-informed education, which includes teaching students about the workings of their own brains, helps foster a growth mindset. This shift in mindset makes students more likely to view learning challenges as opportunities for growth rather than obstacles, ultimately improving motivation and academic outcomes.[9]

---

[9] Goldberg, H. (2022). Growing brains, nurturing minds—neuroscience as an educational tool to support students' development as life-long learners. *Brain Sciences* 12: 1622.

This knowledge helps demystify the complexities of reading, transforming it from a passive act into a dynamic engagement with their cognitive abilities. Moreover, by integrating brain science into literacy instruction, teachers can personalize learning experiences, adapt strategies to individual learning styles, and foster a deeper appreciation for the learning process. Ultimately, teaching about the brain equips students not only to read more effectively but also to approach learning with curiosity, resilience, and a deeper understanding of their own mental capabilities.

Benefits of Teaching About the Brain

For the Teacher	For the Student
✓ Improved instructional strategies	✓ Enhanced learning
✓ Early identification of learning issues	✓ Increased motivation
✓ Personalized learning	✓ Improved reading skills
✓ Enhanced engagement	✓ Better retention
✓ Better classroom management	✓ Self-regulation skills
	✓ Critical thinking support for diverse learners

The Brain and the Science of Reading

Lately, there's been a lot of exciting progress in understanding how our brains work when we read. This new area of research is helping us figure out what happens in our heads when we decode words and understand what we read. These insights are making a big difference in how we approach education. From creating personalized learning plans for students to deciding on school-wide curriculums, the discoveries from brain studies are changing the way we teach. By exploring how our brains handle written language, the *Science of Reading* gives us the tools to develop better teaching methods, support early reading skills, and emphasize the importance of using proven techniques to help all kinds of learners become strong readers. So, what does the Science of Reading say about how our brains play a role in literacy?

Phonological Awareness

Phonological awareness is all about playing with the sounds of language. It's a key skill for learning to read. Kids who are good at this can break down words into individual sounds (phonemes) and blend them back together, which helps with reading and spelling.

When we play with sounds, specific areas in the left side of our brain get busy. These areas help us recognize and process the sounds in words. Research shows that kids who get lots of practice with these skills are better readers. "Repetition fosters the growth of high-quality representations from phonemes and graphemes (letters) to word meanings and grammatical forms."[10] Activities such as clapping out syllables, playing sound-matching games, and singing songs can all enhance phonological awareness.

For kids who find reading challenging, focusing on sounds can be beneficial. Activities that involve breaking down and blending sounds can strengthen the brain's ability to decode words. This is especially beneficial for kids with dyslexia, as their brains can reorganize and create new connections with the right practice.

Interventions that focus on phonological awareness have shown significant benefits. Structured programs that include phonemic awareness tasks, like segmenting words into sounds and blending sounds to make words, can make a big difference. These practices support reading development and improve spelling and overall language skills.

---

[10] Wolf, M. (2018). The science and poetry in learning (and teaching) to read. *Phi Delta Kappan* 100 (4): 13–17. https://doi.org/10.1177/0031721718815667.

Orthographic Processing

Orthographic processing is about recognizing the visual patterns of letters and words. When we read a familiar word, a specific part of our brain lights up quickly, helping us read faster and more accurately.

This skill develops through lots of practice with reading. The more we see and practice words, the better we recognize them instantly. This is why early reading experiences and learning the relationships between letters and sounds are so important. "Theory, experiments on brain circuitry for reading, and education research all currently point to the superiority of grapheme-phoneme teaching methods."[11] Activities like sight word drills, word searches, and repeated reading of familiar texts help reinforce these visual patterns.

Different languages have different ways of matching sounds to letters. Some languages, like Spanish, have consistent letter-sound correspondences, while others, like English, are more variable. Understanding these differences can help teachers tailor their instruction to match the specific needs of their students. For instance, focusing on consistent patterns can accelerate reading fluency in languages with transparent orthographies.

Teachers can design instructional activities that promote automatic recognition of sight words and decoding skills for unfamiliar words. Games that involve matching letters to sounds, memory exercises with word cards, and practice with writing can all strengthen orthographic processing. This helps students become more confident and fluent readers.

Neuroplasticity and Learning

Our brains are incredibly flexible, a concept known as *neuroplasticity*. This means they can change and form new connections throughout our lives. Effective reading instruction can change the brain, making it better at reading.

---

[11] Cook, G. (2010). The brain and the written word. *Scientific American Mind* 21 (1): 62–65. https://doi.org/10.1038/scientificamericanmind0310-62.

Our brain structure changes when we learn to read, especially with methods like phonics. Areas involved in processing sounds and understanding text become more robust. This is why early and targeted reading instruction is so powerful. For instance, neuroimaging studies have shown increased gray matter volume in regions associated with phonological processing and reading comprehension after systematic phonics instruction. "Neuroplasticity underlies key aspects of reading, from forming new circuits to recycling neurons and adding branches over time. This plasticity makes the reading brain malleable and influenced by environmental factors, including what and how it reads, and how the reading circuit is formed."[12]

Early intervention is crucial, especially for struggling readers. Programs that focus on intensive, structured practice in phonemic awareness and phonics can lead to significant improvements. "Theory, experiments on brain circuitry for reading, and education research all currently point to the superiority of grapheme-phoneme teaching methods."[13] These interventions leverage the brain's ability to adapt and rewire in response to learning experiences, supporting the development of strong reading skills.

Every reader is unique. Some might be great at sounding out words but struggle with comprehension, while others might have solid vocabulary but need help with phonics. Understanding these differences helps teachers provide personalized support.

Using tools to assess each student's strengths and weaknesses allows teachers to create customized learning plans. This way, every student gets the help they need to become a confident reader. For example, assessments can identify specific areas where a student may need extra support, such as phonological awareness or comprehension strategies.

Teachers can use differentiated instruction techniques to meet the needs of diverse learners. This might include small group work, one-on-one tutoring, or using technology to provide additional practice and support. Educators can help all students achieve their reading potential by recognizing and addressing individual differences.

---

[12] Wolf, M. (2018). The science and poetry in learning (and teaching) to read. *Phi Delta Kappan* 100 (4): 13–17. https://doi.org/10.1177/0031721718815667.

[13] Cook, G. (2010). The brain and the written word. *Scientific American Mind* 21 (1): 62–65. https://doi.org/10.1038/scientificamericanmind0310-62.

Teaching Strategies

Insights from brain research have given us powerful tools for teaching reading. Effective strategies include systematic phonics instruction, building vocabulary, teaching comprehension skills, and promoting reading fluency.

Incorporating fun, multisensory activities makes learning more engaging. When lessons are interactive and connect different parts of the brain, students are more likely to enjoy reading and become better at it. Techniques like using tactile letters, visual aids, and interactive read-alouds can make learning to read an exciting adventure.

By understanding how the brain learns to read, teachers can use evidence-based practices to help all students succeed. This blend of science and education is a powerful way to ensure every child becomes a proficient reader. Ongoing professional development and access to the latest research can help educators stay informed and effective in their teaching practices.

Reading is a complex but excellent skill that our brains are designed to master. With the right strategies and support, everyone can enjoy the magic of reading!

> "I've always been interested in the brain, but when I found out how it works to actually learn how to read I was amazed. Connecting the brain to speaking, listening, and reading is such a complex aspect. Students have to know that they can grow their brain sometimes when they get to fourth grade or higher, they seem to think that they're either a good reader, or a bad reader already. When we talk about the brain, they figure out that they can actually continue to grow their brain and that they're not stuck."
>
> -Susan Neumeier, 4th Grade, Freedom Elementary, Ohio

Interest and the Brain

Have you ever reflected on reading lessons you've given and wondered why one went really well and another didn't? As a teacher always trying to improve, I wanted to identify factors that positively impact a successful reading lesson. I didn't realize until much later in my career that a student's interest level in the text or the subject matter in the text is directly related to their success in comprehension.

When you first begin reading a text, whether a book or an article, one of the initial processes that occurs in your brain is an assessment of your interest in the material. Your brain quickly decides if the content captures your interest. This decision sets off different neural pathways: one if you are interested and another if you are not. Research emphasizes the role of brain plasticity and how interest can trigger deeper processing and more effective learning, supporting the idea that our initial emotional response to a text significantly impacts how we process and retain information.[14]

If the material piques your interest, your brain engages more actively, enhancing memory retention, recall, and overall comprehension. In contrast, if you find the content uninteresting, your brain's response is slower and less motivated. This lack of interest increases cognitive tension and decreases your brain's reward response, making the reading process less engaging and less effective. Understanding these brain processes can help us appreciate the importance of finding and fostering interest in reading materials to improve comprehension and retention.

> Think back to Chapter 3, where I discussed the importance of getting to know your readers. Do you see the connection between understanding who your students are and the power of interest and curiosity? If you know and understand who your students are and what they like and dislike, you can use this information to design lessons and select texts that will pique their interest, automatically increasing their reading comprehension.

---

[14] Ardila, A. and Bertolucci, P. (2010). Illiteracy: the neuropsychology of cognition without reading. *Oxford Journals* 25: 689–712.

Think of yourself as a reader. How does curiosity and interest impact your ability to successfully read and comprehend text in your everyday personal and professional life?

Understanding the factors contributing to reading comprehension success is a key focus in educational and cognitive neuroscience research. Curiosity and interest stand out as particularly influential. These elements enhance the enjoyment of reading and significantly impact how well readers understand and retain information. Studies show that when students are curious or interested in the material, they engage more deeply, which significantly enhances both comprehension and memory retention. For instance, research from *Educational Psychology Review* emphasizes that fostering interest in reading materials—whether through autonomy, relevant content, or engagement strategies—improves motivation and comprehension. Interest-driven motivation is connected to the activation of neural pathways associated with pleasure and reward, which in turn strengthens cognitive engagement and learning.[15] We can gain valuable insights into effective reading strategies and educational practices by examining how curiosity and interest affect the brain.

Curiosity, a desire to learn and discover, and *interest*, an engagement with the material, activate specific brain regions and mechanisms that facilitate comprehension. This interaction between emotional and cognitive processes underscores the importance of fostering curiosity and interest in educational settings to improve reading outcomes. The following sections delve into the specific ways these factors influence reading comprehension through various brain functions.

Brain Functions and Comprehension
- Dopamine Release
- Engagement & Attention
- Prior Knowledge Activation

---

[15] Peterson, E.G. and Hidi, S. (2019). Curiosity and interest: current perspectives. *Educational Psychology Review* 31: 781–788. https://doi.org/10.1007/s10648-019-09513-0.

Dopamine Release

Curiosity triggers the brain's reward system, releasing dopamine, a neurotransmitter that significantly enhances attention and motivation. When dopamine is released, it acts on various brain regions to increase alertness and focus, making the reading experience more engaging. This heightened state of attention ensures that readers are more likely to absorb and understand the material they are reading. Dopamine's role in improving motivation also means that readers are more willing to invest the effort to comprehend complex texts.

Additionally, dopamine plays a crucial role in memory encoding and retrieval. When readers are curious, the increased dopamine levels facilitate the encoding of new information into long-term memory. This makes it easier to recall information later, leading to better retention of what has been read. Dopamine plays a crucial role in reward-motivated learning, and curiosity activates these reward pathways. The release of dopamine in the hippocampus strengthens memory consolidation processes, making it easier to retain and recall information. This effect is especially prominent when curiosity-driven learning engages the brain's reward system, which reinforces the learning experience.[16] Furthermore, higher dopamine levels enhance cognitive flexibility, allowing readers to adapt to new and complex reading materials readily. This adaptability is essential for processing unfamiliar concepts and integrating new knowledge with existing understanding.

Engagement and Attention

When readers are genuinely interested in the material, their engagement and focus increase significantly. This heightened engagement improves comprehension as readers are more attentive and less likely to be distracted. Sustained attention allows for deeper processing of the text, enabling readers to grasp nuances and underlying themes that might be missed with a more superficial reading approach. For example, a 2020 study by Liu and Gu investigated how attention and engagement influence reading

---

[16] Marvin, C. (2015). Columbuia Academic Commons How curiosity drives actions and learning: Dopamine, reward, and information seeking https://doi.org/10.7916/D8V40TX6.

comprehension, particularly in situations where readers faced interruptions or distractions. The study found that when students were highly engaged with the material, their ability to focus remained strong, leading to improved comprehension scores. The research highlighted that this sustained attention, driven by genuine interest, allowed readers to process deeper layers of the text, grasping nuances and underlying themes that are often overlooked in more distracted or superficial reading conditions.[17]

Engaged readers are also more likely to employ active reading strategies, such as annotating the text, asking questions, and summarizing key points. These strategies further enhance understanding by encouraging interaction with the material. By actively engaging with the text, readers can clarify their thoughts, make connections between different ideas, and reinforce their comprehension. This active involvement is crucial for transforming passive reading into a more dynamic and practical learning experience.

Prior Knowledge Activation

Interest in a topic often correlates with existing knowledge, which helps readers connect new information with what they already know. This connection facilitates schema activation, a process where prior knowledge structures are used to understand and organize new information. Readers can better integrate and remember the material by linking new content to existing schemas.

Activating prior knowledge provides a context for interpreting new content, making it easier to understand and recall. "Deep reading is always about connection—connecting what we know to what we read, what we read to what we feel, what we feel to what we think, and how we think to how we live out our lives in a connected world."[18] Readers who relate new information to familiar concepts are more likely to retain and apply it in different contexts. This contextual understanding enhances comprehension by allowing readers to see the relevance and application of the material, making the reading experience more meaningful and memorable.

---

[17] Liu, Y. and Gu, X. (2020). Media multitasking, attention, and comprehension. *Springer Nature* 68 (1): 67–87. https://www.jstor.org/stable/10.2307/48727429.

[18] Wolf, M. (2018). The science and poetry in learning (and teaching) to read. *Phi Delta Kappan* 100 (4): 13–17. https://doi.org/10.1177/0031721718815667.

	Activating Prior Knowledge
KWL Chart	Have students fill out a chart with three columns: "What I Know," "What I Want to Know," and "What I Learned." Start by discussing the first two columns.
Think-Pair-Share	Ask a question related to the topic of the text. Students think about their answer, discuss it with a partner, and then share with the class.
Brainstorming	Write a keyword or phrase from the text on the board and have students call out related words or concepts. Record these ideas for reference.
Word Association	Present a key term or concept from the text and have students quickly write down or share words they associate with it.
Anticipation Guide	Create a list of true/false or agree/disagree statements related to the text. Students respond before reading and revisit their responses after reading to see how their understanding has changed.
Quick Write	Give students a prompt related to the text and have them write for a few minutes about what they know or think about the topic.
Graphic Organizers	Use Venn diagrams, concept maps, or other organizers to help students visually connect new information with what they already know.
Questioning	Pose open-ended questions about the text's topic to spark curiosity and discussion.
Predicting	Show students the title, cover, or a key image from the text and have them predict what the text will be about.
Personal Connections	Ask students to relate the topic to their own experiences or prior knowledge.

Emotional Connection

Emotionally engaging content stimulates the amygdala, a brain region involved in emotional processing and memory consolidation. When readers form positive emotional connections with the material, their ability to remember and recall information improves. Research suggests that emotionally engaging content not only captures attention more effectively but also enhances the depth of processing, leading to better memory retention over time. Emotional stimuli tend to consume more cognitive resources, leading to heightened attention and deeper engagement, which are critical factors for improving learning and recall.[19] This emotional engagement can increase intrinsic motivation, encouraging readers to delve deeper into the text and persist through challenging sections.

Positive emotional connections can also reduce anxiety, making the reading experience more enjoyable and less stressful. When readers feel emotionally connected to the content, they are more likely to find personal relevance. This personal relevance enhances memory retention and makes the content more impactful, as readers can relate it to their experiences and emotions.

Neuroplasticity

Curiosity-driven learning promotes neural neuroplasticity, the brain's ability to reorganize itself by forming new neural connections. This increased plasticity facilitates acquiring and integrating new information, enhancing the brain's capacity to adapt and respond to changing demands. Neuroplasticity is crucial for developing higher-order thinking skills, such as critical analysis and problem-solving, essential for comprehending complex texts.

A 2017 study by Chai et al. examined the relationship between emotional engagement and memory retention, finding that emotional stimuli capture attention more effectively and lead to deeper cognitive processing. This deeper engagement results in improved long-term retention of the material. The study highlights that emotional content requires

---

[19] Bradley, M. and Sambuco, N. (2022). Emotional memory and amygdala activation. *Frontiers in Behavioral Neuroscience* 16: 896285.

more cognitive resources, specifically engaging brain regions such as the amygdala and hippocampus, which are crucial for memory consolidation. This increased attention and engagement enhance the ability to recall information later, making emotional stimuli particularly effective in educational contexts.[20]

As the brain forms new connections, it becomes more adept at processing and retaining information. This adaptability allows readers to build on their knowledge and develop a deeper understanding of the material. By promoting neuroplasticity, curiosity-driven learning supports continuous cognitive growth and the ability to tackle increasingly challenging reading materials.

Intrinsic Motivation

Reading out of genuine interest fosters intrinsic motivation, a powerful long-term learning and comprehension driver. Intrinsically motivated readers are likelier to set personal reading goals and persevere through complex texts. This sustained motivation encourages a deeper exploration of topics, leading to a more comprehensive understanding of the material.

Intrinsic motivation supports self-directed learning, allowing readers to take ownership of their education and pursue subjects that captivate their interest. This autonomy in learning fosters a sense of curiosity and engagement, making the reading experience more enjoyable and fulfilling. By nurturing intrinsic motivation, readers are more likely to develop a lifelong love of learning and continue to seek out new knowledge independently.

A study published in *Educational Psychology Review* highlights how teacher-student interactions can significantly promote self-regulated learning (SRL) in elementary school students. This research emphasizes that when teachers provide high-quality instructional support, tailored to the needs of their students and focused on autonomy, it enhances students' intrinsic motivation. The study found that fostering autonomy allows students to take more control of their learning, fueling curiosity and deeper engagement with the material. This, in turn, helps students develop self-regulation strategies, which are

---

[20] Tyng, C., Amin, H., Saad, M., and Malik, A. (2017). The Influences of emotion on learning and memory. *Frontiers in Psychology* 8: 1454.

essential for lifelong learning. By encouraging students to become intrinsically motivated, they are more likely to pursue knowledge independently and develop a lasting love of learning.[21]

Metacognition

Interested readers are more likely to engage in *metacognitive strategies*, such as self-questioning, summarizing, and reflecting on their understanding. These strategies help readers monitor their comprehension and adjust as needed, leading to a deeper engagement with the text. Metacognitive awareness allows readers to identify gaps in their knowledge and seek clarification, enhancing their overall understanding.

By fostering metacognitive skills, readers can develop a more strategic approach to reading, using techniques that enhance comprehension and retention. These strategies encourage active participation in the reading process, making assimilating and applying new information easier. As readers become more adept at monitoring their understanding, they can better manage their learning and improve their ability to comprehend complex texts. I talk more about metacognition in Chapter 7.

Closing

Teaching students about how the brain works when they read is not just an intriguing addition to the curriculum; it is an essential component for fostering deeper understanding and engagement in literacy. By educating students on the brain's structure and processes, such as the roles of the lobes in reading and the functions of neurons and dendrites, we empower them with valuable insights into their learning mechanisms. This knowledge transforms reading from a passive activity into an active exploration of their cognitive abilities, encouraging them to take ownership of their learning journey.

Understanding the brain's role in reading helps demystify the complexities involved in the process. Students gain a clearer perspective on how different brain parts collaborate to decode words, comprehend text, and retain information. This not only boosts their

---

[21] de Ruig, N.J., de Jong, P.F., and Zee, M. (2023). Stimulating elementary school students' self-regulated learning through high-quality interactions and relationships: a narrative review. *Educational Psychology Review* 35: 71. https://doi.org/10.1007/s10648-023-09795-5.

confidence but also enhances their ability to employ effective reading strategies tailored to their unique cognitive strengths. When students understand that their brains grow and adapt through practice and perseverance, they develop resilience and a growth mindset, which are crucial for academic success and lifelong learning.

> "I spend the first two weeks of school doing all of these comprehension lessons. It has allowed my students to believe they are readers and can do hard things. I really believe these lessons are life-changing because I've even had my students in special education tell me that now they know they can read. Our class mascot is Billy Bob the brain cell and is inspired from the lesson on neurons and dendrites. I love these lessons and they have changed the way I teach my students in more engaging and exciting ways."
>
> -Angie Thompson, 3rd Grade, Freedom Prep Academy-Provo Elementary, Utah

Moreover, integrating brain education into literacy instruction has far-reaching benefits beyond improved reading skills. It fosters empathy, cognitive awareness, and effective communication, as students learn to appreciate the intricate processes behind their thoughts and actions. This holistic approach to education nurtures well-rounded individuals who are better equipped to face challenges and engage meaningfully with the world around them.

Ultimately, teaching about the brain in the context of reading not only enhances students' literacy skills but also instills a profound appreciation for their cognitive capabilities. It empowers them to become self-aware, resilient learners who are curious about the world and motivated to achieve their full potential. By making brain education a cornerstone of literacy instruction, you lay the foundation for a future where students are not just proficient readers but also enthusiastic, lifelong learners.

Consider these questions as you ponder this issue more and try the following lessons.

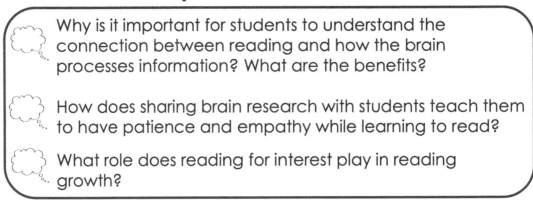

Lessons to Try

Remember that you can access these lesson for free at `http://www.cieraharristeaching.com/ttrlessons` using the passcode: `literacy for all`.

"A Reader's Brain" Lesson

The lesson plan "A Reader's Brain" provides an in-depth look at how different parts of the brain contribute to the process of reading. The objective of the lesson is for students to understand the main parts of the brain and how each part aids in reading. It covers the functions of the frontal, temporal, parietal, and occipital lobes, explaining their roles in speech production, verbal memory, language comprehension, and visual identification of letters. The lesson includes interactive activities where students create a brain diagram, coloring and labeling each part to reinforce their understanding.

Teaching this lesson is important because it bridges the gap between biological functions and cognitive skills. By understanding how the brain works, students can gain insights into their learning processes, which can help them develop strategies to improve their reading skills. This knowledge empowers students to become more self-aware and active participants in their learning journey, making them better equipped to tackle challenges in reading and other areas.

The benefits of teaching this lesson extend beyond reading comprehension. It encourages critical thinking and scientific inquiry, as students explore the connection between brain anatomy and function. This multidisciplinary approach not only enhances their reading abilities but also fosters a deeper appreciation for science and the human body. Additionally, the hands-on activities promote engagement and retention, making the learning experience enjoyable and memorable.

Quick Tip

When teaching this lesson, use real-life examples and relatable contexts to explain each brain function. This will help students connect the scientific concepts to their everyday experiences, making the information more relevant and easier to grasp.

"Neurons and Dendrites" Lesson

The lesson plan "Neurons and Dendrites" focuses on helping students understand the biological basis of learning by exploring how the brain grows and functions when acquiring new skills. The lesson begins with essential questions about neurons and dendrites, and why practice and hard work are crucial for brain development. It involves showing students images of neurons, labeling their parts (dendrites, axon, nucleus), and explaining how these components help the brain communicate and store information. Through hands-on activities like drawing and connecting neurons, students visualize how their efforts in learning lead to stronger neural connections.

Teaching this lesson is vital because it links the abstract concept of learning to concrete biological processes, making it easier for students to grasp why practice leads to improvement. By understanding that neurons strengthen their connections through repeated practice, students can appreciate the importance of persistence and effort in mastering new skills. This insight not only motivates students but also fosters a growth mindset, where they recognize that their abilities can improve with dedication and hard work.

The benefits of this lesson extend beyond a better understanding of neuroscience. It encourages students to approach challenges with resilience, knowing that each attempt contributes to their brain's growth. The lesson also integrates science with literacy, making learning interdisciplinary and engaging. By involving students in interactive activities, it ensures that the information is memorable and enjoyable, promoting long-term retention and application of the concepts learned.

Quick Tip: When teaching this lesson, use relatable analogies to explain the function of neurons and dendrites, such as comparing dendrites to hands reaching out to communicate. This helps students visualize and understand the concepts better, making the lesson more effective and engaging.

"Interests and the Brain" Lesson

The lesson plan "Interests and the Brain" aims to help students understand how their personal interests can enhance their focus and effectiveness as readers. The lesson begins by engaging students with questions about their reading preferences, using examples like choosing between books on spinach or ice cream to illustrate how interest influences their brain's reaction. The plan explains that when students read material that interests them, their brains produce positive chemical reactions, stimulating the brain's reward system. This reaction increases focus, memory, and motivation, leading to better retention and a more enjoyable reading experience.

The importance of this lesson lies in its ability to connect the concept of interest with cognitive engagement and learning efficiency. By highlighting the brain's role in processing interesting information, students learn to value their preferences and are encouraged to select reading materials that resonate with them. This approach not only enhances their reading skills but also fosters a lifelong love of learning by making the process enjoyable and relevant to their personal lives. Understanding these mechanisms empowers students to make informed choices about their reading, leading to improved academic performance and personal growth.

The benefits of teaching this lesson are multifaceted. It promotes a growth mindset by showing students that their brain's response to interesting material can be leveraged to improve learning outcomes. The introduction of interest book clubs provides a practical application of this concept, allowing students to explore topics they are passionate about in a supportive, collaborative environment. This method reduces the pressure of traditional assignments and fosters a sense of community and shared learning. Additionally, the flexibility of the lesson, with options for both in-person and virtual implementation, ensures that it can be adapted to various educational settings.

Quick Tip

When introducing the concept of interest book clubs, involve students in the selection process by allowing them to suggest and vote on topics. This increases their investment in the activity and ensures that the chosen subjects genuinely reflect their interests, leading to higher engagement and participation.

CHAPTER 5

SCHEMA: THE POWER OF PERSPECTIVE

Cognitive Science of a Reader

Explore the neurological and cognitive processes behind reading, emphasizing the importance of schema.

Understanding and utilizing schema is a powerful tool in the realm of literacy education. Schema, the mental framework that helps us organize and interpret information, plays a crucial role in how students connect prior knowledge with new information to enhance comprehension. This chapter aims to emphasize the importance of teaching schema intentionally and continuously throughout the school year, transforming how students interpret texts and leading to deeper and more meaningful reading experiences.

Schema is not just a one-time lesson but an ongoing strategy that teachers need to integrate into their curriculum. When students activate their schema, they draw upon their previous knowledge and experiences, which helps them make sense of new information. For example, if a student has a schema for a "birthday party," they might expect cake, games, and presents whenever they read about one. This mental structure allows students to quickly understand and predict what might happen in a new situation, thus aiding in comprehension and retention.

The significance of schema extends beyond mere reading skills. It fosters critical thinking and analytical abilities as students learn to make inferences, predictions, and connections within the text and their own experiences. By understanding and leveraging schema, educators can help students become more engaged readers who are capable of navigating complex texts with ease and insight. This chapter delves into the definition of schema, its types, and its pivotal role in reading comprehension, supported by current research and practical examples.

This chapter explores strategies to activate and use schema before, during, and after reading. By connecting new information to existing knowledge, students can enhance their understanding and retention of texts. This approach not only improves literacy outcomes but also fosters a lifelong love of reading and learning. Educators find practical guidance on how to implement schema-based instruction in their classrooms, ensuring that every student can benefit from this essential cognitive tool.

Chapter 5 Objectives

 The readers will understand and articulate the concept of schema and its role in cognitive processing and reading comprehension.

 The readers will recognize and differentiate between content, conceptual, procedural, cultural, and metacognitive schema.

 The readers will learn strategies to activate and use schema before, during, and after reading to enhance comprehension.

 The readers will develop the ability to connect new information to existing knowledge, improving understanding and retention of texts.

 The readers will utilize schema to make inferences and predictions and critically analyze texts, leading to a deeper engagement with the material.

What Is Schema?

Schema is the most powerful tool that a child has and brings with them when they come to your classroom. It's the number one strategy a student can use when reading. As a teacher, that's pretty important to know. Teachers need to teach schema intentionally at the beginning of the year and support it throughout the year. Schema isn't something that you talk about and teach one time. If you do, then you are entirely underutilizing this tool that students have and could be using to improve their comprehension. Students come with all of this knowledge. They need to know how, when, and where to use it to become better at reading.

You know from Chapter 1 that students already possess an essential part of the reading process: thinking. We tell them they are readers because they can think. This thinking comes from them using information they already know (their schema) and combining it with the text they are reading. So, they already have half of the equation. They have prior knowledge and know how to think, so we embrace this and support it by teaching them how to intentionally use schema as a reading strategy that will take their understanding of a text from the surface to an extended level.

Definition: schema A mental framework that a student uses to understand and organize information. This includes their prior knowledge, experiences, beliefs, and skills. In reading, a student's schema helps them make sense of new texts by connecting what they already know with what they are learning, enhancing comprehension and retention.

So we keep using the word *schema*, but we haven't stopped considering what it means. The process of connecting known information to new information takes place through a series of networkable connections known as schema.[1] It is a mental framework that helps us organize and interpret information. Think of it as a sort of cognitive blueprint or map

---

[1] Neumann, K.L. and Kopcha, T.J. (2018). The use of schema theory in learning, design, and technology. *TechTrends* 62 (5): 429–431. https://doi.org/10.1007/s11528-018-0319-0.

that our brains use to understand the world around us. When students encounter new information, they use their existing schema to make sense of it. For example, if a child has a schema for a "birthday party," they might expect cake, games, and presents whenever they hear about one. This mental structure lets them quickly understand and predict what might happen in a new situation.

Schema is the most powerful tool that a child has and brings with them when they come to your classroom.

Students develop their schema through experiences and interactions with their environment. These experiences can come from various sources, including family, school, community, media, and personal activities. Every time a child learns something new, whether it's about animals, math concepts, or social rules, they build and refine their schema. This process is continuous, meaning that as students grow and have more experiences, their schema becomes more complex and sophisticated.

While schema and background knowledge are closely related, they are not exactly the same. A study published in the *Journal of Cognitive Neuroscience* by van Kesteren et al. (2014) sheds light on the relationship between schema and background knowledge, highlighting that while they are related, they are not the same. Background knowledge refers to factual information stored in memory, whereas schemas are cognitive structures that help organize and interpret that information. The study found that schemas assist in learning by integrating new information into preexisting knowledge frameworks, allowing for more efficient processing. This process differs from simply recalling background knowledge, as schemas involve the application and connection of knowledge in meaningful ways to enhance learning and memory retention.[2]

Current research in the Science of Reading emphasizes the critical role of schema in reading comprehension. According to this research, students who can connect new information to their existing schema can better understand and remember what they read. This is because their schema provides a context for new information, making it easier to integrate and recall later. A study led by James Kim at the Harvard Graduate School of Education found that students who develop strong schemas—mental frameworks that help organize and apply knowledge—can better connect new information to their prior knowledge. This connection allows them to comprehend and retain new material more effectively. The study specifically highlighted how expanding students' background knowledge through a content-rich curriculum in subjects like science significantly improved their reading comprehension over time. By linking new concepts to existing schemas, students were able to tackle more complex reading tasks with greater success.[3] For teachers, activating students' prior knowledge before reading and helping them build new schema related to the text can significantly enhance their comprehension and

---

[2] Kesteren, M., Rijpkeme, M., and Ruiter, D. (2014). Building on prior knowledge: Schema-dependent encoding processes relate to academic performance. *Journal of Cognitive Neuroscience* 26 (20): 2250–2261. https://doi.org/10.1162/jocn_a_00630.

[3] Kim, J., Burkhauser, M., and Relyea, J. (2023). A longitudinal randomized trial of a sustained content literacy intervention from first to second grade: transfer effects on students' reading comprehension. *American Psychological Association* 115 (10): 73–98.

retention. By recognizing and nurturing schema development, educators can create more effective and engaging learning experiences for their students.

> **Places Where Students Get Schema**
> - Family interactions and conversations
> - School lessons and educational activities
> - Books, stories, and reading materials
> - Personal experiences and observations
> - Cultural traditions and practices
> - Media, including TV shows, movies, and digital content
> - Community events and social interactions
> - Travel experiences and exposure to different environments
> - Extracurricular activities such as sports, arts, and clubs
> - Internet and online resources

Why Is Schema Important?

Brain science in Chapter 4 shows that neurons and dendrites grow as information and experiences are repeated. This is the basis of understanding to show that accessing schema to something students know and that's already in their brains is essential to make stronger connections and support memory and recall.

Schema plays a pivotal role in literacy and reading comprehension by serving as a mental framework that helps readers make sense of text. When students activate their schema while reading, they draw upon their prior knowledge and experiences to connect with the content. This process significantly enhances their ability to understand and retain information. It makes good sense that to comprehend a story or text readers will need a threshold of knowledge about the topic. Without such knowledge, it becomes difficult to construct a meaningful mental model of what the text is about.[4]

The activation of schema enables readers to engage more deeply with the text. Students can make predictions, ask relevant questions, and connect ideas within the text and their

---

[4] Neumann, K.L. and Kopcha, T.J. (2018). The use of schema theory in learning, design, and technology. *TechTrends* 62 (5): 429–431. https://doi.org/10.1007/s11528-018-0319-0.

experiences by relating what they are reading to what they already know. This active engagement improves comprehension and fosters critical thinking skills for analyzing and interpreting complex texts.

Research in literacy emphasizes that effective reading comprehension strategies, such as predicting, summarizing, and making inferences, are closely linked to schema activation. A 2020 study, "The Effects of Schema Activation and Reading Strategy Use on L2 Reading Comprehension," found that students who activated prior knowledge before reading could better predict and infer meanings, leading to improved comprehension. By using schema, students connect background knowledge to the text, enhancing their ability to engage with and understand complex material.[5] When students access their schema, they are better equipped to apply these strategies effectively, leading to improved comprehension outcomes. For example, students with activated schema can more readily contextualize and understand the new information when encountering unfamiliar vocabulary or concepts.

For example: "Literacy experts often recommend that science teachers focus on comprehension tools such as visualizing, predicting, summarizing, questioning, making connections, and inferring. We argue, however, that without sufficient background knowledge, none of these tools will be effective."[6]

Without activating schema, students may struggle to comprehend texts effectively. The text can appear disjointed or irrelevant when readers fail to connect new information to their existing knowledge base. This disconnect hinders their ability to make predictions, infer meaning, and draw conclusions, essential skills for deep comprehension. For instance, without schema, students may encounter difficulties understanding context-specific vocabulary or cultural references embedded within the text. This lack of connection to prior knowledge can lead to frustration and disengagement from reading

---

[5] Cho, Y. and Ma, J. (2020). The effects of schema activation and reading strategy use on L2 reading comprehension. *English Teaching* 75 (3): 49–68.
[6] Marzano, R.J. (2024). Association for Supervision and Curriculum Development Building background knowledge for academic achievement: research on what works in schools.

activities. Think back to Chapter 1, which listed a variety of medical terms that would be impossible to understand without the proper background knowledge.

> "I grew up feeling dumber than a box of rocks. My sister, a year younger than me, and my brother, a year older than me, are both very intellectual. They are naturally very logistical thinkers and seem to gather and retain information just by breathing. I, on the other hand, had to bust my butt for every C I earned. I did not think like they did (them, left brain vs. me, out the door right brain). I thought I knew nothing, had nothing to offer, brought nothing to the table. I had nicknames like "bonehead" and "density" because I just didn't get it the first, second, or even third times around. Learning about schema and how to present it to my 4th graders has helped me realize I had more to offer than anyone thought but I just didn't know it. My students WILL know how very important they are, and how much incredible stuff they already know and bring to the table as readers."
>
> -Jenny Altensee, 5th Grade, Fairborne Intermediate School, Ohio

Moreover, without schema, students may rely solely on surface-level reading skills, such as decoding words or identifying literal meanings. This approach limits their ability to engage critically with the text and explore deeper layers of meaning. "Put simply, the more you know about a topic, the easier it is to read a text, understand it, and retain information. Previous studies have shown that background knowledge plays in an enormous role in reading comprehension."[7] By contrast, activating schema allows students to approach reading as a dynamic process of constructing meaning, actively integrating new information with what they already know. This enhances comprehension and encourages lifelong learning habits that extend beyond the classroom. Thus, the intentional use of schema in literacy instruction is crucial for nurturing proficient readers who can navigate and interpret texts effectively across various subjects and genres.

---

[7] Neumann, K.L. and Kopcha, T.J. (2018). The use of schema theory in learning, design, and technology. *TechTrends* 62 (5): 429–431. https://doi.org/10.1007/s11528-018-0319-0.

"So last week we were continuing our lessons. When we got to 'Accessing My Schema,' I followed the lesson plans exactly. We did the t-Chart with a book about Mt. Everest and one about Chihuahua dogs. As expected, kids had much more schema about Chihuahua dogs than Mt. Everest. I gave them the Brain Break, then I read the books I had checked out. After reading the books, I started to write the new information kids learned from the Mt. Everest book and the Chihuahua dogs book. As we started listing fact after fact that they remembered from the book about Chihuahuas, one of my students had an 'aha moment' and made the connection that when they had more schema about a topic, it was easier to learn new information about that topic. Home run!!!"

-Mily Ramos Pena-5th Grade-Gonzalo & Sofia Garcia Elementary School, Texas

Benefits of Using Schema

Approaching each text as new information can be overwhelming and confusing. By accessing your students' schema, you ensure they know the content, vocabulary, imagery, and information they will be confronted with when they read. This gives your students an edge. There are many benefits to taking time and using schema in your reading instruction. Let's break them down!

- **Enhanced understanding:** Activating schema allows students to connect new information to what they already know, providing a framework that aids in understanding complex ideas and relationships within the text. This process helps students make sense of unfamiliar concepts by relating them to familiar ones.
- **Improved memory:** Schema activation enhances memory retention by organizing new information into existing mental frameworks. Background knowledge is like Velcro. It helps new information adhere. The more background knowledge you develop and use, the more you can make sense of and remember new information.[8] When students

---

[8] Zimmermann, S. and Hutchins, C. (2003). *7 Keys to Comprehension: How to Help Your Kids Read It and Get It!* Three Rivers Press.

connect new content to their schema, recalling and retaining information become easier over time, as the schema provides a structured context for storage and retrieval.
- **Increased engagement:** Students are more engaged when they can relate to the content they are reading. Schema activation encourages active participation in reading by making the material more personally relevant, promoting sustained interest and motivation.
- **Effective problem-solving:** Students can effectively problem-solve within the text by applying schema. They use their prior knowledge to predict outcomes, analyze situations, and draw conclusions based on the information presented. This critical thinking skill is essential for deeper comprehension and analytical reasoning.
- **Enhanced inference skills:** Schema helps students make informed inferences about the text by filling in gaps and making connections based on their background knowledge. This ability to infer meaning beyond the literal text contributes to a deeper understanding of implicit messages and underlying themes.
- **Facilitated text comprehension:** Through schema activation, understanding the context, themes, and perspectives presented in a text becomes more accessible. Students can better interpret and analyze the author's intentions and the implications of the information presented.
- **Cultural understanding:** Schema enables students to interpret cultural nuances and references embedded in texts. By activating cultural schema, students gain insights into diverse perspectives, practices, and beliefs, promoting cultural literacy and sensitivity. "Content schema is part of the individual's cultural orientation, and since culture affects all aspects of life, it certainly has a major impact on all elements of reading."[9]
- **Improved vocabulary acquisition:** Schema facilitates vocabulary acquisition by providing context for unfamiliar words encountered in the text. Students can deduce meanings and nuances of words based on their schema, expanding their vocabulary and comprehension skills.
- **Enhanced metacognition:** Reflecting on how their schema influences comprehension encourages metacognitive awareness. Students become more aware of their thinking processes and strategies, enabling them to monitor and adjust their

---

[9] Gilakjani, A.P. and Ahmadi, S.M. (2011). The relationship between L2 reading comprehension and schema theory: a matter of text familiarity. *International Journal of Information and Education Technology* 1 (2): 142–149.

comprehension strategies effectively. Remember to check out Chapter 7 for more information on metacognition.

- **Promotion of lifelong learning skills:** Utilizing schema fosters a habit of connecting new learning to prior knowledge. This practice supports lifelong learning by encouraging students to build upon existing knowledge, connect across subjects and disciplines, and continuously expand their understanding of the world around them.

Understanding Schema on a Deeper Level

Schema is a broad concept encompassing a wide range of topics and ideas. It's one thing to understand schema's importance and benefits. Still, it's essential to understand where schema comes from and to be able to utilize that information and incorporate it into your literacy instruction. So, what are the different schema types, and how do you use this information to support comprehension? Let's look at the various kinds of schema in the following sections.

Type of Schema	Definition
Content Schema	knowledge of specific facts and details about subjects, aiding comprehension by connecting new information to existing knowledge
Cultural Schema	awareness of cultural norms and practices, aiding interpretation of characters' motivations and contextual influences in texts
Conceptual Schema	understanding abstract ideas and relationships, enabling analysis of complex text themes and theories
Procedural Schema	knowledge of procedures and strategies for tasks, supporting navigation of instructional texts, and application of reading skills
Metacognitive Schema	awareness of one's thinking processes and strategies, facilitating self-regulated learning and effective reading practices

Content Schema

Content schema is the knowledge of specific facts and details about subjects, aiding comprehension by connecting new information to existing knowledge.

This type of schema relates to specific knowledge about topics, events, and facts. For instance, understanding the life cycle of a butterfly or the causes of the American Revolution falls under content schema. Content schema is essential in literacy because it gives students background knowledge that helps them comprehend texts more deeply. Students with prior knowledge of the subject matter can better anticipate what they will read, make connections within the text, and infer meaning from the content. For example, knowing that the earth orbits the sun or that George Washington was the first president of the United States.

A peer-reviewed study titled "Effects of Prior Knowledge on Comprehending Text About Learning Strategies" published in *Frontiers in Psychology* (2020) supports the claim that students with prior knowledge are better able to anticipate what they will read, make connections within the text, and infer meaning from the content. The study found that students who possessed prior knowledge about a topic demonstrated better comprehension, as they could more effectively integrate new information with their existing knowledge. This allowed them to make logical inferences and connections, which facilitated a deeper understanding of the material. The research also emphasized that students who valued and utilized prior knowledge strategies showed enhanced comprehension, particularly when reading complex texts.

This study underscores the importance of building and activating prior knowledge to improve reading comprehension, as it helps students anticipate content, make connections, and infer meanings more effectively.[10]

Conceptual Schema

Conceptual schema involves understanding abstract ideas and relationships, enabling analysis of complex text themes and theories.

---

[10] Kikas, E., Silinskas, G., Madamurk, K., and Soodle, P. (2021). Effects of prior knowledge on comprehending text about learning strategies. *Frontiers in Education* 6: 766589.

This includes understanding principle and relationships. It encompasses broader concepts that transcend specific details, such as understanding democracy, gravity, or justice. The conceptual schema supports literacy by enabling students to grasp complex themes and theories presented in texts. By activating conceptual schema, students can analyze and synthesize information, identify main ideas, and connect across different texts and contexts.

For example, understanding the concept of gravity or comprehending the idea of democracy.

Procedural Schema

Procedural schema refers to knowledge of procedures, sequences, and task completion strategies. It supports navigation of instructional texts and application of reading skills. It includes understanding how-to instructions, steps in problem-solving processes, or strategies for writing a persuasive essay. Procedural schema supports literacy by equipping students with the skills to navigate and comprehend instructional texts, procedural manuals, and academic writing. Understanding procedural schema helps students follow text structures, apply reading strategies effectively, and engage in active reading practices.

For example, knowing how to follow a recipe to bake a cake or understanding the steps to solve a math problem.

Cultural Schema

Cultural schema involves knowledge about cultural norms and practices, values, traditions, and practices of different groups or societies. It aids interpretation of characters' motivations and contextual influences in texts. It includes understanding cultural references, idiomatic expressions, and perspectives shaped by cultural backgrounds. Cultural schema is crucial in literacy because it helps students interpret and appreciate diverse perspectives and contexts represented in texts. "Students need to have direct access to meaningful and relevant texts, and the classroom library is the optimal location. As the United States population becomes more diverse, educators must focus not only on developing their own cultural awareness but also on assisting their students in developing their cultural awareness."[11] By activating cultural schema, students can better understand characters' motivations, interpret figurative language, and analyze the impact of cultural contexts on the text's themes and messages.

For example, understanding gestures that indicate politeness in different cultures or recognizing the significance of holidays like Diwali or Hanukkah.

Metacognitive Schema

Metacognitive schema pertains to knowledge and awareness of one's thinking processes and strategies, facilitating self-regulated learning and effective reading practices.

It includes understanding how to monitor comprehension, apply reading strategies, and reflect on learning experiences. The metacognitive schema supports literacy by fostering self-regulated learning behaviors and adaptive reading strategies. When students activate metacognitive schema, they can evaluate their understanding, adjust their reading approaches, and employ effective comprehension strategies to enhance their reading proficiency.

For example, when you reflect on your reading comprehension by asking yourself, "Do I understand what I just read?" or "Which reading strategy should I use to tackle this text?"

Reflect: Think about a recent text you've read. Which type of schema (content, conceptual, procedural, cultural, or metacognitive) did you activate most while reading? How did it help you understand the material better?

How Schema Influences Reading Comprehension

Understanding these schema types is essential for educators because it allows them to tailor instruction and support based on students' diverse cognitive strengths and needs.

---

[11] Howlett, K.M. and Young, H.D. (2019). Building a classroom library based on multicultural principles: a checklist for future k-6 teachers. *Multicultural Education* 26 (3-4): 40–46.

Educators can help students build connections between prior knowledge and new information by recognizing and activating different schema types, facilitating deeper comprehension, critical thinking, and engagement with texts across various subjects and genres. Moreover, fostering awareness of schema types encourages students to recognize the value of their background knowledge and apply it strategically to enhance their reading and learning experiences.

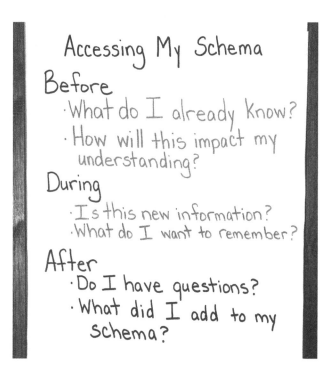

Remember that the goal in literacy is always comprehension; how do schema and comprehension truly connect? When we think of comprehension, teachers typically think of reading skills such as main idea and theme. Understanding how schema influences reading comprehension involves recognizing its impact on these reading skills. Here's an expanded explanation with a chart illustrating how schema supports different skills.

Reading Skill	How Schema Supports It
Main Idea	Schema helps readers identify the central topic or message by connecting key details to their existing knowledge. When activated, schema helps readers discern the most significant information in the text.
Theme	Understanding themes involves recognizing recurring ideas or messages in a text. Schema allows readers to relate these themes to broader concepts and experiences, facilitating a deeper grasp of the author's intended message.
Inference	Making inferences requires readers to draw conclusions based on implicit information. Schema aids in filling gaps in the text by leveraging prior knowledge to deduce meaning and make logical connections.
Visualization	Visualizing involves creating mental images based on textual descriptions. Schema enables readers to draw upon personal experiences and sensory details to imagine scenes and events described in the text vividly.
Predictions	Predicting involves anticipating what might happen next in the text. Schema supports predictions by allowing readers to use prior knowledge to forecast outcomes based on patterns, context clues, and character motivations.
Context Clues	Understanding context clues helps readers decipher the meaning of unfamiliar words or phrases. Schema provides contextual knowledge that aids in interpreting vocabulary within the broader context of the text.
Text Structure	Recognizing text structure involves identifying how information is organized (e.g., cause and effect, chronological order). Schema helps readers navigate text structures by recognizing familiar patterns and sequences.
Critical Thinking	Schema fosters critical thinking by encouraging readers to evaluate and analyze information within the text. It supports questioning, comparing, and contrasting ideas based on prior knowledge and experiences.
Summarizing	Summarizing requires condensing key information from a text. Schema assists in selecting and synthesizing relevant details, enabling readers to construct concise summaries that effectively capture the main points

It's obvious here that schema can support any and all reading skills we ask students to complete. It's integral to reading comprehension as it empowers readers to navigate texts with greater understanding, interpretive insight, and cognitive flexibility. By leveraging schema, readers can effectively decode, analyze, and derive meaning from diverse texts across various genres and subjects.

Three Steps to Using Schema in Your Reading Classroom

You should now understand that schema is an integral part of the reading process. But what does it look like inside the classroom? I've taken all that's known about schema and turned it into a simple three-step process.

3 Steps to Using Schema in Your Reading Classroom
1. Get to Know Your Students' Schema
2. Plan with Schema in Mind
3. Activate Schema Before, During, and After Reading

Step 1: Get to Know Your Students' Schema

Understanding your students' schema is crucial at the beginning of the school year. Head back to Chapter 3 for more information on how best to get to know your students. This knowledge provides a foundation for practical instruction and meaningful learning experiences. Getting to know your students' backgrounds, interests, and experiences helps you to tailor your teaching to meet their unique needs and to connect new content to their existing knowledge. "Too often we think of a student in regard to a predetermined reading level (e.g., M, magenta, 16), when in reality, as this and other studies have shown, a student's reading level varies depending on his or her interest in the text, as well as other factors, including background knowledge."[12] Students come from diverse backgrounds

---

[12] Duke, N.K., Pearson, P.D., Strachan, S.L., and Billman, A.K. (2011). International Reading Association 51-93 essential elements of fostering and teaching reading comprehension.

and bring a wealth of prior knowledge that can enrich the learning environment. Investing time in understanding their cultural, familial, and educational experiences creates a classroom atmosphere that values and builds upon their strengths.

In addition to backgrounds, learning about your students' likes and dislikes is crucial. Knowing their interests can help you select reading materials and design activities that are more engaging and relevant to them. When students see connections between their interests and classroom content, they are more motivated to participate and invest in their learning. "Importantly, texts or materials that trigger or capitalize on a student's interests contribute to motivation."[13] Similarly, being aware of their dislikes can help you avoid potential disengagement and create strategies to make less preferred subjects more interesting.

Understanding your students' reading habits and experiences is another key aspect of getting to know their schema. Some students may have rich reading experiences with a wide range of genres, while others might have had limited exposure to books. By gaining insight into their reading histories, you can better support their literacy development and choose appropriate texts to challenge and interest them. Knowing what types of books they enjoy, how often they read, and their comfort level with different reading materials helps create a more personalized learning journey that fosters a love for reading and builds strong comprehension skills.

Step 2: Plan with Schema in Mind

When teachers understand the schema that their students have and do not have, they can plan more effectively to support their literacy development. This intentional approach ensures that lessons are engaging and accessible, building on existing knowledge while addressing gaps.

---

[13] Duke, N.K., Pearson, P.D., Strachan, S.L., and Billman, A.K. (2011). International Reading Association 51-93 essential elements of fostering and teaching reading comprehension.

When Students Have the Schema

When teachers identify that students already possess relevant schema, they can design lessons that extend and deepen this knowledge. Here are some ways to leverage existing schema:

- **Providing advanced texts and projects:** Provide more challenging reading materials that push students to think critically and make deeper connections. Use complex texts that build on their existing knowledge, encouraging higher-order thinking and analysis.
- **Supplying enrichment activities:** Design enrichment activities that allow students to explore topics more deeply. This could include research projects, debates, or creative assignments that require them to apply their knowledge in new ways.
- **Facilitating discussions:** Use discussions to allow students to share and expand their schema. Encourage them to bring in personal experiences and prior knowledge during class discussions, fostering a collaborative learning environment where students learn from each other.
- **Connecting new concepts:** Introduce new concepts by linking them to what students already know. Use analogies and comparisons to make new information more relatable and easily understood.

When Students Lack the Schema

Teachers must provide foundational knowledge and scaffold learning experiences for students lacking the necessary schema. Here are strategies to build schema:

- **PRE-teaching vocabulary and concepts:** Before reading a new text, introduce key vocabulary and concepts. Use visuals, real-life examples, and simplified explanations to ensure students grasp the basics.
- **Building background knowledge:** Incorporate activities that build background knowledge relevant to the text. This could include watching educational videos; reading related, more straightforward texts; or engaging in hands-on activities that provide context.

- **Providing scaffolded instruction:** Break down complex texts and concepts into manageable chunks. Provide guided reading sessions, targeted questions, and step-by-step instructions to help students gradually build their understanding.
- **Using interactive read-alouds:** Use read-alouds to model thinking and connect new information to what students might already know. Pause frequently to ask questions, make connections, and explain concepts in simpler terms.

Quick Tip: Let students experience reading with no schema. How does it feel? Why was it hard to read and remember? Let them see and feel the power behind schema!

Step 3: Activate Schema Before, During, and After Reading

Activating schema is a critical component of reading comprehension, but it's a process that extends beyond just the beginning of the lesson. Many teachers make the mistake of only activating schema before reading, which, while important, is just one part of the process. To fully utilize schema, students must connect what they learn to their existing knowledge throughout the entire reading experience—before, during, and after reading.

Before Reading

Before reading, activating schema involves preparing students to connect their existing knowledge to the new content they will encounter. This stage helps set the stage for comprehension and engagement. By tapping into students' prior knowledge, teachers can stimulate their interest and provide a context for new information. The study "Prior Knowledge and Its Activation in Elementary Classroom Discourse" (2019) emphasizes the importance of activating schema before reading to improve comprehension. This research demonstrates that when teachers engage students in discussions that activate their prior knowledge before they begin reading, it enhances their ability to understand and retain new information. By preparing students to connect what they already know with the new content they will encounter, schema activation fosters engagement and sets a strong foundation for comprehension.[14]

Questions to Ask:
- What do you already know about this topic?
- Have you ever experienced something similar to what the text is about?
- What will this text be about based on the title and pictures?

Activities to try activating schema before you read the text:

- **KWL charts:** Have students fill out what they already know (K) and what they want to know (W) about the topic. This primes their thinking and sets a purpose for reading. After reading, they can fill in what they learned (L), which helps connect new information to prior knowledge.
- **Brainstorming sessions:** Conduct a group brainstorming session where students share their thoughts and knowledge about the topic. Write down their ideas to create a visual connection to their schema. This collaborative activity can also reveal different perspectives and gaps in knowledge.

During Reading

While reading, it's essential to keep students engaged with the text by continually connecting it to their prior knowledge. This ongoing connection helps them make sense of new information, maintain focus, and deepen their comprehension. A child is much more apt to remember stories, books, and incidents that are meaningful because they connect

---

[14] Hattan, C. and Alexander, P.A. (2020). Prior knowledge and its activation in elementary classroom discourse. *Reading and Writing* 33: 1617–1647. https://doi.org/10.1007/s11145-020-10022-8.

to other things in their life.[15] Encouraging students to actively think about how new information fits into what they already know makes the reading experience more interactive and meaningful.

> **Questions to Ask:**
> - How does this text part relate to what you already know?
> - Can you think of a time when you experienced something similar to what is happening in the story?
> - What does this remind you of?

Activities to try activating schema while you read the text:

- **Using think-alouds:** Model the thought process of making connections by thinking aloud while reading a text. Show how you relate new information to your own experiences and knowledge. This strategy demonstrates how to connect schema and shows students that it is a normal part of reading comprehension.
- **Annotating texts:** Encourage students to annotate by writing notes in the margins about how different text parts relate to their schema. This keeps them actively engaged and thinking about connections as they read. Annotating helps track thoughts and connections, which can be revisited during discussions or reviews.

After Reading

After reading, students must reflect on how the new information they've gained fits into their schema. This reflection solidifies their understanding and helps them retain the latest knowledge. It also allows students to evaluate how their initial ideas have changed or expanded.

---

[15] Zimmermann, S. and Hutchins, C. (2003). *7 Keys to Comprehension: How to Help Your Kids Read It and Get It!* Three Rivers Press.

> **Questions to Ask:**
> - How has your understanding of the topic changed after reading this text?
> - What new information did you learn that connects to what you already knew?
> - How can you apply what you learned from this text to other situations?

Activities to try activating schema after you read the text:

- **Summarizing and reflecting:** Have students summarize the text and reflect on how it connects to their prior knowledge. This can be done through written reflections or group discussions. Summarizing reinforces comprehension, and reflecting allows students to see the growth in their understanding.
- **Concept mapping:** Ask students to create concept maps showing the connections between the new information and their schema. This visual representation helps them see the relationships and reinforces their learning. Concept maps can also be used as a study tool to organize thoughts for future assignments or discussions.

Activating schema is a continuous process that should occur before, during, and after reading. By asking thoughtful questions and incorporating engaging activities at each stage, teachers can help students make meaningful connections to their prior knowledge. This enhances comprehension and fosters a deeper understanding and retention of the material. The study "Activating Prior Knowledge to Improve Reading Comprehension" (2020) provides statistical evidence supporting the claim that activating schema before, during, and after reading enhances student comprehension. In this research, third-grade students who received explicit instruction on making connections between their prior knowledge and the text showed significant academic gains. The intervention group improved their vocabulary scores by 40%, and their reading comprehension scores by 20% compared to the control group. These findings illustrate how engaging students with their schema across all stages of reading leads to better comprehension and retention of material, further supporting the continuous activation of schema throughout the reading process.[16] When students are consistently encouraged to link new information to what they already know, they become more active and effective readers, capable of navigating complex texts with greater ease and insight.

Building Schema in Your Students

One of the issues teachers face these days in the classroom is the lack of schema in students. In "The Knowledge Gap," Natalie Wexler discusses the significant impact of limited life experiences, interactions, and robust environments on students' knowledge acquisition and academic success. Wexler argues that the root of many educational disparities lies in the lack of exposure to a rich and varied set of experiences, which are crucial for building background knowledge. This deficiency in knowledge then hinders students' ability to comprehend complex texts and engage in higher-order thinking tasks.

Wexler emphasizes that while schools often focus on teaching isolated skills, such as reading strategies, they frequently overlook the importance of content knowledge. She explains that students struggle to understand and retain new information without a solid foundation of background knowledge, leading to a widening knowledge gap. This gap is especially pronounced among students from disadvantaged backgrounds who may not have access to the same enriching experiences as their more privileged peers.

In her book, Wexler highlights the importance of providing students with opportunities to engage with various topics and experiences inside and outside the classroom. She writes, "The fundamental problem with the way reading is taught in American schools isn't with the phonics aspect of reading instruction, but rather with the content that students are—or aren't—learning once they can decode words on a page."[17] This quote underscores her argument that content knowledge is crucial for reading comprehension and overall academic success.

---

[16] Cho, Y. and Ma, J. (2020). The effects of schema activation and reading strategy use on L2 reading comprehension. *English Teaching* 75 (3): 49–68.
[17] Wexler, N. (2019). *The Knowledge Gap: The Hidden Cause of America's Broken Education System - and How to Fix It*. Avery.

Wexler also points out that a lack of robust environments where children are exposed to diverse vocabulary and concepts significantly affects their schema-building ability. Schema, or background knowledge, is essential for connecting and understanding new information. Without these experiences, students are disadvantaged, with fewer cognitive frameworks to draw upon when learning new material.

To address this issue, Wexler advocates for a more integrated approach to education that prioritizes content-rich curricula and real-world experiences. By exposing students to a wide range of topics and contexts, educators can help bridge the knowledge gap and provide all students with the tools they need to succeed academically. This approach supports reading comprehension and fosters critical thinking, problem-solving, and a lifelong love of learning.

So, how do you take your understanding that the lack of knowledge is an issue and make choices in your classroom that support fixing this issue?

Strategies to Help Build Schema

Building schema enhances students' reading comprehension and overall academic success. Teachers can employ effective strategies to help students develop and expand their background knowledge across different subjects and contexts.

6 Strategies To Help Build Schema
- Diverse Exploration of Nonfiction Texts
- Integrating Science and Social Studies
- Multimedia Exploration and Real-World Connections
- Encouraging Collaborative Learning
- Building Vocabulary
- Interactive Read-Alouds and Pre-Reading Activities

Strategy 1: Diverse Exploration of Nonfiction Texts

Providing diverse reading materials, including nonfiction texts, is essential for building a robust foundation of knowledge. Nonfiction texts cover science, history, biographies, and more. This exposure allows students to acquire knowledge in multiple domains, fostering a broader understanding of the world. "Simply activating background knowledge at the beginning of a reading comprehension lesson is not enough. We must activate background knowledge that is specific to the text. Additionally, you may need to build background knowledge of students who have little to no contact knowledge of the topic."[18] By regularly engaging with nonfiction, students learn to analyze text features like headings, captions, and diagrams, which are crucial for extracting and synthesizing information. Projects that involve choosing and analyzing nonfiction books further enhance engagement and deepen students' appreciation for reading while building their schema.

Strategy 2: Integrating Science and Social Studies

Integrating science and social studies into reading assignments and classroom activities provides real-world contexts that enrich students' background knowledge. Exploring scientific concepts or historical events through reading enhances comprehension and encourages critical thinking and inquiry. A study titled "Integrating Science and Literacy: An Innovative Instructional Model" (Anderson et al., 2017) integrated literacy skills like reading, writing, listening, and speaking into science lessons. The study provides students with real-world contexts to apply their literacy learning, which in turn strengthens their background knowledge on the subject.

Additionally, the study shows that this interdisciplinary approach promotes critical thinking and problem-solving. It emphasizes how students, through inquiry-based learning, can create hypotheses, analyze data, and solve problems—all while developing their reading and writing abilities. This integration not only helps students better understand the science content but also enhances their overall reading comprehension, aligning with your claim that this approach encourages critical thinking and inquiry-based learning in real-world contexts.[19] Hands-on activities and projects related to these subjects, such as STEM projects or historical research presentations, allow students to apply theoretical

---

[18] Kemeny, L. (2020). *7 Mighty Moves*. Scholastic.
[19] Anderson, E., Dryden, L., Garza, E., and Goodwin, P. (2017). Integrating science and literacy: an innovative instructional model. *English in Texas* 47 (1): 24–28.

knowledge in practical ways. This integration helps students connect classroom learning to their lives, communities, and the broader world, filling gaps in their knowledge and enhancing schema development.

Strategy 3: Multimedia Exploration and Real-World Connections

Utilizing multimedia resources and real-world connections is a powerful strategy for building students' background knowledge. Incorporating documentaries, educational videos, and interactive websites provides visual and auditory stimuli that complement textual information. These resources offer diverse perspectives and contexts, making abstract concepts more concrete and relevant to students' lives. Guiding students to analyze and discuss multimedia sources helps them extract valuable information and evaluate different sources of knowledge. Guest speakers or virtual visits from experts further deepen students' understanding by providing firsthand insights and experiences, bridging the gap between classroom learning and real-world applications.

Strategy 4: Encouraging Collaborative Learning

Collaborative learning fosters a dynamic environment where students can share their knowledge, perspectives, and experiences with their peers. Group discussions, peer teaching, and collaborative projects enable students to learn from each other and build on their collective understanding. "Recognizing that comprehension is an active and often collaborative process of making meaning, effective teachers of reading comprehension tend to employ classroom discussion to help readers work together to make meaning from the texts they encounter."[20] By working together, students fill gaps in their knowledge and gain new insights into the material. Collaborative activities that involve research, presentations, or cooperative reading tasks promote active engagement and deepen

---

[20] Duke, N.K., Pearson, P.D., Strachan, S.L., and Billman, A.K. (2011). International Reading Association 51-93 essential elements of fostering and teaching reading comprehension.

comprehension. This strategy enhances schema development and cultivates important social and communication skills essential for academic success.

Strategy 5: Building Vocabulary

A strong vocabulary is essential for understanding and engaging with complex texts. "As students acquire vocabulary, they tap into existing knowledge networks and simultaneously build connections. Their depth of vocabulary knowledge often reflects their understanding of related concepts."[21] Teachers can support vocabulary development through word walls, vocabulary journals, and interactive activities. Word walls display critical terms related to the curriculum, providing visual reinforcement and aiding retention. Vocabulary journals encourage students to record new words, meanings, and usage examples, reinforcing their understanding over time. Interactive vocabulary games and activities make learning new words enjoyable and help students connect vocabulary to their existing knowledge. By expanding their vocabulary, students enhance their ability to comprehend texts across different subjects and contexts, facilitating deeper schema development.

Strategy 6: Interactive Read-Alouds and Pre-Reading Activities

Interactive read-alouds and pre-reading activities engage students in active participation and preparation for understanding new content. "Interactive read aloud builds community and engagement, as well as comprehension."[22] During interactive read-alouds, teachers model thinking processes such as making connections, asking questions, and predicting outcomes. This modeling helps students understand how to apply their background knowledge to comprehend texts effectively. Pre-reading activities like anticipation guides, K-W-L charts, and brainstorming sessions activate students' prior knowledge

---

[21] Hennessy, N.L. (2021). *The Reading Comprehension Blueprint: Helping Students Make Meaning from Text*. Paul H. Brookes Publishing Co.

[22] Harvey, S. and Ward, H. (2021). *From Striving to Thriving: How to Grow Confident, Capable Readers*. Scholastic.

and set a purpose for reading. These activities create a foundation for connecting new information to existing schema, making learning more meaningful and improving overall comprehension.

By implementing these strategies consistently and purposefully, educators can empower students to build robust schema, deepen their understanding of content, and effectively bridge the knowledge gap. Each strategy contributes to creating a supportive learning environment where students actively acquire and apply knowledge across various subjects and contexts. Remember, schema isn't something that can simply be an afterthought. It needs to be an initial part of teachers' planning process when thinking through their reading lessons.

Closing

> "All of the things taught here have supported the best practice teaching instruction I receive from SOR, Lead4Ward and our district testing analysis consultant. However, this course took information from concept to concrete, just like we need to do for students. I'm exceptionally confident that I have the materials and support to make great gains this year. I've never felt this positive about going back to school."
>
> -Sarah Forren, K-5 Special Education, Marble Falls Elementary, Texas

Schema is a powerful tool that significantly impacts students' reading comprehension and overall learning experience. By intentionally teaching and activating schema, educators can help students bridge the gap between prior knowledge and new information, leading to a richer understanding of texts. This chapter has explored the different types of schema and their roles in comprehension, providing practical strategies for incorporating schema-based instruction in the classroom.

The journey of understanding and utilizing schema doesn't end here. It is a continuous process that evolves as students grow and encounter new experiences. By fostering an environment that values and builds upon students' schema, educators can create a dynamic and engaging learning experience. This approach enhances reading comprehension and promotes critical thinking, cultural understanding, and lifelong learning skills. Embracing the power of schema allows students to become more effective and confident readers, ready to tackle complex texts and diverse subjects with greater ease and insight. Consider these questions as you ponder this issue more and try the following lessons.

End of Chapter Reflection Questions:

What role does schema play in a reader's understanding of a text?

What do we need to teach students about their schema?

Why must we teach schema FIRST? (How is schema related to every single skill and strategy?)

What if a student does not have the schema for a topic they are reading about?

Lessons to Try

As a reminder, you can access the complete lessons for free at `http://www.cieraharristeaching.com/ttrlessons` using the passcode: `literacy for all`.

"What Is Schema" Lesson

The lesson plan on "What Is Schema?" focuses on helping students understand the concept of schema and its significance in reading comprehension. The lesson begins with a discussion to establish that everyone's brain contains preexisting knowledge, which forms their schema. The teacher models this by visualizing their schema on butcher paper, which includes various categories like foods, places, and experiences. This interactive approach engages students and visually demonstrates how schema comprises everything we know and have experienced. The lesson aims to make students aware that their unique schema impacts their ability to understand and connect with new information they encounter in texts.

Teaching students about schema is crucial because it directly influences their reading comprehension skills. Readers can better understand, interpret, and retain new information when they activate their prior knowledge. The lesson underscores that schema is dynamic and can be expanded by gaining new experiences and knowledge. By encouraging students to identify and discuss their schema, the lesson fosters a deeper connection to reading materials, making the learning process more relevant and effective. This awareness helps students become more strategic readers who can more efficiently navigate and comprehend diverse texts.

Another benefit of teaching about schema is that it promotes inclusivity and appreciation of diverse perspectives in the classroom. Recognizing that each student's schema is unique and shaped by their experiences and background encourages respect and understanding among peers. It also supports collaborative learning, as students share their schema and learn from each other. The lesson enhances social learning and critical thinking skills by integrating activities where students work together to explore and expand their schema.

Quick Tip

When teaching this lesson, emphasize the value of students sharing their schema. This helps them generate more ideas and builds a classroom culture of collaboration and mutual respect. Encouraging students to work in groups and discuss their different experiences will enrich the learning experience and make the concept of schema more tangible and relatable.

"Accessing My Schema" Lesson

The "Accessing My Schema" lesson plan is designed to help students understand the importance of activating their prior knowledge or schema when reading. The lesson begins by explaining schema and its role in reading comprehension, emphasizing that a reader's background knowledge significantly influences their ability to understand and retain new information. Students engage in activities that illustrate the difference in comprehension when they have prior knowledge about a topic versus when they don't. This exercise involves using familiar and unfamiliar issues to create a T-chart, where students write down their existing knowledge and observe how it affects their understanding of the texts read during the lesson.

This lesson is crucial as it equips students with strategies to enhance their reading comprehension by tapping into their schema. By recognizing when and how to access their prior knowledge, students can better connect with new information, making it more relatable and more accessible to remember. This practice improves comprehension and encourages active engagement with the text, fostering a deeper understanding and retention of the material. Moreover, the lesson addresses potential comprehension challenges when students lack sufficient schema, helping them develop strategies to bridge these gaps.

Teaching students to access their schema has numerous benefits. It promotes metacognitive skills as students learn to think about their thinking and become more aware of how their background knowledge influences their reading. This awareness can lead to more effective learning strategies across subjects. Additionally, it encourages active reading, where students continuously relate new information to what they already know, ask questions, and seek to fill knowledge gaps. This approach not only boosts academic performance but also nurtures lifelong learning habits.

Quick Tip

When teaching this lesson, use various engaging and relatable topics to ensure students can easily connect with at least one. Incorporate interactive elements like drawing or acting out scenarios to make the lesson more dynamic and memorable. This will help reinforce the concept and keep students engaged throughout the lesson.

"Multiple Perspectives" Lesson

The lesson on multiple perspectives aims to help students understand how their unique experiences, or "schema," influence their interpretation of texts. The lesson begins with an engaging activity where students discuss what they see in an ambiguous image, highlighting how different backgrounds lead to varied perceptions. This sets the stage for the main lesson, where students read scenarios and share their interpretations based on their schema. Through guided discussions and reflections, students learn that their personal experiences shape their understanding of stories and that it's natural for different readers to have different takeaways from the same text.

This lesson is essential because it fosters critical thinking and empathy in students. By recognizing that everyone has a unique perspective, students learn to appreciate diverse viewpoints and understandings. This is particularly important in a multicultural and interconnected world where students encounter various perspectives. Teaching students to value different interpretations enhances their reading comprehension and promotes a more inclusive and understanding classroom environment.

One significant benefit of teaching this lesson is encouraging active student participation and discussion. This interactive approach makes learning more engaging and memorable. Additionally, by continuously practicing and discussing multiple perspectives, students will become more adept at considering and respecting different viewpoints. This skill is invaluable both in academic settings and in everyday interactions.

Quick Tip

Use a variety of texts and scenarios to illustrate the concept of multiple perspectives. This will allow you to cater to your students' diverse backgrounds, making the lesson more relatable and impactful.

Schema: The Power of Perspective

CHAPTER 6

CURIOSITY: THE MOTIVATION MAXIMIZER

Cultivating Metacognitive Thinkers

Focus on strategies to maintain curiosity, develop metacognitive skills, and apply effective reading techniques to engage students.

In the journey of literacy development, curiosity emerges as a powerful catalyst that can significantly enhance student engagement and learning. This chapter delves into the profound impact of curiosity on reading and literacy. Curiosity, the intrinsic desire to learn, understand, and explore, drives individuals to seek new information and experiences. This natural inclination is evident from early childhood as children ask countless questions each day, demonstrating their inherent drive to discover the world around them.

Neurologically, curiosity triggers dopamine release, making learning a pleasurable experience and activating memory centers in the brain. Psychologically, it motivates individuals to fill gaps in their knowledge, leading to deeper engagement with reading materials. This chapter explores various strategies to cultivate and sustain curiosity in the classroom, emphasizing creating a positive and stimulating environment, understanding students' interests, and employing dynamic book introductions and inquiry-based projects. By fostering curiosity, educators can transform the educational experience into a more enriching and enjoyable journey, ultimately helping students develop a lifelong love for learning.

Chapter 6 Objectives

The readers will understand the definition and importance of curiosity in learning.

The readers will explore the neurological and psychological mechanisms that enhance learning through curiosity.

The readers will learn how curiosity improves reading comprehension and engagement.

The readers will discover practical strategies for fostering curiosity in the classroom.

The readers can implement specific techniques to create a stimulating and curiosity-driven learning environment.

What Is Curiosity?

Curiosity is the desire to learn, understand, and explore. It is the mind's intrinsic motivator, driving us to seek new information and experiences. This natural inclination is present from a very young age, as evidenced by the countless daily questions preschoolers and kindergarteners ask. Their curiosity is a powerful force, propelling them to discover the world around them.

> **Definition: curiosity** A strong desire to know or learn something, often characterized by inquisitiveness, exploration, and a thirst for knowledge

Curiousness plays a pivotal role in the context of reading. When students are curious about a topic, their engagement with the text increases significantly. This heightened interest activates their cognitive processes, enabling them to process information rapidly, retain details more effectively, and stay focused longer. Curiosity plays a significant role in enhancing students' engagement with reading, as it activates cognitive processes such as rapid information processing, better retention, and sustained focus. A study published in *Psychonomic Bulletin & Review* (2021) demonstrated that curiosity creates a positive feedback loop that drives information-seeking behavior and learning. When students are curious about a subject, they engage more deeply with the text, leading to better learning outcomes. The study also found that curiosity enhances cognitive engagement, motivating students to explore topics more deeply and retain information more effectively.[1] Essentially, curiosity acts as a catalyst for deeper comprehension and learning.

Unfortunately, as children grow older, this innate curiosity often diminishes. Various factors contribute to this decline, including the way adults respond to their questions. When children's inquiries are met with dismissive remarks like, "Now is not the right time," or "We're in math class, don't ask that," they internalize the message that their curiosity is not valued. Over time, this can lead them to stop asking questions and, eventually, to stop thinking curiously.

This is a significant issue because curiosity is beneficial and essential for effective learning. It enhances reading comprehension by making students more invested in what they are reading. When students are curious, their brains engage more fully with the material.

---

[1] Wade, S. and Kidd, C. (2019). The role of prior knowledge and curiosity in learning. *Psychonomic Bulletin and Review* 26: 1377–1387. https://doi.org/10.3758/s13423-019-01598-6.

A 2014 study by Matthias J. Gruber, Bernard D. Gelman, and Charan Ranganath published in *Neuron* found that curiosity enhances memory retention by activating the hippocampus and dopaminergic circuits, regions of the brain associated with memory and reward. The study demonstrated that when curiosity is sparked, students are more focused and able to process and retain information more effectively. This suggests that fostering curiosity in the classroom can lead to better academic outcomes and deeper learning.[2] This engagement leads to better memory retention, a deeper understanding of the content, and a greater ability to connect what they are reading and already know.

To foster a classroom environment where curiosity thrives, teachers must create a positive, welcoming, and encouraging atmosphere. Curiosity should be nurtured across all subjects, not just reading. Teachers can achieve this by getting to know their students and understanding their interests. This knowledge allows teachers to present material that resonates with students' natural curiosities. This chapter dives into the world of curiosity to see just how impactful this neurological concept can be in literacy.

The Science Behind Curiosity

Curiosity is a fascinating aspect of human nature and profoundly impacts literacy. Curiosity is driven by a neurological and psychological interplay that encourages us to seek new knowledge and experiences. When we're curious, our brains release dopamine, a neurotransmitter associated with pleasure and reward. This release makes learning enjoyable, turning acquiring new information into a rewarding experience. "When learners' curiosity was piqued by questions and their answers, the parts of the brain associated with pleasure, reward, and creation of memory underwent an increase in activity."[3] For students, curiosity can transform reading from a task into an adventure, making them more likely to engage with texts profoundly and thoughtfully.

Psychologically, curiosity operates as a motivational force. When students are curious, they desire to fill the gaps in their knowledge. Teachers can harness this drive to create

---

[2] Gruber, M., Gelman, B., and Ranganth, C. (2014). States of curiosity modulate hippocampus-dependent learning via the dopaminergic circuit. *Neuron* 84: 486–496.

[3] Ness, M. (2016). When readers ask questions: inquiry-based reading instruction. *Reading Teacher* 70 (2): 189–196. https://eric.ed.gov/?id=EJ1112129.

literacy experiences that are both engaging and educational. By tapping into students' natural curiosity, educators can design reading activities that are more personalized and relevant to their interests, fostering a more profound connection to the material and enhancing comprehension.

Neurologically, curiosity activates several brain parts involved in learning and memory. The hippocampus, a region crucial for forming new memories, becomes particularly active when we are curious. This heightened activity helps students retain the information they read. Neurologically, curiosity activates several brain regions involved in learning and memory, particularly the hippocampus, which is essential for forming new memories. A 2019 review by Gruber and Ranganath discusses how curiosity enhances hippocampus-dependent memory by engaging the dopaminergic circuit. This heightened brain activity during curious states not only improves the retention of the target information but also incidental information encountered during the curious state. This suggests that curiosity plays a pivotal role in enhancing learning efficiency and memory retention.[4] When a student encounters a text that piques their curiosity, the hippocampus works overtime, encoding the details more efficiently and making recall easier in the future. This is why students often remember stories or facts that genuinely interest them.

Moreover, the prefrontal cortex, which is responsible for higher-order thinking and decision-making, also plays a significant role in curiosity. This brain region helps students analyze and synthesize information, leading to better critical thinking and problem-solving skills. The prefrontal cortex, specifically the dorsolateral and ventromedial regions, plays a crucial role in curiosity by supporting higher-order thinking and decision-making. A study published in *Frontiers in Neuroscience* demonstrated that the prefrontal cortex is heavily involved in decision-making processes, especially under conditions where individuals are allowed free choice. This brain region is responsible for analyzing and synthesizing information, which leads to better critical thinking and problem-solving abilities. When students engage their curiosity, the prefrontal cortex helps them assess different possibilities and choose optimal solutions, enhancing their learning and decision-making

---

[4] Gruber, M., Ranganath, C. 2019. OSH Preprints. How curiosity enhances hippocampus-dependent memory. https://doi.org/10.31219/osf.io/5v6nm.

capabilities.[5] When reading, a curious mind actively engages with the text, asking questions, making connections, and predicting outcomes. This dynamic interaction with the material enhances comprehension and retention, making learning more effective and enjoyable.

Curiosity also engages the brain's reward system, particularly the striatum. When students satisfy their curiosity by finding answers in a text, the brain releases dopamine, reinforcing the learning experience with feelings of pleasure and satisfaction. This positive feedback loop encourages students to continue seeking new knowledge, creating a sustainable and self-reinforcing cycle of learning and exploration.

In the context of literacy, these neurological and psychological mechanisms highlight the importance of fostering curiosity in the classroom. By creating a learning environment that values and stimulates curiosity, teachers can help students develop a lifelong love of reading. This approach improves literacy skills and nurtures a broader enthusiasm for learning as students become more confident and capable of navigating and understanding the world through the written word.

Ultimately, curiosity is a powerful tool in the literacy toolkit. It bridges the gap between mere reading and profound understanding, turning the act of reading into a deeply personal and fulfilling journey. Educators can unlock students' potential by understanding and leveraging the mechanisms behind curiosity, guiding them toward more affluent, meaningful educational experiences.

Curiosity and Reading Abilities

Curiosity is a powerful driving force in students' reading skills development. When students are curious, they naturally seek out information, ask questions, and explore topics that interest them. This intrinsic motivation leads them to read more frequently and with greater engagement. As they delve into books, articles, and other reading materials, they encounter a variety of vocabulary and sentence structures, which enhances their language skills. Curiosity transforms reading from a chore into an adventure, making learning enjoyable and fulfilling.

---

[5] Funahashi, S. (2017). Prefrontal contribution to decision-making under free-choice conditions. *Frontiers in Neuroscience* 11 (431).

One of the most significant impacts of curiosity on reading skills is the accelerated vocabulary acquisition. When students are genuinely interested in a topic, they are more likely to pay attention to new words and phrases, seeking to understand and remember them. A meta-analysis of vocabulary acquisition in students shows a strong correlation between vocabulary knowledge and reading comprehension, especially when students are motivated by curiosity and interest in the subject matter. The findings suggest that students' reading interest significantly boosts their vocabulary retention, making curiosity a powerful tool in language learning.[6] This context-driven learning helps them grasp the meanings of words more effectively than rote memorization. Over time, a rich vocabulary becomes a crucial tool for comprehension, allowing students to understand and appreciate more complex texts.

Curiosity also fosters deeper comprehension skills. When curious, students don't just passively read; they actively engage with the material. They ask questions, make predictions, and draw connections between new information and what they already know. This active engagement promotes critical thinking and helps students develop a more nuanced understanding of the text. "Motivation increases a reader's application of comprehension strategies (Schiefele et al., 2012) and significantly affects reading comprehension beyond a reader's background knowledge" (Taboada et al., 2009).[7] Curiosity-driven readers are more likely to infer meaning, recognize themes, and appreciate the subtleties of language, all of which contribute to stronger reading comprehension.

> Curiosity bridges the gap between mere reading and profound understanding, turning the act of reading into a deeply personal and fulfilling journey.

Curiosity and Struggling Readers

For struggling readers, curiosity can be a game-changer. Often, these students may feel frustrated or discouraged by their reading difficulties, leading to a lack of motivation.

---

[6] Santi, E., Kholipa, R., Putri, M., and Mujiono. (2021). Reading interest strength and vocabulary acquisition of EFL Learners: a meta-analysis. *Journal of Language and Linguistic Studies* 17 (30): 1225–1242.

[7] Liebfreund, M.D. (2021). Cognitive and motivational predictors of narrative and informational text comprehension. *Reading Psychology* 42 (2): 177–196. https://doi.org/10.1080/02702711.2021.1888346.

However, when teachers tap into their natural curiosities and provide reading materials aligned with their interests, these students can experience a renewed sense of purpose and enthusiasm. "As teachers use and leverage these research based principles of reading interest—cultivating individual interests, fostering situational interest, selecting texts with interest-enhancing elements, and teaching interest self-regulation strategies—simply surviving can be transformed into thriving."[8] This personalized approach makes reading more enjoyable and helps them build confidence as they start to see progress in their skills.

On the other hand, proficient readers can use their curiosity to refine further and expand their abilities. Since they already possess foundational solid skills, their curiosity can lead them to explore more challenging and diverse texts. This exploration broadens their literary horizons and deepens their understanding of different genres, cultures, and perspectives. Curiosity keeps proficient readers intellectually stimulated and continually pushes them to higher levels of achievement.

However, there are differences in how curiosity affects struggling and proficient readers. Curiosity can provide struggling readers with the motivation to overcome obstacles and persist in their efforts. "Students who are motivated and engaged in reading read often and enjoy the experience. They also are more likely to use strategies to help them through difficulties, have higher overall comprehension and achievement, and develop expertise on particular topics."[9] It can help them focus on the enjoyment of discovery rather than the mechanics of reading. Curiosity catalyzes advanced learning and intellectual growth for proficient readers, encouraging them to tackle more sophisticated material and think critically about complex issues.

Fostering curiosity in all students is essential for developing robust and lifelong reading habits. Teachers can play a pivotal role by creating a classroom environment that encourages exploration and questioning. Providing diverse reading materials, incorporating

---

[8] Harvey, S. and Ward, H. (2021). *From Striving to Thriving: How to Grow Confident, Capable Readers*. Scholastic.

[9] Robinson, D.A. and Padesky, C.J. (2020). Keeping students interested: interest-based instruction as a tool to engage. The Reading Teacher 73 (5): 575–586.

student interests into lessons, and celebrating curiosity-driven achievements can all contribute to a vibrant, literacy-rich atmosphere. When students' natural curiosity is nurtured, their reading skills flourish, leading to a more profound love of learning and a lifelong passion for reading.

Curiosity and Reading Comprehension

Curiosity enhances reading comprehension by driving students to engage more deeply with the text. When students are curious about a subject, they are more likely to ask questions, make predictions, and seek out additional information, all of which are fundamental components of active reading. "The benefits of this deep, topic-focused reading are twofold: Readers improve their reading abilities as they practice skills through extensive, sustained reading, and they develop expertise on a topic as they build deep background knowledge."[10] This intrinsic motivation leads to a more meaningful interaction with the text, as students are not merely reading to complete an assignment but are genuinely interested in understanding the material. Curiosity encourages students to think critically and analytically, which enhances their ability to infer, synthesize, and evaluate information, thereby improving comprehension.

Furthermore, curiosity helps students connect new information with their existing knowledge. When curious, students are more likely to draw upon their prior experiences and background knowledge to make sense of new concepts. "Connecting new information to what they already know facilitates deeper understanding and retention. Researchers have found that traditional reading level assessments matter less when students are interested in their reading material; in other words, students can read harder texts when those texts are of interest to them."[11] As students explore topics they are curious about, they develop

---

[10] Harvey, S. and Ward, H. (2021). *From Striving to Thriving: How to Grow Confident, Capable Readers*. Scholastic.

[11] Springer, S.E., Harris, S., and Dole, J.A. (2017). From surviving to thriving: four research-based principles to build students' reading interest. *The Reading Teacher* 71 (1): 43–50. https://doi.org/10.1002/trtr.1574.

a more robust and nuanced understanding of the material, enhancing their ability to comprehend and recall information.

Curiosity also fosters a love for reading, essential for developing strong reading comprehension skills. When curious, students are more inclined to seek out books and other reading materials independently. This self-directed exploration improves their reading fluency and exposes them to various genres and writing styles, further enhancing their comprehension abilities. A study published in *Frontiers in Psychology* investigated the role of independent reading in enhancing literacy skills among young students. The research found that when students are motivated by curiosity, they tend to choose books that interest them, leading to more frequent and engaged reading. This self-directed exploration exposes students to diverse genres and writing styles, which improves their fluency and overall comprehension. The study highlights that students who engage in independent reading due to their curiosity show marked improvements in their ability to decode new words, understand complex texts, and retain information.[12] By cultivating a genuine interest in reading, students are more likely to become lifelong learners with strong critical thinking skills.

Identifying and Nurturing Curiosity to Improve Understanding of Texts

Teachers can identify and nurture curiosity in their students by creating a learning environment that values and encourages curiosity. One way to do this is by paying attention to students' questions during lessons. Questions that go beyond the surface level and show a desire to understand a topic's "why" and "how" are strong indicators of curiosity. Teachers can also observe students' engagement during activities and discussions, noting which topics or themes spark the most interest and enthusiasm.

---

[12] Silinskas, G., Senechal, M., Torppa, M., and Lerkkanen, M. (2020). Home literacy activities and children's reading skills, independent reading, and interest in literacy activities from kindergarten to grade 2. *Frontiers in Psychology* 11 (1528).

Nurturing curiosity involves providing students with opportunities to explore topics that intrigue them. This can be done through choice-based assignments, where students select books or research projects based on their interests. Additionally, incorporating open-ended questions and inquiry-based learning activities encourages students to take ownership of their learning and pursue their curiosity. By allowing students to explore and ask questions, teachers can help them better understand the material.

Encouraging curiosity also means creating a classroom culture that values questions and exploration. Teachers can model curiosity by sharing their interests and questions with students and demonstrating how to seek answers. By fostering a supportive and interested classroom environment, teachers can help students feel comfortable expressing their curiosity and taking intellectual risks, which is essential for deep learning and comprehension.

Three Steps to Foster Curiosity and Reading Comprehension

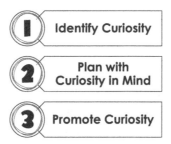

This section breaks down the process of fostering curiosity and reading comprehension into three steps—identifying curiosity, planning with curiosity in mind, and promoting curiosity.

Identify Curiosity

Student surveys: Use surveys or interest inventories at the beginning of the year to understand students' interests, hobbies, and questions about the world. This information can guide the selection of reading materials and topics.

Observation: Respond to the questions students ask during lessons and discussions. Note which topics generate the most interest and engagement.

Conferences: Hold one-on-one or small group conferences to discuss students' interests and what they are curious about. These conversations can provide deeper insights into their passions and motivations.

Plan with Curiosity in Mind

Choice boards: Create choice boards that offer a variety of reading materials and activities aligned with students' interests. This allows students to select tasks they are curious about and more likely to engage deeply.

Inquiry-based projects: Design projects that start with a compelling question or problem for students to investigate. This approach encourages students to explore topics in-depth and develop their understanding through research and exploration.

Thematic units: Develop thematic units that align with students' interests. For example, if many students are curious about space, create a unit that includes a variety of texts related to space exploration, astronomy, and science fiction.

Promote Curiosity

Question-driven discussions: Encourage students to ask and explore their questions during reading discussions. Use strategies like "think-pair-share" to allow students to discuss their questions with peers before sharing with the larger group.

Curiosity journals: Have students keep curiosity journals in which they write down questions that arise while reading and research the answers. This practice reinforces the habit of questioning and seeking knowledge.

Interactive reading activities: Incorporate interactive reading activities such as literature circles or Socratic seminars that promote discussion and critical thinking. These activities allow students to explore different perspectives and deepen their comprehension through dialogue.

> **What Is a Socratic Seminar?**
>
> A Socratic seminar is a structured discussion where students explore texts through open-ended questions guided by a teacher or student moderator. Participants engage deeply with the material, discussing themes and ideas collaboratively. This format fosters critical thinking, communication skills, and a nuanced understanding of texts, making it a valuable tool in education for promoting active and thoughtful learning.

Educators can create an environment that nurtures curiosity and significantly enhances reading comprehension by integrating these strategies into their teaching. Curiosity-driven learning engages students deeper, making reading a more meaningful and enriching experience.

Curiosity and Intrinsic Motivation

Fostering curiosity within students significantly contributes to their intrinsic motivation for reading. When curiosity is sparked, students become more eager to explore reading materials for assignments and out of genuine interest. "Importantly, intrinsic motivation transcended text type and proved to be a consistent energizer for narrative and informational text comprehension. While the effect of cognitive variables maybe dependent on variables related to the text (including text type), intrinsic motivation appears to be an area that may influence comprehension regardless of text type."[13] This intrinsic motivation stems from a deep-seated desire to understand and discover rather than simply comply with academic requirements. For instance, when students are curious about a historical event or a scientific concept, they are more likely to engage actively with related texts,

---

[13] Liebfreund, M.D. (2021). Cognitive and motivational predictors of narrative and informational text comprehension. *Reading Psychology* 42 (2): 177–196.

leading to improved comprehension and retention. Curiosity encourages students to ask questions, seek answers, and make connections, essential skills in developing a robust literacy foundation.

The relationship between curiosity and a lifelong love of reading is symbiotic. Curiosity acts as a catalyst, propelling students to seek books and topics that align with their interests. This exploration fosters a broader appreciation for literature beyond what is required in the classroom. When students experience the joy of discovering new ideas through reading, they develop a habit of reading for pleasure. This habit, cultivated through curiosity-driven exploration, extends into adulthood, shaping individuals who see reading as a skill and a source of enjoyment and personal growth.

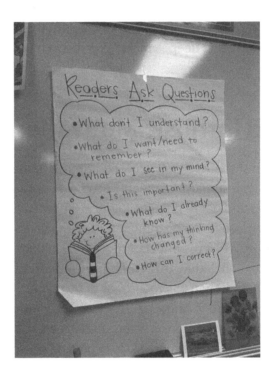

Creating a classroom environment that nurtures and sustains curiosity involves several strategies. First, teachers can provide diverse reading materials catering to different interests, abilities, and cultural backgrounds. Offering choice empowers students to select books that resonate with their curiosity, enhancing their motivation to read. "It appears that students who are allowed to choose their own reading materials are more motivated to read, expend more effort, and gain better understanding of the text."[14] Moreover, integrating inquiry-based learning approaches encourages students to ask questions, conduct research, and critically analyze text information. This process deepens their understanding and reinforces reading as a tool for exploration and discovery.

In addition to curating a rich literary environment, teachers can model curiosity themselves. By demonstrating enthusiasm for books, sharing personal reading experiences, and engaging in discussions that encourage curiosity-driven inquiries, educators inspire students to view reading as a dynamic and interactive process. The study titled "The Impact of Curiosity on Teacher-Student Relationships" (2022) highlights the role teachers play in fostering curiosity in students by modeling enthusiasm for reading. The research found that when teachers share their personal experiences with books and engage students in curiosity-driven discussions, it positively impacts student engagement. By demonstrating their own passion for reading and asking open-ended, thought-provoking questions, teachers inspire students to approach reading with a sense of exploration. This modeling helps students see reading as an interactive process and motivates them to seek out reading materials independently, improving their overall comprehension and critical thinking skills.[15] Teachers can also foster curiosity by incorporating interdisciplinary connections and real-world applications into reading activities. For example, relating literature to current events or inviting guest speakers can pique students' curiosity and illustrate the relevance of reading beyond academic settings.

Furthermore, creating opportunities for collaborative learning, such as book clubs or literature circles, allows students to discuss and explore texts together. These discussions deepen comprehension and encourage students to share their interpretations and questions, fostering a sense of community around reading. Emphasizing the importance of questioning and inquiry in the classroom culture promotes a growth mindset where curiosity is valued as a precursor to learning and understanding.

---

[14] Gambrell. 1996. Seven Rules of Engagement.
[15] Neto, R., Golz, N., Polega, M., and Stewart, D. (2022). The impact of curiosity on teacher-student relationships. *Journal of Education* 202 (1): 15–25.

To sustain curiosity over time, teachers must regularly assess and adjust their instructional approaches based on students' evolving interests and needs. Flexibility in teaching methods allows educators to adapt to the changing dynamics of curiosity within the classroom, ensuring that students continue to find reading meaningful and engaging. Additionally, celebrating curiosity-driven achievements and milestones reinforces the value of exploration and discovery, encouraging students to persist in their pursuit of knowledge through reading.

Fostering curiosity among students enhances their intrinsic motivation for reading and cultivates a lifelong love of literature. Teachers empower students to see reading as a pathway to exploration, understanding, and personal enrichment by creating a classroom environment that supports inquiry, choice, and meaningful connections. Educators can inspire a curiosity-driven approach to reading beyond academic requirements through intentional and nurturing practices, shaping individuals who embrace reading as a source of joy, discovery, and lifelong learning.

Practical Strategies to Promote Curiosity

Curiosity in reading can be sparked through various means, including engaging introductions to books, exploration of authors' backgrounds, and opportunities for inquiry-based learning. By nurturing students' innate curiosity and providing meaningful reading experiences, teachers can foster a lifelong love for learning through literature.

To ignite and maintain curiosity about reading among elementary students, teachers can employ a variety of effective methods:

- **Dynamic book introductions:** Start lessons with dynamic book talks or captivating book trailers that highlight vital aspects of the story, such as characters, settings, and themes. For example, a suspenseful reading of an exciting chapter or a visually appealing trailer can immediately capture students' interest and motivate them to delve deeper into the book.
- **Author studies:** Explore the lives and works of authors who write engaging stories for children. Discuss their inspirations, writing processes, and the themes they explore in their books. Encourage students to delve into multiple works by the same author to identify recurring motifs or narrative techniques, fostering curiosity about storytelling diversity.

- **Inquiry-based projects:** Design projects that encourage students to investigate topics related to their readings. For instance, after reading a historical fiction novel, students could research primary sources from that period to better understand the historical context portrayed in the book. This approach enhances comprehension and encourages curiosity-driven exploration of interdisciplinary connections.
- **Interactive read-alouds and discussions:** Engage students in interactive read-aloud sessions where they actively predict outcomes, analyze characters' motivations, or discuss the story's themes. Encourage students to ask questions about the text and explore their interpretations, fostering a sense of ownership and curiosity-driven exploration.
- **Utilize "Wonder Walls" or "I Wonder Boards":** Create a designated space in the classroom where students can post questions, thoughts, or observations about the books they are reading. This visual display validates students' curiosity and encourages ongoing peer inquiry and discussion.

Photo Credit: www.carlyandadam.com

Curiosity: The Motivation Maximizer

- **Literary journals or response notebooks:** Provide students with journals or notebooks to record their reflections, questions, and connections to the texts they read. Encourage them to revisit and expand upon their entries over time, fostering a habit of curiosity-driven reflection and personal engagement with literature.
- **Guest readers and author visits:** Invite guest readers from the community to enrich students' reading experiences or arrange virtual author visits. Hearing directly from authors or community members can inspire curiosity about the creative process and provide insights into the stories behind the books.
- **Parking lot for questions:** Implement a "parking lot" in the classroom—a poster or piece of anchor chart paper labeled as such—where students can write down questions about the readings or any topic of interest. Students can use sticky notes or directly write on the poster. Periodically, allocate time to address these questions as a class, demonstrating that their inquiries are valued and encouraging a culture of curiosity.

Asking Open-Ended Questions

Open-ended questions foster curiosity and promote critical thinking during reading activities. Unlike closed questions that elicit brief responses, open-ended questions encourage students to think deeply, analyze information, and construct their understanding. By posing open-ended questions, teachers can:

- **Encourage diverse perspectives:** Questions like "What do you think might happen if...?" or "Why do you think the character chose to...?" invite students to consider different possibilities and viewpoints, stimulating curiosity about alternative storylines or motivations.
- **Promote higher-order thinking:** Questions that ask students to evaluate, analyze, or synthesize information from the text (e.g., "How does the author's use of imagery contribute to the mood of the story?") prompt critical thinking and deeper engagement with the text, fostering curiosity about literary techniques and thematic exploration.
- **Support inquiry and exploration:** Open-ended questions facilitate inquiry-based learning by empowering students to ask questions, investigate topics of interest, and pursue deeper understanding independently or collaboratively.

Open-Ended Questions for Promoting Curiosity in Reading

Question Type	Examples of Questions
Predictive Thinking	What do you predict will happen next? How do you think the story will end?
Character Analysis	Why do you think the main character made that decision? How might the story change if a character acted differently?
Theme Exploration	What message or lesson is the author trying to convey through this story? How does this theme relate to real life?
Connection to Real Life	Can you relate this story to an experience you've had? How would you react if you were in the character's situation?
Author's Intent	Why do you think the author chose to include this detail? What do you think the author wants readers to understand about this character?
Comparative Analysis	How does this book compare to others we've read? What similarities or differences do you notice in the characters or plot?
Reflection and Evaluation	What surprised you most about this story? How has your perspective changed after reading this book?

By incorporating these open-ended questions into classroom discussions, literature circles, and reflective writing activities, teachers can cultivate a culture of curiosity and critical inquiry among elementary students. These questions encourage students to explore diverse perspectives, engage deeply with texts, and develop a lifelong passion for reading and learning.

Reflect: How often do you use open-ended questions in your literacy instruction? How do you see them being a powerful tool for curiosity and inclusion of all students' reading abilities?

Choice and Autonomy

Choice and autonomy play pivotal roles in nurturing curiosity and enhancing reading comprehension among elementary students. When students can select their reading materials through independent reading selections or participation in book clubs and literature circles, they engage more deeply with the content. Teachers can support this by curating a diverse classroom library that reflects students' interests and reading levels. Educators foster a sense of ownership over their learning journey by allowing students to choose books they find intriguing, sparking intrinsic motivation and curiosity-driven exploration.

Independent Reading Selections

Maintaining a diverse classroom library is essential for cultivating a love for reading among students. By offering a wide range of genres and reading levels, educators empower students to explore their interests and preferences freely. Regularly scheduled independent reading time encourages students to choose books that captivate their curiosity and ignite their imaginations. Furthermore, urging students to delve into various genres and discover new authors expands their literary horizons, fostering a deeper appreciation for diverse narratives and writing styles.

Book Clubs or Literature Circles

Incorporating book clubs or literature circles enriches students' reading experiences through collaborative learning. These small group discussions enable students to select books collectively, promoting engagement and shared exploration. Rotating roles within groups—such as discussion leader, summarizer, and connector—encourages active participation and fosters a sense of responsibility among students. Providing guiding questions or prompts sparks critical thinking and encourages deeper text analysis, enhancing comprehension and discourse.

Project-Based Learning Activities

Integrating reading into project-based learning activities empowers students to interact with texts creatively and meaningfully. Educators nurture creativity and personal expression by allowing students to choose how they engage with the material—whether through multimedia presentations, alternative endings, or designing book covers. These projects deepen students' understanding of the text and enable them to showcase their interpretations and insights, fostering a deeper connection to literature and learning.

Reading Challenges and Goals

Encouraging students to set and achieve personal reading goals cultivates a sense of accomplishment and motivation. Whether aiming to read a specific number of books or exploring different genres, students benefit from tracking their progress and celebrating their achievements. Offering rewards or incentives further incentivizes students to surpass their reading goals, reinforcing the value of perseverance and personal growth through reading.

Flexible Reading Groups

Supporting flexible reading groups allows students to engage with texts in ways that cater to their interests and learning preferences. Allowing self-selection of reading groups based on personal interests promotes autonomy and engagement. Rotating through different genres or themes accommodates diverse interests and learning styles, ensuring all students have opportunities to explore topics that resonate with them. Tailoring support and resources to each group's dynamics and individual needs fosters a supportive environment for collaborative learning and deeper comprehension.

Student-Led Book Recommendations

Creating opportunities for student-led book recommendations nurtures a community of enthusiastic readers. Through book talks, reviews, or presentations, students can share their enjoyment of particular books and articulate why they believe others would find them engaging. This practice enhances communication skills and promotes empathy and appreciation for diverse literary tastes within the classroom community.

Choice in Assessments and Projects

Offering students choices in how they demonstrate their understanding of texts fosters creativity and deeper engagement with literature. Educators honor students' unique perspectives and learning styles by allowing varied assessments—such as essays, creative projects, or debates. Empowering students to select topics or themes for exploration encourages personal investment in their academic growth and promotes a deeper understanding of literary concepts. Providing constructive feedback acknowledges students' contributions and supports their development as critical thinkers and communicators.

Creating opportunities for student-led book recommendations further enriches the reading experience. Through activities like book talks or reviews, students articulate why certain books are worth exploring, fostering a community of readers who share and appreciate diverse literary interests. By implementing these strategies, educators nurture a love for reading and empower students to become independent learners who actively seek knowledge and understanding through literature and beyond.

Closing

It is essential to recognize the profound impact of curiosity on literacy and overall learning. Curiosity is not merely a fleeting interest but a fundamental driving force that can transform how students engage with reading materials. By fostering curiosity, educators can ignite a lifelong passion for learning, making the educational journey more enjoyable and meaningful for students.

This chapter has explored various strategies to cultivate and sustain curiosity in the classroom. From creating a stimulating environment and understanding students' interests to employing dynamic book introductions and inquiry-based projects, these approaches can significantly enhance student engagement. When curiosity is nurtured, students are more likely to delve deeply into texts, ask meaningful questions, and make connections that lead to a richer understanding of the material.

Moreover, the neurological and psychological mechanisms behind curiosity emphasize its role in enhancing memory and comprehension. By leveraging curiosity, educators can activate students' cognitive processes, making learning a pleasurable and rewarding experience. This approach improves literacy skills and fosters critical thinking and problem-solving abilities, essential for students' academic and personal growth.

In essence, curiosity is a powerful tool in the literacy toolkit. Educators can help students develop a genuine love for reading and learning by creating a classroom culture that values and stimulates curiosity. This chapter should remind you that by tapping into students' natural curiosity, you can transform the educational experience, guiding them toward more profound, meaningful, and lifelong learning adventures.

Consider these questions as you ponder this issue more and try the following lessons.

End of Chapter Reflection Questions:

- How do we manage the abundant curiosity of our students?

- What is the power of student choice? How do I manage it?

- What do we do with our students who struggle to express curiosity? Conversely, how do I balance that with my students, who seem to have endless questions/curiosity and meet both groups' needs?

Lessons to Try

You can access the complete lesson for free at `http://www.cieraharristeaching.com/ttrlessons` using the passcode: `literacy for all`.

"Building Curiosity" Lesson

The lesson plan on "Building Curiosity" is designed to foster a sense of wonder and inquisitiveness in students, guiding them to understand how curiosity can lead to deeper engagement and knowledge acquisition. The lesson begins with an introduction to curiosity, emphasizing its importance in learning and personal growth. Students are shown a series of photographs intended to spark their curiosity, prompting them to ask questions and express their interests. This interactive approach helps students identify topics that intrigue them, leading to a deeper exploration through reading and discussion.

The significance of this lesson lies in its ability to encourage students to take an active role in their learning process. The lesson taps into their intrinsic motivation by allowing students to choose genuinely curious topics, making the learning experience more engaging and enjoyable. This method enhances their reading skills and helps build their background knowledge on various subjects. Additionally, the lesson promotes critical thinking and inquiry-based learning, as students are encouraged to ask questions, seek answers, and share their findings with their peers.

One key benefit of teaching this lesson is that it helps students develop a lifelong love for learning. By nurturing their curiosity, teachers can create a classroom environment where students feel valued and inspired to explore new ideas. Furthermore, the lesson supports the development of essential skills such as collaboration, communication, and problem-solving. As students work together to learn about their chosen topics, they also learn to appreciate diverse perspectives and interests.

Quick Tip

When implementing this lesson, create a supportive and open environment where all questions are welcomed and valued. Encourage students to share their thoughts and questions without fear of judgment, as this will help build their confidence and eagerness to learn.

"Asking Questions" Lesson

The "Asking Questions" lesson plan aims to enhance students' reading comprehension by encouraging them to ask questions actively while reading. The lesson begins with a fun and engaging activity where students use three brown paper bags containing unknown items to learn the value of questioning. Through a series of questions, students try to guess the contents of the bags, moving them closer to the finish line with each question. This hands-on activity demonstrates how asking questions leads to better understanding and knowledge acquisition.

The importance of this lesson lies in its ability to transform students from passive readers to active learners. The lesson promotes critical thinking and deeper engagement with the text by teaching students to ask questions. Asking questions helps students clarify their understanding, make connections, and predict outcomes, all essential skills for adequate reading comprehension. Moreover, this practice helps students retain information better and fosters a curiosity-driven approach to learning, which can be applied across all subjects.

One key benefit of teaching this lesson is that it equips students with a lifelong learning strategy. The habit of asking questions can significantly improve students' academic performance and boost their confidence as readers. Additionally, it helps students develop a growth mindset, where they view challenges as opportunities to learn rather than obstacles. By fostering a curious attitude, teachers can create a more dynamic and interactive classroom environment that encourages exploration and discovery.

Quick Tip

During the lesson, encourage all types of questions and create a safe space where students feel comfortable sharing their thoughts. Reinforce the idea that there are no wrong questions and that every question asked brings them closer to understanding the text better. This will help build students' confidence and promote a positive learning atmosphere.

"Creating a Curiosity Routine" Lesson

The "Creating a Curiosity Routine" lesson plan aims to instill a habit of curiosity in students while they read. It begins with an engaging activity where the teacher pretends to look for a note in their bag, emphasizing the need for an organized place to capture thoughts and questions. This leads to the introduction of the concept of a reader's notebook, a personal space for students to document their curiosity, questions, visualizations, and reflections as they read. By recording thoughts in a routine, the lesson ensures that students become more active and engaged readers.

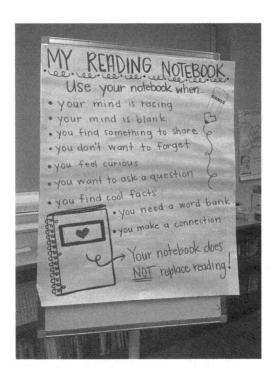

The importance of this lesson lies in its ability to transform how students interact with texts. Curiosity drives deeper comprehension and retention of information, as students who ask questions and seek answers are more likely to understand and remember what they read. The lesson also helps students develop critical thinking skills by connecting new information with what they already know and articulating their thoughts and questions. By fostering a habit of curiosity, students are encouraged to become lifelong learners who view reading not just as a task but as an opportunity for exploration and discovery.

One key benefit of teaching this lesson is supporting diverse learning styles and encouraging self-directed learning. Students can use their reader's notebooks to suit their needs best, whether through writing, drawing, or listing new vocabulary. This flexibility makes the lesson accessible and engaging for all students, promoting a more inclusive classroom environment. Moreover, by regularly practicing curiosity, students build confidence in their ability to navigate and understand complex texts, essential for academic success across all subjects.

Quick Tip

When implementing the curiosity routine, model using the reader's notebook yourself. Show examples of how you document your thoughts and questions while reading, and regularly share your entries with the class. This provides students with concrete examples to follow and reinforces that curiosity is a valuable and ongoing part of the learning process.

CHAPTER 7

METACOGNITION: INQUIRY AND INDEPENDENCE

Cultivating Metacognitive Thinkers

Focus on strategies to maintain curiosity, develop metacognitive skills, and apply effective reading techniques to engage students.

One pivotal skill you can impart to your students in the journey of fostering literacy is metacognition—thinking about one's thinking. This chapter delves into the essence of metacognition and its transformative power in reading comprehension. Despite emphasizing foundational literacy skills, many students still struggle to understand texts deeply. This gap often arises from a lack of metacognitive strategies, where students read the words but fail to engage actively with the content.

Metacognition acts as a golden key, unlocking students' potential to become readers, thinkers, and inquirers. "Metacognition influences students' reading achievement, as students proactively set goals, select and use strategies, and self-monitor the effectiveness of their reading to achieve goals."[1] By teaching them to plan, monitor, and reflect on their reading processes, you enable them to take control of their learning. This chapter explores the components of metacognition, its practical applications in the classroom, and the profound benefits it brings to students' academic and personal growth.

Chapter 7 Objectives

 The readers will understand the definition and components of metacognition.

 The readers will explore the benefits of metacognition in enhancing reading comprehension and overall learning.

 The readers will examine the role of self-regulation and reflection in students' reading processes.

 The readers will identify ways to integrate metacognitive strategies into their literacy instruction to foster independent and critical thinkers.

What Is Metacognition?

I have worked with thousands of teachers over the years, and over that time, one specific reading crisis has revealed itself. Teachers come to me saying, "I follow the Science of Reading guidelines, and I'm teaching the five components of literacy, but my students are still struggling with comprehension. They read beautifully but don't understand what they are reading!" This is one of the issues I've noticed the Science of Reading craze has had on the reading community—too much emphasis on the early components of literacy and not

---

[1] Afflerback, P., Cho, B., Kim, J., and Crassas, M. (2013). What else matters besides strategies and skills? *International Literacy Association and Wiley* 66 (6): 440–448.

194   The Thinking Reader

enough on the end goal. Remember, the end goal is that your students fully understand the text they are reading, that they are comprehending the text and not consuming it.

When students read a text beautifully but struggle to understand it, it's due to a lack of metacognitive strategies. This means they, the reader, were not actively participating in their reading. They were saying the words but not making much sense of what was happening in the text.

Metacognition is a golden key to ensuring students can read and participate actively in a text. So, what is metacognition?

Metacognition is a powerful and essential skill that we must explicitly teach children. It empowers them to be aware of their thinking, giving them the tools to navigate their thoughts effectively. To put it simply, metacognition means thinking about your thinking. It's being conscious of what's happening in your mind, recognizing your thoughts, and listening to your brain. "Metacognitive experiences are feelings, judgements and task-specific knowledge that reflect what the person is aware of and feels during task performance."[2] Surprisingly, I don't recall learning about this concept in college. No one emphasized its importance for teaching kids, but it is crucial.

> Metacognition acts as a golden key, unlocking students' potential to become readers, thinkers, and inquirers.

Definition: text complexity

Refers to characteristics of individual texts, such as sentence length and word complexity, regardless of readers or tasks. Therefore, a text's complexity is determined in relation to other texts.

Metacognition is the hallmark of an active reader. Think of it as an umbrella under which various reading strategies reside. Visualizing, making connections, determining

---

[2] Furnes, B. and Norman, E. (2015). Metacognition and reading: comparing three forms of metacognition in normally developing readers and readers with Dyslexia. *Dyslexia* 21 (3): 273–284.

importance, and synthesizing are all metacognitive strategies. As discussed in Chapter 8, these strategies all fall under the broader category of metacognition. Metacognitive strategies promote critical thinking by making students aware of their thought processes, which is the first step toward evaluating, analyzing, and understanding a text.

Metacognition involves two key components: self-regulation and reflection. Self-regulation is managing one's thoughts and behaviors to achieve goals. It includes planning, monitoring, and evaluating progress. "There is a special focus in today's schools on students' ability to engage in self-regulation, defined as the extent to which learners are 'metacognitively, motivationally and behaviorally active participants in their own learning process' (Zimmerman, 1986, p. 308)."[3] Conversely, reflection involves looking back at what has been done to understand successes and areas for improvement. Together, these components help students become more effective and independent learners.

When students practice metacognition, they better understand their learning processes. "It is this internal reflection and conscious control of the learning process that goes to the heart of metacognition."[4] They become more adept at identifying their strengths and weaknesses, allowing them to focus on areas that need improvement. This self-awareness leads to better study habits and more efficient problem-solving techniques, ultimately enhancing their overall academic performance.

In the context of reading, metacognition helps students become more engaged and active readers. They learn to ask questions, make predictions, and summarize information as they read, which improves comprehension and retention. By being aware of their thought processes, students can identify when they are confused or distracted and take steps to regain focus.

 Reflect: How can you see metacognition as an important part of your literacy block?

Metacognition is a critical skill that supports lifelong learning. It encourages students to take ownership of their education and develop a growth mindset. By teaching

---

[3] Furnes, B. and Norman, E. (2015). Metacognition and reading: comparing three forms of metacognition in normally developing readers and readers with Dyslexia. *Dyslexia* 21 (3): 273–284.
[4] Alleva, P. and Gundlach, J. (2016). Learning intentionally and the metacognitive task. Journal of Legal Education 65.

metacognitive strategies, you equip your students with the tools they need to succeed academically and in their future endeavors.

Active Reader (uses metacognition)	Inactive Reader (does not use metacognition)
Plans Reading Strategies Sets goals for reading Previews the text before reading	**Reads Without a Plan** Starts reading without setting any goals Dives into reading without previewing
Monitors Understanding Checks comprehension regularly Recognizes when they don't understand	**Does Not Monitor Understanding** Continues reading without checking for understanding Does not notice when they are confused
Adjusts Reading Strategies Uses strategies like re-reading or summarizing Adjusts pace based on difficulty of text	**Does Not Adjust Reading Strategies** Continues reading without changing approach Reads at the same pace regardless of text difficulty
Engages with the Text Asks questions while reading Makes predictions and inferences	**Reads Passively** Rarely asks questions about the text Does not predict or infer from the text
Reflects on Reading Summarizes and reviews key points Thinks about how the information connects to other knowledge	**Does Not Reflect on Reading** Does not summarize or review after reading Reads without connecting to prior knowledge
Self-Corrects Goes back to clarify misunderstandings Revisits difficult sections	**Does Not Self-Correct** Continues reading despite confusion Avoids re-reading challenging parts
Evaluates and Critiques Critically analyzes the text's arguments Reflects on the quality and credibility of the text	**Does Not Evaluate or Critique** Accepts information without questioning Takes the text at face value
Applies Metacognitive Strategies Uses prior knowledge to understand new information Thinks about their own thought process	**Lacks Metacognitive Strategies** Struggles to connect new information to what they know Is unaware of their own thought process

Metacognition Broken Down

I've established that metacognition is the awareness of one's thinking. But what does this mean or look like concerning reading a text? When readers engage in metacognition, they actively monitor and regulate their understanding and thought processes while reading. This involves being aware of when comprehension is breaking down, knowing how to apply strategies to fix these issues, and reflecting on the effectiveness of these strategies. Metacognition transforms a passive reading experience into an interactive one, where the reader is constantly engaged with the text.

- **Planning and goal setting:** Metacognition begins with planning and goal setting. This involves setting specific objectives for what you want to achieve from your reading session. It could be understanding a particular concept, gathering information for a project, or simply enjoying a story. Previewing the text to get an overview is also crucial. This helps decide which reading strategies to employ, such as skimming for main ideas or reading slowly to absorb complex information.

- **Monitoring comprehension:** While reading, an active reader continuously monitors their comprehension. "Metacognitive awareness enables students to understand what they know, what they don't know, and what they need to know to fill the gaps in their knowledge."[5] This means checking their understanding as they go along, recognizing when they do not grasp something, and pinpointing confusing parts of the text. It's about being conscious of whether the material makes sense and identifying gaps in understanding that must be addressed.

- **Applying fix-up strategies:** When comprehension breaks down, metacognitive readers apply fix-up strategies to resolve the issue. This might include re-reading unclear sections, adjusting their reading speed depending on the difficulty of the text, and summarizing information to ensure they've captured the essential points. "The best

---

[5] Gizem, F. and Berk, A. (2023). Metacognitive awareness, reflective thinking, problem solving, and community of inquiry as predictors of academic self-efficacy in blended learning. *Turkish Online Journal of Distance Education* 24 (1): 23.

fix-up strategy of all is cultivating awareness: to be so engaged with the text that when that engagement starts to waver, just like a car veering from its lane, they immediately recognize it and can take steps to get back on course."[6] They also ask questions and seek answers within the text, using context clues to decipher unfamiliar words and concepts.

- **Reflecting on reading:** Reflection is a vital component of metacognition after reading. It involves summarizing and reviewing the key points to solidify understanding. "Students who have reflective thinking skills are cognizant of their learning experiences and apply them to different problem situations to deal with these situations (Yilmaz, 2020). They also understand what they need to do in order to accomplish more difficult tasks when they are aware of their learning experiences."[7] Reflective readers think about how the new information fits into their existing knowledge base, assess the effectiveness of the strategies they used, and evaluate the quality and credibility of the text. Reflection helps retain information and improve future reading experiences.

- **Engaging with the text:** Engagement with the text is another hallmark of metacognitive reading. This includes predicting what might happen next; drawing connections to personal experiences or other texts; and visualizing scenes, characters, and concepts described in the material. Active engagement leads to a more profound and personal interaction with the text, enhancing comprehension and enjoyment.

- **Self-regulation:** Self-regulation is crucial for maintaining focus and attention while reading. A 2019 study on self-regulation in strategic reading education found that students who are taught self-regulation techniques show significant improvements in reading comprehension, motivation, and focus. By learning to manage their attention and behavior, students can better maintain focus on the material, even when

---

[6] Zimmermann, S. and Hutchins, C. (2003). *7 Keys to Comprehension: How to Help Your Kids Read It and Get It!* Three Rivers Press.

[7] Gizem, F. and Berk, A. (2023). Metacognitive awareness, reflective thinking, problem solving, and community of inquiry as predictors of academic self-efficacy in blended learning. *Turkish Online Journal of Distance Education* 24 (1): 22.

distractions arise. This not only boosts comprehension but also allows students to take charge of their learning, leading to more effective problem-solving and information retention.

This research underscores the importance of incorporating self-regulation strategies in reading instruction, as these skills help students control their cognitive processes, stay on task, and achieve their learning goals more effectively.[8]

This involves managing distractions, taking breaks when necessary, and setting a clear purpose for reading. Adjusting this purpose as needed ensures that the reader remains aligned with their goals and makes the most of their reading session.

- **Evaluating and adapting strategies:** Metacognitive readers continuously evaluate and adapt their strategies. They assess the success of their comprehension techniques and are open to trying different methods for various types of texts. Learning from past experiences helps refine their approach, making them more efficient and effective readers.

Benefits of Teaching Metacognition

I want you to take a second and look at your curriculum pacing guide. I almost guarantee that metacognition is nowhere on the outline of reading skills and strategies they ask you to teach. So why should you listen to me and take time out of your busy year to teach it?

As I mentioned, metacognition is the one concept that will ensure students become active readers. Chapter 1 discussed the difference between reading skills and strategies. Metacognition falls directly into this discussion. Metacognitive strategies create an active reading experience. They are "student-centric." Other reading skills are more "text-centric" and don't involve the reader's brain, only the text.

---

[8] Turkben, T. (2019). The effect of self-regulation based strategic reading education on comprehension, motivation, and self-regulation skills. *International Journal of Progressive Education* 15 (4).

Metacognitive Strategies (Student-Centric)	Non-Metacognitive Strategies (Text-Centric)
Visualizing Involves creating mental images based on the text, which engages the reader's imagination and personal interpretation.	**Main Idea** Involves identifying the central message or concept of the text, focusing solely on the text content.
Making Connections Encourages relating the text to personal experiences, other texts, or world events, deepening understanding.	**Text Structure** Involves recognizing the organization of the text, such as chronological order or compare and contrast, without personal engagement.
Synthesizing Involves combining new information from the text with existing knowledge to form new ideas or insights.	**Plot** Focuses on the sequence of events in a story, which is an element of the text itself rather than the reader's thought process.
Determining Importance Requires identifying the most critical elements or messages in the text, which involves personal judgment and analysis.	**Cause & Effect** Involves identifying the relationship between events in the text, focusing on textual content.
Asking Questions Involves generating questions before, during, and after reading to enhance comprehension and engagement.	**Theme** Focuses on identifying the underlying message or lesson in the text without requiring personal engagement or reflection.
Using Schema Engages prior knowledge and experiences to understand and interpret new information from the text.	**Point of View** Involves recognizing the perspective from which the story is told, focusing on text content.

Metacognitive strategies are deeply rooted in the student's active involvement with the text. "Thinking about reading involves being aware of what your mind does as you create meaning. It's about playing an active role in tracking understanding and knowing how to fix comprehension when you get lost."[9] These strategies require students to use their prior knowledge (schema), continuously assess their understanding, and engage in self-regulation and reflection. Non-metacognitive strategies primarily focus on extracting and handling information directly from the text. These strategies do not require the same level of personal engagement or self-awareness.

As the chart shows, focusing on and teaching metacognitive strategies ensures that our students are at the center of the thinking process, creating an active reader experience. In addition, teaching metacognition to your students has many other benefits.

- **Deeper understanding:** Metacognitive strategies such as visualizing, making connections, and synthesizing information help students engage more deeply with the material. "It is only when they link the text to their own experiences that the text will begin to matter, and it may then evoke more rigorous attention, reflection, and analysis."[10] By creating mental images, relating concepts to personal experiences, and integrating new knowledge with existing understanding, students develop a more profound grasp of the content.

- **Enhanced memory:** Actively employing metacognitive techniques improves memory retention. When students consciously monitor their understanding and use strategies like summarizing or asking questions, they reinforce learning and retention of key information.

- **Autonomous learning:** Metacognition empowers students to take control of their learning process. "Variables such as community of inquiry, metacognitive awareness, problem solving and reflective thinking were significant and strong predictors of students' academic self-efficacy."[11] By setting goals, monitoring their comprehension, and applying fix-up strategies independently, students become more self-directed

---

[9] Zimmermann, S. and Hutchins, C. (2003). *7 Keys to Comprehension: How to Help Your Kids Read It and Get It!* Three Rivers Press.

[10] Beers, K. and Probst, R. (2017). *Disrupting Thinking: Why How We Read Matters*. Scholastic.

[11] Gizem, F. and Berk, A. (2023). Metacognitive awareness, reflective thinking, problem solving, and community of inquiry as predictors of academic self-efficacy in blended learning. *Turkish Online Journal of Distance Education* 24 (1): 32.

learners. They learn to identify when they need to adjust their approach, enhancing their ability to learn effectively and independently.
- **Self-assessment:** Through metacognition, students develop the ability to assess their learning progress. They gain insights into their strengths and weaknesses, enabling them to make informed decisions about improving their understanding and performance.
- **Analytical skills**: Metacognition fosters critical thinking by encouraging students to evaluate information critically. By reflecting on their thinking processes and evaluating the effectiveness of different strategies, students develop the analytical skills necessary for understanding complex concepts and solving problems creatively. According to Strampel and Oliver (2007), developing students' reflective thinking skills can facilitate understanding, support conceptual change, and foster critical evaluation and knowledge transfer. Therefore, designing an effective learning environment that promotes a culture of reflection must be one of the primary goals of teachers.[12]

Metacognitive strategies fundamentally change the way students interact with text by placing them at the center of the learning process. Unlike surface-level approaches to reading, metacognition encourages students to become active participants in their own comprehension journey. This involves not only being aware of their thinking but also knowing when and how to adjust their strategies for better understanding. By fostering this level of engagement, students develop a sense of ownership over their learning, which leads to a deeper connection with the material.

Additionally, metacognitive instruction shifts the focus from merely completing tasks to cultivating lifelong learning habits. This empowers students to think critically about their approach to reading and problem-solving, enabling them to transfer these skills across subjects and real-world scenarios. The benefits are not limited to academic achievement; they extend to building confidence, enhancing motivation, and equipping students with tools to handle challenges effectively. Through consistent practice, students learn to view themselves as capable, adaptable learners

---

[12] Palle, A. (2020). Developing students' reflective thinking skills in a metacognitive and argument-driven learning environment. *International Journal of Research in Education and Science* 6 (3): 467–483.

who can navigate complex information and apply their understanding in meaningful ways.

- **Problem-solving:** When faced with challenges in understanding, students who use metacognitive strategies can identify the root causes of their difficulties and apply appropriate strategies to overcome them. This problem-solving ability extends beyond academic tasks to real-world situations.
- **Active participation:** Engaging in metacognitive practices makes learning more meaningful and engaging for students. "When the reader notices what's going on inside himself and feels the emotion or raises the question that the text evokes, he is doing more than simply decoding . . . he is instead opening himself up to the text, interacting with it . . . accepting its invitation into its world and using it to help him make sense of his own experience."[13] By encouraging them to actively think about how they learn, teachers can ignite curiosity and enthusiasm for learning. This active involvement enhances motivation and persistence in tackling challenging tasks.
- **Motivation:** Understanding their learning processes and seeing improvements through metacognitive strategies boosts students' confidence. This sense of accomplishment and progress fosters intrinsic motivation as students recognize their capacity to learn and grow.
- **Higher achievement:** Students who regularly use metacognitive strategies tend to achieve higher academic success. "Integrating metacognition in teaching improves student achievement and cultivates independent learning among students."[14] By improving comprehension, retention, and problem-solving skills, metacognition equips students with the tools to excel academically across subjects.
- **Skill transfer:** Metacognitive skills are transferable across various subjects and tasks. Students learn to apply strategies like asking questions, using prior knowledge, and evaluating their understanding universally, enhancing overall academic performance.

---

[13] Beers, K. and Probst, R. (2017). *Disrupting Thinking: Why How We Read Matters*. Scholastic.
[14] Palle, A. (2020). Developing students' reflective thinking skills in a metacognitive and argument-driven learning environment. *International Journal of Research in Education and Science* 6 (3): 467–483.

- **Adaptability:** Metacognition instills lifelong learning skills by teaching students to reflect on and adapt their learning strategies. They develop a growth mindset, understanding that learning is a continuous improvement process.
- **Continuous improvement:** Through metacognition, students cultivate a habit of self-reflection and continuous improvement. They become more resilient learners, capable of overcoming challenges and adapting to new learning environments and demands.
- **Articulation of thoughts:** Metacognition helps students articulate their thoughts and ideas more clearly. By reflecting on their learning processes, students improve their ability to communicate effectively with peers and teachers.
- **Collaborative learning:** Students who understand their learning processes can contribute more effectively to group projects and discussions. They can share insights and strategies, fostering a cooperative learning environment where peers support each other's learning.
- **Stress reduction:** Understanding their learning strengths and weaknesses through metacognition can reduce anxiety and stress related to academic challenges. Students feel more confident in their ability to manage academic tasks effectively.

Teaching metacognition equips elementary students with essential cognitive, academic, and personal skills. By fostering more profound understanding, independence, critical thinking, and motivation, metacognition prepares students for academic success, lifelong learning, and personal growth.

 Reflect: Which benefit(s) do you see affecting your students the most when implementing metacognition into your literacy instruction?

Tips for Teaching Metacognition

Metacognition must be explicitly taught, like any other reading skill or strategy. Students need to know the word "metacognition" and understand what it means. They must understand metacognition and be repeatedly reminded to use it while reading. You want them to be THINKERS! But how do you teach such a concept when it's not concrete?

Teach Different Types of Thinking

In teaching metacognition, it's essential to introduce students to the three distinct types of thinking they might experience while reading. By familiarizing students with these types and helping them observe and recognize each, you enhance their ability to monitor and regulate their cognitive processes effectively.

Thinking Type	What does it mean?
Distracting Thoughts	A reader's mind wanders to unrelated thoughts instead of focusing on the text.
Interacting Thoughts	Students actively engage with the text. These thoughts involve accessing prior knowledge (schema), connecting ideas, or pausing to clarify information.
Reacting Thoughts	Students respond behaviorally or emotionally to the text. This could involve asking questions for clarification, expressing surprise at a plot twist, or reflecting on a character's motivations.

The first type of thinking is *distracting thinking,* where a reader's mind wanders to unrelated thoughts instead of focusing on the text. This can hinder comprehension and engagement with the material. Students learn to recognize when their attention drifts by identifying distracting thoughts and developing strategies to refocus on the reading task.

The second type is *interacting thoughts,* which occur when students actively engage with the text. These thoughts involve accessing prior knowledge (schema), connecting ideas, or pausing to clarify information. Interacting thoughts are crucial for deepening understanding and making meaning from the text. Encouraging students to notice and articulate these thoughts helps them become more aware of how their background knowledge and cognitive processes contribute to comprehension.

The final type of thinking is *reacting,* which occurs when students respond behaviorally or emotionally to the text. This could involve asking questions for clarification, expressing surprise at a plot twist, or reflecting on a character's motivations. Reacting thoughts highlight students' emotional engagement with the text and ability to analyze their reactions, fostering empathy and deeper connections to the content.

To effectively teach these types of thinking, consider using modeling as a primary strategy. Display thoughts related to a text on sentence strips or notecards as you read aloud. Arrange these thoughts on a board or anchor chart in the order they occur, demonstrating the sequence of your cognitive processes. This modeling helps students observe firsthand how different types of thinking unfold during reading. After reading, facilitate a discussion where students collaboratively categorize these thoughts into distracting, interacting, and reacting categories. Encourage them to justify their classifications and reflect on how each type of thinking contributes to their understanding of the text.

Differentiate Between Thoughts and Text

Emphasizing the connection between text and students' thoughts is foundational in teaching metacognition, as it enhances their ability to engage deeply with reading material. By prompting students to reflect on their thoughts while reading actively, educators foster metacognitive strategies that bolster comprehension and promote critical thinking skills. You want to create a "When I read this, I think this" situation. This approach encourages students to go beyond surface-level understanding by continually assessing their understanding and making connections between the text and their prior knowledge.

Such metacognitive practices enable students to navigate complex texts more effectively, empowering them to extract and articulate meaningful insights.

Moreover, integrating metacognitive strategies into reading instruction shifts students toward a more analytical and evidence-based approach to learning. When students recognize and evaluate their thought processes during reading, they become better equipped to support their interpretations with textual evidence. This skill is crucial in academic settings where students are often required to justify their answers and demonstrate a thorough understanding of the material. By linking textual evidence to their insights and interpretations, educators prepare students for academic success, lifelong learning, and critical analysis in various contexts.

TRY THIS!

Practical activities such as using notecards with thoughts or reflections related to a text are highly effective in implementing and reinforcing this skill. By asking students to match these thoughts to specific sections in the text and justify their placements, educators encourage students to articulate their understanding coherently. This activity promotes collaborative learning as students engage in discussions to compare their interpretations and reasoning. Through these interactions, students gain exposure to diverse perspectives and deepen their understanding of the text's nuances. By consistently reinforcing the correlation between their thoughts and textual content, educators nurture students' metacognitive awareness and equip them with the essential skills needed for deeper comprehension and critical thinking across all academic disciplines.

Model by Thinking Out Loud

One of the most effective ways to teach metacognition to elementary students is by modeling your thinking processes aloud. For example, a 2021 study highlights how "think-aloud" modeling encourages students to engage in self-regulated learning and develop critical problem-solving skills. Teachers who model their thinking help students reflect on their own learning, allowing them to identify strategies that work best for them. This process fosters independence and deeper engagement with tasks (Philippakos, 2021).[15] When you're reading a story together, pause to verbalize your thoughts: "I'm predicting what might happen next based on what we've read so far." This demonstrates to students how to actively engage with their thoughts while learning, encouraging them to adopt similar strategies independently. Additionally, you can vary the types of texts you read and the contexts in which you model thinking. By showing them how to apply these strategies across different subjects and activities, students learn that metacognition is a flexible tool that enhances understanding in various situations. This approach also builds their confidence in using these strategies independently, fostering independence and deeper comprehension.

It's crucial to model metacognition consistently and explicitly. When students hear you verbalize your thinking processes, they internalize the idea that thinking about one's thinking is a valuable skill in learning. In literacy, when encountering a challenging passage, you could model thinking aloud by saying, "I'm going to try a different reading strategy because this one isn't helping me understand the main idea." This openness clarifies the reading process, prompting students to tackle difficulties methodically. Furthermore, encourage students to reflect on their thinking processes by asking questions like, "What strategy did you use to understand that section of the text?" or "Why did you choose that particular strategy when reading?" You create a classroom culture that celebrates thinking critically and learning from mistakes by consistently modeling and encouraging metacognitive reflection.

---

[15] Philippakos, Z. (2021). Think aloud modeling: expert and coping models in writing instruction and literacy pedagogy. *The Language and Literacy Spectrum* 31 (1).

Encourage Self-Reflection

Foster a habit of self-reflection by regularly prompting students to think about their learning experiences. After completing a task or a lesson, ask questions like, "What did you find challenging about this activity?" or "How did you figure out the answer?" This encourages students to think critically about their learning processes, promoting awareness of their strengths and areas for improvement. Moreover, students should be encouraged to keep journals or learning logs where they can record their reflections regularly. This practice reinforces the habit of metacognitive thinking and allows students to track their progress over time, which can be motivating and insightful.

Self-reflection in literacy involves more than just looking back—it's also about planning for future learning. Encourage students to set specific goals based on their reflections after reading a challenging text. For example, if a student struggles with understanding character motivations in a novel, their goal might be to use annotation strategies to track character development more effectively. Guide them in breaking down these goals into practical steps, such as annotating key passages or discussing character motives with classmates. By linking reflection to goal-setting, students cultivate a proactive approach to enhancing their comprehension skills and becoming more independent readers.

Additionally, create opportunities for students to discuss their reflections with peers in small group settings or during class discussions. This collaborative exchange reinforces their metacognitive abilities and fosters a supportive classroom environment where students can learn from each other's insights and perspectives. Through these interactions, students refine their reading strategies and develop empathy and critical thinking skills as they engage in meaningful literary discussions.

Reflection Questions to Use with Any Text		
Before Reading	**During Reading**	**After Reading**
What do you already know about this topic? What are you expecting to learn from this text? How can you connect this text to what you already know? What strategies can you use if you find the text difficult? What goals do you have for understanding this text?	What predictions can you make based on the title/cover? What questions do you have as you read? Are there any parts of the text that are unclear to you? How does this information relate to what you've read before? Are there any words or phrases that stand out to you? How does the author's tone or perspective influence your understanding?	How did your predictions compare to what actually happened? Did you encounter any challenging words or concepts? How did you tackle them? What was the main idea of the text? Can you summarize the text in your own words? What did you learn from reading this text? How does this text connect to other texts you've read?

These questions prompt students to think actively about their reading process at different stages—before, during, and after reading. They encourage students to set goals, monitor their understanding, make connections, and reflect on their comprehension and learning strategies. Teachers can use these questions to guide discussions, journal prompts, or individual reflections, fostering metacognitive awareness and enhancing students' ability to engage critically with texts.

Teach Metacognitive Strategies Explicitly

Introduce specific metacognitive strategies in a clear and structured manner. For instance, teach students how to use graphic organizers like mind maps or concept maps to organize their thoughts before writing a story. Explain the purpose of each strategy and guide them through using it effectively, gradually shifting the responsibility for using these strategies independently. Furthermore, provide opportunities for students to apply these strategies in different contexts and encourage them to reflect on which strategies work best for them personally. This personalized approach helps students develop metacognitive flexibility, enabling them to choose and adapt strategies based on the task. Chapter 8 covers more about metacognitive strategies.

Explicit instruction of metacognitive strategies involves breaking down complex processes into manageable steps. For example, when teaching students how to monitor their understanding during reading, you might start by demonstrating how to ask themselves questions like, "Does this make sense?" or "What can I do if I don't understand?" Encourage them to use these prompts independently as they read, gradually incorporating more sophisticated strategies such as summarizing or predicting outcomes. Additionally, scaffold their learning by providing support and feedback as they practice these strategies. For instance, during writing workshops, provide opportunities for peer or teacher conferences where students can discuss their writing process and receive guidance on improving their metacognitive skills. By scaffolding their learning and providing timely feedback, you empower students to participate actively in their learning process.

Provide Opportunities for Discussion

Engage students in discussions about their learning strategies and problem-solving approaches. Encourage them to share how they tackled a particular math problem or how they inferred the meaning of an unfamiliar word while reading. By discussing these processes openly, students learn from each other's strategies and develop a broader repertoire of metacognitive skills. Additionally, facilitate peer feedback sessions where students can provide constructive insights into each other's thinking processes. This collaborative learning environment deepens their understanding of metacognition and strengthens their communication and reasoning skills.

Discussions about metacognition should emphasize the importance of reflecting on successes and challenges. Encourage students to share what strategies worked for them, what didn't, and why. This reflective dialogue helps students gain insights into their own thinking and problem-solving approaches and those of their peers. It also fosters a growth mindset by reinforcing that learning is a dynamic process involving continuous improvement and adaptation. Moreover, provide structured opportunities for students to apply metacognitive strategies collaboratively, such as group projects or problem-solving tasks. Encourage them to articulate their thinking to their peers, fostering more profound engagement with metacognition and promoting a supportive classroom culture where students learn from and inspire each other.

Set Goals and Monitor Progress

Help students set achievable goals for their learning and monitor their progress. In The Reading Comprehension Blueprint, page 178, it says: "The skilled reader sets his or her own standards or criteria for comprehension depending on the reading situation, which includes the reader's perception of the task, the demands of the text, and his or her abilities and attitudes. The reader sets goals before and during reading and determines what degree of understanding is good enough to accomplish the intended result."[16] Guide them in identifying specific steps or strategies they can use to reach their goals. For instance, if students want to improve their spelling, help them create a plan that includes practicing spelling words daily and reviewing mistakes. Moreover, self-monitoring encourages students to periodically review and adjust their goals based on their progress and changing learning needs. This iterative process of goal-setting and self-monitoring cultivates a habit of metacognitive awareness, empowering students to take ownership of their learning journey.

Goal-setting in metacognition goes beyond academic achievements; it also encompasses personal growth and skill development. Encourage students to set goals related to their learning strategies, such as improving their focus during class discussions or managing their time more effectively during assignments. Teach them to break down larger goals into smaller, manageable tasks and to celebrate their progress along the way. By fostering a growth-oriented approach to goal-setting, you help students develop resilience and perseverance in facing challenges.

Additionally, provide opportunities for students to share their goals with peers and to receive feedback and encouragement. This collaborative aspect enhances motivation and reinforces the importance of metacognition as a lifelong learning skill.

---

[16] Hennessy, N.L. (2021). *The Reading Comprehension Blueprint: Helping Students Make Meaning from Text*. Paul H. Brookes Publishing Co.

Sample Goals Students Can Set That Support Metacognition

Struggling Readers	On-Level Readers	Advanced Readers
Monitoring Comprehension: I will stop periodically while reading to check if I understand what I've read so far.	**Predicting Outcomes:** Before reading, I will predict what might happen next in the story based on the information I have.	**Analyzing Author's Intentions:** I will think about why the author chose specific words or wrote the story in a certain way, and how it affects the meaning.
Clarifying Confusion: I will ask myself questions when I don't understand a word or sentence and try to figure out its meaning from context clues.	**Summarizing:** After reading each section, I will summarize the main ideas or events to check my understanding.	**Evaluating Perspectives:** I will consider different viewpoints presented in the text and evaluate their strengths and weaknesses.
Setting Reading Goals: I will set a goal to read for 10 minutes without stopping to improve my focus and stamina.	**Making Connections:** I will connect what I'm reading to my own experiences, other books I've read, or things I've learned in school.	**Synthesizing Information:** I will combine information from different parts of the text to form new ideas or conclusions.
Visualizing Text: I will try to create mental images of what I'm reading to help me understand and remember the story better.	**Monitoring Understanding:** I will pay attention to when I start to lose focus or don't understand something, and use strategies to clarify my understanding.	**Self-Regulating Learning:** I will adjust my reading speed and strategies based on the difficulty of the text and my comprehension level.
Reflecting on Strategies: I will think about which reading strategies help me the most and use them more often.	**Using Text Features:** I will use headings, illustrations, and other text features to help me understand the structure and content of the text.	**Critiquing Texts:** I will analyze the quality of the evidence and arguments presented in non-fiction texts and form my own opinions.

Metacognition and Complex Texts

A critical reminder about implementing metacognition into your literacy instruction is that metacognition won't naturally occur unless a text is complex enough to support it. If a text is too simple, there's nothing essential to think about. To practice metacognition and metacognitive strategies, the text needs to be deep and complex enough to support the critical thinking we are asking our students to do.

Check your reading or literacy state standards for me quickly. You probably noticed the words "complex text" somewhere if you did. This vague term has entered the Common Core Standards and many other state standard lists! Unfortunately, the standards don't go into too much detail about what that term means! That leaves it to the teachers to figure it all out! So, let's dive in! Let's chat about text complexity and what it all means!

Why the Term "Complex Text"?

It's important to understand WHY standards have started using this term in the first place. Colleges found that a vast majority of their students were coming to them not able to read at the capacity needed for collegiate texts. This information then trickled down into high schools to try and get students "college and career ready." And BOOM, it ended up in the state standards.

But just because it's on the standards list doesn't mean there's enough information to help with the issue! There isn't! Many teachers are still very confused about what constitutes a "complex text."

What Is Text Complexity?

Unfortunately, there isn't a black-and-white definition of a "complex text." It's based upon multiple factors, and those factors change from situation to situation, not allowing us to define this term concretely.

> **Definition: text complexity** Refers to characteristics of individual texts, such as sentence length and word complexity, regardless of readers or tasks. Therefore, a text's complexity is determined in relation to other texts

Text complexity varies from reader to reader. A text can be complex for one student and not complex for another. It's hard to identify whether or not one specific text is genuinely complex. As adult readers, we know when a text is complex by using our metacognition. As we read, we need to slow down, re-read, define words, clarify information, and do "extras" to understand the text. But what about students? Can they do this?

"Four qualitative factors that make texts easier or more complex are (1) levels of meaning (e.g., single or multiple) or purpose (e.g., explicit or implicit), (2) structure (e.g., simple or complex), (3) language conventionality and clarity (e.g., literal or figurative), and (4) knowledge demands (e.g., few or many assumptions about readers' knowledge" (NGA Center & CCSSO, 2010).[17] Inside a text that typically has high text complexity, we would find a few consistencies:

- More implicit meanings of concepts
- The use of unconventional text structures (flashbacks, flash-forwards, multiple points of view)
- Figurative language and unfamiliar language (academic or domain-specific)
- A literal meaning that is intentionally at odds with the underlying meaning (the purpose of the text is hidden)

How to Measure Text Complexity?

Because there's no concrete definition of a complex text, each must be measured individually. But how?

---

[17] Strong, J., Amendum, S., and Smith, K. (2018). Supporting elementary students' reading of difficult texts. *International Literacy Association and Wiley*.

There are three (technically four) parts to measuring text complexity: analyzing the qualitative data from the text, analyzing the quantitative data from the text, and analyzing the reader and task. "The comprehension process is often considered an interaction between reader, text, and activity, surrounded by the sociocultural context (RAND Reading Study Group, 2002). The possible difficulties that a text presents are a result of the quantitative and qualitative aspects of text complexity, as well as characteristics of the reader and the associated tasks. For a teacher to determine what makes a text difficult for his or her students, all three aspects must be considered. We discuss measures of each of these aspects of text difficulty."[18]

Each of these components measures different aspects:

- **Qualitative Data** refers to the data in the actual words and language. This isn't something that a computer can measure. It's all about the text structure, the language's clarity, and conventions. It also includes vocabulary difficulty and the knowledge demands of the reader.

- **Quantitative Data** refers to the data that can be counted (think numbers/quantity). This refers to the sentence length, the number of words or syllables, word frequency, and so on. This is what the Lexile Level is all about! (That is also why we can't justify using Lexile as a determining factor for leveling texts!)

---

[18] Stong, J., Amendum, S., and Smith, K. (2018). Supporting elementary students' reading of difficult texts. *International Literacy Association and Wiley* 72 (2): 201–212.

- **Reader and Task.** This final component has two parts. First, the reader at hand. Who will be reading the text? What knowledge do they possess? What language do they speak? Each text can have a varying complexity level from reader to reader. Finally, the task paired with the text itself adds to the complexity level. What is the reader being asked to do with the text?

"Whether the quantitative measure is unidimensional or multidimensional, many researchers recommend supplementing the measure with considerations of qualitative complexity; that is, aspects of text complexity that can only be judged by an attentive human reader."[19]

When thinking about text complexity, consider these points:

- **Read the text before presenting it to students:** To determine whether the text is complex, you must give it the time needed to read it yourself and consider the above factors and how they will impact your readers.
- **Consider your targeted standards and curricular goals:** How does the text you selected support them? Not every text will support the objectives you wish to focus on.
- **Ensure the text provides opportunities for critical thinking:** Does the text provide opportunities for students to examine and analyze thoroughly, make inferences, uncover new insights, and so on? How is the text going to challenge their thinking? The text complexity isn't high enough if you know it won't.

Incorporating metacognition for teachers and students is crucial in understanding and navigating complex texts. Teachers must reflect on their reading processes to identify complexities and anticipate student difficulties. Students should be taught metacognitive strategies to monitor their comprehension, such as asking themselves questions about the text, summarizing paragraphs, and predicting upcoming content. You can better prepare your students to tackle complex texts confidently and competently by fostering these skills.

---

[19] Hennessy, N.L. (2021). *The Reading Comprehension Blueprint: Helping Students Make Meaning from Text*. Paul H. Brookes Publishing Co.

Understanding Complex Texts

© Ciera Harris Teaching, 2020

	Extremely Complex	**Very Complex**	**Average Complexity**	**Slightly Complex**
Purpose	☐ Hard to determine purpose. Implied or subtle	☐ Purpose not stated, but simple to deduce.	☐ Purpose not stated but very simple to deduce.	☐ Plainly stated in text. Concrete to readers
Text Structure	☐ Text features are crucial to understanding of text ☐ Graphics are sophisticated and necessary to analyze ☐ Relationship between ideas in text are deep. Text organization is specialized	☐ Text features help to greatly heighten reader's comprehension ☐ Graphics are important and some of them may be necessary to analyze to comprehend text ☐ Relationship between ideas are deeper than normal, often implicit. Text organization may exhibit traits common to specific discipline	☐ Text features heighten reader's comprehension ☐ Graphics are supplementary to the text ☐ There is a relationship between some ideas in the text that are implicit. Text organization is generally sequential	☐ Text features help reader understand content but are not essential ☐ Graphics are simple and unnecessary in comprehending the text ☐ Relationship between ideas are concrete and stated. Organization of text is clear and easy to predict
Language	☐ Complex – contains figurative language ☐ Vocabulary is unfamiliar and subject-specific. Includes academic language ☐ Complex sentence structure	☐ Complex – contains some figurative language ☐ Vocabulary is sometimes unfamiliar ☐ Contains many complex sentences	☐ Mainly unambiguous and easy to follow ☐ Vocabulary is familiar and conversational ☐ Simple and compound sentences used	☐ Very straightforward and literal. Easy to follow and understand ☐ Vocabulary is conversational language ☐ Mostly simple sentences
Knowledge Demands	☐ Board knowledge base needed on specific or specialized content	☐ Moderate level of specific or specialized content	☐ Everyday practical knowledge sprinkled with some specific or specialized content	☐ Everyday, practical knowledge

Metacognition Activities

Metacognition isn't something to hit at the beginning of the year and never return to. It's a concept that needs to be reviewed, reminded, encouraged, and modeled frequently throughout the school year. Here are some quick and straightforward metacognition activities you can try any time of the year AFTER you have introduced what metacognition is to your students.

Sorting Types of Thinking

To enhance students' metacognitive awareness and comprehension skills, teachers prepare index cards with different types of thinking, such as predicting, questioning, and summarizing. These cards are distributed to students before they engage with a selected text. The goal is for students to read the text and categorize each card into three categories: distracting thoughts (unrelated to the text), interacting thoughts (directly related to the text), and reacting thoughts (emotional or personal responses). This activity prompts students to identify the types of cognitive processes they experience while reading and justify their categorizations with evidence from the text itself. Students develop a deeper understanding of how their thinking influences their comprehension by actively sorting and discussing these cards.

Matching Thinking with Text

In this lesson, teachers prepare by underlining various segments of a text that elicit different types of thinking, such as making connections, asking questions, or visualizing. Corresponding index cards are created with examples of these thinking types. Students are tasked with matching each underlined segment of the text with the appropriate index card, identifying both the type of thinking involved and categorizing it as distracting, interacting, or reacting. This dual classification encourages students to recognize patterns in their thinking and understand how specific parts of the text stimulate different cognitive responses. Through discussion and reflection on their choices, students gain insights into how various thinking strategies can enhance their comprehension and engagement with the text.

Partner Metacognitive Listening

In this collaborative activity, students work in pairs, each receiving a text and a chart listing metacognitive strategies such as asking questions, making predictions, and summarizing. One student reads aloud while the other listens attentively, noting instances where the reader demonstrates these strategies. After the first reading session, students switch roles. Each time a strategy is observed, the listener makes a tally mark in the corresponding section of the chart. This activity encourages active listening and heightens students' awareness of how their peers employ metacognitive strategies to enhance understanding. In the subsequent discussion, students reflect on which strategies were most effective in aiding comprehension, sharing insights on how they might incorporate these strategies into their reading practices to improve their metacognitive skills.

Creating a Metacognitive Mind Map

To visually represent their metacognitive processes during reading, students are given a blank game board labeled from start to finish and a key associating different metacognitive strategies with specific colors. As students read independently, they use the colored markers to annotate the game board, indicating where and how they applied each strategy throughout the text. This visual mapping helps students monitor their thinking in real time and encourages them to reflect on their cognitive processes and the effectiveness of each strategy in aiding their comprehension. After completing their reading, students review their mind maps, identifying which strategies were used most frequently and analyzing why specific strategies enhanced their understanding of the text more effectively. Through this reflective process, students develop a deeper awareness of their thinking habits and learn to make deliberate choices about which strategies to employ in future reading tasks.

Annotating Thinking in Text

In this lesson focused on text annotation, students are provided with a text and a key linking specific metacognitive strategies, such as predicting, questioning, and clarifying, to different colors. As they read, students underline sections of the text where they encounter each type of thinking and annotate these instances with thought bubbles or margin notes explaining their thoughts and reactions. This dual annotation process not only helps students track their thinking patterns but also encourages them to articulate and reflect on the effectiveness of their cognitive strategies in enhancing comprehension. In a concluding discussion, students share their annotations, discussing which types of thinking were most prevalent and how these thoughts influenced their understanding of the text. Through this collaborative reflection, students gain insights into their thinking processes and develop strategies to improve their metacognitive skills in future reading and learning experiences.

Closing

As you finish this chapter on metacognition, inquiry, and independence, it's essential to reflect on the transformative power of metacognitive strategies in the classroom. By fostering metacognitive awareness, we enable students to become active participants in their learning journey. They learn not just to read, but to think about their reading, to question and engage with the text, and to apply strategies that enhance their comprehension and retention. This shift from passive to active reading is crucial in developing critical thinking and lifelong learning skills.

Implementing metacognitive strategies requires dedication and consistent effort from both teachers and students. However, the rewards are profound. Students who master these strategies become more independent learners, capable of self-regulation and reflection. They are better equipped to tackle complex texts, identify their strengths and areas for improvement, and apply their learning across various contexts. As educators, our role is to guide and support them in this process, providing the tools and opportunities they need to succeed. By doing so, we help them unlock their full potential and prepare them for future academic and personal success. Consider these questions as you ponder this issue more and try the following lessons.

End of Chapter Reflection Questions:

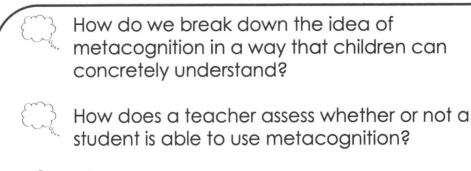

- How do we break down the idea of metacognition in a way that children can concretely understand?
- How does a teacher assess whether or not a student is able to use metacognition?
- How do we choose texts that promote metacognition?
- What is a complex text?

Lessons to Try

You can access the complete lesson for free at `http://www.cieraharristeaching.com/ttrlessons` using the passcode: `literacy for all`.

"Drive Your Own Reading with Metacognition" Lesson

The "Drive Your Own Reading with Metacognition" lesson plan is designed to help students develop the crucial skill of metacognition, which involves being aware of and regulating their thinking while reading. This lesson begins with a relatable analogy, comparing the steps of driving a car to the reading process to illustrate the concept of metacognition engagingly and understandably. Students learn to monitor their thoughts before, during, and after reading, ensuring they actively engage with and comprehend the text more deeply.

The importance of this lesson lies in its ability to transform students from passive readers into active thinkers. By teaching metacognitive strategies, educators enable students to take control of their reading processes, leading to improved comprehension and retention. Metacognition helps students recognize when they do not understand something and equips them with strategies to address these gaps in understanding. This self-awareness and adaptability are key to becoming proficient readers and successful learners across all subjects.

The benefits of teaching metacognition extend beyond reading comprehension. Students who practice metacognitive strategies become more independent learners, capable of setting goals, monitoring their progress, and reflecting on their learning experiences. These skills foster a growth mindset, encouraging students to view challenges as opportunities for growth rather than obstacles. Additionally, by integrating metacognitive practices into their daily routines, students develop lifelong learning habits that will benefit them academically and personally.

Quick Tip: When teaching this lesson, consistently model metacognitive strategies by thinking aloud during reading activities. This practice helps students understand how to apply these strategies and reinforces the importance of awareness of their thinking processes.

"Reading Uncertainties" Lesson

The "Reading Uncertainties" lesson plan aims to teach students that it's okay to encounter difficulties while reading and to equip them with strategies to overcome these challenges. The lesson begins with a relatable activity where the teacher reads a passage aloud, intentionally making mistakes, and then discusses these mistakes with the students. This activity helps to normalize the experience of reading uncertainties and sets the stage for introducing specific strategies that students can use to address their reading challenges.

This lesson is important because it encourages students to view mistakes as a natural part of the reading process rather than a sign of failure. Students can become more resilient and independent readers by recognizing and addressing their uncertainties. Teaching these strategies also promotes metacognitive skills as students learn to monitor their understanding and apply appropriate strategies when encountering difficulties. This self-awareness and problem-solving ability are crucial for academic success and lifelong learning.

The benefits of teaching this lesson are manifold. Students who learn to identify and address their reading uncertainties can improve their reading comprehension and overall academic performance. These skills also help build confidence and reduce anxiety related to reading, making students more willing to engage with challenging texts. Additionally, the lesson's focus on practical strategies empowers students to actively participate in their learning actively, fostering a growth mindset and a positive attitude toward reading.

Quick Tip: When teaching this lesson, create a supportive classroom environment where students feel safe making mistakes and sharing their uncertainties. Encourage open discussions about reading challenges and celebrate students' efforts to use strategies to overcome them.

"Author vs. Me" Lesson

The "Author vs. Me" lesson plan aims to help students understand the collaborative reading process by distinguishing between the author's information and the reader's thoughts. This lesson focuses on enhancing students' metacognitive skills by encouraging them to actively engage with the text, creating a more meaningful reading experience. By recognizing that both the author and the reader play crucial roles in constructing meaning, students learn to appreciate the dynamic relationship between the text and their cognitive processes.

The importance of this lesson lies in its ability to foster deeper comprehension and critical thinking. Students often approach reading as a passive activity, solely relying on the author's words to understand the content. This lesson challenges that notion by demonstrating how readers' thoughts, questions, connections, and reflections can significantly enrich their understanding of the text. This approach improves comprehension and empowers students to become more active and engaged readers, capable of interacting with texts on a more profound level.

Teaching the "Author vs. Me" lesson offers numerous benefits. It encourages students to practice metacognition, the awareness and regulation of their thinking processes. This skill is essential for academic success across all subjects, as it helps students monitor their understanding and adjust their strategies accordingly. Additionally, the lesson promotes collaborative learning by incorporating group discussions and shared reflections, which can enhance social skills and build a supportive classroom community.

Quick Tip

When implementing this lesson, it's crucial to model the metacognitive process explicitly and provide ample opportunities for guided practice before expecting students to perform independently. This gradual release of responsibility ensures students build confidence and competence in using their metacognitive skills effectively.

CHAPTER 8

METACOGNITIVE STRATEGIES FOR SUCCESS

Cultivating Metacognitive Thinkers

Focus on strategies to maintain curiosity, develop metacognitive skills, and apply effective reading techniques to engage students.

This chapter explores the pivotal role of metacognitive strategies in literacy instruction. As you learned in Chapter 7, metacognition, or "thinking about thinking," is crucial for developing active, engaged readers who can navigate complex texts with confidence and comprehension. This chapter delves into various metacognitive strategies that educators can integrate into their teaching practices to foster these skills in students to help take their learning a step further.

The chapter highlights how metacognitive strategies help students monitor their understanding, recognize when they are confused, and employ appropriate strategies to resolve difficulties. Through practical examples and research-based methods, I demonstrate how teachers can guide students in becoming self-regulated learners.

The chapter also addresses common challenges educators face when teaching metacognitive strategies and provides solutions to overcome these obstacles. It discusses the significance of creating a classroom environment that encourages reflective thinking and continuous learning. By the end of the chapter, you will have a comprehensive understanding of how to implement metacognitive strategies effectively, ultimately leading to improved literacy outcomes for your students.

Chapter 8 Objectives

 The readers will understand the concept of metacognition and its relevance in literacy instruction.

 The readers will learn various metacognitive strategies to enhance students' reading comprehension.

 The readers will be able to identify and address challenges in teaching metacognitive strategies.

 The readers will explore practical examples and methods for integrating metacognitive strategies into their teaching practices.

 The readers will recognize the importance of fostering a reflective and supportive classroom environment for metacognitive development.

Introduction to Metacognitive Strategies

Chapter 7 emphasized the critical role of teaching and incorporating metacognition into literacy instruction. The goal is to cultivate students who are not just passive receivers of information but active participants in their reading experiences. Reading is a dynamic interaction between the author and the reader, where both parties contribute to the meaning-making process. The author provides the content, but it is the reader's responsibility to engage with it actively. By employing metacognitive strategies, students keep their minds alert and interact deeply with the text, thereby enhancing comprehension and retention. "Mounting evidence shows that students who are able to self-regulate their learning achieve higher learning outcomes" (e.g., Dignath, Buettner, & Langfeldt, 2008; Pintrich & DeGroot, 1990; Zimmerman & Martinez-Pons, 1986).[1]

When students are actively involved in their reading, they move beyond mere word decoding to truly understanding and interpreting the text. This active involvement requires them to think critically and reflectively about what they read, ask questions, make connections, and draw inferences. In this way, reading becomes a give-and-take relationship where the reader is as engaged and invested as the author.

Understanding Metacognitive Strategies and Their Role in Reading

Metacognition, often described as "thinking about thinking," encompasses a wide range of reading strategies. It is a comprehensive term that includes various techniques and approaches aimed at enhancing understanding and engagement with a text. "Metacognitive strategies including planning, monitoring and evaluation increase metacognitive awareness that enhances the quality of the learning process (Karaoglan Yilmaz, Olpak, & Yilmaz, 2018)."[2] Metacognitive strategies are particularly powerful because they require readers to be actively involved in their learning process, rather than passively absorbing information.

---

[1] Baas, D., Castelijns, J., Vermeulen, M. et al. (2015). The relation between assessment for learning and elementary students' cognitive and metacognitive strategy use. *The British Journal of Educational Psychology* 85 (1): 33–46.

[2] Gizem, F. and Berk, A. (2023). Metacognitive awareness, reflective thinking, problem solving, and community of inquiry as predictors of academic self-efficacy in blended learning. *Turkish Online Journal of Distance Education* 24 (1): 20–36.

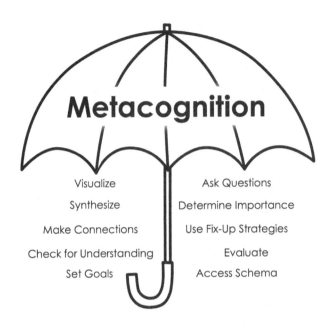

Consider visualization, a fundamental metacognitive strategy. Visualization involves creating mental images of the text to enhance understanding and memory. However, this process is not possible without accessing prior knowledge, or schema. For instance, when a reader encounters a passage describing a bustling marketplace, their ability to visualize it depends on their previous experiences and knowledge of such places. If they have no memory or background knowledge of marketplaces, their visualization will be limited, and their comprehension of the text will suffer. Therefore, effective visualization requires readers to draw on their existing knowledge and experiences.

Similarly, other metacognitive strategies, such as making connections, asking questions, and determining importance, also rely heavily on the reader's active engagement and prior knowledge. These strategies are designed to keep readers' minds actively working as they read, ensuring that they are continuously processing and making sense of the information.

The Necessity of Explicitly Teaching Metacognitive Strategies

"Unfortunately, not all children spontaneously develop the required strategies and engage in strategic processes when encountering a text that is difficult to comprehend. This is, however, empirical evidence that reading comprehension strategies can be taught to help readers process texts more actively and deeply."[3] Metacognitive strategies need to be explicitly taught and modeled for students to use them effectively. Teachers play a crucial role in this process, demonstrating how and when to use each strategy and explaining its purpose. Through direct instruction and modeling, students can see how experienced readers approach a text and manage their comprehension.

Each metacognitive strategy has a unique purpose and is used in specific contexts. For example, asking questions can help students engage with a narrative by clarifying confusing parts of a text and encouraging deeper thinking about the content. Determining importance can help students focus on key elements of the story, thereby increasing their understanding and retention of essential information. Accessing schema, or drawing on prior knowledge, allows students to make connections with the text, enhancing their comprehension and making the material more relatable and memorable. "Metacognitive awareness enables students to understand what they know, what they don't know, and what they need to know to fill the gaps in their knowledge. It also enables students to understand how to control their cognitive processes and what cognitive strategies lead them to learn (Jaleel, 2016)."[4]

However, not every text will require the use of all strategies. Proficient readers are adept at recognizing what's happening inside their brains as they read and can select the most appropriate strategy for the task at hand. A 2020 study published in the *Journal of Research in Reading* found that proficient readers are adept at employing metacognitive strategies, such as

---

[3] de Koning, B.B. and van der Schoot, M. (2013). Becoming part of the story! Refueling the interest in visualization strategies for reading comprehension. *Educational Psychology Review* 25 (2): 261–287. https://doi.org/10.1007/s10648-013-9222-6.

[4] Gizem, F. and Berk, A. (2023). Metacognitive awareness, reflective thinking, problem solving, and community of inquiry as predictors of academic self-efficacy in blended learning. *Turkish Online Journal of Distance Education* 24 (1): 20–36.

> By providing students with the tools to actively engage with texts, educators can transform passive reading into an interactive and dynamic experience.

monitoring their comprehension and adjusting their reading approaches when needed. They are more likely to engage in behaviors like making inferences, adjusting strategies when comprehension falters, and using background knowledge to understand complex texts. These abilities allow them to effectively navigate and understand various types of reading materials, leading to improved comprehension.

Additionally, proficient readers exhibit greater awareness of their own thinking, which enables them to use different strategies flexibly depending on the demands of the reading task. This metacognitive awareness is key to their ability to succeed in reading, as it allows them to both monitor and regulate their understanding in real time.[5] They might decide to visualize a particularly descriptive scene in a novel, ask questions to understand a complex argument in a non-fiction text, or summarize key points after reading a dense academic article.

To develop these skills, students need ample opportunities to practice metacognitive strategies in various reading contexts. This practice should be supported by ongoing feedback and reflection, helping students to refine their use of strategies and become more self-aware and strategic readers. The following table provides a detailed breakdown of each metacognitive strategy, including explanations and examples of when and how to use them. This resource can serve as a valuable reference for both teachers and students as they work to incorporate metacognition into their reading practices.

> "Skills before strategies. I think too many teachers, myself included, were starting the year teaching character traits or main idea instead of going over how to ask and answer questions or something from the strategies column that will help them succeed better in the skills column."
>
> -Valerie Keehler, 3rd Grade, Climax Springs Elementary, Missouri

---

[5] Soto, C., Blume, A., and Bernal, M. (2020). The role of meta-cognitive cues on the comprehension of proficient and poor readers. *Journal of Research in Reading* 43 (3): 272–289.

By fostering metacognitive awareness and skill in your students, you empower them to take control of their reading and learning. "In terms of motivation, self-regulated learners have an intrinsic interest in learning and report high levels of self-efficacy. Cognitively, self-regulated learners optimize their learning environment by selecting learning strategies and structuring their environment."[6] This not only improves their comprehension and academic performance but also instills a lifelong love of reading and learning. Through metacognition, students become more reflective, self-aware, and effective readers, capable of navigating a wide range of texts and learning experiences.

Metacognitive strategies need to be explicitly taught and modeled in order for students to understand their purpose. Each strategy has its own purpose and reason to be used while reading. Not every text a reader approaches will need the use of all of the strategies. Strong readers recognize what's happening inside their brains while reading and specifically choose a strategy that will help them work through the text. The following table breaks down each metacognitive strategy and explains when the strategy should be used. You will learn more about each strategy later in the chapter.

Metacognitive Strategies and When They Should Be Used

Visualize	**When to Use:** When struggling to understand descriptive or complex passages. **Explanation:** Visualization helps students create mental images of the text, making it easier to understand and remember details. For example, when reading a story with rich descriptions of settings or characters, students can visualize the scenes to deepen comprehension.

---

[6] Baas, D., Castelijns, J., Vermeulen, M. et al. (2015). The relation between assessment for learning and elementary students' cognitive and metacognitive strategy use. *The British Journal of Educational Psychology* 85 (1): 33–46.

Make Connections	**When to Use:** When the text feels abstract or disconnected from prior knowledge. **Explanation:** Making connections involves linking the text to personal experiences (text-to-self), other texts (text-to-text), or world knowledge (text-to-world). This strategy helps students relate to the content and better understand the text. For instance, when reading about a historical event, students can connect it to what they've learned in history class.
Ask Questions	**When to Use:** When confused about the text's content or purpose, or to engage more deeply with the material. **Explanation:** Asking questions encourages active reading and critical thinking. Students can pose questions about the text's content, purpose, and meaning. For example, they might ask, "Why did the character make that choice?" or "What will happen next?"
Access Schema (Prior Knowledge)	**When to Use:** When encountering new or challenging topics. **Explanation:** Accessing prior knowledge helps students draw on what they already know to understand new information. Before reading, they can brainstorm what they know about the topic. During reading, they can use this knowledge to make sense of the text.
Set Goals	**When to Use:** When needing to focus attention and effort on specific aspects of the text. **Explanation:** Setting goals gives students a purpose for reading and helps them focus. Goals can be about understanding the main idea, finding specific information, or enjoying the story. For example, a student might set a goal to identify the main argument in a persuasive text.

Synthesize	**When to Use:** When needing to integrate new information with existing knowledge. **Explanation:** Synthesizing involves combining new information from the text with existing knowledge to form new ideas or insights. This strategy is useful for summarizing information or creating a deeper understanding of the text. For example, students can synthesize details from different parts of a story to understand a character's development.
Determine Importance	**When to Use:** When needing to identify key ideas and details in dense or informational texts. **Explanation:** Determining importance helps students focus on key information and main ideas rather than getting bogged down by minor details. This strategy is particularly useful when reading informational texts. For example, students can identify the main arguments and supporting details in a news article.
Check for Understanding	**When to Use:** When unsure about comprehension or to verify understanding periodically. **Explanation:** Checking for understanding involves self-monitoring comprehension. Students can pause periodically to summarize what they've read, clarify confusing parts, and ensure they understand the text. This can involve re-reading difficult sections or discussing the text with peers.
Fix-It Strategies	**When to Use:** When encountering comprehension breakdowns or misunderstandings. **Explanation:** Fix-it strategies are used to address comprehension problems as they arise. These strategies include re-reading, looking up unknown words, and seeking help from peers or teachers. For example, if a student doesn't understand a paragraph, they might re-read it or use a dictionary to look up unfamiliar terms.

Evaluate	**When to Use:** When reflecting on the text's content, purpose, and effectiveness.
	Explanation: Evaluating involves critically assessing the text's content, purpose, and effectiveness. Students can reflect on whether the text met their expectations, how it compares to other texts, and what they learned from it. This strategy promotes higher-order thinking and comprehension.

The Metacognitive Cycle

Metacognitive strategies play a crucial role in enhancing students' reading comprehension and overall learning experience. A study published in *The Reading Teacher* (2007) demonstrated that third-grade students who received explicit instruction in metacognitive strategies, such as comprehension monitoring and summarization, showed significant improvement in both reading comprehension and vocabulary. The intervention group outperformed the control group in post-test assessments, with marked increases in comprehension scores after a five-week program. This statistical evidence highlights how metacognitive strategies help students become more aware of their thinking processes, allowing them to adjust their reading techniques and better understand complex texts. By actively engaging with the text and monitoring their understanding, students were able to improve both their reading comprehension and vocabulary development.[7] By teaching these strategies explicitly, students learn not only how to use them but also when and why they are effective. This process can be broken down into two main steps: teaching each strategy independently and introducing students to the metacognitive cycle.

---

[7] Boulware-Gooden, R., Carreker, S., Thornhill, A., and Joshi, M. (2007). Instruction of metacognitive strategies enhances reading comprehension and vocabulary achievement of third-grade students. *The Reading Teacher* 61 (1): 70–77.

Step One: Explicitly Teach Each Individual Strategy

Metacognitive strategies, like other reading skills, require deliberate and structured instruction. "Direct instruction is required in the use of different comprehension skills in order to advance students' ability to independently comprehend texts. Being able to make connections is an important reading comprehension strategy which allows students make meaning of what they are reading."[8] To achieve this, educators should adopt a methodical approach known as the gradual release of responsibility. This involves several stages: introducing each strategy one at a time, explaining its purpose and relevance, and demonstrating the strategy in action. Teachers should show students how to apply the strategy while reading a text, thinking aloud to reveal the cognitive processes involved.

Following this, provide opportunities for students to practice the strategy with support. This could involve group work, partner activities, or teacher-led sessions where students apply the strategy to selected texts. Finally, encourage students to use the strategy on their own, providing feedback and monitoring their progress to ensure they are using the strategy effectively.

By following this sequence, students gain a thorough understanding of each metacognitive strategy, learning to recognize its utility and integrate it into their reading practice. You will learn more about how to teach each strategy later in the chapter.

Gradual Release of Responsibility

I do	We do	We do	You do
The teacher introduces the metacognitive strategy, reviews the material, goes over the anchor chart, explains today's lesson, models the strategy, and discusses (5 minutes)	The teacher guides the students through *same* strategy – different variation – asks questions – clarifies thinking (5 minutes)	The teacher puts the students into groups – try out the same strategy, different variation, walks around, and gives support where needed (10 minutes)	The teacher gives a quick exit ticket to collect data (5 minutes)

---

[8] Yaghmour, L.S. and Obaidat, L.T. (2022). The effectiveness of using direct instruction in teaching comprehension skill of third-grade students. *International Journal of Instruction* 15 (2): 373–392.

Step Two: Introduce the Metacognitive Cycle

Once students are familiar with individual strategies, it's important to introduce them to the metacognitive cycle. The metacognitive cycle represents the process that proficient readers go through before, during, and after reading a text. When readers first approach a text, they stop to think about the overall topic, what the text might be about, and access their prior knowledge on the topic. They begin to think about any goals or purposes they may have when reading the text, creating a plan to achieve the best comprehension and understanding. As they read, the reader applies strategies to better support their understanding of the text, using metacognition to monitor their thinking and becoming aware of any uncertainties that arise. Finally, when the text is complete, they reflect on their overall level of understanding and the success of meeting the goals they set for themselves. This cyclical process helps students to approach reading as an active, strategic endeavor, enhancing their comprehension and fostering a deeper engagement with the text.

By engaging in this comprehensive approach, students learn to approach reading as an active, strategic process. They become more adept at planning, monitoring, and evaluating their understanding, which leads to improved reading comprehension and overall academic performance. Explicitly teaching metacognitive strategies and introducing the metacognitive cycle equips students with essential tools for effective reading and learning. This structured approach not only enhances their immediate reading skills but also fosters lifelong learning habits. As students become more skilled in using these strategies, they gain confidence and independence in their reading, setting a strong foundation for future academic success.

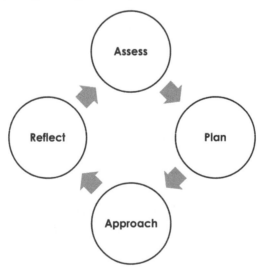

Assess

Actions:

- Examine the title, headings, and any available summaries.
- Skim through the text to get a sense of its structure and length.
- Identify the overall topic and potential themes.
- Recall prior knowledge and experiences related to the topic.

Questions to ask:

- What is the text about based on the title and headings?
- What do I already know about this topic?
- What are my initial thoughts or feelings about this text?
- How does this topic relate to what I have learned before?

Plan

Actions:

- Set specific reading goals or purposes (e.g., understanding the main idea, gathering information for a project).
- Decide on which metacognitive strategies to use (e.g., visualization, summarizing, questioning).
- Determine how much time to allocate to reading and how to break up the reading session if necessary.

Questions to ask:

- What do I want to achieve by reading this text?
- Which strategies will help me understand this text better?
- How should I pace myself through this text?
- What resources (e.g., dictionary, notes) might I need?

Approach

Actions:

- Read the text actively, applying the chosen metacognitive strategies.
- Monitor comprehension and be alert to any confusion or difficulty.
- Adjust strategies as needed (e.g., re-reading, looking up unfamiliar words).
- Take notes or highlight key points to aid understanding and retention.

Questions to ask:

- Am I understanding what I am reading?
- What strategies am I using right now, and are they effective?
- Where am I getting confused, and how can I clarify my understanding?
- What are the key points or ideas in this section of the text?

Reflect

Actions:

- Review the text and summarize the main ideas or arguments.
- Evaluate how well the reading goals were met.
- Reflect on the effectiveness of the strategies used.
- Consider how the new information fits with existing knowledge and how it might be applied in the future.

Questions to ask:

- Did I achieve my reading goals?
- What strategies worked well, and which did not?
- What are the main points or takeaways from this text?
- How does this new information integrate with what I already know?
- What can I do differently next time to improve my reading comprehension?

The Metacognitive Cycle in Action

Sometimes it's easier to understand by seeing an example. The fictional story titled "The Mystery of the Missing Lunchbox" in the following sidebar is one such example. Student A is the reader and they are using the metacognitive cycle to ensure they are going to be an active thinker and a participant in the reading process.

> ## "The Mystery of the Missing Lunchbox"
>
> Greenfield Elementary School was bustling with the morning rush of students heading to their classes. Among them was Emma, a bright and spirited third-grader known for her infectious smile and love for lunchtime. Each day, Emma eagerly anticipated opening her trusty green lunchbox, packed lovingly by her mom with her favorite sandwich and snacks. It was a highlight of her day, until one fateful Wednesday morning when disaster struck—Emma's cherished lunchbox had mysteriously disappeared!
>
> Emma's heart sank as she realized her lunchbox was missing. She retraced her steps from the cafeteria back to her classroom, carefully scanning under tables, peeking into cubbies, and asking her friends if they had seen it. With each unanswered inquiry, her worry deepened. Where could her lunchbox have vanished to? It seemed to have disappeared into thin air.
>
> Determined not to give up, Emma decided to search the school grounds thoroughly. She checked the playground, the library, and even the lost and found, but her lunchbox was nowhere to be found. As frustration started to set in, Emma took a deep breath and reminded herself that she needed to approach this problem like a detective.
>
> She enlisted the help of her best friend, Lucas, who was known for his keen observational skills. Together, they brainstormed possible scenarios: Was it misplaced in another classroom? Did someone accidentally take it? Or was there a miscommunication at the cafeteria? They even considered the possibility of a lunchbox thief prowling the school, though it seemed unlikely.

Their investigation led them to Mrs. Thompson, the kind-hearted school librarian who knew every nook and cranny of Greenfield Elementary. Mrs. Thompson listened attentively as Emma explained her predicament, nodding thoughtfully. "Let's think logically," she said, "If I were a lunchbox, where would I go?"

Emma and Lucas exchanged puzzled glances, unsure of how to respond. Mrs. Thompson chuckled softly and pointed toward the cafeteria bulletin board. "Sometimes, things end up where they belong, but we just don't see them right away," she suggested cryptically.

Perplexed but intrigued, Emma thanked Mrs. Thompson and headed back to the cafeteria with Lucas. There, pinned neatly on the bulletin board amidst colorful flyers and announcements, was a small green lunchbox. Emma's eyes widened in disbelief. "How did it get there?" she wondered aloud.

Lucas grinned triumphantly. "Looks like your lunchbox decided to go on an adventure of its own," he teased.

Relieved and overjoyed, Emma carefully retrieved her lunchbox from the bulletin board. It seemed that someone had found it and placed it there for safekeeping, assuming its owner would eventually come looking. Emma couldn't contain her gratitude as she hugged her lunchbox tightly. "Thank you, Mrs. Thompson!" she exclaimed, knowing that the wise librarian's words had guided her to this unexpected resolution.

As they returned to their classroom, Emma couldn't stop smiling. The mystery of the missing lunchbox had been solved, and she felt a sense of accomplishment knowing that she and Lucas had tackled the problem together. From that day on, Emma made sure her lunchbox was securely zipped and tucked away in her backpack after lunch, never taking its presence for granted again. And whenever she passed by the cafeteria bulletin board, she couldn't help but smile knowingly at her lunchbox's brief but memorable escapade.

Little did she know, this adventure would become one of many cherished stories shared with her classmates and teachers at Greenfield Elementary School, forever adding to the school's rich tapestry of memories.

Let's consider student A's journey through the metacognitive cycle.

Step 1: Assess

Action: Student A carefully examined the cover of the book titled "The Mystery of the Missing Lunchbox." The illustration showed a school hallway with lockers. Student A recalled reading mysteries a few weeks prior with their teachers. They remembered mysteries being a type of genre where there is typically a problem with clues to help solve the mystery. To ensure comprehension, Student A remembered that they are working on slowing down and reading carefully with their teacher. This meant paying close attention to the illustrations and title to predict what the story might be about and how the mystery might unfold.

Step 2: Plan

Action: Student A set their reading goal: "I want to understand why Emma's lunchbox disappeared and how she finds it. I'm going to read slowly to catch all the details and think about where I would look if I lost something." To ensure comprehension, they planned to:

- Visualize the scenes described in the story.
- Make predictions about what might happen next.
- Ask questions about the characters' actions and motivations.
- Summarize sections of the text in their own words.

Step 3: Approach

Action: As Student A delved into the story, they actively visualized themselves searching for the lunchbox. They imagined the school hallway, the cafeteria, and the playground, picturing Emma's movements and expressions. In addition to visualizing, they decided to:

- Ask questions like "Why did Emma check the playground?" and "What could Lucas do to help?"
- Make connections between the story and their own experiences, such as losing something valuable.

- Read slowly and carefully, stopping to re-read parts that were confusing or important.
- Monitor their comprehension by summarizing each paragraph in their own words and predicting what might happen next.

Step 4: Reflect

Action: After finishing the story, Student A took a moment to reflect on what they read. They thought about how well they understood the story and what they learned from Emma's adventure. They realized that because they read slower, they were better able to pick up on the clues that led to the solution of the mystery in the story. They also realized that:

- Visualizing helped them feel like they were a part of the story, making it more engaging.
- Asking questions led them to finding clues they hadn't found while reading the first time.
- Summarizing sections in their own words helped clarify the story's events and improved their memory of the plot.
- Making connections between the story and their own experiences made the story more relatable and easier to understand.

The metacognitive cycle is a dynamic and individualized process, varying significantly from one student to another and from one story to the next. Each student's unique strengths and weaknesses influence the choice of strategies they employ, while the specific demands of the text also play a crucial role in determining the most effective approaches for enhancing comprehension. A study on metacognitive strategy intervention in reading comprehension, published in *Metacognition and Learning* (2021), demonstrates that proficient readers often adjust their strategies based on both their individual capabilities and the specific demands of the text. For instance, students with strong vocabulary skills may rely on context clues to infer meaning, while those who struggle with decoding might benefit more from re-reading or focusing on phonetic strategies. The complexity of the text also dictates the approaches students choose, such as using summarization for simpler texts or monitoring comprehension for more challenging content.

This individualized approach allows students to optimize their learning by adapting their strategies to meet the demands of the material, ultimately leading to better comprehension and retention.[9] For instance, a student with a strong vocabulary might focus on inferencing and critical thinking, whereas another with less confidence in their reading skills might benefit more from visual aids and repeated readings. Despite these differences, the consistent application of metacognitive strategies can foster a deeper understanding and appreciation of reading. By systematically guiding students through this reflective process, we not only help them recognize the importance of these strategies but also empower them to become more self-aware, autonomous learners. Over time, this dedicated support will lead to significant improvements in their reading proficiency and overall academic success.

Three Most Impactful Metacognitive Strategies

As you've seen so far from this chapter, there are many metacognitive strategies that readers can choose to use while reading. These strategies can be incredibly diverse, ranging from simple techniques like determining importance within the text to more complex approaches like evaluating the author's intent and the effectiveness of their arguments. Have you ever thought about which ones have the most impact on a reader's comprehension? It's an intriguing question, especially considering how different readers might find different strategies more effective based on their unique learning styles and preferences.

Out of the 10 strategies discussed so far, there are 3 that stand out the most in terms of their profound impact on enhancing a reader's understanding and engagement with the text:

- Visualization
- Asking Questions
- Making Connections

---

[9] Green, J.A. (2021). Teacher support of metacognition and self-regulated learning: a compelling story and a prototypical model. *Metacognition Learning* 16: 651–666. https://doi.org/10.1007/s11409-021-09283-7.

These strategies not only help in grasping the content better but also make the reading experience more interactive and enjoyable.

Visualization involves creating mental images of the scenes, characters, and events described in the text. This technique can transform the reading experience from a mere absorption of words to an immersive journey through the story. "A central factor in differentiating proficient readers from less proficient readers appears to be their ability to actually visualize text context themselves. In line with this, Hibbing and Rankin-Erickson (2003) argued that readers who lack the ability to create visual mental images when reading often experience comprehension problems."[10] When readers visualize, they are more likely to remember details and understand the narrative's flow and emotional nuances.

Asking Questions is another powerful strategy. By actively questioning the text, readers engage in a dialogue with the material. They might ask questions about the characters' motivations, predict what might happen next, or seek clarification on confusing points. "The purpose of teaching students to formulate their own questions is not just for attaining the goal of having students select and retain information, although this goal will be achieved in active comprehension, but also to teach students a process of reading and learning from text which emphasizes the reader's purposes and the dynamic interaction between the reader and the printed page, including selective attention to those aspects of text that are relevant to satisfying students' curiosity".[11] This constant questioning keeps readers engaged and encourages a deeper exploration of the text.

Making Connections, the third standout strategy, involves linking the content of the text to the reader's own experiences, other texts, or broader world knowledge. This connection-making enriches the reading experience, as it allows readers to see the relevance of the material in their own lives and understand it within a larger context. When students connect new information with their own experiences or prior knowledge, they can better reflect on and understand the material. This process deepens engagement

---

[10] de Koning, B.B. and van der Schoot, M. (2013). Becoming part of the story! Refueling the interest in visualization strategies for reading comprehension. *Educational Psychology Review* 25 (2): 261–287.

[11] Singer, H. (1978). Active comprehension: from answering to asking questions. *The Reading Teacher* 31 (8): 901–908.

and allows for a more meaningful interpretation of the text, as students view the content within a broader context that relates to their lives or world events.[12]

These three strategies—Visualization, Asking Questions, and Making Connections—are particularly effective because they actively involve the reader in the reading process, making comprehension a dynamic and interactive activity. By mastering these strategies, readers can significantly enhance their ability to understand and enjoy a wide range of texts.

The following sections break these down even further!

Visualization

Visualization is a powerful metacognitive strategy that plays a critical role in reading comprehension. As Albert Einstein famously said, "If I can't picture it, I can't understand it." This emphasizes the importance of being able to create mental images to grasp and retain information effectively. Visualization not only aids in understanding but also places the reader in the driver's seat of their reading experience, transforming them into more engaged and critical thinkers. "Visualizing . . . can lead to learning—learning defined as the process of grappling with difficult issues; making connections between and among multiple texts; and cultivating a heightened awareness of the way we see the word and world."[13]

> **Definition: visualization**
> The mental process through which readers create images, scenes, or pictures in their mind based on the descriptions provided in the text

---

[12] Correia, M. and Bleicher, R. (2008). Making connections to teach reflection. *Michigan Journal of Community Service Learning* 14 (2): 41–49.

[13] Park, J.Y. (2012). A different kind of reading instruction: using visualizing to bridge reading comprehension and critical literacy. *Journal of Adolescent & Adult Literacy* 55 (7): 629–640. https://doi.org/10.1002/JAAL.000.

Contrary to the assumption that children are naturally imaginative and can easily visualize, many students, particularly those with poor comprehension skills, require explicit instruction to develop this ability. Visualization allows these students to use a nonverbal tool to associate, retrieve, and store information, making abstract concepts more concrete. This bridging of verbal and visual representational systems fosters deeper comprehension, better recall, and more connections.

Visualization is linked to many other skills, making it an indispensable tool for reading comprehension. For instance, it is one reason why nonfiction texts can be harder for students to grasp. Nonfiction often contains abstract concepts that are challenging to visualize. By developing strong visualization skills, students can create richer reading experiences, enhancing their understanding and retention of the material.

When teaching visualization, several factors should be considered to ensure effectiveness:

- Identifying and introducing key vocabulary ahead of time is essential. This helps students create mental images of the words, especially when accompanied by pictures or examples.
- Assessing prior knowledge is also crucial, as students need to have the necessary schema to visualize effectively.
- Sharing visuals ahead of time can be particularly beneficial for students who lack the background knowledge related to the text.
- Explicit modeling and think-aloud demonstrations are vital in teaching visualization. Teachers can verbalize their thought processes, showing students how to create mental images from the text. This involves describing the mental images that come to mind while reading and explaining how these images aid in understanding the text. It's important to balance attention to phrasing and punctuation with the focus on visualization, as overemphasis on the former can detract from the latter.

Comparing different visuals can enhance visualization skills. For example, comparing a photo with a drawing after listening to or reading a text, or engaging in activities like read/draw/swap, where students read a passage, draw their visualization, and then swap with peers to compare and discuss. This process helps students clarify and refine their mental images, making the abstract more tangible.

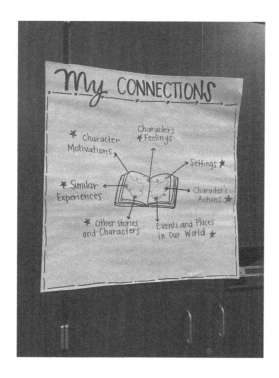

For struggling students, guiding questions can be instrumental in leading them to form mental images. These questions can focus on specific story elements, helping students break down the text into manageable parts that they can visualize. Repetition is also key; reading a text twice, once without pictures and once with, allows students to build and refine their mental images. This repetition helps reinforce the mental images, making them more vivid and detailed.

Using the RIDER Strategy—Read, Imagine, Describe, Evaluate, Repeat

The RIDER strategy is an effective approach to structured visualization. "In this reading comprehension strategy, the students make use of visual imagery when they learn new material by transforming what is to be learned into meaningful visual, auditory, or kinesthetic images of the information. In this regard, the students make images in their head to develop visualization skills in both literal and inferential comprehension."[14]

> **RIDER Strategy**
> 1. **Read**: Carefully reading the text to understand the content.
> 2. **Imagine**: Creating a mental image of what is being read.
> 3. **Describe**: Verbally or in writing, describing the mental image formed.
> 4. **Evaluate**: Assessing the accuracy and completeness of the mental image against the text.
> 5. **Repeat**: Re-reading and refining the mental image as needed.

By following the RIDER strategy, students can systematically develop their visualization skills, enhancing their overall comprehension and critical thinking abilities. This strategy empowers students to take control of their reading experience, making them more active participants in the process.

Choosing the Right Text

Choosing the right text is also crucial for developing visualization skills. Texts with rich, descriptive language provide ample opportunities for students to practice creating detailed mental images. These texts can serve as excellent starting points for introducing visualization techniques and for modeling the RIDER strategy.

Visualization is an essential metacognitive strategy that enhances reading comprehension by transforming abstract concepts into concrete images. It empowers students to take control of their reading experience, making them more engaged and critical thinkers. "Successful reading comprehension depends on the construction of a coherent meaning-based mental representation of the situation described in a text (Kintsch 1988; Van den Broek 2010). This so-called situation model representation is gradually constructed by

---

[14] Nadhif, A. and Hidayat, W. (2019). Rider strategy to improve students' reading skill. *Kodifikasia: Journal Penelitian Islam* 17 (1).

continuously updating information from different text dimension . . . and integrating this information with the reader's background knowledge, as text unfolds."[15] By incorporating explicit instruction, guided practice, and structured strategies like RIDER, teachers can help all students, especially those with poor comprehension skills, develop their visualization abilities. This, in turn, creates a richer, more connected reading experience, fostering deeper understanding and retention of the material.

Quick Tips for Teaching Visualization

- **Identify words ahead of time:** Since teaching visualization isn't as concrete as we would like it to be, we need to take a step back and start small. Don't jump right into using a text, as that can overwhelm students. Start by visualizing words or phrases. For example, say, "When I say tree, what do you see in your mind?" Show students how their schema plays a large role in their ability to comprehend. Use common, relatable words that students encounter in everyday life. Create a list of such words and practice them with the class. Extend this practice to different settings typically found in stories. For instance, tell students the word "park" and have them visualize or describe what they would see at a park. Once students have mastered this with individual words, phrases, and settings, slowly introduce short passages and eventually full stories.

- **Assess prior knowledge:** A strong schema of a topic or idea is essential for effective visualization. Think about a topic you know little about and imagine reading a passage on it. Visualizing would be difficult, right? Before reading, assess students' prior knowledge. This can be done through discussions, K-W-L charts (Know, Want to know, Learned), or quick written assessments. If students lack schema, build it through sharing photos, images, or conducting picture walks. This provides a visual basis for students to begin with. Encourage students to connect the new content with their personal experiences, enhancing their ability to visualize.

---

[15] de Koning, B.B. and van der Schoot, M. (2013). Becoming part of the story! Refueling the interest in visualization strategies for reading comprehension. *Educational Psychology Review* 25 (2): 261–287.

- **Don't focus on fluency:** There is a time and place to teach fluency, but not during a visualization lesson. Stopping students for fluency errors can disrupt their focus on visualizing the text. During visualization lessons, let minor fluency issues slide. Keep the primary objective—visualization—at the forefront. Encourage students to read naturally and visualize the content. The more they stop, the harder it is to maintain their mental imagery. Address fluency in separate lessons dedicated to improving reading flow and accuracy.
- **Show them the power:** Visualization is a powerful tool, but students need to understand its value. Demonstrate how making mental images of a text enhances comprehension. Conduct mini-lessons where you read a short text, draw your visual(s), and then answer comprehension questions using only your drawings. This practice shows students that their mental images can help them recall and understand the text better. If answers aren't found in their visualizations, encourage students to reflect on their visualization process and improve it.

Visualization is a crucial strategy for enhancing reading comprehension. Many teachers assume that students automatically know how to visualize, but explicit instruction is often necessary. These tips provide a structured approach to teach visualization effectively, ensuring students build strong mental imagery skills to support their reading comprehension.

Asking Questions

Engaging with a text through questioning is a powerful metacognitive strategy that transforms passive reading into an active, critical thinking process. "Questions lead readers deeper into a piece, setting up a dialogue with the author, speaking to the readers' minds. If you ask questions as you read, you are awake. You are thinking. You are interacting with the words."[16] When students learn to value their own questions, their confidence increases, and their thinking capabilities expand. This active involvement encourages them to engage deeply with the material, enhancing their comprehension and retention.

---

[16] Zimmermann, S. and Hutchins, C. (2003). *7 Keys to Comprehension: How to Help Your Kids Read It and Get It!* Three Rivers Press.

> **Definition: asking questions** A strategy where readers actively pose questions about the text before, during, and after reading. This technique helps to engage with the material, clarify understanding, and deepen comprehension.

Questioning taps into the natural human impulse for curiosity, a trait often seen in young children who incessantly ask "why" about the world around them. "Children are naturally curious and come to our elementary classrooms well versed in posing questions to their parents and caregivers. On an average day, children ages 2–10 typically ask their mothers an average of 288 questions" (Frazier, Gelman, & Wellman, 2009).[17] However, as students grow older and face more structured educational environments, this innate sense of curiosity can diminish, particularly when reading. One reason for this loss is the traditional focus on answering questions posed by teachers, which can make reading feel like a test rather than an exploration. Head back to Chapter 6 to learn more about how to support your students' curiosity.

Authentic questioning—where students generate their own questions about the text—can reignite their curiosity and motivation to seek answers. Students who engage in generating their own questions are more likely to deepen their understanding of the material and remain actively engaged in their learning. This strategy encourages students to explore beyond the text, fostering a sense of ownership over their learning process. By formulating authentic questions, students are motivated to investigate answers independently, which enhances their comprehension and critical thinking skills.[18] This process sets up a dialogue between the reader and the author, fostering a more interactive and engaged reading experience. As active thinkers, students are no longer passively absorbing information but are instead critically analyzing and interpreting the text.

---

[17] Ness, M. (2016). When readers ask questions: inquiry-based reading instruction. *The Reading Teacher* 70 (2): 189–196. https://doi.org/10.1002/trtr.1481.

[18] Ness, M. (2019). When students generate questions: participatory-based reading instructions in elementary classrooms. *Educating the Young Child* 17.

For teachers, the types of questions they ask should serve as models for the kinds of questions they want their students to develop. Questions should be varied, encouraging a range of responses, and should include higher-order questions that require deep thinking and analysis. Teachers should also reflect on their questioning practices, asking themselves if their questions promote student engagement and critical thinking, or if they are doing most of the talking, which can stifle student participation.

Encouraging students to ask their own questions increases their responsibility for their learning and raises their awareness of their thinking processes. "Student-generated questions are at the heart of inquiry-based classrooms, which are student-centered and teacher-guided (Wilhelm, 2007). In inquiry-based classrooms, students' questions and curiosities, rather than a teacher-directed curriculum, drive learning. Inquiry-based classrooms focus on questions in an attempt to address real-world questions. The benefits of inquiry-based instruction are well documented; students hold more ownership and control of their learning (Short et al., 1996), engage in collaborative learning (Myers & Beach, 2001), develop their metacognitive skills (Wells, 1999), and are more motivated and engaged in learning tasks" (Wilhelm, 2007).[19] This shift from answering questions to asking them is at the heart of metacognitive strategies. It helps struggling readers understand that their questions are just as valid and valuable as those from more proficient readers, breaking down the barrier that often exists between different levels of reading ability.

Types of Questions

- **Clarifying**: These kinds of questions help clear up confusion for the reader. The answer can be found right in the text.
- **Revealing**: These kinds of questions help the reader think more deeply about the character/events/topic. The reader needs to use schema and infer in order to figure out the answer.
- **Extending**: These kinds of questions go beyond the text itself. They take the reader outside of the text to consider what the author was thinking or possibly pushes the reader to consider their own viewpoint on the text.

---

[19] Ness, M. (2016). When readers ask questions: inquiry-based reading instruction. *The Reading Teacher* 70 (2): 189–196.

Even advanced readers benefit from this strategy. By being explicit about how questioning can affect comprehension, teachers can help all students, regardless of their reading level, become more thoughtful and engaged readers. This approach moves away from the traditional "guess what's in the teacher's head" method and empowers students to take ownership of their reading experience.

Ultimately, fostering a classroom environment where questioning is encouraged and valued can lead to a more dynamic and interactive learning experience. "Instruction must focus on meaningful ways to encourage and honor the questions that children naturally ask. When teachers create time and space for children's questions, powerful learning and interactions occur."[20] Students become more confident in their ability to think critically and engage with texts on a deeper level. By making questioning a central part of reading instruction, educators can help students develop the metacognitive skills necessary for lifelong learning and critical thinking.

Tips for Teaching Asking Questions

- **Encourage Students to Ask Questions:** Cultivate a classroom culture where questioning is valued not just for finding answers but for nurturing curiosity and deepening understanding. Integrate questioning seamlessly into daily routines to encourage students to engage actively with their learning. By emphasizing the process of inquiry, educators empower students to become more thoughtful and engaged readers who actively seek meaning and connections within the material.
- **Find Ways to Integrate Questioning:** Integrate questioning into everyday classroom practices by establishing dedicated times for students to ask and explore inquiries. Whether during morning meetings, before embarking on a new chapter, or as part of end-of-day reflections, providing structured opportunities for questioning fosters

---

[20] Ness, M. (2016). When readers ask questions: inquiry-based reading instruction. *The Reading Teacher* 70 (2): 189–196.

a habit of curiosity and reflection. Utilize thinking stems such as "I wonder why . . ." or "How might . . ." to scaffold students' ability to formulate meaningful questions that provoke deeper thinking and exploration.

- **Ask Thick vs. Thin Questions:** Educate students on discerning between thick and thin questions to enhance their ability to inquire effectively. Thin questions, which typically begin with interrogative words like who, what, when, and where, solicit factual responses. In contrast, thick questions, starting with words like why and how, demand deeper analysis and critical thinking. Encourage students to move beyond surface-level inquiries by prompting them to explore underlying themes, motivations, and implications within the text. This approach not only strengthens their comprehension skills but also nurtures a capacity for insightful inquiry and exploration of complex ideas. According to a review on questioning techniques and reading comprehension, teaching students to ask thick questions fosters critical thinking, as they are encouraged to explore underlying themes and motivations in the text rather than just recall facts. This approach not only strengthens comprehension but also enhances students' ability to make inferences and engage with complex ideas.[21]

- **When to Ask Questions:** Developing the discernment to ask insightful questions at strategic moments is essential for students as it empowers them to delve beyond the surface of texts, uncover nuanced meanings, and forge connections that enrich their comprehension and engagement with the material. This skill cultivates a habit of critical thinking and curiosity, fostering a deeper, more interactive learning experience where students actively shape their understanding through purposeful inquiry.

Consider the key moments and strategies for guiding students on when to ask questions.

---

[21] Joseph, L., Alber-Morgan, S., Cullen, J., and Rouse, C. (2016). The effects of self-questioning on reading comprehension: a literature review. *Reading & Writing Quarterly* https://doi.org/10.1080/10573569.2014.891449.

Key Moment	Teacher Strategy	Sample Questions
When I'm Curious	Encourage students to ask questions driven by curiosity to explore topics further, like when encountering a new concept or an intriguing storyline.	- "Why did the character make that choice?" - "What would happen if the story took place in a different setting?"
When I Want to Make Predictions	Before reading, prompt students to make predictions based on clues from the text or prior knowledge. This helps activate prior knowledge and prepares them to engage with the text actively.	- "What do you think will happen next based on the title and cover?" - "How might this character's actions affect the outcome of the story?"
When I Need to Clarify Something	During reading, encourage students to ask questions to clarify confusing or ambiguous points. This fosters comprehension and helps students stay engaged with the material.	- "I'm not sure what this word means. Can we look it up together?" - "Could you explain why the character reacted that way?"
When I Need to Think Deeper	Prompt students to ask questions that encourage deeper thinking and analysis. These questions go beyond surface-level understanding and require students to make connections and draw conclusions.	- "Why do you think the author chose to start the story this way?" - "What are the underlying themes in this poem, and how do they relate to real-life experiences?"
When I Need to Focus My Reading	Teach students to ask questions that help them focus their reading on specific aspects of the text, such as character development, plot structure, or literary devices.	- "How does the author use symbolism to convey the story's message?" - "What techniques does the author use to create suspense in this chapter?"
When I Need to Understand the Author's Intent	Encourage students to question why authors make certain choices in their writing, such as character development, plot twists, or narrative style. This helps students understand the author's purpose and perspective.	- "What message is the author trying to convey through this character's journey?" - "How does the author's background influence the themes explored in this book?"
When I Need to Understand How Characters Develop	Guide students to ask questions that delve into the motivations, emotions, and growth of characters throughout the text. This fosters empathy and a deeper understanding of narrative elements.	- "How has the main character changed from the beginning to the end of the story?" - "What internal conflicts does this character face, and how do they affect the plot?"

By teaching students when to ask questions—whether driven by curiosity, to make predictions, clarify confusion, think deeply, focus their reading, understand author's intent, or develop characters—educators empower them to become active, reflective readers who engage deeply with texts and enhance their overall comprehension skills.

Encouraging Curiosity and Deeper Thinking

Foster a sense of curiosity by using questioning as a tool to engage students in active learning. "Asking questions is about furthering passions and satisfying curiosities. Questions indicate engagement. They are a fundamental part of being human. They are a key ingredient in building superb readers."[22] Encourage them to ask questions that stimulate predictions, seek clarification, or prompt deeper reflections on the material. For example, "What might happen next?" not only encourages discussions on plot development but also invites exploration into character motivations and the consequences of their actions.

Focusing Reading and Understanding Author's Intent

Questions play a pivotal role in guiding students to focus their reading and uncover the author's intent. By prompting questions such as, "What message is the author trying to convey?" students learn to read with purpose, extracting deeper meanings from the text. Additionally, exploring questions about characters' motivations, conflicts, and growth enhances their comprehension and empathy toward literary figures.

Questioning in Different Contexts

Teach students to pose questions within and beyond the text to deepen their engagement and critical thinking skills. Within-the-text questions focus on comprehension of the material, while beyond-the-text questions encourage students to connect the story with their prior knowledge or experiences.

	Purpose	**Examples**
Within-the-Text Questions	These questions focus on understanding the literal meaning and details directly stated in the text. Within-the-Text questions help students comprehend the story's plot, characters, setting, and events by directly referencing the text.	• What is the main character's name? • Where did the story take place? • How did the main character solve the problem in the story? • What was the main idea of the passage we just read?

---

[22] Zimmermann, S. and Hutchins, C. (2003). *7 Keys to Comprehension: How to Help Your Kids Read It and Get It!* Three Rivers Press.

Beyond-the-Text Questions	These questions encourage students to think beyond the literal text and make connections with their own experiences, knowledge, and the world around them. Beyond-the-Text questions prompt students to relate the text to their personal experiences, prior knowledge, and broader contexts, fostering deeper connections and understanding.	• How would you have felt if you were in the main character's situation? • Can you relate any similar experiences you've had to what happened in the story? • Why do you think the author included this particular event in the story? • How does this story remind you of another book or movie you've seen?

Enhancing Comprehension

Guide students in evaluating the quality of their questions to ensure they contribute effectively to their comprehension of the text. Encourage self-reflection on how different types of questions enhance understanding across genres such as fiction, non-fiction, poetry, and drama. Discussing these distinctions helps students tailor their questioning strategies to suit different literary contexts.

Specific Texts and Examples

Select texts that are rich in content and provide ample opportunities for generating thick questions. Show students concrete examples of how questioning can evolve within a text, illustrating how inquiry leads to a deeper appreciation and analysis of literature. This approach not only enhances comprehension but also cultivates a lifelong habit of critical thinking and inquiry.

Teaching students to ask questions is a multifaceted approach that involves integrating questioning into daily routines, using tools and activities to make it engaging, and focusing on the types and timing of questions to enhance comprehension and foster deeper thinking. By doing so, students become more curious, thoughtful, and independent readers.

Making Connections

Making connections while reading cultivates a profound and multifaceted engagement with texts, significantly enhancing students' comprehension and fostering a deeper appreciation for literature. When students relate what they read to their own experiences, they forge personal connections that bring the text to life in meaningful ways. These connections allow students to empathize with characters, recognizing shared emotions and experiences that resonate on a personal level. "A child is much more apt to remember stories, books, and incidents that are meaningful because they connect to other things in his life."[23] For example, a student encountering a character grappling with loss might reflect on their own experiences of sadness or separation, thereby understanding the character's motivations and actions more profoundly. This empathetic engagement not only enriches their comprehension of character dynamics but also encourages students to explore complex themes such as resilience, empathy, and identity within the narrative context.

> **Definition: making connections**
> A strategy that involves relating the text they are reading to their own experiences, other texts, or the world around them. This technique enhances comprehension and engagement by linking new information to prior knowledge

Moreover, making connections to other texts expands students' literary horizons and deepens their understanding of genre conventions, authorial styles, and thematic explorations. By drawing parallels between different texts or authors, students uncover recurring motifs, narrative structures, and symbolic elements that transcend individual stories.[24]

---

[23] Zimmermann, S. and Hutchins, C. (2003). *7 Keys to Comprehension: How to Help Your Kids Read It and Get It!* Three Rivers Press.
[24] Yaghmour, K.S. and Obaidat, L.T. (2022). The effectiveness of using direct instruction in teaching comprehension skill of third-grade students. *International Journal of Instruction* 15 (2): 373–392.

> "Being able to make connections is an important reading comprehension strategy which allows students to make meaning of what they are reading. When connections are made to the texts read by students, it helps them not only to make meaning/sense out of what they read, but also to aid better retention of such information and connect more with the text itself."
> *The Effectiveness of Using Direct Instruction in Teaching Comprehension Skill of Third-Grade Students*

Additionally, connecting the text to the broader world encourages students to consider the societal, historical, and cultural contexts that shape narratives and influence their interpretation. Text-to-world connections prompt students to critically examine how literature reflects and critiques societal norms, values, and conflicts. For example, analyzing a novel set during a historical period of social upheaval may prompt students to explore parallels with contemporary social issues, fostering a deeper understanding of the enduring relevance and impact of literature on collective consciousness. By engaging with texts through multiple lenses—personal experience, intertextual analysis, and socio-cultural inquiry—students not only deepen their comprehension but also develop a nuanced appreciation for the complexities and enduring relevance of literature in their lives and in society.

Making connections helps students create mental images of what they're reading, making the text more vivid and immersive. "The reader works with the author's exact words and sentences and the text base while simultaneously surfacing background knowledge to make meaning of the text. The student engages in multiple cognitive processes-extracting meaning units, integrating ideas, monitoring understanding, elaborating on understanding-which results in the student reader constructing a mental model of the text."[25] When they can visualize scenes and scenarios based on personal or learned experiences, it keeps them engaged and prevents boredom, fostering a continuous and

---

[25] Hennessy, N.L. (2020). *The Reading Comprehension Blueprint: Helping Students Make Meaning from Text*. Paul H. Brookes Publishing Co.

enjoyable reading experience. This mental imagery not only aids in comprehension but also strengthens memory retention by associating textual information with vivid mental pictures, thereby enhancing overall cognitive engagement with the material. Furthermore, visualization allows students to infer details not explicitly stated in the text, encouraging deeper analysis and interpretation of themes and characters.

Encouraging students to make connections sets a purpose for their reading. Whether they relate the text to their own lives (text-to-self), connect it to other texts they've read (text-to-text), or place it in a broader context (text-to-world), these connections help students find relevance and meaning in what they're reading. This purposeful reading keeps them focused and actively involved in the material. Additionally, by establishing a clear purpose, students develop a deeper appreciation for the significance of the text within different contexts, fostering critical thinking and analytical skills essential for academic and personal growth. Understanding how texts connect to their lives and the world around them also encourages students to think critically about societal issues and their own perspectives.

> "It was incredible to watch even our lowest 1st grader grasp these very hard concepts in order to make connections from their reading to what they already know."
>
> -Jamie Brown Patton, K-12 Interventionist, Deer Creek School, Mississippi

Connections between what students read and what they already know (schema) aid in memory retention and comprehension. By linking new information to existing knowledge, students not only remember what they've read better but also develop a habit of questioning and seeking deeper understanding. A 2020 study published in *Reading Research Quarterly* examined how activating prior knowledge before reading improves attention and advanced comprehension compared to introducing entirely new knowledge. The study found that students who had their background knowledge activated before reading demonstrated better attention and comprehension skills, emphasizing the importance of connecting new information to what students already know for deeper understanding and critical thinking.[26] This process of building connections encourages curiosity and a thirst for knowledge, as students actively seek to expand their mental frameworks and make sense of complex ideas. Moreover, the act of making connections reinforces neural pathways associated with learning, promoting long-term memory formation and intellectual growth.

Types of Connections

Text-to-Self	Relating the text to personal experiences, feelings, and memories helps students connect emotionally to the material and understand how it relates to their own lives. This emotional connection can deepen their engagement with the text and enhance their ability to relate its themes and messages to their own experiences, fostering empathy and self-reflection.
Text-to-Text	Making connections between the text and other books, authors, genres, or themes expands students' understanding by drawing parallels and comparisons across different texts. This comparative analysis encourages students to recognize recurring patterns, themes, and motifs in literature, thereby broadening their literary knowledge and critical thinking skills.
Text-to-World	Connecting the text to real-world events, historical contexts, or current issues broadens students' perspectives and encourages critical thinking about the impact of literature on society. This contextual understanding allows students to consider how literature reflects and shapes cultural norms, societal values, and historical events, fostering a deeper appreciation for the relevance and influence of literature beyond the classroom.

---

[26] Kaefer, T. (2020). When did you learn it? How background knowledge impacts attention and comprehension in read-aloud activities. *Reading Research Quarterly* 55 (S10).

Every student brings unique background knowledge (schema) to their reading. This prior knowledge shapes their interpretation of texts and influences how they connect with and understand the material. Recognizing and building upon students' schema helps teachers cater to diverse learning needs and foster deeper comprehension. By activating and expanding students' existing schema, educators can enhance their ability to make meaningful connections between new information and prior knowledge, facilitating deeper understanding and retention of complex concepts.

Before reading, discussing potential connections with students prepares them to actively engage with the text. For example, introducing unfamiliar topics by relating them to broader concepts or personal experiences helps bridge knowledge gaps and sparks interest in the material. This pre-discussion not only primes students for deeper comprehension but also cultivates their ability to approach reading with curiosity and critical awareness. Additionally, discussing connections encourages collaborative learning and allows students to benefit from diverse perspectives, promoting a richer understanding of the text and its implications.

Connection Type	Breakdown
Text-to-Self	Connecting text to: Personal experiences (e.g., overcoming fear), Relationships (e.g., like those with family or friends), Holidays/Vacations (e.g., similar events or emotions), Personal feelings (e.g., how characters' emotions relate to theirs), Places visited or seen (e.g., settings similar to ones they know)
Text-to-Text	Connecting text to: Genre (e.g., fantasy, mystery), Structure (e.g., chapters, narrative style), Author (e.g., other works by the same author), Theme (e.g., similar themes explored in other books), Plot (e.g., similar plot twists or developments), Characters (e.g., similarities between characters), Vocabulary (e.g., new words learned)
Text-to-World	Connecting text to: TV shows/Movies (e.g., similar themes or characters), Radio/Newspaper (e.g., related news events or articles), Historical events (e.g., how historical context influences the story), Current events (e.g., connections to present-day issues), Conversations (e.g., topics discussed in everyday life)

Encouraging students to recognize when they lack relevant background knowledge or struggle to make connections promotes metacognitive awareness. This self-awareness empowers students to take ownership of their comprehension process, motivating them to seek out information and deepen their understanding independently. By fostering responsibility for their learning, educators empower students to become proactive learners who actively seek to expand their knowledge and skills, preparing them for lifelong learning and intellectual growth.

Recognizing that everyone's connections to a text are unique fosters inclusive classroom discussions. By valuing and exploring diverse perspectives and interpretations, teachers can enrich students' understanding through shared insights and collaborative learning experiences. This diversity of perspectives encourages critical thinking and respectful dialogue, as students learn to appreciate differing viewpoints and constructively engage with complex ideas. Moreover, encouraging discussion cultivates a supportive learning environment where students feel empowered to express their thoughts and insights, promoting deeper engagement with the text and fostering a sense of community within the classroom.

Teachers play a crucial role in modeling effective connection-making strategies. "Direct instruction is required in the use of different comprehension skills in order to advance students' ability to independently comprehend texts. Being able to make connections is an important reading comprehension strategy which allows students make meaning of what they are reading."[27] By demonstrating how to make meaningful connections and explaining their significance, educators empower students to apply these strategies autonomously. This modeling not only enhances students' comprehension skills but also cultivates their ability to engage critically with texts. By modeling thoughtful questioning, inference-making, and connection-building, educators equip students with the tools and strategies necessary to navigate complex texts and extract deeper meaning independently.

---

[27] Yaghmour, L.S. and Obaidat, L.T. (2022). The effectiveness of using direct instruction in teaching comprehension skill of third-grade students. *International Journal of Instruction* 15 (2): 373–392.

Making connections encourages students to invest emotionally and intellectually in what they read, fostering a deeper connection to the material. This investment not only enhances comprehension but also promotes independence in reading and learning, as students learn to monitor their own thinking and evaluate their level of understanding. By encouraging students to actively seek connections and draw conclusions based on evidence from the text, educators promote self-directed learning and critical thinking skills essential for academic success and lifelong learning.

Tips for Teaching Making Connections

- **Use a variety of questions/prompts to get students thinking about their connections:** When prompting students to make connections, it's beneficial to employ a diverse range of questions and prompts that encourage them to draw upon their personal experiences and emotions related to the text. For instance, asking questions like "What does this remind you of in your life?" prompts students to reflect on parallels between their own experiences and those of the characters or situations in the text. Similarly, prompting them with questions such as "How is this similar to your life?" encourages deeper introspection into shared themes or events. Additionally, questions like "What were your feelings when you read this?" help students articulate emotional responses, fostering a deeper connection with the text. By using a variety of prompts, educators can stimulate different aspects of students' connections, enriching their engagement with the material.

What can teachers ask to prompt connections?	
Connection	**Questions Teachers Can Ask**
Text-to-Self	• How does this remind you of something that has happened in your life? • Can you relate this character's experience to something you've experienced? • What emotions did this part of the story evoke in you? Have you felt similar emotions before? • What lessons or morals can we learn from this story that apply to our lives? • How does this text challenge or reinforce your beliefs or understanding of the world?

Text-to-Text	• How does this situation in the story compare to events or situations in other books you've read? • Can you draw parallels between this character's actions and decisions and those of people you know or historical figures? • Have you seen similar themes or ideas in movies, TV shows, or video games? How do they compare to what we're reading?
Text-to-World	• Does this story remind you of any current events or issues in the world today? • How does this text relate to cultural or societal norms you're familiar with?

- **When being intentional about this strategy, pre-select texts where you know students will be able to make a variety of types of connections:** Intentionally choosing texts that resonate with students' backgrounds, interests, and experiences enhances their ability to make meaningful connections. Students who read personalized texts exhibited higher motivation, enjoyment, and engagement compared to those reading non-personalized texts. While comprehension scores did not significantly differ between the two groups, the personalized group demonstrated greater overall enthusiasm and connection with the material, suggesting that resonance with personal experiences fosters deeper engagement.[28] By selecting texts that evoke emotions or situations familiar to students, educators create opportunities for deeper engagement and relevance. Pre-selecting texts ensures that students encounter content that facilitates various types of connections—whether personal, thematic, or cultural—thereby enriching their overall comprehension and critical thinking skills.
- **Use rubrics to help assess and share expectations:** Rubrics are valuable tools for assessing and communicating expectations regarding connection-making skills. A well-designed rubric can outline criteria such as clarity, relevance, depth of reflection, and integration of personal experience. By providing clear guidelines, rubrics

---

[28] Ertem, I. (2013). The influence of personalization of online texts on elementary school students' reading comprehension and attitudes toward reading. *International Journal of Progressive Education* 9 (3): 218–228.

empower students to understand what constitutes effective connection-making and encourage them to strive for higher levels of engagement and understanding. Moreover, rubrics facilitate constructive feedback, enabling educators to support students in refining their connection-making abilities across various texts and contexts. Below is an example rubric that teachers can use to assess students' connections.

Criteria	Exemplary	Proficient	Developing	Needs Improvement
Adds to Mental Image	The connection vividly enhances the mental picture of the text, providing rich detail and clarity.	The connection provides a clear mental image related to the text, though some details could be more developed.	The connection attempts to add to the mental image but lacks specific details or clarity.	The connection does not contribute to a clear mental image of the text.
Helps Understand How Characters Are Feeling	The connection demonstrates a deep understanding of character emotions, providing insightful analysis.	The connection shows an understanding of character emotions, though it may lack depth or insight.	The connection attempts to address character emotions but does so superficially.	The connection does not relate to character emotions.
Helps You Feel Like You're in the Story	The connection effectively immerses the reader in the narrative, fostering a strong sense of presence and engagement.	The connection contributes to a sense of being in the story, though the immersion could be more vivid or sustained.	The connection attempts to create a sense of presence in the story but is not fully engaging.	The connection does not help the reader feel involved in the story.
Doesn't Distract You or Make You Forget	The connection seamlessly integrates with the text, enhancing comprehension without disrupting flow.	The connection is relevant and generally does not disrupt understanding, though it may occasionally divert focus.	The connection occasionally distracts from the main text or interrupts comprehension.	The connection frequently distracts from the text or significantly disrupts understanding.
It Adds to Your Thinking	The connection sparks deep reflection and critical thinking about the text, leading to new insights or perspectives.	The connection prompts some reflection and stimulates thinking about the text's themes or ideas.	The connection raises basic questions or thoughts but does not lead to significant reflection or new understanding.	The connection does not contribute to thinking about the text.

> **Explanation of Rubric Categories**
> - **Exemplary:** Demonstrates exceptional depth and clarity in enhancing understanding and engagement with the text.
> - **Proficient:** Shows solid understanding and contributes effectively to comprehension and engagement.
> - **Developing:** Indicates attempts at making connections but may lack depth or consistency.
> - **Needs Improvement:** Shows little to no evidence of meaningful connection-making or detracts from understanding.

- **Explicitly explain what makes connections meaningful:** It is crucial to explicitly define what constitutes a meaningful connection in the context of reading comprehension. Educators can explain that meaningful connections enhance understanding by adding to mental images, helping grasp characters' emotions, or immersing oneself deeper into the narrative without detracting from the main ideas. Emphasizing these points helps students recognize the value of their connections and encourages them to seek connections that contribute to their overall comprehension and critical thinking skills.

- **Teaching students to manage making connections is also important, especially for younger students:** Teaching students how to manage their connection-making process is essential, particularly for younger learners who may become overly enthusiastic or distracted by attempting to make numerous connections. Strategies like "hands up, hands down"—where students raise their hands to indicate they've made a connection—help maintain focus and regulate when connections are shared. By encouraging students to reflect on the relevance and depth of their connections before sharing them, educators support the development of thoughtful and intentional connection-making skills, enhancing overall comprehension and engagement with the text.

- **Focus on the question—does this connection extend our learning and understanding of the story?** Encouraging students to evaluate the significance of their connections fosters deeper comprehension and critical thinking. By focusing on whether a connection extends their learning and understanding of the story, students learn to differentiate between shallow and deep connections. This approach prompts them to consider how their connections contribute new insights, perspectives, or emotional resonance to their interpretation of characters, themes, or plot developments, thereby enhancing their overall engagement and analytical skills.

	Examples of Connections That Extend Learning	**Examples of Connections That Do Not Extend Learning**
Text-to-Self	"Cinderella's perseverance despite adversity reminds me of when I had to work hard to achieve a goal, just like she did to attend the ball."	"Cinderella's glass slipper reminds me of a pair of shoes I once saw in a store." (shallow connection)
Text-to-Text	"Cinderella's journey and transformation parallel the challenges and growth of the protagonist in 'Beauty and the Beast,' where characters undergo personal change and self-discovery."	"Cinderella's stepsisters remind me of characters in a completely unrelated fairy tale." (irrelevant connection)
Text-to-World	"Cinderella's transformation from rags to riches reflects the 'American Dream' where hard work leads to success."	"Cinderella's ball gown is similar to fashion trends seen in modern celebrity culture." (misplaced connection)

- **For learners who struggle to write—have them draw and label their drawings:** For students who find writing challenging, providing alternative means of expression, such as drawing and labeling, can facilitate connection-making. Asking students to illustrate scenes or characters from the text that evoke personal connections allows them to visually represent their thoughts and feelings. Visual representations serve as a starting point for discussions about connections, enabling educators to scaffold students' comprehension and encourage meaningful engagement with the text.

- **Hard to make meaningful connections after a first read:** Recognizing that meaningful connections often require multiple readings of a text is crucial for developing deep comprehension skills. Educators can facilitate this process by using familiar stories or allowing students to become more familiar with the content before focusing on making connections. Repeated readings enable students to notice subtleties, make deeper connections, and develop a nuanced understanding of characters, themes, and narrative elements over time, thereby enhancing their ability to engage critically with the text.
- **Think of the types of connections as different levels of understanding:** Understanding connections as varying levels of comprehension—text-to-self, text-to-text, and text-to-media/world—helps students develop broader insights and critical thinking skills. Text-to-self connections relate directly to personal experiences, providing a foundational understanding of the text's relevance. Text-to-text connections involve comparing themes, characters, or events across different texts, fostering broader insights and analytical skills. Text-to-media/world connections encourage students to relate the text to broader cultural, historical, or contemporary contexts, promoting deeper understanding and synthesis of ideas.
- **Pull out pieces of text/sentences and have students make very obvious connections to the text:** Selecting specific excerpts that prompt clear connections to personal experiences, other texts, or external media helps students practice identifying and articulating different types of connections. By guiding students to describe the type of connection—whether text-to-self, text-to-text, or text-to-media/world—educators encourage deeper reflection and critical analysis. Additionally, prompting students to explain how these connections enhance their understanding of the text's themes or characters promotes active engagement and comprehension skills development. This approach supports students in making meaningful connections that contribute to their overall comprehension and appreciation of literature.

Reflect: Consider how metacognitive strategies like visualizing, making connections, and asking questions are currently being used in your classroom. Which of these strategies do your students seem to struggle with the most, and what adjustments could you make to better support their development in this area?

Closing

This chapter has thoroughly explored the concept of metacognition and its integral role in literacy instruction. It began by defining metacognition and underscoring its significance in the reading process. By understanding how metacognitive strategies empower students to monitor and regulate their thinking, educators can foster a more profound and engaged approach to reading. These strategies help students become aware of their cognitive processes, enabling them to tackle challenging texts with greater confidence and skill.

The chapter delved into various practical strategies that teachers can incorporate into their classrooms, such as think-alouds, self-questioning, and summarizing. These techniques not only enhance students' reading comprehension but also promote critical thinking and self-reflection. By providing students with the tools to actively engage with texts, educators can transform passive reading into an interactive and dynamic experience. The examples and methods discussed in this chapter serve as a foundation for teachers to build upon and customize according to their unique classroom needs.

Moreover, the chapter addressed the challenges that educators might face when teaching metacognitive strategies and offered solutions to overcome these obstacles. Creating a classroom environment that supports reflective thinking and continuous learning is paramount. By encouraging students to think about their thinking, teachers can help them develop into self-regulated learners who take ownership of their educational journey. This approach not only improves literacy outcomes but also equips students with lifelong learning skills.

The use of metacognitive strategies is essential for enhancing a reader's thinking and comprehension abilities. By integrating these strategies into literacy instruction, educators can cultivate active, engaged, and self-aware readers. The knowledge and techniques presented in this chapter provide a robust framework for teachers to help their students achieve academic success and become thoughtful, independent learners. As you move forward, I encourage you to continue to prioritize metacognitive development in your educational practices, ensuring that every student has the opportunity to thrive as a confident and capable reader. Consider these questions as you ponder this issue more and try the following lessons.

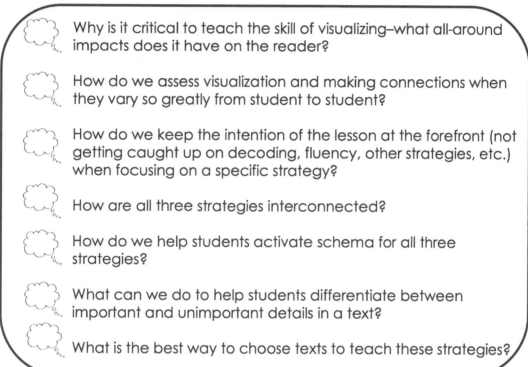

End of Chapter Reflection Questions:

- Why is it critical to teach the skill of visualizing—what all-around impacts does it have on the reader?
- How do we assess visualization and making connections when they vary so greatly from student to student?
- How do we keep the intention of the lesson at the forefront (not getting caught up on decoding, fluency, other strategies, etc.) when focusing on a specific strategy?
- How are all three strategies interconnected?
- How do we help students activate schema for all three strategies?
- What can we do to help students differentiate between important and unimportant details in a text?
- What is the best way to choose texts to teach these strategies?

Lessons to Try

Remember that you can access the lessons for free at `http://www.cieraharristeaching.com/ttrlessons` using the passcode: `literacy for all`.

"Visualization" Lesson

The lesson plan on visualization focuses on helping students understand and utilize visualization as a critical reading strategy. The lesson begins with an engaging activity where students close their eyes and visualize memories associated with different scents, such as banana, peppermint, and rain. This initial activity serves to illustrate the natural process of creating mental images and sets the stage for discussing the concept of visualization. Following this, the teacher introduces the term "visualization" and collaborates with students to create an anchor chart outlining the benefits of this strategy. The lesson progresses with the teacher modeling the visualization process using a read-aloud text and visualization grids, before guiding students to practice the technique themselves.

The importance of this lesson lies in its ability to make students active participants in their reading process. Visualization helps students to connect more deeply with the text by transforming abstract words into concrete mental images, thereby enhancing comprehension and retention. By drawing their visualizations, students can better recall details and understand the narrative structure of the text. Additionally, the lesson addresses common misconceptions, such as the assumption that students naturally know how to visualize while reading, emphasizing the need for explicit instruction in this strategy.

Teaching visualization offers numerous benefits, including encouraging students to be more engaged and thoughtful readers. It allows them to draw on their personal experiences and prior knowledge, making the reading experience more meaningful and memorable. Furthermore, visualization helps students focus on key details and improves their overall comprehension and recall of the text. By incorporating visualization into literacy instruction, teachers can foster a more interactive and personalized reading experience for their students, ultimately leading to improved reading skills.

Quick Tip

When teaching this lesson, ensure to validate and celebrate the diversity of students' visualizations. Emphasize that there is no single correct way to visualize a text and that each student's mental images are unique and valuable. This will help build students' confidence and encourage them to engage more deeply with the reading material.

"Types of Questions" Lesson

This lesson focuses on helping students understand how to ask and categorize different types of questions while reading. The lesson begins by reviewing the purpose of asking questions, emphasizing that readers ask questions to deepen their understanding of a text. The lesson introduces three categories of questions: clarifying, revealing, and extending. Students are guided through identifying and sorting example questions into these categories using an anchor chart and interactive activities.

Next, the teacher models the questioning process by reading a story and showing students how to categorize questions based on the text. Students participate by sorting provided questions into the appropriate categories, discussing why each question fits where it does. The lesson continues with a small group activity where students collaborate to sort questions from a second story into the same categories, promoting critical thinking and engagement. The teacher monitors discussions, asking guiding questions to deepen students' understanding.

The lesson concludes with an exit ticket where students individually categorize questions, providing data for the teacher to use in identifying students who may need additional support. This reflective element encourages independent thinking and allows for targeted reteaching if necessary.

Quick Tip

Encourage students to create their own questions after reading a text and categorize them. This helps reinforce the concept and promotes ownership of their learning.

"Making Connections" Lesson

The "Making Connections" lesson plan is designed to enhance students' comprehension skills by teaching them how to make connections between their own experiences and the texts they read. The lesson begins with engaging questions that help students recognize their prior knowledge and experiences, leading to a discussion about how these connections can impact their understanding of new material. By drawing parallels between familiar topics and new content, students can better retain and comprehend the information they encounter.

This lesson is essential because it leverages students' existing schema, or background knowledge, to facilitate deeper understanding and retention of new information. Making connections is a fundamental strategy in reading comprehension, helping students to relate personally to the material, understand it in a broader context, and remember it more effectively. When students see the relevance of what they are learning to their own lives, they are more likely to be engaged and motivated in their learning process.

Teaching students to make connections also prepares them for more advanced critical thinking and analytical skills. As they practice linking new information to what they already know, they develop the ability to synthesize information, draw inferences, and evaluate content more critically. This skill is not only vital for academic success but also for lifelong learning.

Quick Tip

Encourage students to share their connections during discussions, as this not only validates their experiences but also provides a richer understanding of the text for the whole class. Diverse perspectives can enhance the learning experience and show students the value of multiple viewpoints.

CHAPTER 9

TALKING (MEANINGFULLY) ABOUT TEXTS

Communication & Critical Thinking

Highlight the importance of meaningful dialogue about texts and the development of critical thinking skills in reading.

Academic discussions about texts play a crucial role in developing students' critical thinking, comprehension, and communication skills. "While students and teachers are interacting with each other they are using language as a tool for understanding the world (Lave and Wenger, 1991). Learning unfolds in context and can occur in planned and unplanned ways (Twiner et al., 2014). As they actively participate in a group, individuals contribute ideas that advance everyone's comprehension" (Wells, 1999).[1] While many students

---

[1] Paterson, D. (2019). Engaging elementary students in higher order talk and writing about text. *Journal of Early Childhood Literacy* 19 (1): 34–54.

are naturally adept at social conversations, engaging in meaningful academic dialogue requires a different set of skills and understandings. Social conversations are typically informal and spontaneous, whereas academic discussions demand a more structured approach, often involving complex vocabulary, higher-order thinking, and a nuanced understanding of social cues. This chapter explores how educators can bridge this gap, equipping students with the tools necessary for productive and insightful text discussions.

The ability to talk about texts meaningfully is not an innate skill for most students; it must be taught explicitly. By setting clear expectations and teaching the various components of a successful academic conversation, educators can create a classroom environment where rich, text-based discussions flourish. This involves helping students understand the give-and-take nature of these conversations, the importance of active listening, and the ways to effectively use agreements, disagreements, extensions, questions, clarifications, and reactions to build a deeper understanding of the text.

Moreover, fostering an environment where academic conversations are valued and cultivated from the beginning of the school year can significantly impact students' learning experiences. When students are taught how to navigate and contribute to discussions thoughtfully, they become more confident and engaged learners. Jeff Zwiers and Marie Crawford highlight in *Academic Conversations: Classroom Talk That Fosters Critical Thinking and Content Understandings* how regular participation in academic conversations not only enhances students' critical thinking but also builds their ability to engage thoughtfully with peers, leading to deeper comprehension across content areas. They argue that well-facilitated discussions help students practice essential communication skills such as elaborating on ideas, supporting opinions with evidence, and engaging in meaningful dialogue, which are critical for both academic and real-world success.[2] This not only enhances their comprehension of texts but also prepares them for various academic and real-world scenarios where effective communication and critical thinking are essential.

The following sections delve into specific strategies and techniques that educators can use to facilitate these discussions. From understanding the fundamental differences between social and academic conversations to practical tips and activities designed to

---

[2] Zwiers, J. and Crawford, M. (2011). *Academic Conversations: Classroom Talk That Fosters Critical Thinking and Content Understandings*. Stenhouse Publishers.

encourage meaningful dialogue, this chapter aims to provide a comprehensive guide for teachers looking to enhance their students' conversational skills around texts.

Chapter 9 Objectives

 The readers will understand the key differences between social conversations and academic discussions.

 The readers will learn strategies for explicitly teaching students the components of effective academic conversations.

 The readers will explore various techniques to foster a classroom environment conducive to rich text-based discussions.

 The readers will gain insights into practical activities and exercises that promote deeper engagement and critical thinking during text discussions.

 The readers will be equipped with tools to assess and reflect on the effectiveness of their students' academic conversations, ensuring continuous improvement and growth.

Don't Make Assumptions

Many teachers assume that students naturally know how to talk and engage in conversations. However, social conversations differ significantly from academic discussions, and this assumption can lead to challenges in the classroom.

Students are adept at chatting with friends and enjoying casual conversations during recess and lunch. They also engage in conversations at home with their families. But when it comes to discussing academic concepts in school, the dynamics change, adding a layer of pressure and significance to these interactions. For instance, research highlights how peer relationships and teacher support

When students are taught how to navigate and contribute to discussions thoughtfully, they become more confident and engaged learners.

Talking (Meaningfully) About Texts

shape academic engagement. While students may enjoy the ease of social interactions outside the classroom, academic discussions involve structured dialogue, often increasing anxiety and pressure to perform well, particularly when there is an expectation to articulate complex ideas and demonstrate understanding. This creates a stark contrast between casual conversations and academic discourse, where students feel more self-conscious about their contributions in front of teachers and peers.[3]

Students may struggle with academic conversations for several reasons:

- **Lack of familiarity with academic language:** Unlike the casual, informal language used in social conversations, academic discussions require more formal, subject-specific vocabulary.
- **Increased cognitive demand:** Academic conversations involve higher-order thinking skills, such as analysis, synthesis, and evaluation, which are less frequently used in social interactions.
- **Different social cues and expectations:** The social cues in academic settings are often more nuanced and formal, requiring students to adapt their behavior and communication style.
- **Structured environment:** Unlike the free-flowing nature of social conversations, academic discussions often follow a structured format, which can be unfamiliar and challenging for students.

Given these differences, it's crucial to set clear expectations for academic conversations at the beginning of the school year. Conversations are complex, involving various components, options, and skills. By teaching students the different elements of conversations, including the give and take and understanding social cues, you can help them meet these expectations in partner work, group discussions, and small group settings.

Explicitly teaching these skills lays the groundwork for deeper academic discussions. In school, listening skills are part of the curriculum, and there are many reasons to explicitly teach conversation skills. By dedicating time at the beginning of the year to teach

---

[3] Vitaro, F., Colpin, H., Tieskens, J., and van Lier, P.A.C (2022). How peers and teachers shape elementary school children's academic and socioemotional development.

students how to have academic conversations, you prepare them to talk about texts in depth, leading to higher comprehension and a more meaningful learning experience.

Social Conversations vs. Academic Conversations

Aspect	Social Conversations	Academic Conversations
Purpose	Building relationships, having fun, sharing personal experiences	Exploring ideas, understanding concepts, learning from others
Context	Informal settings (e.g., playground, lunch, home)	Formal settings (e.g., classroom, study groups)
Language Used	Casual, slang, informal	Formal, subject-specific vocabulary
Tone	Relaxed, playful	Serious, focused
Participants	Friends, family	Peers, teachers
Structure	Free-flowing, unstructured	Structured, often guided by prompts or questions
Topics	Personal interests, daily life	Academic subjects, texts, complex ideas
Listening Skills	Basic listening	Active listening, critical thinking
Social Cues	Casual, flexible	Specific, often more formal cues
Feedback	Immediate, informal	Constructive, reflective
Role of Questions	General curiosity, maintaining flow	Deepening understanding, prompting analysis
Empathy and Respect	Basic courtesy	Emphasis on respectful disagreement, empathy
Preparation Needed	None	Often requires preparation and prior knowledge

This chapter explores the significance of guiding students in academic discussions about texts, aiming to equip them with the skills needed for productive and insightful conversations.

What Is an Academic Conversation?

As you can see from the previous table, academic conversations and social conversations are very different. Even the ways students converse socially differ from household to household based on cultural and social backgrounds. Understanding the parts of an academic conversation is a great place to start introducing your students to the world of text discussions.

In a basic academic conversation, there are six essential parts:

- Agreements
- Disagreements
- Extensions
- Questions
- Clarifications
- Reactions

Engaging in meaningful academic conversations requires students to utilize various conversational strategies to deepen their understanding and facilitate insightful dialogue. Agreements play a crucial role in these discussions, as they not only validate peers' ideas but also build a collaborative atmosphere. When students agree on interpretations of a text, it fosters a sense of unity and shared purpose, encouraging them to delve further into the material together. However, disagreements are equally vital, as they challenge students to consider alternative viewpoints and justify their own interpretations. These disagreements can lead to richer discussions, prompting students to think critically and defend their perspectives with evidence from the text.

Extensions allow students to build upon each other's ideas, adding depth and complexity to the conversation. By contributing additional insights or connecting different aspects of the text, students can collectively explore themes, characters, and plot developments in greater detail. Asking questions is another essential element, as it drives the conversation forward and helps clarify any uncertainties. Through thoughtful questioning, students can uncover deeper meanings and explore the nuances of the text. Clarifications, on the other hand, ensure that everyone is on the same page, preventing misunderstandings and ensuring a coherent discussion. Lastly, reactions, whether emotional or intellectual, provide immediate feedback and keep the conversation dynamic and engaging. These spontaneous responses show active listening and encourage further exploration of ideas.

> **Definition: academic conversation** A structured dialogue focused on exploring ideas, understanding concepts, and learning from others. It typically involves formal language, active listening, the use of evidence, and higher-order thinking skills such as analysis and evaluation. Academic conversations aim to deepen comprehension and foster collaborative learning through respectful engagement and critical analysis.

Incorporating these conversational components effectively can transform a simple discussion into a profound learning experience. By practicing agreements, disagreements, extensions, questions, clarifications, and reactions, students develop essential communication skills that enhance their ability to analyze texts and articulate their thoughts. This structured approach to conversation not only improves comprehension but also fosters a collaborative learning environment where students feel valued and heard. "The teacher is more collaborator than evaluator and creates an atmosphere that challenges students and allows them to negotiate and construct the meaning of the text."[4] As they become more adept at using these strategies, students will be better equipped to engage in meaningful academic discourse, ultimately leading to a deeper understanding and appreciation of the texts they study.

Agreements:

- **Definition:** Expressions of concord or support for another person's ideas or statements.
- **Purpose:** Agreements help to build rapport and show that you value and understand the other person's perspective.
- **Example:** "I completely agree with your analysis of the protagonist's motivations in the story. It really seems like she was driven by a sense of justice."

---

[4] Goldenberg, C. (1992). Instructional conversations: promoting comprehension through discussion. *International Literacy Association and Wiley* 46 (4): 316–326.

Disagreements:
- **Definition:** Expressions of dissent or differing opinions from another person's ideas or statements.
- **Purpose:** Disagreements introduce different viewpoints and promote critical thinking. They are essential for a balanced and thorough discussion.
- **Example:** "I see your point, but I disagree that the author intended the ending to be optimistic. The tone throughout the final chapter felt quite somber to me."

Extensions:
- **Definition:** Contributions that add to or build upon another person's ideas or statements.
- **Purpose:** Extensions help to deepen and expand the conversation, introducing new information or perspectives.
- **Example:** "That's a great point about the theme of friendship. Additionally, I think the author's use of setting also highlights the importance of community."

Questions:
- **Definition:** Inquiries aimed at gaining more information, clarity, or understanding about another person's ideas or statements.
- **Purpose:** Questions drive the conversation forward, encourage deeper thinking, and clarify any ambiguities.
- **Example:** "Can you explain more about why you think the antagonist's actions were justified?"

Clarifications:
- **Definition:** Requests or efforts to make another person's ideas or statements more clear and understandable.
- **Purpose:** Clarifications ensure that all participants have a clear and accurate understanding of the topic, preventing misunderstandings.
- **Example:** "When you mention 'symbolism in the novel,' could you clarify which symbols you are referring to specifically?"

Reactions:
- **Definition:** Immediate responses to another person's ideas or statements, which can include emotional or intellectual feedback.
- **Purpose:** Reactions provide immediate feedback, showing engagement and allowing for real-time adjustments in the conversation.
- **Example:** "Wow, that's an interesting perspective on the main character's development! I hadn't thought about her growth in that way before."

By explaining each of these conversational components, you provide students with a toolkit of strategies to actively participate in discussions. This empowers them to make informed choices about how to contribute to conversations, whether through agreements, disagreements, extensions, questions, clarifications, or reactions. Each component serves as a distinct avenue for engagement, allowing students to navigate and enrich their discussions effectively. By understanding these options, students can tailor their responses to the flow of the conversation, thereby fostering a more dynamic and interactive dialogue.

Furthermore, outlining these components sets clear expectations for the nature and quality of classroom discussions. By specifying what effective academic conversations should look and sound like, you establish a standard for respectful, thoughtful, and productive exchanges. Specifying what academic conversations should look and sound like helps students understand the expectations for engaging in productive dialogue. When teachers model conversation strategies, students grasp how to contribute thoughtfully and respectfully to discussions. This clarity encourages more focused and meaningful academic exchanges (Center for the Professional Education of Teachers, 2023).[5] This clarity helps students recognize the importance of each component in contributing to a holistic and balanced discussion. It also encourages them to practice these skills, knowing that their efforts align with the class's communicative goals.

---

[5] Midgette, L. (2023). Center for Professional Education of Teachers. Building Student-Led Academic Conversations. https://cpet.tc.columbia.edu/news-press/building-student-led-academic-conversations

> "With appropriate teacher scaffolding, students will begin to use moves similar to those modeled or promoted by the teacher. For example, when a teacher affirms students' use of evidence, they begin to use more evidence and also request that other students provide textual evidence for ideas."
> *Strategy Instruction Shifts Teacher and Student Interactions During Text-Based Discussions*

Setting these expectations early on helps create a classroom environment where academic dialogue is valued and cultivated. Students become more confident in their ability to engage in complex discussions, knowing they have a structured approach to rely on. As a result, the overall quality of classroom conversations improves, leading to deeper comprehension and more meaningful interactions with the texts and with each other. By teaching and reinforcing these conversational components, we are not only enhancing students' academic skills but also preparing them for effective communication in various contexts beyond the classroom.

How to Talk About a Text

Now that I have established a foundational understanding of what an academic conversation entails, I can delve into how this knowledge enhances our ability to discuss a text. Academic conversations around a text are instrumental in allowing students to express their ideas, ask probing questions, validate their opinions, and absorb new perspectives from their peers. "These types of discussions benefit all children, including children from low-income families (Applebee, Langer, Nystrand, & Gamoran, 2003; Murphy et al., 2009; Nystrand, 2006) and language-minority backgrounds who are most at risk for reading problems" (August & Shanahan, 2006; Goldenberg, 2010).[6] These discussions are not just about surface-level comprehension but about engaging deeply with the material, analyzing themes, characters, and plot developments, and making connections to broader contexts.

---

[6] Matsumura, L., Garner, H., and Spybrook, J. (2012). The effect of content-focused coaching on the quality of classroom text discussions. *Journal of Teacher Education* 63 (3): 214–228.

To facilitate such rich discussions, it is imperative that you first teach your students the mechanics of a structured conversation. They need to understand how to articulate agreements to show appreciation for their peers' insights, how to respectfully voice disagreements to challenge and refine ideas, and how to extend conversations by adding new layers of thought. Teaching them to ask clarifying questions ensures that misunderstandings are minimized and that everyone in the discussion maintains a clear and accurate grasp of the text. Encouraging students to react in the moment, whether through intellectual or emotional responses, keeps the conversation lively and engaging, fostering a vibrant academic environment.

By mastering these conversational components, students become adept at navigating discussions that are both respectful and intellectually stimulating. This skill set transforms the classroom into a collaborative space where ideas are freely exchanged, and critical thinking is the norm. Students learn to appreciate the value of diverse perspectives, understanding that their peers can offer insights that might illuminate aspects of the text they had not previously considered. This process not only enhances their comprehension of the text but also hones their ability to think critically and articulate their thoughts clearly and confidently.

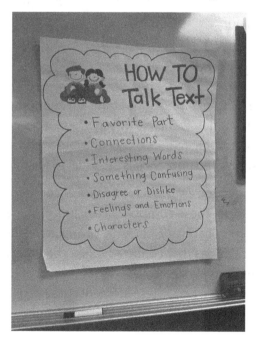

Moreover, these skills are not confined to the classroom. The ability to engage in thoughtful, respectful, and productive conversations is a lifelong skill that will benefit students in all areas of their lives. From academic settings to professional environments and personal relationships, the ability to discuss ideas, ask meaningful questions, and listen to others is invaluable. By teaching students how to have conversations centered around a text, you are equipping them with tools that will serve them well beyond their academic years.

"Lifelong learning abilities, including competencies like effective communication, contribute to personal and professional success, with impacts observed in various contexts such as education and career development."[7]

Ultimately, the goal is to foster a learning environment where students feel confident and equipped to delve into complex discussions. This environment not only enhances their understanding of the texts but also encourages a culture of mutual respect and intellectual curiosity. As students become more proficient in these conversational skills, they will be better prepared to tackle challenging texts and engage in discussions that push the boundaries of their thinking. This is the essence of academic growth and the foundation for a lifelong love of learning.

Step 1: Teach Parts of a Text

Engaging students in meaningful discussions about a text often begins with providing them a starting point. Many times, when we assign group work or think-pair-share activities, students may initially struggle to initiate or contribute to a conversation. Therefore, equipping them with a structured approach is essential to foster productive dialogue.

In teaching literature, we recognize several foundational components of a text that serve as entry points into discussion. These components include a student's favorite part of the text, intriguing or unfamiliar vocabulary, personal connections they have made to the text, aspects of the plot or themes that confused them, characters and their development throughout the story, emotions evoked by the narrative, and opinions or arguments they agree or disagree with within the text. These elements provide a framework for students to begin engaging with the text in a structured and meaningful way.

---

[7] Thwe, W.P. and Kalman, A. (2024). Lifelong learning in the educational settings: a systematic literature review. *Asia-Pacific Education Researcher* 33: 407–417.

By highlighting these basic parts of a text, you can enable students to articulate their thoughts and reactions more effectively. This structured approach not only supports comprehension but also encourages students to explore deeper meanings and perspectives within the text. It empowers them to actively participate in discussions, share insights, and build upon each other's ideas, thereby enriching their overall understanding and appreciation of literature.

When initiating discussions about texts, students often benefit from specific starting points to guide their exploration. These foundational components of a text serve as essential entry points into meaningful conversations.

Parts of a Text to Converse About

- ❖ Favorite Part: A section of the text that resonates personally with the reader, often due to its emotional impact, significance to the plot, or the way it captures their interest.

- ❖ Interesting Words: Vocabulary or phrases that stand out for their uniqueness, complexity, or relevance to the themes or tone of the text.

- ❖ Connections Made: Personal associations or parallels drawn between elements of the text and the student's own experiences, beliefs, or other texts they have encountered.

- ❖ Confusions: Aspects of the plot, themes, or characters that are unclear or raise questions in the student's mind, prompting further exploration and discussion.

- ❖ Characters: Individuals portrayed in the text, their traits, motivations, relationships, and development throughout the story.

- ❖ Feelings Experienced: Emotions evoked by the text's events, characters, or themes, influencing the reader's engagement and interpretation.

- ❖ Agreements or Disagreements: Ideas, perspectives, or actions within the text that resonate with the reader's beliefs or challenge them, prompting reflection and debate.

Talking (Meaningfully) About Texts

These components provide structured points of entry for students to express their thoughts, engage critically with the text, and participate actively in discussions. By encouraging students to explore these elements, educators foster deeper comprehension, analytical thinking, and collaborative learning experiences.

Step 2: Combine

Now that you have equipped your students with an understanding of the essential components of both conversation and text analysis, the next step is to integrate and apply these skills through structured practice. Becoming proficient in academic conversations is a gradual process that requires consistent practice, patience, and supportive guidance, including modeling by teachers.

To begin, select short or well-known texts that are accessible to students. Engage a few students in a modeling session where they demonstrate a conversation about the text. This can start with a specific question prompt related to the text or simply an open-ended invitation to discuss their thoughts and insights. Visual aids, such as posters or digital reminders, displaying the different parts of a conversation and the components of a text, serve as helpful prompts during these discussions.

During the modeling session, guide the students through a structured conversation, highlighting how to incorporate elements like agreements, disagreements, extensions, questions, clarifications, and reactions. This collaborative exercise allows students to observe effective communication strategies in action and encourages them to actively participate.

Fishbowl Strategy for Modeling Conversational Practice

Try using the Fishbowl strategy to effectively model and practice conversational skills with your students. Here's a streamlined approach:

1. Setup: Arrange chairs in two circles – one for active participants and another for observers.

2. Select Participants: Choose a small group of students for the inner circle to discuss a text or topic.

3. Set Clear Objectives: Define specific conversation goals like asking questions or using text evidence.

4. Modeling: Start with a prompt related to the text and model effective conversation techniques.

5. Observation: The outer circle observes and notes effective strategies and contributions.

6. Debrief: Discuss what worked well, areas for improvement, and effective strategies observed.

7. Rotate Roles: Rotate students between inner circle participants and observers for continued practice.

The Fishbowl strategy is a structured way to foster meaningful discussions and enhance students' conversational and analytical skills.

After trying the Fishbowl strategy, involve the entire class in a reflective analysis of the conversation. Discuss the dynamics observed: Did one student dominate the discussion, or was there balanced participation? Did everyone contribute their thoughts, or were some hesitant to participate? Identify factors that facilitated or hindered the conversation's flow and effectiveness.

This debriefing phase is crucial, as it encourages students to critically evaluate their communication skills and recognize areas for improvement. It also reinforces the importance of active listening, respectful dialogue, and inclusive participation in academic discussions. Through repeated practice and thoughtful reflection, students develop confidence and proficiency in engaging with texts and each other in meaningful and productive ways, laying a solid foundation for deeper comprehension and analytical thinking skills.

Step 3: Surface-Level Conversations to Deep Conversations

Are your conversations going to sound amazing the first time out of the gate? Of course not. Through time and modeling you'll show students how to take a basic textual conversation and mold it into a more in-depth conversation.

Transitioning students from surface-level conversations to deep, meaningful discussions about texts involves cultivating their ability to engage critically and reflectively. Building on their understanding of the parts of a conversation and the components of a text, we empower students to delve deeper into texts, making connections between the material and their own lives through metacognitive strategies.

Metacognition plays a pivotal role in this process. By encouraging students to ask questions that extend beyond literal comprehension, such as probing the author's intent or considering alternative viewpoints, you prompt them to think critically about the text's underlying meanings. "Higher order talk and writing about text shows promise as an instructional component, not only because it can increase the motivation and engagement of students, but also because it can contribute to diverse students' growth and achievement in reading" (Bigelman & Peterson, 2016; Peterson & Taylor, 2012; Taylor et al., 2003).[8] Making connections becomes essential as students relate the text to their personal experiences, beliefs, and prior knowledge, fostering a deeper engagement with the material.

Visualizing and synthesizing information further enhances comprehension. Visualizing scenes or concepts from the text helps students create mental images that aid in understanding and retention. Synthesizing involves integrating various elements of the text to form new insights or interpretations, encouraging students to think analytically and creatively.

To make the text about them, students must reflect on how the text impacts their thinking and lives. This reflective questioning process involves considering how the text challenges their perspectives, influences their beliefs, or resonates with their personal experiences. By connecting the text to their own lives, students not only deepen their comprehension but also develop a more profound connection to the material.

In the following table, you'll find a breakdown of different levels of depth in textual conversations. These levels are designed to help educators and students understand the progression from basic comprehension to more nuanced and critical engagement with texts. Each level outlines specific characteristics and examples that demonstrate how students can deepen their understanding and analysis as they interact with literature. This framework not only serves as a guide for assessing students' depth of comprehension but also encourages them to reflect on their own contributions and strive for deeper insights during discussions. By utilizing this table, teachers can scaffold learning experiences effectively, support peer and self-assessment, and ultimately foster a classroom environment where meaningful conversations about texts flourish.

---

[8] Paterson, D. (2019). Engaging elementary students in higher order talk and writing about text. *Journal of Early Childhood Literacy* 19 (1): 34–54.

Levels of Depth in Textual Conversations

Depth Level	Characteristics	Example
Level 1: Surface-Level Understanding	• Focuses on basic plot summary and literal comprehension. • Describes events and characters without deeper analysis. • Responses recall facts from the text.	"The main character in the story is a brave knight who defeats a dragon."
Level 2: Textual Understanding	• Demonstrates comprehension of themes, motifs, and literary devices. • Begins to interpret the text's meaning beyond literal understanding. • Provides evidence from the text to support interpretations.	"The repeated use of light and darkness imagery symbolizes the protagonist's internal struggle."
Level 3: Personal Connection	• Relates the text to personal experiences, beliefs, or emotions. • Makes connections between the text and broader societal issues or personal values. • Considers how the text relates to their own life or worldview.	"The character's journey reminds me of a challenge I faced last year, and how I overcame it."
Level 4: Critical Analysis	• Analyzes the text's themes, characters, and events in depth. • Evaluates the author's choices and intentions, considering multiple perspectives. • Synthesizes information from the text with external sources or other texts.	"The protagonist's moral dilemma reflects broader societal issues of justice and fairness."
Level 5: In-Depth or Critical Conversations	• Engages in sophisticated analysis and evaluation of complex themes and ideas. • Challenges assumptions and explores alternative interpretations. • Considers implications of the text beyond the immediate narrative.	"The author's use of unreliable narration challenges traditional storytelling conventions, inviting readers to reconsider their trust in narrative perspectives."

Using the table:

- **Assessment:** This table serves as a tool for assessing and tracking students' progression in textual discussions. Teachers can observe and evaluate the depth of students' engagement with the text based on their contributions across these levels.
- **Instruction:** Encourage students to aim for higher levels of conversation depth by providing specific prompts and questions tailored to each level. Prompt students to move beyond simple summary toward deeper analysis, personal connection, and critical evaluation.
- **Reflection:** After discussions, prompt students to reflect on their own contributions and identify ways to deepen their understanding and engagement in future conversations. Encourage them to consider which level of depth their contributions align with and how they can push themselves to engage more deeply with the text and with their peers' ideas.
- **Scaffolded learning:** Use the table to scaffold learning experiences, gradually guiding students from lower to higher levels of conversation depth. Start with more structured discussions focusing on surface-level understanding and gradually introduce more complex prompts and challenges to foster critical thinking and analysis.
- **Peer and self-assessment:** Encourage students to use the table for peer assessment, evaluating the depth of their classmates' contributions during discussions. Additionally, students can use it for self-assessment, reflecting on their own growth in engaging with texts over time.

Tips for Encouraging Conversations in Your Classroom

Effective classroom discussions are more than just exchanges of ideas—they are opportunities to foster critical thinking, enhance literacy skills, and cultivate a collaborative learning environment. "When the culture of the classroom is one that fosters a sense of community and caring, where students are challenged to enquire and explore together, and where the process of learning is valued as highly as the product, then students can become self-motivated and efficacious learners" (Wells, 1999).[9] To ensure discussions are engaging and productive, educators can implement several strategies that prioritize thoughtful communication and active participation. Central to this approach is the art of questioning: by crafting strong, open-ended questions, teachers encourage students to explore diverse perspectives, analyze information critically, and construct well-supported arguments. These questions serve as catalysts for deeper inquiry, guiding students toward a deeper understanding of complex topics while honing their ability to articulate their thoughts clearly.

> "While particular elements can be picked out and identified—just as threads of different color can be picked out and identified on a cloth—instruction and conversation are woven into a seamless whole: The conversation is instructional, and the instruction is conversational."
> *Instructional Conversations: Promoting Comprehension Through Discussion*

Moreover, it is crucial not to assume that students inherently possess the skills necessary for effective conversation. Explicit instruction in communication techniques equips students with the tools to listen actively, express ideas cogently, and engage respectfully with their peers. The study The Impact of Explicit Instruction in Communication on Elementary Students' Social Interactions (2020) focuses on how teaching communication techniques to elementary students equips them to actively listen, express their ideas clearly, and engage in respectful dialogue with their peers. Conducted by researchers at the University of Michigan, the study demonstrates that students who receive explicit instruction in communication skills show significant improvement in classroom discussions, conflict resolution, and peer collaboration.

The researchers found that students who were taught active listening and respectful engagement strategies were more likely to participate in meaningful conversations and demonstrate empathy toward their peers. Additionally, the study highlighted that these

---

[9] Paterson, D. (2019). Engaging elementary students in higher order talk and writing about text. *Journal of Early Childhood Literacy* 19 (1): 34–54.

communication skills contributed to improved academic performance due to clearer expression of ideas and better collaboration in group settings.

"Explicit instruction in communication techniques led to notable improvements in students' abilities to listen attentively, articulate their thoughts cogently, and interact with peers in a respectful and constructive manner" (Smith et al., 2020).[10]

Clear expectations for participation and behavior during discussions further support a collaborative learning environment, emphasizing the importance of evidence-based reasoning, constructive feedback, and mutual respect. By integrating these strategies, educators empower students to actively contribute to discussions, fostering a culture where every voice is valued and where learning extends beyond the mere exchange of information to encompass critical analysis and meaningful dialogue. The following sections describe tips to follow when implementing conversations into your classroom.

A Successful Discussion Is All About Questioning

Effective classroom discussions hinge on the quality of questions posed. Open-ended questions not only stimulate critical thinking but also encourage students to explore multiple perspectives and delve deeper into the topic at hand. "Discussions can provide students space to examine ideas and learn new ways of thinking and speaking (Knickerbocker & Rycik, 2006). They also provide a forum for students to interact with others from diverse backgrounds and with differing perspectives" (Eeds & Wells, 1989).[11] When planning discussions, consider questions that prompt analysis, evaluation, and creativity rather than those with straightforward answers. These questions should challenge students to articulate their thoughts clearly, support their ideas with evidence, and consider alternative viewpoints. By fostering a culture of questioning, students learn to engage critically with texts and ideas, honing their literacy skills while developing their ability to construct and defend arguments based on evidence.

---

[10] Salamondra, T. (2021). Effective communication in schools. *BU Journal of Graduate Studies in Education* 13 (1): 22–26.

[11] Hall, L. (2012). The role of reading identities and reading abilities in student's discussions about texts and comprehension strategies. *Journal of Literacy Research* 44 (3): 239–272.

Don't Assume Your Students Know How to Have a Conversation

Teaching strong communication skills is foundational to productive discussions. Explicitly instruct students on how to listen actively, ask probing questions, and respectfully respond to others' viewpoints. Emphasize the importance of clarity and coherence in their verbal expression, as well as active listening techniques such as paraphrasing and seeking clarification. By equipping students with these skills, you empower them to participate meaningfully in discussions, enhancing both their literacy development and their ability to engage critically with complex topics.

Make Sure You Outline Clear Expectations

Clearly defining expectations for classroom discussions sets the stage for productive interaction. Specify criteria such as active listening, respectful disagreement, evidence-based reasoning, and contributions that build on others' ideas. Clarity in expectations not only guides students in their participation but also cultivates a culture of accountability and mutual respect. By linking these expectations to literacy goals, such as constructing well-supported arguments and evaluating diverse sources, students learn to communicate effectively while engaging critically with texts and peers.

Criterion	Exceeds Expectations (4)	Meets Expectations (3)	Approaching Expectations (2)	Below Expectations (1)
Active Listening	Consistently demonstrates attentive listening by summarizing others' points and asking clarifying questions.	Demonstrates attentive listening most of the time, occasionally summarizing others' points or asking questions.	Shows some evidence of listening but seldom summarizes or asks questions.	Rarely listens attentively; often distracted or interruptive.
Respectful Disagreement	Always disagrees respectfully, using "I" statements and providing clear reasons for their perspective.	Usually disagrees respectfully, though sometimes lacks clarity in reasoning.	Occasionally disagrees respectfully but often lacks clarity or becomes confrontational.	Rarely disagrees respectfully, often confrontational or dismissive.
Evidence-Based Reasoning	Consistently supports arguments with strong, relevant evidence from texts or other credible sources.	Usually supports arguments with relevant evidence, though not always strong or fully explained.	Sometimes supports arguments with evidence, but it may be weak or not fully relevant.	Rarely uses evidence to support arguments, relies mostly on opinions.

Building on Others' Ideas	Frequently builds on others' ideas, making connections and extending the conversation thoughtfully.	Often builds on others' ideas, though not always extending the conversation significantly.	Occasionally builds on others' ideas, but contributions may be minimal or repetitive.	Rarely builds on others' ideas, contributions often disconnected or off-topic.
Constructing Well-Supported Arguments	Consistently constructs well-supported, logical arguments, integrating multiple sources and perspectives.	Generally constructs well-supported arguments, though integration of sources may be limited.	Sometimes constructs arguments, but support and integration of sources are often lacking.	Rarely constructs well-supported arguments, minimal use of sources.
Evaluating Diverse Sources	Regularly evaluates and incorporates diverse sources, showing an understanding of varying perspectives.	Often evaluates and incorporates diverse sources, though depth of understanding may vary.	Occasionally evaluates and incorporates diverse sources, but may show limited understanding.	Rarely evaluates or incorporates diverse sources, limited perspective.

> "I feel SO much more confident with setting up the year for success. I felt a little aimless last year and just dove right into the lessons. Now, I see holes in my thought process AND how to fix it to move forward on a better foot."
>
> -Cassie Barnes, 5th Grade, Hickory Creek Elementary, Florida

Every Discussion Needs a Clear Focus

Establishing a clear focus or guiding question directs students' attention and efforts during discussions. This focus should articulate the purpose or central theme of the conversation, guiding students in their exploration and analysis of relevant content. By aligning the discussion's focus with literacy objectives—such as analyzing authorial intent, evaluating evidence, or synthesizing information—students develop critical thinking skills while deepening their understanding of complex texts and ideas.

Provide Students with Sentence Stems (Accountable Talk)

Sentence stems serve as scaffolding for students to articulate their thoughts clearly and coherently during discussions. These prompts encourage students to engage in accountable talk by prompting them to provide evidence, offer explanations, or seek clarification. By incorporating sentence stems that promote critical thinking—such as "I think ___ because ___," or "Can you clarify ___?"—students learn to construct well-reasoned arguments, support their assertions with evidence, and engage in meaningful dialogue that enhances their literacy skills.

Consider these sentence stems that students can use to help hold textual conversations.

Sentence Stems Students Could Use to Help Hold Textual Conversations:	
Purpose	Sentence Stem Suggestions
Expressing Opinion	• "I think the author's intention was ___ because ___." • "In my view, ___ is significant because ___." • "From my perspective, ___ is important because ___."
Agreeing or Disagreeing	• "I agree with ___'s point that ___ because ___." • "I respectfully disagree with ___ because ___." • "While I understand ___'s argument, I find ___ more compelling because ___."
Asking for Clarification	• "Could you clarify what you meant by ___?" • "I'm not sure I understand how ___ connects to ___ in the text. Could you explain?" • "Can you elaborate on the evidence you mentioned regarding ___?"
Seeking Evidence	• "What specific passage or example supports your interpretation of ___?" • "Can you provide textual evidence to back up your claim about ___?" • "Where did you find support for that assertion in the text?"
Building on Ideas	• "Adding to what ___ said about ___, I also think ___." • "Expanding on the theme of ___, another example from the text is ___." • "I agree with ___'s analysis of ___. Additionally, I would add ___."
Summarizing	• "So, if I understand correctly, the main idea of this section is ___." • "In summary, the author argues that ___ because ___." • "To recap, the key point in this paragraph is ___."
Challenging Ideas	• "I see where you're coming from, but could there be an alternative explanation for ___?" • "What about considering ___ as another perspective on this issue?" • "While your interpretation is plausible, I'm inclined to question it because ___."
Making Connections	• "This passage reminds me of ___ because ___." • "I see a parallel between ___ in this text and ___ in another piece we've read." • "The way the character handles ___ is similar to ___ in real-world situations."
Offering a Counterargument	• "Have we considered the implications of ___ in relation to ___?" • "What if we looked at this issue from the perspective of ___ instead?" • "While ___'s argument has merit, it overlooks the impact of ___."
Proposing a Solution or Conclusion	• "To address this issue, one possible solution could be ___." • "In conclusion, the author suggests ___ to resolve ___." • "A potential outcome of ___ could be ___."

Always Give Students Time to Brainstorm Before Talking

Prioritizing brainstorming and reflection time before discussions allows students to organize their thoughts and formulate coherent responses. This process supports literacy development by encouraging students to consider multiple perspectives, analyze complex information, and construct arguments based on evidence. Pausing during discussions to allow students to gather their thoughts reinforces the importance of thoughtful communication and enables them to contribute more effectively to the conversation.

Give Students Roles (Secret Missions) During Discussions

Assigning roles during discussions encourages active participation and accountability among students. These roles—such as summarizer, skeptic, or synthesizer—provide specific tasks that guide students in engaging critically with the content and contributing meaningfully to the discussion. By linking roles to literacy goals, such as evaluating sources, synthesizing information, or challenging assumptions, students develop essential skills in critical thinking and collaborative communication.

Conversational Jobs

The Scribe	The Captain	The Encourager	Time Keeper
• Write down notes, answers, and other written responsibilities for the group. • Ensure neat handwriting and accurately reflect the group's decisions.	• Hold the group accountable and on task. • Lead discussions and ensure all voices are heard. • Read directions aloud and ask questions to keep the conversation going.	• Uplift team members and give praise for thoughtful contributions. • Prevent arguing and fighting within the team. • Stay positive.	• Manage the stopwatch or timer for the group. • Keep track of time and ensure the group stays on task. • Remind group members of time respectfully.
The Checker	**Materials Manager**	**Volume Manager**	**The Presenter**
• Ensure everyone in the group understands what is going on. • Double-check answers with all group members and re-teach if necessary.	• Collect and distribute materials needed for the activity. • Ensure materials are used respectfully and returned correctly.	• Maintain appropriate noise levels during group work. • Remind group members respectfully when they get too loud.	• Present the final product or assignment to the teacher or class if needed. • Speak clearly and confidently to be heard and represent the group's work.

Allow Students to Decide on the Focus Question(s)

Providing students with opportunities to choose discussion topics or questions promotes ownership and engagement. This student-driven approach fosters intrinsic motivation and encourages deeper exploration of topics that resonate with their interests and experiences. "In a seminal study on classroom discourse, Mishler (1978) found that when teachers posed questions, students gave short responses, but when students posed questions to one another, the students responded with more elaboration. Regardless of who is asking the questions, discussion styles that move away from recitation models toward models of shared reasoning garner greater levels of engagement in discussions from students, higher quality of discourse, and greater equity in participation across various levels of achievement" (Chinn, Anderson, & Waggoner).[12] By empowering students to shape the direction of discussions, educators cultivate a classroom environment that values diverse perspectives and encourages critical inquiry, enhancing both literacy skills and students' ability to engage critically with complex ideas.

Remind Students of Different Ways to Engage with the Conversation

Supporting struggling students involves reminding them of various strategies to participate meaningfully in discussions. Encourage them to ask clarifying questions, provide evidence to support their views, draw connections between ideas, or offer alternative perspectives. By reinforcing these engagement strategies, students develop critical thinking skills and gain confidence in their ability to contribute thoughtfully to discussions while enhancing their literacy skills through active participation and dialogue.

---

[12] Boardman, A., Boele, A., and Klinger, J. (2018). Strategy instruction shifts teacher and students interactions during text-based discussions. *International Literacy Association and Wiley* 53 (2): 175–195.

Talk About Acceptable Struggle and Strategies to Progress

Acknowledging and discussing the concept of "acceptable struggle" empowers students to navigate challenges during discussions independently. Encourage students to embrace moments of uncertainty or difficulty as opportunities for growth and learning. Provide strategies, such as collaborative problem-solving, revisiting previous discussions, or seeking additional resources, to help students overcome obstacles and move forward in their understanding. By fostering resilience and perseverance, educators support students in developing critical thinking skills and strengthening their literacy competencies through reflective engagement in discussions.

Better Questions, Even Better Conversations

"Research has also shown that answering and generating a variety of questions about the texts they read positively impacts on students' comprehension, especially when engaging with complex texts" (Graham & Hebert, 2010; NICHHD, 2000; Wilkinson & Hye Son, 2009).[13] In the dynamic environment of a classroom, the types of questions posed by teachers can significantly influence the quality of student engagement and learning. Open-ended questions, which cannot be answered with a simple "yes" or "no," play a crucial role in fostering deeper conversations and enhancing the educational experience. By encouraging students to think critically and creatively, these questions transform the classroom into a vibrant space for exploration and discovery.

One of the primary benefits of open-ended questions is that they allow students to express their creativity and engage in deep thinking. Unlike closed questions that seek specific answers, open-ended questions invite students to explore various perspectives and construct unique responses. The study "Open-Ended Questions to Assess

---

[13] Paterson, D. (2019). Engaging elementary students in higher order talk and writing about text. *Journal of Early Childhood Literacy* 19 (1): 34–54.

Critical-Thinking Skills in Indonesian Elementary Schools" (2021) supports the claim that open-ended questions allow students to express their creativity and engage in deep thinking. Conducted with elementary students, the research demonstrated that open-ended questions led to increased cognitive engagement, fostering originality and elaboration in student responses. The flexibility of open-ended questions encouraged students to explore multiple perspectives and think more critically about problems.[14] This not only stimulates their intellectual curiosity but also helps them develop a more profound understanding of the subject matter. When students are given the freedom to think outside the box, they are more likely to produce original and insightful answers.

	Open-Ended Questions	**Closed Questions**
Definition	These questions prompt more extended responses and invite the reader to think critically or express opinions.	These questions typically require short, specific answers.
Purpose	They encourage deeper analysis, reflection, and interpretation of the text.	They are used to confirm understanding or gather specific details.
Example using The Three Little Pigs	"What do you think motivated the wolf to blow down the houses, and how do you think the pigs felt during each encounter?"	"Did the wolf blow down the houses?"

---

[14] Kartikasari, I. and Usodo, B. (2022). The effectiveness of open-ending learning and creative problem solving models to teach creative thinking skills. *Pegem Journal of Education and Instruction* 12 (4): 29–38.

Open-ended questions naturally provide scaffolding for students of all abilities. These questions can be approached at different levels of complexity, allowing each student to contribute according to their understanding and skills. This inclusivity ensures that every student is engaged in the discussion, not just the one who is called upon. By catering to a diverse range of abilities, open-ended questions help create an inclusive classroom environment where every student feels valued and supported.

Critical thinking is an essential skill that students need to develop to succeed in both academic and real-world settings. Open-ended questions challenge students to analyze information, evaluate different viewpoints, and justify their reasoning. In work by authors (Peterson, 2013; Taylor et al., 2003, 2002a), results showed that higher order responses occurred when teachers posed higher order questions and then asked students to write their personal responses or talk with partners. These types of activities required every student to formulate his or her own interpretation of the text and allowed for lengthier responses and deeper elaborations of meaning.[15] This process enhances their critical thinking skills and prepares them for complex problem-solving tasks. By regularly incorporating open-ended questions into classroom discussions, teachers can help students become more adept at thinking critically and making informed decisions.

Engaging in conversations that stem from open-ended questions also helps students build their language and vocabulary skills. As they articulate their thoughts and ideas, they learn to use language more effectively and expand their vocabulary. This practice is especially beneficial for students who are learning English as a second language or those who need additional support with language development. Through these discussions, students become more confident in their ability to communicate clearly and persuasively.

---

[15] Paterson, D. (2019). Engaging elementary students in higher order talk and writing about text. *Journal of Early Childhood Literacy* 19 (1): 34–54.

	Easy	→		Hard
Summarizing	What do you remember so far in the story?	What events were too unimportant to include in the summary?	How might the title help you create your summary?	How does your summary compare to your partner's summary?
Point of View	Whose point of view do you wish the story was told from? Why?	If you were telling the story, how would it be different?	How does the point of view of the text support the perspective the character/author has?	How might the story change if it were told through _____'s POV?
Plot	What part of the plot surprised you the most?	What was your favorite part of the plot?	What event would you add or change in the plot?	How did the character's traits affect the plot of the story?
Theme	How can you connect to the theme of the story?	What other texts can you remember that had a similar theme?	Which event do you believe gives the most evidence for the theme?	How did the plot support the theme of the text?
Main Idea	Where do we see evidence of the Main Idea throughout the text?	What detail might you have added that also supports the main idea?	What might be another title for the story?	How do the smaller main ideas in the paragraph support the larger main idea of the text?

Genres	Which genre do you believe is the hardest to understand? Why?	If you were to write a story with a specific genre, which would it be and why?	How did the genre of the text affect your ability to make connections?	How does the plot of the story give evidence toward the genre?
Cause & Effect	How might ____ affect ____?	What is another way to get the same results?	What might result if _____?	What are some other effects that could happen from _____?
Making Inferences	How did the picture in the text help support your inferences?	How did you schema affect your ability to make inferences in this story?	What was the most important inference you made throughout the text?	Were the inferences you made vital to the plot of the story?
Sequencing	How would you change the sequencing of the events in the text?	Why do you think the author arranged the events in the order that he/she did?	What events do you think happened before the first event in the story?	How do you think the sequel of the story would occur?
Author's Purpose	Which of the purposes do you think is more fun to read? Why?	When do you think the author determined the purpose of the story in his/her writing process?	How does the author's purpose support the genre of the story?	If you were to change the author's purpose of the text, which events could stay and which would have to go?

Talking (Meaningfully) About Texts

Character	How can you relate to this character?	Do you agree or disagree with the choices that the character is making?	What would NOT be a strong character trait to describe ____?	How do the character's relationships effect the plot of the story?
Setting	How does the author describe the setting in the story?	How important is the setting to the plot of the story?	What other words could the author have used in the text to describe the setting?	If you could put the character in another story setting, how would he/she act?
Problem/ Solution	How might you have solved the problem differently?	How did the events in the plot lead up to this specific problem?	How would you evaluate the character's ability to solve the problem?	How did the solutions affect the remainder of the plot?
Text Structure	How do the text features found in the text support the text structure?	How could you organize the facts in the text in a different way?	How does the text structure help the author develop his/her ideas?	What sections of the text are organized differently than this section?
Compare/ Contrast	In what ways are ____ & ____ same/different?	Why would the author want you to compare these two topics?	How do the similarities or differences between ____ affect the plot of the story?	Which character from a different story is more similar to _____ than _____?

Fact & Opinion	How do the facts & opinions in the story support the genre of the text?	What do the facts & opinions in the text say about the author's perspective?	Do you share any opinions found within the text? Why?	Where in the text could you add in your opinion about the topic?
Perspective	Because the story is told through ____'s POV, how does the author showcase that character's perspective?	How would the story change if the author's perspective were different?	How do the events in the text support the author's or character's perspective?	Is your perspective about ____ similar or different from the character/author?
Making Connections	Where did you make your strongest connection in the story?	How did making connects support your understanding of the text?	What was the first connection you made?	Did you connect more to the plot or the characters? Why?
Visualizing	How did the words in the text support your ability to visualize the story?	How did the author's voice help you visualize the story?	Where in your visualizations can you see text evidence and where do you see your schema?	How did your schema affect the outcome of your visual?
Determining Importance	Why do we need to pay attention to ____?	How did the text features support the important parts of the text?	What clues did you find throughout the story that were important?	Why did the author include unimportant events such as ____?

Talking (Meaningfully) About Texts

Open-ended questions encourage students to reflect on their own ideas, thoughts, and feelings. A study published by *Responsive Classroom* in 2023 supports the claim that open-ended questions encourage students to reflect on their own ideas, thoughts, and feelings. The study highlights how such questions promote deeper thinking by allowing students to express themselves more fully and to connect their personal experiences with their learning. For example, prompts like "What strategies did you use today?" or "How did this activity make you feel?" help students process their thoughts, fostering both emotional and cognitive reflection.[16] This self-reflection helps them develop a deeper understanding of themselves and their beliefs. It also fosters emotional intelligence, as students learn to articulate their emotions and consider how their experiences shape their perspectives. By giving students the opportunity to explore their inner worlds, open-ended questions promote personal growth and self-awareness.

Collaboration is a key component of modern education, and open-ended questions are an effective tool for promoting respectful dialogue among students. These questions teach students how to listen to different viewpoints, agree or disagree respectfully, and build upon each other's ideas. This collaborative process not only enhances their communication skills but also prepares them for working effectively in diverse teams. By learning to engage in constructive conversations, students develop the social skills necessary for success in both academic and professional settings.

Students are more likely to remember the answers they come up with in response to open-ended questions. According to research conducted by Columbia University's Center for Teaching and Learning, open-ended questions stimulate peer discussion and allow students to explore their understanding of key concepts more deeply. This process strengthens their memory of the material because they must articulate their thoughts and reflect on them during discussions.[17] The process of thinking deeply and constructing a thoughtful response engages their cognitive skills and reinforces their learning. When

---

[16] 2023 Responsive Classroom Training minds one question at a time. https://www.responsiveclassroom.org/training-minds-one-question-at-a-time/

[17] Columbia Center for Teaching and Learning. Learning through discussion. https://www.responsiveclassroom.org/training-minds-one-question-at-a-time/

students are actively involved in generating their answers, they form stronger connections to the material and retain information more effectively. This deeper level of engagement helps ensure that their learning is both meaningful and lasting.

> "There is so much that plays into reading and comprehension beyond the words on the pages. The critical components are WHAT one does when they read- the questioning that takes place, the mind movies that are made, the conversations that can happen. All of these can help boost comprehension."
>
> -Sarah Adderley, 3rd Grade, Roosevelt Elementary School, Washington

Finally, open-ended questions focus more on the process of finding the answer rather than just the answer itself. This emphasis on the journey of discovery encourages students to explore different approaches and develop their problem-solving skills. By valuing the process, teachers help students understand that learning is not just about getting the right answer but about developing the skills and strategies needed to find solutions. This mindset prepares students for lifelong learning and continuous improvement.

Open-ended questions are a powerful tool for fostering better conversations and enhancing the educational experience. They encourage creativity, critical thinking, and collaboration while building language skills and promoting self-reflection. By incorporating open-ended questions into their teaching strategies, educators can create a more engaging, inclusive, and effective learning environment.

Make Conversations FUN!

Talking about a text doesn't have to be boring. Shake things up and get yourself out of the "Think-Pair-Share" rut by including some new and engaging conversational strategies to get your students talking! When students are more engaged in the activity and conversation, they are more likely to derive meaningful insights from the experience. Engaged readers, especially in elementary settings, show higher levels of comprehension and are more likely to internalize and derive deeper insights from their reading experiences. It emphasizes that engagement is not only tied to immediate academic success but also contributes to long-term literacy development by encouraging critical thinking and active involvement in the learning process.[18]

Effective conversation about a text goes beyond merely answering questions; it involves exploring ideas, making connections, and deepening understanding. Engaged students are more likely to remember what they've learned and apply it in meaningful ways. The key to achieving this is by creating a vibrant and interactive learning environment where students feel motivated to participate actively.

Moreover, fostering a culture of open dialogue and respectful exchange of ideas can significantly enhance students' communicative skills. By engaging in structured, meaningful conversations, students develop skills such as active listening, critical thinking, and the ability to articulate their ideas clearly and respectfully. This method has been shown to improve both academic outcomes and social cohesion.[19] As they articulate their thoughts and listen to others, they develop a deeper appreciation for multiple perspectives. This process enriches their understanding of the text and helps them build essential skills for collaborative learning and critical thinking.

The following sections consider some whole-group conversational strategies you can try with any text!

Speed Dating

Speed Dating is a dynamic and engaging classroom activity designed to promote student interaction and discussion. To implement this strategy, provide students with a basic recording sheet and present a broad question or topic for discussion. Students then pair up and move from partner to partner, discussing the given topic. This movement keeps

---

[18] Lee, Y. and Jang, B. (2021). A systematic review of reading engagement research: what do we mean, what do we know, and where do we need to go? *Reading Psychology* 42 (5): 540–576.

[19] Carrion, R. and Aguileta, G. (2020). Implications for social impact of dialogic teaching and learning. *Frontiers in Psychology* 11: 140.

the energy high and allows students to hear multiple perspectives in a short period. As they converse, students should record key highlights from each conversation on their recording sheets. This activity not only fosters communication skills but also helps students to synthesize information from different viewpoints, enhancing their understanding of the topic.

Save the Last Word

In the Save the Last Word strategy, students participate in small group discussions where one person initiates the conversation. The unique twist is that the person who starts the discussion must not speak again until the end. Instead, they listen to the contributions of their peers. Once everyone has shared their thoughts, the initiator summarizes the entire conversation. This method encourages active listening and ensures that the discussion is driven by a variety of voices. It also helps the initiating student to practice summarization skills, distilling the conversation into its most important points.

Buzz Words

Buzz Words is an interactive small group activity that keeps conversations focused and lively. Each group is given a stack of cards, each with a different "buzz word" related to the topic of discussion. Every few minutes, a new card is drawn, and the group shifts their focus to include the new buzz word in their conversation. This technique helps students to explore different facets of a topic and keeps discussions from becoming stagnant. By continually introducing new keywords, students are encouraged to think critically and connect various concepts, deepening their overall comprehension.

Stoplight Discussion

Stoplight Discussion is a visual and participatory method that helps gauge student comfort levels during discussions. Provide students with red, yellow, and green cards (or cups). During the discussion, students display the card that corresponds to their comfort level: red means they are not comfortable contributing, yellow indicates they have something to add but are hesitant, and green shows they are ready to share. This system allows students to participate at their own pace and provides a non-verbal way for teachers to monitor engagement and support students accordingly. It creates an inclusive environment where all students can contribute when they feel ready.

Quick Tip

Make sure to always model these strategies before jumping in! Try it once (or twice) with the teacher involved, then see how the students do without you.

Top Three

The Top Three strategy involves transforming a question into a "top three" list to deepen student analysis and engagement. For instance, instead of asking, "What was your favorite part of the story?" rephrase it to, "What are the top three most memorable parts of the story?" This approach requires students to think more critically and rank their responses, providing reasons for their choices. It promotes higher-order thinking as students evaluate and prioritize different aspects of a topic. This method can be used across various subjects to encourage detailed and thoughtful responses.

Facts of Five

In the Facts of Five activity, students begin by writing down five main thoughts on their text or topic. They then form groups of three and share their lists, analyzing and combining them into a collective top five list. Next, these small groups merge with other groups, reducing their combined lists of 10 to a refined top 5 list. This iterative process encourages collaboration and critical thinking, as students must negotiate and justify their choices to create a cohesive list. It helps students to see the value in different perspectives and work toward a common understanding.

Colored Conversations

Colored Conversations is an engaging strategy that uses colored marbles or pom-poms to represent student contributions. Divide students into small groups and assign each color to a student. Every time a student contributes to the discussion, they place their colored item into a central container. This visual representation helps students to be aware of their participation level and encourages equitable involvement. It can also serve as a reflective tool for students to assess their own engagement and for teachers to ensure that all voices are heard in the discussion.

Fishbowl

The Fishbowl strategy involves placing a few students in an inner circle (the "fish") to discuss a topic while the rest of the class forms an outer circle, observing and taking notes.

This setup allows for an in-depth conversation among the inner circle participants while providing the outer circle with an opportunity to listen and reflect. After a set period, roles can be switched, giving more students the chance to participate actively. This method fosters active listening, critical thinking, and respectful observation, making it an effective way to delve deeply into complex topics.

Hot Seat

Hot Seat is a role-playing activity where one student sits in the "hot seat" and pretends to be a specific character or object from the text. The rest of the class asks the "hot seat" student questions, and they must respond in character. This strategy enhances comprehension and engagement by encouraging students to think from different perspectives. It also promotes creativity and deeper understanding of the material as students must thoroughly know their character or object to answer questions accurately.

Snowball Discussion

Snowball Discussion starts with students in pairs discussing a topic. After a designated time, pairs join another pair to form a group of four, sharing their ideas and building on the discussion. This process continues, with groups merging and discussions expanding, until the entire class forms one large group. This method allows for progressive idea building and ensures that every student has a voice in the discussion. It fosters collaboration, critical thinking and a sense of community as students collectively explore and expand on their ideas.

Reflect: Which strategy do you see your students enjoying the most?

Benefits to Having Text Discussions

Engaging in discussions about a text that students have read offers a multitude of benefits that significantly enhance their learning experience. One of the primary advantages is the opportunity to hear diverse perspectives. When students share their interpretations and insights, they are exposed to a variety of viewpoints that may differ from their own. A study titled "Negotiating Diverse Perspectives: Early Elementary Students Cultivate Empathy Through Children's Literature and Dramatic Inquiry" (2019) highlights that when students engage in discussions about literature, they are exposed to a variety of perspectives, which not only broadens their understanding but also fosters empathy. This study demonstrates that early elementary students, through interactive discussions and inquiry-based engagements with texts, develop critical thinking and empathetic understanding by considering alternative interpretations and experiences.

These discussions help students process their peers' diverse perspectives, which can significantly deepen their understanding of the text and promote a more inclusive and empathetic classroom environment.[20]

This exposure can broaden their understanding and foster empathy as they consider alternative interpretations and experiences.

Additionally, discussing a text allows students to validate their own thoughts and interpretations. By articulating their ideas and hearing responses from their peers, students can gauge whether their understanding aligns with others or if they have missed key points. This process of validation can boost their confidence in their analytical abilities or prompt them to reassess and refine their interpretations.

Moreover, discussions provide a valuable platform for students to ask questions about parts of the text they found confusing or intriguing. This interactive element encourages curiosity and active engagement with the material. When students inquire about unclear sections, they are often prompted to revisit the text, which promotes deeper comprehension and retention of the material.

---

[20] Deliman, A. (2019). *Negotiating Diverse Perspectives: Early Elementary Students Cultivate Empathy Through Children's Literature and Dramatic Inquiry*. Indiana University.

The collaborative nature of discussions also leads to the discovery of new ideas. As students listen to and build on each other's contributions, they can develop a richer and more nuanced understanding of the text. This collective brainstorming can reveal connections and themes that might have been overlooked during individual reading.

Furthermore, talking about a text helps students create a more solid understanding of the material. Verbalizing their thoughts and hearing feedback helps solidify their grasp of the content and encourages them to think more critically about what they have read. This critical thinking is essential for developing higher-order cognitive skills, such as analysis, synthesis, and evaluation.

"Small-group instruction within a 30-minute period should include several brief, targeted, and engaging activities. This is because students will benefit from listening to the thoughts and opinions of their peers related to the new concepts they are learning."[21]

In addition to these benefits, discussions can also enhance students' communication skills. Articulating their ideas clearly and listening to others respectfully are crucial skills that are cultivated through regular practice in a supportive environment. These skills are not only vital for academic success but also for effective communication in everyday life.

Engaging in discussions about a text enriches the reading experience by fostering a deeper understanding, encouraging critical thinking, and enhancing communication skills. These conversations transform reading from a solitary activity into a dynamic and collaborative learning process, ultimately leading to a more profound and comprehensive grasp of the material.

Build a Culture of Collaboration

Teachers often voice frustration with statements like, "My students just won't collaborate! They won't get along during group activities. They don't know how to collaborate." It's a

---

[21] Donegan, R. and Wanzek, J. (2021). Effects of reading interventions implemented for upper elementary struggling readers: a look at recent research. *Reading and Writing* 34: 1943–1977.

common scenario where students struggle with group tasks, even when presented with exciting and engaging activities. This isn't necessarily the students' fault. Teachers sometimes overlook the crucial step of preparing their classroom environment to support successful collaboration. Establishing a culture of collaboration is essential.

> **Building a Culture of Collaboration**
> - Embrace student differences
> - Consider how you are grouping students
> - Navigate peer rejections and acceptance
> - Build student confidence
> - Build trust with your students
> - Move around, ask questions
> - Stop seeking the 'right' answer

For genuine collaboration to occur, teachers must create a classroom atmosphere that encourages student interaction and empowers students to take active roles in the learning community. This involves relinquishing some control over talk-time and content coverage. True collaboration requires teachers to invest time in building a collaborative culture and then stepping back to let it unfold. Let's explore how to achieve this.

Embrace Student Differences

The first step is to embrace student differences. A leader's job is to touch every one of those people so they know they're free to think and do things better. Ask yourself if your students feel free to think and innovate. Consider how students would react knowing their uniqueness is celebrated and that their diverse perspectives enrich the learning experience. Imagine a classroom where each student's contributions are genuinely valued. Commit to understanding the depth of your students' thinking by providing multiple opportunities for them to demonstrate their cognitive abilities in various ways.

Group Students Thoughtfully

Next, consider how you are grouping your students. Are you giving them a choice of group? Are you using mixed ability groups, face-buddies, shoulder-buddies, or strategic grouping? Desk arrangements also play a crucial role in facilitating collaboration. For instance, a U-shaped arrangement can allow the teacher to be part of the conversation. Teachers' informed judgments make each grouping scenario work. These decisions are based on teaching styles, experiences with students, and trust in each student's unique gifts. Provide structured opportunities for students to engage in meaningful conversations. My Engagement Strategy Cards offer over 60 different ideas to get you started.

Create a Safe Environment

Navigating peer rejection and acceptance is another critical aspect. Research shows a direct correlation between participation and self-concept in students. Peer rejection can significantly diminish self-concept and participation. Our job as teachers is to create an environment where students feel safe to participate. To achieve this, ask deep, thought-provoking questions that allow all students to reflect and respond. Use quick writes, quick draws, and pair discussions before whole-group discussions to encourage participation.

Build Confidence and Trust

Building confidence is essential for collaboration. Students need to feel validated and heard. This increases their confidence and willingness to collaborate. Facilitate confidence by validating students' answers, encouraging them to share with others, and not accepting incorrect answers.

Trust is a pillar of a collaborative classroom, beginning with the teacher's belief in students' capabilities. Do you trust that students can learn from each other, especially because of their differences? Do you believe they have amazing things to share? Encourage self-trust in students by building their confidence. What are you doing to help your students trust in themselves?

Walk the Classroom

Walking around and following through during activities is crucial. Encourage participation by moving around, asking questions, and holding students accountable. Consistency in expectations fosters a collaborative environment where students enjoy and expect interaction.

Avoid "Right" Answers Only

In higher-order thinking tasks, move away from seeking the "right" answer. Instead, allow students to evaluate their learning, justify their answers, and appreciate diverse viewpoints. This fosters rich, whole-group conversations where students learn to agree and disagree respectfully.

Reflect on these steps and consider your own classroom. What are your thoughts on the importance of student interaction? What have you observed about students who succeed or struggle in your classroom? How can you promote peer acceptance and reduce peer rejection? How evident is trust in your classroom? What can you do this week to increase trust and confidence? How can trust and accountability coexist in your classroom?

The next time collaborative efforts fall short, revisit these steps. What changes can you make to support your students and enhance their collaborative skills? Sometimes, the smallest adjustment can have the most significant impact.

Closing

As this chapter on fostering meaningful text discussions concludes, it's important to reflect on the transformative impact these conversations can have on students' learning experiences. By explicitly teaching the skills necessary for academic dialogue, educators empower students to engage deeply with texts, think critically, and articulate their ideas with clarity and confidence. These discussions not only enhance comprehension and analytical abilities but also foster a collaborative classroom environment where diverse perspectives are valued and explored.

Implementing the strategies and techniques discussed in this chapter requires dedication and consistent practice. However, the benefits are profound. Students who are adept at participating in academic conversations are better equipped to tackle complex texts, engage in thoughtful debates, and develop a lifelong love for learning. They learn to listen actively, respect differing viewpoints, and construct well-reasoned arguments, skills that are essential not only in academic settings but in their future personal and professional lives as well.

In essence, by prioritizing and cultivating meaningful text discussions, educators lay the groundwork for a rich and dynamic learning environment. This chapter has provided a comprehensive guide to achieving this goal, from understanding the foundational differences between social and academic conversations to implementing practical activities that encourage deeper engagement. As you move forward, remember that fostering these skills is an ongoing process, one that will continue to evolve and grow as your students develop into confident, critical thinkers and communicators. Consider these questions as you ponder this issue more and try the following lessons.

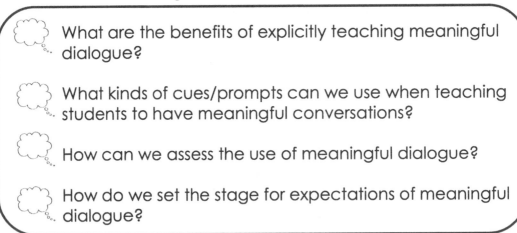

End of Chapter Reflection Questions:

- What are the benefits of explicitly teaching meaningful dialogue?
- What kinds of cues/prompts can we use when teaching students to have meaningful conversations?
- How can we assess the use of meaningful dialogue?
- How do we set the stage for expectations of meaningful dialogue?

Lessons to Try

Remember that you can access the complete lessons for free at `http://www.cieraharristeaching.com/ttrlessons` using the passcode: `literacy for all`.

"Successful Conversations" Lesson

The lesson plan titled "Successful Conversations" is designed to help students develop and refine their conversational skills. The primary objective is for students to understand what constitutes a conversation and to practice the various components that make up effective communication. The lesson begins with a demonstration by the teacher, who models a conversation with a volunteer student on a fun topic. This interactive approach helps students visualize the conversation process and recognize the different elements involved, such as asking questions, making extensions, and agreeing or disagreeing.

The importance of this lesson lies in its focus on explicit teaching of conversational skills, which are often overlooked in academic settings. By breaking down a conversation into manageable parts, students can better understand and practice each component. This method not only improves their ability to hold meaningful discussions but also enhances their overall communication skills, which are crucial for academic success and personal interactions. The use of anchor charts, bookmarks, and discussion cards further reinforces these concepts, providing students with tangible tools to aid their learning.

One of the key benefits of teaching this lesson is that it equips students with the ability to engage in productive conversations across various contexts, both in and out of the classroom. The practice activities, such as rolling a die to determine the next conversational move, make learning interactive and enjoyable, fostering a positive classroom environment. Additionally, the lesson's adaptability for virtual learning ensures that students can develop these essential skills regardless of the setting.

Quick Tip: Encourage students to practice these skills at home with family members, helping to reinforce their learning and build confidence in their conversational abilities.

"Let's Talk Text" Lesson

The "Let's Talk Text" lesson plan aims to enhance students' ability to engage in meaningful conversations about texts they read. The lesson integrates the fundamentals of successful conversations with textual discussions, providing students with a framework to articulate their thoughts and deepen their comprehension. The lesson begins with a modeled conversation between the teacher and a student about a recently read book, emphasizing conversational components such as questioning, reacting, and agreeing. Following this, students analyze the conversation to identify the discussed parts of the book, promoting an understanding that discussing texts helps to process, clarify, and expand their understanding through shared insights.

The importance of this lesson lies in its ability to foster critical thinking and comprehension among students. By encouraging students to talk about texts, the lesson helps them to not only retain information but also to engage with it on a deeper level. This process allows students to consider multiple perspectives, ask questions, and make connections between the text and their own experiences. These discussions can significantly enhance their comprehension and retention of the material, making reading a more interactive and reflective activity. Furthermore, the lesson's emphasis on there being no "right or wrong" way to discuss a text helps to create a safe and open environment for students to express their thoughts and ideas.

Teaching this lesson offers numerous benefits. It equips students with conversational skills that are essential for academic success and lifelong learning. By practicing how to articulate their thoughts and listen to others, students develop important communication skills. Additionally, the lesson's structure supports differentiated learning by allowing students to express their understanding in various ways, whether through verbal discussion, written notes, or illustrations. This inclusivity ensures that all students, regardless of their learning style, can participate and benefit from the lesson.

 Quick Tip Consistently model enthusiastic and active participation in discussions, as this sets a positive example and encourages students to engage more fully in their conversations about texts.

"Read, Think, Talk" Lesson

The lesson plan "Read Think Talk" aims to enhance students' ability to have text-based conversations by integrating metacognition, journal writing, and active thinking. The lesson begins with a review of conversational skills and the importance of thinking while reading. Students are guided to stop at predetermined points in a text to reflect and discuss their thoughts. This structured approach helps students practice identifying key moments in the text where they need to pause and process the information, fostering deeper comprehension and engagement with the material.

This lesson is crucial as it addresses a common issue where students tend to read passively without reflecting on the content. By incorporating regular pauses for reflection, students learn to engage actively with the text, enhancing their understanding and retention. The exercise also emphasizes the importance of metacognition, encouraging students to be aware of their thought processes while reading. This awareness not only improves reading comprehension but also promotes critical thinking skills, which are essential for academic success across subjects.

Furthermore, the lesson fosters collaborative learning by having students work in groups to discuss the text and rate each other's conversational skills. This peer interaction helps students learn from one another, develop communication skills, and build confidence in expressing their ideas. The use of visual aids like pom-pom balls to track participation ensures that all students are actively involved in the conversation, creating an inclusive learning environment. By practicing these skills in a structured and supportive setting, students are better prepared for more advanced academic discussions.

Quick Tip

To ensure a smooth and effective lesson, model the process thoroughly before having students practice in groups. Demonstrating how to stop and reflect at key points in the text and showing how to use the conversation checklists will provide students with a clear example to follow. This preparation will help them feel more confident and engaged during their discussions.

CHAPTER 10

FOSTERING CRITICAL THINKING IN THE CLASSROOM

Communication & Critical Thinking

Highlight the importance of meaningful dialogue about texts and the development of critical thinking skills in reading.

In today's rapidly evolving world, the ability to think critically is not just an academic skill but a vital life competency. Critical thinking empowers students to engage deeply with content, analyze information, and make reasoned judgments. "Critical thinking is more than a set of subskills. It is a stance or disposition of being actively reflective (Dewey, 1933) and, therefore, is situated in a constructivist theoretical perspective. Dewey called this disposition reflective thinking, in which learners actively persist in careful consideration of evidence and rationale to establish a belief."[1] It is the bedrock of informed decision-making, enabling students to navigate complex problems both in their academic pursuits and daily lives.

---

[1] Pilgrim, J., Vasinda, S., Bledsoe, C., and Martinez, E. (2019). Critical thinking is critical. *The Reading Teacher* 73 (1): 85–93.

This chapter delves into the crucial role of critical thinking in education, providing practical strategies for teachers to foster these skills in the classroom. It explores how critical thinking enhances students' ability to evaluate evidence, synthesize information, and draw well-informed conclusions—skills essential for academic success and real-world problem-solving.

As you journey through this chapter, you'll gain insights into the key components of critical thinking, effective strategies to promote these skills among elementary students, and techniques to design classroom activities that encourage deep engagement with texts and complex ideas. Additionally, you will read about methods for assessing and evaluating students' critical thinking abilities and explore ways to integrate critical thinking into various subject areas and curriculum standards.

By the end of this chapter, you will be equipped with the knowledge and tools to cultivate a classroom environment that nurtures critical thinkers, preparing your students to excel academically and thrive in an increasingly complex world. Get ready to embark on this journey so you can understand and implement the essence of critical thinking in the educational landscape.

Chapter 10 Objectives

 The readers will understand the key components of critical thinking and their significance in the learning process.

 The readers will learn effective strategies to promote critical thinking skills among elementary students.

 The readers will be able to design classroom activities that encourage deep engagement with texts and complex ideas.

 The readers will develop techniques for assessing and evaluating students' critical thinking abilities.

 The readers will explore integrating critical thinking into various subject areas and curriculum standards.

What Is Critical Thinking?

Critical thinking actively engages with information to analyze, evaluate, and synthesize it. This process involves rigorous questioning, careful assessment of evidence, and thoughtful reflection. "We understand critical thinking to be purposeful, self-regulatory judgment which results in interpretation, analysis, evaluation, and inference, as well as explanation of the evidential, conceptual, methodological, criteriological, or contextual considerations upon which that judgment is based."[2] Unlike rote memorization or passive learning, critical thinking requires individuals to actively interrogate information, identify biases, and draw connections between disparate pieces of information. It is a disciplined approach to processing information essential for deep understanding and effective problem-solving.

The essence of critical thinking lies in its systematic approach. Critical thinkers do not accept information at face value. Instead, they dialogue with the content, asking probing questions and seeking clarification. They aim to understand the underlying principles and assumptions that shape the information they encounter, leading to more nuanced and well-informed conclusions.

Fostering critical thinking in the classroom is not merely an academic exercise; it is a crucial life skill that prepares students for the complexities of the modern world.

Definition: critical thinking

Critical thinking is the disciplined process of actively analyzing, evaluating, and synthesizing information to form reasoned judgments. It involves questioning assumptions, assessing evidence, and making well-informed decisions.

---

[2] Abrami, P., Bernard, R., Borokhovski, E. et al. (2015). Strategies for teaching students to think critically: a meta-analysis. *Review of Educational Research* 85 (2): 275–314.

Critical thinking encompasses a variety of cognitive skills and dispositions, each contributing to a more thorough and reflective understanding of information. Four of the critical components include:

- **Analysis:** Breaking down information into constituent parts to understand its structure and meaning. For example, a critical thinker identifies the main argument, supporting evidence, and underlying assumptions when reading a text.
- **Evaluation:** Assessing information and arguments' credibility, relevance, and validity. This includes questioning the sources' reliability and the evidence's strength.
- **Synthesis:** Integrating information from multiple sources to create a coherent understanding. Critical thinkers connect new information with prior knowledge, identifying patterns and relationships.
- **Inference:** Drawing logical conclusions based on the analyzed and evaluated information, leading to reasoned judgments and decisions.

These skills are interrelated and often overlap in practice. For example, analyzing a text may involve evaluating its sources, and synthesizing information from multiple texts requires analysis and evaluation. These skills enable critical thinkers to navigate complex information landscapes with discernment and clarity.

Consider the four components of critical thinking (analysis, evaluation, synthesis, and inference). Which of these skills do your students tend to struggle with the most? How can you modify your instruction to better support their development in this area?

Importance of Critical Thinking in Academic and Real-World Contexts

Critical thinking is indispensable in academic settings. It enables students to move beyond surface-level understanding and engage deeply with content. A study titled

"Critical Thinking Skills and Their Impacts on Elementary School Students" published in the *Malaysian Journal of Learning and Instruction* in 2021 examined the critical thinking skills of fifth-grade students. The research found that while many students struggled with critical thinking tasks initially, there was evidence that critical thinking interventions helped improve their ability to analyze, interpret, and make inferences. However, it also noted that students often relied on memorization rather than understanding, which hindered their deep engagement with the content. The study emphasized the importance of systematic instruction and practice in fostering these critical thinking skills, showing that targeted strategies can help students move beyond surface-level learning.[3]

For instance, critical thinking allows students to evaluate primary sources, understand differing perspectives, and construct well-supported arguments in subjects like history and science. This depth of engagement is crucial for mastering advanced coursework and contributing meaningfully to academic discussions.

Beyond academics, critical thinking is equally vital in everyday life. It equips individuals with the tools to make informed decisions, solve problems, and navigate the complexities of modern society. A study conducted by Butler in 2024 emphasizes the importance of critical thinking in everyday decision-making, demonstrating how these skills enable individuals to process information effectively and solve problems creatively. The study highlights that fostering critical thinking in students from an early age allows them to apply these abilities in various contexts, ranging from personal decisions to navigating societal complexities. By promoting critical thinking through structured assessments and educational strategies, students are better prepared to engage with the challenges of modern life.[4] Whether evaluating news stories, making financial decisions, or understanding social and political issues, critical thinking helps individuals distinguish between credible information and misinformation. This ability to critically assess information is essential in a world where the volume of available information is vast and varied in quality.

---

[3] Sarwanto, S., Widi, L.E.F., and Chumdari (2021). Critical thinking skills and their impacts on elementary school students. *Malaysian Journal of Learning and Instruction* 18 (2): 161–187.

[4] Butler, H. (2024). Predicting everyday critical thinking: a review of critical thinking assessments. *Journal of Intelligence* 12: 16.

Levels of Thinking

Understanding the progression toward critical thinking can be facilitated by considering different levels of thinking, each with specific characteristics and activities.

Levels of Critical Thinking

Level	Definition	What Readers Do
Remembering	Recall basic facts and concepts	Memorize definitions, list main characters, recall dates and events
Understanding	Comprehend and interpret information	Summarize paragraphs, explain concepts in own words, describe sequences
Applying	Use information in new contexts	Solve problems using learned concepts, apply theories to real-life examples
Analyzing	Break down information into parts and understand relationships	Identify arguments, distinguish between facts and opinions, analyze text structure
Evaluating	Judge the value and credibility of information	Assess the reliability of sources, critique arguments, compare different viewpoints
Creating	Combine information to form new ideas	Write original essays, design experiments, develop new solutions
Critical Thinking	Integrate analysis, evaluation, and synthesis to form reasoned judgments	Question assumptions, evaluate evidence, synthesize multiple perspectives, reflect on biases

At each level, readers engage with texts in increasingly sophisticated ways. Critical thinking represents the highest level, where readers understand and use information and critically assess and integrate it to form well-reasoned conclusions.

What Readers Who Think Critically Do

Readers who engage in critical thinking exhibit several distinctive behaviors, mainly when dealing with complex texts:

- **Question assumptions:** They do not take information at face value. Instead, they scrutinize the text's assumptions, asking why the author holds particular views and what evidence supports them.
- **Evaluate evidence:** Critical readers assess the quality and relevance of the evidence presented. They consider the credibility of sources, data validity, and arguments' logical coherence.
- **Synthesize information:** They integrate information from various texts and sources, identifying patterns and drawing connections. This holistic approach allows them to build a more comprehensive understanding of the topic.
- **Reflect:** They reflect, considering how their beliefs and biases influence their interpretation of the text. This reflective practice helps them remain open to new perspectives and adjust their views based on new information.
- **React thoughtfully:** Critical readers actively engage with the text, participating in discussions, asking probing questions, and presenting well-reasoned arguments. They are not passive consumers of information but active participants in the learning process.

Sample Questions That Promote Critical Thinking

Promoting critical thinking in the classroom involves asking questions that encourage deeper engagement with the text. Here are examples of questions that foster critical thinking versus those that do not:

Questions That Promote Critical Thinking	Questions That Do Not Promote Critical Thinking
✓ "What is the author's main argument, and how is it supported?"	• "What is the main idea of the paragraph?"
✓ "How does this text relate to other materials we have studied?"	• "Who is the main character in the story?"
✓ "What assumptions does the author make, and are they justified?"	• "What happened first in the story?"
✓ "What are the strengths and weaknesses of the author's argument?"	• "What are the key points mentioned?"
✓ "How might this information change if viewed from a different perspective?"	

The key difference lies in the required depth of engagement. Critical thinking questions demand analysis, evaluation, and synthesis, while surface-level questions focus on recall and basic comprehension. "By asking questions that probe who is speaking, to whom, about what, and to what end, as well as how the author presents information, infuses perspective, structures argument, and positions readers, teachers can engage students in critical reading that helps them gain a better understanding of text and its subtext, including the author's motives and perspective, the ideologies underpinning the text, the constructedness of knowledge, and the politics of representation."[5]

---

[5] Fang, Z. (2016). Teaching close reading with complex texts across content areas. *National Council of teachers of English* 51 (1): 106–116.

Importance of Critical Thinking with Complex Texts in State Standards

Many state standards now emphasize the importance of critical thinking, mainly when dealing with complex texts. These standards recognize that students must develop the ability to engage deeply with challenging materials to succeed academically and in real-world scenarios. Critical thinking skills are integral to understanding and analyzing complex texts, and they are often featured in state assessments and curricula.

Teachers can help students meet these rigorous standards by incorporating critical thinking into reading instruction. This involves teaching students to comprehend texts and evaluate and synthesize information critically. Such skills are essential for college and career readiness, preparing students to navigate a world where the ability to think critically is increasingly essential.

Understanding and teaching critical thinking is essential for educators. It involves fostering a mindset that actively questions, evaluates, and synthesizes information. By focusing on higher-order thinking skills, teachers can effectively prepare students to navigate complex texts and real-world challenges. "A variety of critical thinking skills (both generic and content specific) and dispositions can develop in students through instruction at all educational levels and across all disciplinary areas using a number of effective strategies."[6] Critical thinking is not just an academic skill but a necessary tool for informed and engaged citizenship. Students can develop into critical thinkers capable of thoughtful analysis and reasoned decision-making through deliberate instruction and practice. This comprehensive approach to reading instruction equips students with the skills they need to succeed in academic and real-world contexts.

---

[6] Abrami, P., Bernard, R., Borokhovski, E. et al. (2015). Strategies for teaching students to think critically: a meta-analysis. *American Educational Research Association* 85 (2): 275–314.

Deep Dive into the Four Components of Critical Thinking

Critical thinking comprises several key components, with analysis, evaluation, synthesis, and inference among the most crucial. These skills are considered essential thinking skills because they involve higher-order thinking processes beyond simple recall or understanding. They require an active engagement with information, questioning its validity and integrating it with prior knowledge to draw well-reasoned conclusions. Each component is vital in developing a comprehensive and nuanced understanding of complex texts and real-world situations.

Analysis from a Teacher's Perspective

Teachers play a critical role in fostering students' analytical skills by teaching them how to break down complex texts and information into their constituent parts. This involves guiding students to identify the main argument, supporting evidence, and any underlying assumptions within a text. Teachers might employ strategies such as highlighting essential text parts, using graphic organizers, asking probing questions, and encouraging students to delve deeper into the material. For instance, during a lesson on persuasive writing, a teacher might ask students to identify the thesis statement, the main points supporting it, and any rhetorical devices used by the author. A study on "Teachers' Role in Fostering Reading Skill" (Jose & Raja, 2011) underscores how educators play a crucial role in developing students' analytical abilities by teaching them to dissect complex texts. Teachers guide students in breaking down texts into their constituent parts, helping them challenge assumptions, evaluate arguments, and engage critically with the material. This type of instruction not only enhances reading comprehension but also prepares students to apply these skills in analyzing real-world information. Teachers achieve this through structured techniques like the SQ3R method (Survey, Question, Read, Recite, Review) and critical reading strategies, encouraging students to move beyond surface-level reading to interpret and evaluate the deeper meaning and implications of the text.[7]

---

[7] Jose, G. and Raja, B. (2011). Teachers' role in fostering reading skill: effective and successful reading. *i-manager's Journal on English Language Teaching* 1 (4): 1–10.

> **The SQ3R Method**
>
> The SQ3R method, created by Francis P. Robinson, helps students engage deeply with texts. It stands for Survey, Question, Read, Recite, and Review:
>
> - **Survey:** Skim headings and summaries to get a big-picture view.
> - **Question:** Turn headings into questions to focus your reading.
> - **Read:** Actively read, looking for answers to your questions.
> - **Recite:** Summarize the material in your own words to reinforce understanding.
> - **Review:** Regularly revisit the material to solidify knowledge.
>
> This approach boosts comprehension and retention by encouraging active engagement with the text.

Analysis from a Reader's Perspective

From the reader's perspective, analysis involves actively engaging with the text to dissect and understand its structure and meaning. In a study published in *Reading and Writing* in 2023, researchers explored how students comprehend and evaluate argumentative texts. The study highlighted that analytical reading strategies, such as identifying main ideas, supporting details, and the text's argumentative structure, are crucial for understanding complex texts. This kind of analysis enables students to grasp both what the text says and how it conveys its message, making it especially important for scientific and argumentative readings. The ability to engage critically with the text and understand its structure leads to improved comprehension and the ability to assess the quality of the arguments presented.[8] Readers identify the main ideas, supporting details, and hidden assumptions that might influence the text's message. This process enables readers to grasp what the text says and how it conveys its message. Analytical reading is crucial when dealing with

---

[8] Diakidoy, I.N., Ioannou, M.C., and Christodoulou, S.A. (2017). Reading argumentative texts: comprehension and evaluation goals and outcomes. *Reading and Writing* 30: 1869–1890. https://doi.org/10.1007/s11145-017-9757-x.

argumentative texts, scientific reports, or any material that requires a detailed understanding of its components. For example, when reading a scientific article, a reader might identify the research question, hypothesis, methodology, results, and conclusions, analyzing how each part contributes to the overall study.

> **Prerequisite Skills for Analysis**
> - Basic comprehension skills to understand the text
> - Ability to identify and understand main ideas and details
> - Familiarity with logical structures and argumentation

When and Why a Reader Utilizes Analysis

Readers utilize analysis when they need to understand an argument's structure or a complex concept's components. This skill is crucial for writing essays, participating in discussions, and solving problems that require a deep understanding of the material. Analysis helps readers to break down complex information into manageable parts, making it easier to understand and evaluate.

Evaluation from a Teacher's Perspective

Teachers help students develop evaluative skills by teaching them how to assess the credibility and relevance of information. This involves guiding students to question the reliability of sources, examine the strength of evidence, and consider the significance of the information to the topic at hand. Teachers might use activities such as comparing different sources, examining biases, and evaluating the logical coherence of arguments. For instance, a teacher might present students with multiple articles on a controversial topic and ask them to evaluate each source's credibility and the argument's validity.

Evaluation from a Reader's Perspective

Readers engage in evaluation by critically assessing the information they encounter. This involves questioning the reliability of sources, examining the strength of the evidence provided, and considering the relevance of the information to the topic. "Reading from a critical perspective involves thinking beyond the text to understand issues such as why the author wrote about a particular topic, wrote from a particular perspective, or chose to include some ideas about the topic and exclude others (McLaughlin & DeVoogd, 2011, 2018). It requires both the ability and the deliberate inclination to think critically—to analyze and evaluate all types of texts, meaningfully question their origin and purpose, and take action."[9] Evaluative reading is essential when readers need to determine the trustworthiness of information, such as when conducting research, making decisions based on multiple sources, or forming opinions on controversial issues. For example, when reading news articles, a critical reader might evaluate the cited sources, check for bias, and assess whether the evidence supports the claims.

> **Prerequisite Skills for Evaluation**
> - Analytical skills to break down information
> - Understanding of credibility indicators (e.g., author's expertise, publication source)
> - Knowledge of logical fallacies and biases

When and Why a Reader Utilizes Evaluation

Evaluation is used when readers need to determine the trustworthiness of information. It ensures that the information used is credible and relevant. This skill is vital for making informed decisions, particularly in situations where the quality of information can significantly impact outcomes, such as in academic research, business decisions, or personal choices.

Synthesis from a Teacher's Perspective

Teachers encourage students to develop synthesis skills by integrating information from various sources to form a cohesive understanding. This involves guiding students to

---

[9] McLaughlin, M. and Devoogd, G. (2020). Critical expressionism. *International Literacy Association and Wiley* 73 (5): 587–595.

combine insights from different texts, identify patterns, and draw connections. Teachers might use concept mapping, comparative analysis, and project-based learning to help students practice synthesis. For example, in a literature class, a teacher might ask students to synthesize themes from multiple novels to discuss a broader literary trend.

Synthesis from a Reader's Perspective

Readers engage in synthesis by combining information from multiple sources to create a new understanding. This process involves connecting new information with prior knowledge, identifying patterns, and integrating diverse perspectives. A study published in *Educational Psychology Review* highlights how students are able to connect new information with prior knowledge, identify patterns, and integrate diverse perspectives. This synthesis process, particularly in reading multiple documents, helps students construct more elaborate and well-organized texts, which enhances their comprehension and critical thinking. The study also emphasizes the importance of selecting relevant information and organizing it coherently, which contributes to a deeper understanding of the subject matter.[10] Synthesis is crucial when readers must develop a comprehensive understanding of a topic, such as during research projects, developing arguments, or creating new ideas or solutions. For instance, a student writing a research paper might synthesize information from various academic articles to construct a well-rounded argument.

Prerequisite Skills for Synthesis
- Analytical skills to understand different sources
- Comprehension skills to grasp the meaning of each source
- Creative thinking to combine information in new ways

---

[10] Barzilai, S., Zohar, A.R., and Mor-Hogani, S. (2018). Promoting integration of multiple texts: a review of instructional approaches and practices. *Educational Psychology Review* 30: 973–999.

When and Why a Reader Utilizes Synthesis

Synthesis is used when readers need to develop a comprehensive understanding of a topic. It allows them to see the bigger picture and make connections across different areas of knowledge. This skill is essential in academic writing, where synthesizing information from various sources can produce more robust and well-supported arguments. A peer-reviewed study titled "Does Text Complexity Matter in the Elementary Grades? A Research Synthesis of Text Difficulty and Elementary Students' Reading Fluency and Comprehension" from 2018 provides strong evidence for the role of synthesis in developing a comprehensive understanding of reading materials. The research highlights how students engage with increasingly complex texts by combining new information with prior knowledge. This synthesis allows them to connect various text elements, like main ideas and supporting details, which leads to improved comprehension, especially as text complexity increases.[11]

Inference from a Teacher's Perspective

Teachers help students develop inferencing skills by drawing logical conclusions based on analyzed and evaluated information. This involves guiding students to make predictions, form hypotheses, and draw conclusions based on evidence. Teachers might use prediction, hypothesis testing, and scenario analysis exercises to develop students' inferencing skills. For example, in a science class, a teacher might ask students to infer the results of an experiment based on the data collected.

Inference from a Reader's Perspective

Readers make inferences by drawing logical conclusions from the information provided, filling in gaps, and making predictions based on the evidence and their understanding. This process involves using context clues and prior knowledge to make sense of

---

[11] Amendum, S.J., Conradi, K., and Hiebert, E. (2018). Does text complexity matter in the elementary grades? A research synthesis of text difficulty and elementary students' reading fluency and comprehension. *Educational Psychology Review* 30: 121–151.

implicit information. Inferencing is crucial for interpreting themes, predicting outcomes, and understanding underlying meanings. For instance, when reading a mystery novel, a reader might infer the culprit's identity based on clues provided throughout the story.

> **Prerequisite Skills for Inference**
> ❖ Analytical skills to understand the text
> ❖ Evaluative skills to assess the quality of information
> ❖ Critical thinking to draw logical conclusions

When and Why a Reader Utilizes Inference

Inference is used when readers need to go beyond the explicit information provided. It helps readers make sense of complex texts and draw deeper insights. This skill is essential for interpreting literature, making predictions, and understanding implicit messages in various forms of communication.

Levels of Critical Thinking Components

Component	Basic Level	Intermediate Level	Advanced Level
Analysis	Identifying main ideas and details	Recognizing arguments and assumptions	Deconstructing complex arguments and underlying assumptions
Evaluation	Questioning source reliability	Comparing multiple sources	Critiquing the strength of arguments and evidence
Synthesis	Combining information from simple texts	Integrating insights from various texts	Creating new perspectives and solutions
Inference	Making simple predictions	Drawing logical conclusions	Formulation hypotheses and theories based on evidence

Levels of Critical Thinking

Understanding the levels of critical thinking components is essential for teachers because it provides a structured framework for progressively developing and assessing students' thinking skills. By recognizing the different stages—basic, intermediate, and advanced—teachers can tailor their instruction to meet students where they are and guide them toward more sophisticated levels of thinking. This awareness helps design activities and assessments that are appropriately challenging, ensuring that all students are engaged and supported in their cognitive development.

Knowing the levels also allows teachers to scaffold instruction effectively. For example, a teacher can start with tasks that focus on identifying main ideas and details (primary analysis) before moving on to more complex tasks like deconstructing arguments and assumptions (advanced analysis). This progression helps students build a solid foundation of critical thinking skills and gradually enhances their ability to handle more complex and abstract concepts. Ultimately, this structured approach fosters a classroom environment where critical thinking is continuously developed and valued, preparing students for academic success and real-world challenges.

Understanding and teaching the components of critical thinking—analysis, evaluation, synthesis, and inference—requires a deep engagement with the material. Teachers must model these processes and provide opportunities for practice at varying levels of complexity. By developing these skills, students can become adept at navigating complex texts and making well-reasoned judgments, preparing them for academic success and informed citizenship. These skills are essential for academic achievement and personal and professional success in a world that increasingly values critical thinking and problem-solving abilities.

Strategies for Developing Critical Thinking Skills

Three of the most effective strategies for developing critical thinking skills in students are through questioning techniques, text analysis, and evaluating information. Questioning techniques involve asking thoughtful, open-ended questions that encourage students to think deeply and engage with the material more profoundly. Text analysis requires students to break down and understand the components of what they read, including identifying main arguments, supporting evidence, and underlying assumptions. Evaluating information involves assessing the credibility and relevance of sources, comparing different perspectives, and making reasoned judgments based on the evidence provided.

- **Questioning techniques:** Asking thoughtful, open-ended questions that encourage deep thinking and active engagement with the material.
- **Text analysis:** Breaking down and understanding the components of a text, including identifying main arguments, supporting evidence, and underlying assumptions.
- **Evaluating information:** Assessing the credibility and relevance of sources, comparing different perspectives, and making reasoned judgments based on the evidence provided.

These strategies support critical thinking by pushing students beyond surface-level understanding and encouraging them to engage with the material actively. Questioning techniques foster curiosity and allow students to explore various angles of a topic. "Higher order questioning requires students to think at a deeper level and to elaborate on their oral and written responses to literature."[12] Text analysis helps them see the structure and purpose of a piece, leading to a deeper understanding of the content. Evaluating information teaches students to discern the sources they encounter and make informed decisions based on evidence.

Schema and metacognition are crucial in supporting these strategies. When students activate their schema, they can better understand and relate to the content. Metacognition, or "thinking about thinking," involves students reflecting on their thought processes. This self-awareness helps them become more effective learners, as they can identify strategies that work best for them and adjust their approach as needed.

Teachers must intentionally utilize these strategies to provide opportunities for students to think critically, as critical thinking does not come naturally. It requires deliberate practice and guidance. For example, in questioning, it is almost a waste of time to ask

---

[12] Peterson, D. and Taylor, B. (2012). Using higher order questioning to accelerate students' growth in reading. *International Literacy Association and Wiley* 65 (5): 295–304.

questions where everyone raises their hands because it indicates that the questions are not challenging enough. If every student knows the answer, the questions are not deep enough to stimulate critical thinking. The ability of students to think critically directly reflects a teacher's ability to ask the right questions and guide them through the process of finding the answers. By crafting questions that require analysis, evaluation, and synthesis, teachers can help students develop these essential skills and become more thoughtful and engaged learners.

Questioning Techniques

Knowing how to ask critical thinking questions is crucial for fostering a classroom environment that promotes deep learning and intellectual engagement. Critical thinking questions are designed to push students beyond mere recall of facts, prompting them to analyze, evaluate, and synthesize information. However, crafting these questions requires intentional preparation. Teachers must pre-read the texts and carefully develop questions to encourage students to think deeply and engage with the material on a higher level. A 2011 study in *Learning Environments Research* highlights that a well-designed classroom environment that fosters critical thinking begins with teachers crafting questions that engage students in higher-order thinking. This preparation not only enhances the quality of classroom discussions but also supports students' development of metacognitive skills and intellectual engagement. By preparing these questions in advance, teachers ensure that their lessons are more effective at promoting deep thinking and reflection.[13] This preparation ensures that questions are aligned with learning objectives and can elicit thoughtful responses that reflect a deeper understanding of the text.

Critical thinking instruction necessitates thorough preparation. Teachers should read the text multiple times to identify key themes, arguments, and potential areas for deeper exploration. This allows them to craft questions that challenge students to make connections, draw inferences, and critically assess the information presented. For instance, instead of asking a simple factual question like, "What happened to the main character?"

---

[13] Mathews, S.R. and Lowe, K. (2011). Classroom environments that foster a disposition for critical thinking. *Learning Environments Research* 14: 59–73.

a teacher might ask, "What motivates the main character's actions, and how do these motivations reflect broader themes in the story?" Such questions require students to go beyond the surface level and consider the underlying elements that drive the narrative.

Teachers can determine if a question supports critical thinking by evaluating whether it requires students to engage in higher-order thinking processes. Questions that promote critical thinking often cannot be answered with a simple "yes," "no," or a straightforward fact. They typically require analysis, evaluation, synthesis, or inference. Teachers can use frameworks like Bloom's Taxonomy to ensure their questions target various cognitive levels, from understanding and applying to analyzing and creating. Additionally, practical critical thinking questions often lead to more questions, encouraging a continuous cycle of inquiry and exploration. By intentionally crafting and preparing these questions in advance, teachers create opportunities for students to engage deeply with the text, fostering an environment where critical thinking thrives.

Open-ended discussions involve collaborative, in-depth talks on various aspects of the text. Teachers can ask broad questions that allow students to explore themes, characters, and plots in detail. This technique encourages deep thinking, multiple viewpoints, and extended dialogue. "These student-led conversations invite open participation and allow students to construct their own interpretations of texts."[14] For example, instead of focusing on factual questions, a teacher might ask, "What themes do you think are most important in this story, and why?" Allowing students to lead the discussion further enhances their engagement and critical thinking.

Encouraging Multiple Perspectives is about considering different viewpoints on an issue or event in the text. Teachers can ask students how different characters

---

[14] Peterson, D.S. (2019). Engaging elementary students in higher order talk and writing about text. *Journal of Early Childhood Literacy* 19 (1): 34–54.

might view a situation differently, which broadens their understanding and appreciation of diverse viewpoints. Role-playing different characters' perspectives can make this exercise more engaging and insightful. For instance, a teacher might ask, "How might the story be different if told from another character's perspective?"

Incorporating Ethical Dilemmas involves presenting moral or ethical questions related to the text. Teachers can pose dilemmas characters face and ask students to debate potential solutions, engaging them in moral reasoning and ethical decision-making. Linking these dilemmas to real-world issues makes the discussion more relevant and impactful. For example, "Was the character justified in lying to protect their friend? Why or why not?"

Facilitating Prediction Questions asks students to predict what might happen next in the text based on their current knowledge and text clues. This promotes inference and logical reasoning. Teachers might ask students questions like, "What do you think will happen next?" This encourages students to use context clues and their understanding of the story to make informed predictions.

Engaging in Reflective Questions involves questions that make students reflect on their thinking process. Teachers can ask students how their understanding of the text evolved as they read. This develops self-awareness and metacognitive skills. Encouraging students to journal their reflections can provide deeper insights into their thinking. For instance, "How did your understanding of the theme change as you read the story?"

Encouraging Justification of Opinions asks students to back up their opinions with evidence from the text. Teachers can ask students to provide textual evidence to support their views, ensuring their opinions are grounded in critical analysis. Modeling how to find and cite evidence is crucial. For example, "Why do you think this character is the story's hero? Can you provide specific examples from the text to support your opinion?"

Using Comparative Questions involves comparing and contrasting elements within or between texts. Teachers can ask students to compare themes, characters, or settings, enhancing analytical skills by identifying similarities and differences. Using Venn diagrams for visual comparison can help students organize their thoughts. For instance, "How does the conflict in this story compare to the conflict in another book we read?"

Promoting Hypothetical Thinking explores "what if" scenarios related to the text. Teachers can pose hypothetical changes to the plot or character actions, encouraging creative thinking and exploring possibilities. Asking questions like, "What if the character had made a different decision? How might the story have changed?" stimulates students' imaginations and critical thinking skills.

Incorporating Bloom's Taxonomy or DOK Level Questions means structuring questions to target various cognitive levels. Teachers can design questions that progress from recall to creation based on Bloom's levels, ensuring engagement with material at multiple levels of complexity. They can start with simple questions and move to more complex ones, such as "Can you summarize the main events of this chapter?" or "How would you rewrite the ending of the story?"

Socratic Questioning involves asking a series of thoughtful, probing questions to explore ideas deeply. Teachers use follow-up questions to examine students' assumptions and reasoning. This technique encourages deep analysis and critical examination. Active listening and frequently asking "Why?" can help delve deeper into students' thought processes.

Encouraging Students to Ask Their Questions teaches students to formulate their questions about the text. This fosters curiosity and ownership of learning. Teachers can start by modeling good questions and gradually guiding students to brainstorm and pose questions. For example, "What questions do you have about the motivations of the characters in this story?"

Teachers can create a dynamic and engaging classroom environment that promotes critical thinking and more profound understanding by integrating these questioning techniques into their instructional practice. These strategies help students understand the text more deeply and develop the ability to think critically and independently about the material.

Quick Tip When planning questions that promote critical thinking, try to use Bloom's Taxonomy as a guide. Start with simpler questions and gradually build to more complex ones. For example, begin by asking students to summarize a text (recall), then move on to asking them to compare the text with another (analysis), and finally, challenge them to create their own argument based on the text (synthesis).

From Basic to Critical Thinking

Critical thinking does not develop overnight, even for the best of readers. "Reading comprehension is one of the most complex behaviors that we engage in on a regular basis. Multiple processes that work interactively contribute to extracting and constructing meaning from text."[15] Reading is not merely about decoding the words on a page; it involves actively engaging with and thinking about the text. This deeper level of engagement requires time and deliberate practice. Even the poorest readers can be exceptional thinkers if they are guided correctly. For elementary-aged students, who are still developing their cognitive abilities, guiding them into critical thinking through structured techniques like tiered questioning is crucial.

Studies on Tiered Questioning

Tiered questioning is a powerful strategy that can be employed in two ways. First, teachers can start with simple questions and gradually move to more advanced ones, providing a scaffold supporting students' thinking as they progress toward answering critical thinking questions. A study was conducted in 2003 where the

---

[15] Hennessy, N.L. (2021). *The Reading Comprehension Blueprint: Helping Students Make Meaning from Text*. Paul H. Brookes Publishing Co.

researchers investigated the effectiveness of teaching higher-order thinking skills through tiered questioning strategies in science classes involving elementary and intermediate-aged students, including low-achieving learners. The study implemented a teaching approach where teachers started with simple, factual questions and gradually progressed to more complex, analytical ones. This method provided a scaffold that supported students as they developed their thinking skills.

Key findings of the study:

- **Improved critical thinking:** Students exposed to tiered questioning showed significant improvement in their ability to analyze, evaluate, and synthesize information.
- **Enhanced engagement:** The gradual increase in question complexity kept students engaged and allowed them to build confidence as they successfully answered simpler questions before tackling more challenging ones.
- **Benefits for all learners:** Notably, even low-achieving students benefited from this approach, debunking the myth that higher-order thinking skills are only accessible to high-achieving students.

The study demonstrates that tiered questioning effectively scaffolds student thinking, enabling them to progress toward answering critical thinking questions. By starting with simple questions and moving to advanced ones, teachers provide the necessary support for students to develop deeper understanding and engage intellectually with the material.[16]

This method builds confidence and comprehension step-by-step. Alternatively, teachers can pose the critical thinking question at the outset, and if students struggle, rephrase it using more straightforward questions to guide them back up to the original question. This approach helps identify where students might be struggling and provides targeted support to help them reach a deeper understanding.

---

[16] Zohar, A. and Dori, Y. (2003). Higher order thinking skills and low-achieving students: are they mutually exclusive? *The Journal of the Learning Sciences* 12 (2): 145–181.

For tiered questioning to be effective, teachers must understand how to transform simple questions into more complex ones. This progression supports students' cognitive development and builds their confidence in tackling challenging material. Here are a few examples to illustrate this process.

Example 1:

- Simple Question: "What is the main idea of the story?"
- More Advanced Question: "Why is the main idea important to the story?"
- Critical Thinking Question: "How does the story's main idea connect to the real world or other texts you have read?"

Example 2:

- Simple Question: "Who is the protagonist in the story?"
- More Advanced Question: "What challenges does the protagonist face?"
- Critical Thinking Question: "How do the protagonist's challenges reflect larger themes or issues in society?"

Example 3:

- Simple Question: "What happened at the beginning of the story?"
- More Advanced Question: "How did the events at the story's beginning set the stage for the climax?"
- Critical Thinking Question: "In what ways do the events at the beginning of the story influence the overall message or theme?"

By mastering the art of tiered questioning, teachers can support their students on their journeys to becoming deep critical thinkers. This method allows for the gradual development of essential thinking skills, ensuring that all students, regardless of their reading level, can engage deeply with texts and develop their analytical abilities. Through thoughtful and intentional questioning, teachers can transform the reading experience into actively exploring ideas and perspectives, fostering a classroom culture where critical thinking thrives.

Text Analysis

Text analysis examines and breaks down written material to understand its structure, meaning, and purpose. This involves identifying key elements such as a text's main ideas, supporting details, arguments, and assumptions. Text analysis supports critical thinking by encouraging students to engage deeply with the content, question its validity, and draw connections to broader themes or concepts. "Teaching students to become critically literate disrupts the status quo and presents alternative perspectives. It involves teaching students to question texts—texts that they may have previously accepted as truth."[17] It helps students move beyond passive reading to become active participants in their learning, enhancing their comprehension and analytical skills.

The importance of teachers modeling text analysis throughout the year cannot be overstated. A study published in *The Reading Teacher* (2020) emphasizes the importance of teachers consistently modeling text analysis for elementary students. The authors, Schutz and Rainey, highlight how this modeling provides students with a clear framework for engaging critically with texts. When teachers regularly demonstrate how to break down and analyze reading materials, students gain both the skills and confidence needed to approach texts independently. This approach enables them to develop deeper reading comprehension and critical thinking skills over time.

By observing their teachers engaging with complex texts, students internalize strategies such as identifying key ideas, evaluating arguments, and making connections between different parts of a text. This consistent exposure helps students understand not just *what* to think about a text but *how* to think about it, which is crucial for fostering independent analysis skills.[18]

By demonstrating how to dissect and understand complex texts, teachers provide students with a clear framework for approaching reading materials critically. This continuous

---

[17] McLaughlin, M. and DeVoogd, G. (2020). Critical expressionism. *International Literacy Association and Wiley* 73 (5): 587–595.

[18] Schutz, K. and Rainey, E. (2020). Making sense of modeling in elementary literacy instruction. *International Literacy Association and Wiley* 73 (4): 443–451.

modeling helps students develop the necessary skills and confidence to analyze texts independently. Additionally, using complex texts is crucial for deep text analysis. More straightforward texts often lack the depth and richness needed to challenge students and foster critical thinking. Complex texts provide the context and substance for meaningful analysis, pushing students to think more deeply and make more sophisticated inferences.

Text analysis can happen at any grade level, with activities tailored to the student's developmental stages. Even young readers in first and second grade can begin to analyze texts by identifying main ideas and simple arguments. In contrast, older third- through fifth-grade students can tackle more intricate texts and sophisticated analytical tasks. This progressive development ensures that students build a strong foundation in critical thinking that will serve them throughout their academic careers and beyond.

Text Analysis by Grade Level	
Grade Level	**Text Analysis**
1st-2nd Grade	• Identify the main idea of a simple story. • Recognize key details that support the main idea. • Discuss the characters and their actions. • Use pictures and context clues to understand new words.
3rd-4th Grade	• Summarize paragraphs and short texts. • Identify arguments and supporting evidence. • Recognize basic assumptions and biases in a text. • Make simple inferences based on the text. • Compare and contrast characters or events.
5th Grade	• Analyze complex texts to identify themes and central ideas. • Evaluate the credibility of sources and the strength of arguments. • Make detailed inferences and predictions. • Identify and discuss the author's purpose and perspective. • Connect text ideas to broader themes and real-world issues.

By aligning text analysis actions with the appropriate grade levels, teachers can help students progressively develop their critical thinking skills and ability to engage deeply with texts. This structured approach ensures that students build a strong foundation for more sophisticated analytical tasks as they advance in their education.

Close Reading: A Strategy to Support Text Analysis

Close reading is an instructional strategy involving purposeful re-reading and analyzing short and complex texts. It is designed to help students uncover layers of meaning and achieve more profound levels of comprehension. "Close reading provides an exciting and enriching learning experience that can help students grow into proficient readers who are capable of accessing, producing, communicating, evaluating, and renovating knowledge across academic content areas."[19] Close reading involves multiple readings of the same text, each with a specific purpose aligned with the ELA Anchor Standards for Reading. These purposes are:

- Key Ideas and Details
- Craft and Structure
- Integration of Knowledge and Ideas

Through close reading, students engage deeply with the text, noticing additional details and refining their understanding with each successive reading.

First Read: Key Ideas and Details

The first read focuses on understanding the key ideas and details of the text. During this initial reading, students are introduced to the text with minimal activation of prior knowledge, allowing them to form their first impressions. They answer text-dependent questions that help them grasp the "big picture" of what the text says. This step is crucial for building a foundational understanding of the content and context of the text.

Second Read: Craft and Structure

The second read shifts the focus to analyzing the craft and structure of the text. Here, students delve into how the text is constructed and why the author made confident stylistic

---

[19] Fang, Z. (2016). Teaching close reading with complex texts across content areas. *National Council of Teachers of English* 51 (1): 106–116.

and structural choices. They examine vocabulary, sentence structure, and the overall organization of the text. By answering questions related to these aspects, students gain insights into the techniques used by the author to convey meaning and engage the reader.

Third Read: Integration of Knowledge and Ideas

The third and final read aims to integrate knowledge and ideas. Students think more deeply about the text at this stage, becoming "experts" on its content. They synthesize their understanding from the previous reads to interpret the broader significance and implications of the text. Students may answer more complex text-dependent questions or engage in writing prompts that require them to articulate their interpretations and connect the text to other knowledge or experiences.

As students progress through these stages, they analyze the text in various ways, such as annotating with a pencil to mark important ideas and details. Teachers can introduce specific text markings to help students highlight critical concepts, questions, and reflections. This annotation practice not only aids in comprehension but also encourages active engagement with the text.

To effectively implement close reading, it is essential to use complex texts. Head back to Chapter 7 to learn more about text complexity! These texts should possess qualitative measures (e.g., themes, figurative language, literary elements), quantitative measures (e.g., Lexile level, word length, sentence length), and appropriate reader and task considerations (e.g., student's background knowledge, interests, and motivation). Complex texts provide the necessary depth and richness for meaningful text analysis, challenging students to think critically and engage deeply with the material.

> "Disciplinary texts are complex for functionally different reasons (Fang, 2016). Close reading is a potentially powerful tool for understanding the how and why of such complexities and their effects on meaning and understanding."
> *Teaching Close Reading with Complex Texts Across Content Areas*

By incorporating close reading into their instructional practices, teachers can support students' development of critical thinking and text analysis skills. "When implementing close reading, teachers need to attend simultaneously to the reader, the text, the task, and the context, with a specific focus on developing students' understanding of how language and other semiotic resources construct meaning, embed value, and structure."[20] This systematic approach ensures that students engage with texts on multiple levels, enhancing their ability to understand, interpret, and critique complex material. As students become more adept at close reading, they are better prepared for the academic challenges ahead and equipped with the analytical tools necessary for lifelong learning.

Three Tips for Incorporating Close Reading

The purpose of close reading is to deepen students' understanding of a text by focusing on specific elements with each read. This structured approach allows students to engage with the material at a more meaningful level, moving from understanding key details to analyzing the author's craft and finally integrating knowledge to form critical insights.

Understanding and Purpose

The first thing teachers need to understand is the purpose of each read. Essentially, this means you are not just re-reading to read. Close reading consists of three reads of the same passage, each focusing on the pillars of literacy: key details and ideas, craft and structure, and integration of our knowledge and ideas.

Teachers must understand what it means to focus on key details and ideas in the first read. The same goes for the second read, which focuses on craft and structure, and the third on integrating knowledge. Knowing the specific purpose of each read allows you to guide students effectively through the layers of text complexity, ensuring a deeper understanding and more meaningful engagement with the material.

---

[20] Fang, Z. (2016). Teaching close reading with complex texts across content areas. *National Council of Teachers of English* 51 (1): 106–116.

Model Annotating

When reading a professional development book, do you highlight essential concepts and jot down quick notes? Many people do this because it helps crucial information stand out in our minds.

Students need to do the same thing when reading a passage. This close reading tip happens during the second read. I call this Reading with a Pencil. While reading, students are now marking up the text in some way. They may be circling unknown words, writing a question mark next to something confusing, or highlighting a critical detail. There is no wrong or right way to annotate a text. Modeling this process helps students understand how to interact with the text actively and thoughtfully.

Not Everything Needs "Close Reading"

When deciding which texts to close read, getting to know your students first is vital. You need to know what kind of text will be complex for students. This means that you may

Fostering Critical Thinking in the Classroom

have multiple versions of the exact text if it is one that you want students to close read. Be explicit about choosing text that you know will be challenging. Students who are not challenged will be bored and not understand how helpful annotating is. Select texts that will push students to think critically and engage deeply with the content, ensuring that the close reading process is meaningful and effective.

By incorporating these tips into your teaching practice, you can ensure that close reading becomes a powerful tool for developing your students' critical thinking and text analysis skills. These strategies help to create a structured yet flexible approach to reading that fosters deeper understanding and engagement with complex texts.

Text Analysis Isn't One Size Fits All

Supporting students with text analysis truly depends on both the text and the student. The complexity and nature of the text dictate the types of thinking required to delve into its intricacies, such as identifying themes, analyzing structure, or interpreting figurative language. Different texts may demand various levels of cognitive engagement, from basic comprehension to sophisticated critical analysis. Understanding these demands helps teachers tailor their instruction to highlight the specific skills and strategies needed to navigate and understand the text deeply.

Supporting students with text analysis requires understanding both the complexity of the text and the individual student's needs. A study by Amendum, Conradi, and Hiebert (2018) highlights the importance of matching the text's difficulty level to a student's reading abilities. Text complexity influences how students engage cognitively—more complex texts may require higher-order thinking skills, such as analyzing structure or interpreting figurative language, while simpler texts may demand basic comprehension strategies. The study found that as the complexity of the text increases, students may struggle with fluency and comprehension if they are not provided with adequate support.[21]

---

[21] Amendum, S.J., Conradi, K., and Hiebert, E. (2018). Does text complexity matter in the elementary grades? A research synthesis of text difficulty and elementary students' reading fluency and comprehension. *Educational Psychology Review* 30: 121–151.

In practice, teachers must carefully choose texts that align with their students' cognitive abilities and provide scaffolding when engaging with more difficult materials. For example, complex texts can introduce students to deeper themes or advanced vocabulary, but these need to be paired with targeted instructional support to avoid overwhelming the learner. This process of balancing text complexity with student capability helps develop critical thinking and text analysis skills incrementally.

This approach underscores that effective text analysis in the classroom is not just about the text itself, but how well the teacher supports the student in engaging with it at the appropriate cognitive level.

Equally important is recognizing each student's individual strengths and weaknesses. Some students may excel in identifying key details but struggle with making inferences or understanding nuanced arguments. Others might have a firm grasp of vocabulary but need support in analyzing the author's purpose or evaluating the credibility of sources. There is no one-size-fits-all approach to text analysis; adequate support requires a nuanced understanding of both the text and the learner. By knowing your text and your students, you can create a tailored critical thinking experience that fosters deeper engagement and understanding, ensuring all students have the tools they need to succeed.

Evaluating Information

Evaluating information is a crucial skill that helps students discern various sources' credibility, reliability, and relevance. "Evaluation of information, regardless of whether the content is paper-based or web-based, requires critical thinking skills, including analyzing, assessing, and reconstructing information" (Foundation for Critical Thinking, 2017).[22] At the elementary level, this process involves asking students critical questions about the information they encounter, such as who the author is, their qualifications, and whether the information is supported by evidence. Prerequisite skills for evaluating information

---

[22] Pilgrim, J., Vasinda, S., Bledsoe, C., and Martinez, E. (2019). Critical thinking is critical. *The Reading Teacher* 73 (1): 85–93.

include basic reading comprehension, recognizing different types of texts (fiction, non-fiction, articles, etc.), and understanding bias and perspective. These foundational skills help students assess the sources of information they read critically.

In practice, evaluating information at the elementary level might include comparing two articles on the same topic and discussing which one seems more reliable and why. Teachers can ask guiding questions such as, "Who wrote this article?" "Why did they write it?" "What evidence does the author provide to support their claims?" and "Do you think this information is accurate and why?" Examples of when students need to evaluate information include researching for a class project, discerning the accuracy of information in a news article, or even evaluating the credibility of a story told by a peer. By developing these skills early on, students learn to become critical thinkers who can navigate the vast array of information they encounter both in and out of the classroom.

The following table provides elementary-level questions to help students evaluate information's credibility, reliability, and relevance. These questions guide students to think critically about their sources, making the evaluation process more accessible and engaging.

Guiding Questions for Evaluating Information

Aspect	Questions
Author Credibility	Who wrote this information? Do you think the author knows a lot about this topic? Is the author a teacher or expert?
Source Reliability	Where did you find this information? Is this a well-known book, website, or magazine? Have you used this source before?
Purpose and Bias	Why do you think this was written? Is the information trying to make you believe something? Does the author show only one side of the story?
Evidence and Support	What proof does the author give to support their ideas? Are there facts or examples in the text? Does the author tell you where they got their information?
Currency	When was this information written? Is the information new or old? Does the date matter for this topic?

Relevance	How does this information help you with your topic? Is this information important for what you are learning? Does it give you useful ideas or facts?
Comparative Analysis	How does this information compare to what you read in other books or websites? Are there different ideas or facts in other sources? Which source do you trust more and why?
Overall Credibility	Do you believe this information? Why or why not? Would you use this information for your school project? What makes this information good or not good?

Evaluating information and using metacognition are deeply interconnected processes that enhance a student's critical thinking ability.[23] When students engage in metacognitive practices, they are more likely to pause and reflect on the information they are processing, asking themselves questions about its credibility, reliability, and relevance. A study by Ku and Ho (2010) found that metacognitive strategies significantly improve students' ability to critically analyze and evaluate information. The researchers observed that students who were more aware of their cognitive processes could better assess information, ask insightful questions, and reflect on the validity of arguments, leading to higher-order critical thinking outcomes. This highlights how metacognitive awareness not only supports the evaluation of information but also fosters deeper, more analytical thinking. This self-awareness allows them to recognize their biases, understand the influence of their prior knowledge, and identify gaps in their understanding that must be addressed.

Without metacognition, students may passively accept information without questioning its validity or considering its source. By fostering a habit of metacognitive thinking, teachers can help students develop a critical eye toward the information they encounter. When students are conscious of their thought processes, they can more effectively evaluate the quality and trustworthiness of the information. This dual approach strengthens their analytical skills and empowers them to become more discerning consumers of information, capable of navigating a complex and often misleading information landscape.

---

[23] Ku, K.Y.L. and Ho, I.T. (2010). Metacognitive strategies that enhance critical thinking. *Metacognition Learning* 5: 251–267.

Situations When Elementary Readers Might Need to Evaluate Information

This section considers situations when elementary readers will need to evaluate the information they read.

During research projects:
- Assessing the reliability of sources for a report on a historical figure.
- Determining which facts are most relevant for a science project.

Reading news articles:
- Evaluating the credibility of a news story they read in a classroom or online.
- Comparing different articles on the same event to identify biases.

Book reports and reviews:
- Deciding whether the information presented in a nonfiction book is accurate and trustworthy.
- Critiquing an author's point of view in a book review.

Classroom discussions and debates:
- Supporting their arguments with reliable information during a classroom debate.
- Evaluating peers' statements for accuracy and credibility in discussions.

Understanding persuasive texts:
- Analyzing the arguments in a persuasive essay or advertisement.
- Identifying the techniques used to persuade and assessing their effectiveness.

Comparing stories or articles:
- Evaluating different versions of a story or article to see which one is more believable.
- Discussing why one source might be more reliable than another.

Using digital resources:
- Identifying credible websites for information on a school project.
- Assessing the accuracy of facts found in online articles or videos.

Reading informational texts:
- Verifying facts and figures presented in textbooks or informational books.
- Checking the sources of information cited in the text.

By recognizing these situations, elementary readers can practice and develop their skills in evaluating information, becoming more discerning and critical thinkers.

We evaluate information in our everyday lives constantly, often without even realizing it. Whether deciding which news articles to trust, determining the credibility of a social media post, or choosing which product to buy based on reviews, we continually assess the reliability and relevance of the information we encounter. This critical evaluation helps us make informed decisions, avoid misinformation, and understand the world. Bringing this awareness into the literacy classroom can significantly enhance students' critical thinking skills. By discussing how they naturally evaluate information daily, teachers can make the process more relatable and accessible to students.

In the literacy classroom, teachers can draw parallels between these everyday evaluations and the skills needed to assess texts critically. For example, comparing the process of evaluating a product review with analyzing a persuasive text can help students understand the importance of questioning the source and evidence. Teachers can encourage students to share their experiences of evaluating information outside of school, fostering discussions highlighting the practical application of these skills. By making these connections, students can see the value and relevance of evaluating information, not just in their academic work but also in their daily lives. This approach helps to cultivate a classroom environment where critical thinking is a natural and integral part of learning.

> "This has totally changed the way I teach and the results are fantastic. I love having third grade teachers tell me they know which students came out of my classroom!"
>
> -Kathryn A. Terdiman, 2nd Grade, West Berwick Elementary, Pennsylvania

Encouraging a Critical Thinking Mindset

Creating a supportive environment that fosters critical thinking is essential for developing students' ability to analyze, evaluate, and synthesize information. A classroom culture that values questioning and curiosity encourages students to explore ideas deeply and express their thoughts without fear of judgment. This environment is foundational to promoting a growth mindset, as discussed in Chapter 11. When students see their questions and ideas are welcomed and valued, they become more willing to take risks and learn from their mistakes. This openness to exploration and learning is crucial for developing a reader's mindset and, ultimately, a critical thinking mindset.

To cultivate such a culture, teachers must actively encourage risk-taking and celebrate the learning that comes from mistakes. This can be achieved by creating opportunities for students to ask questions, explore different viewpoints, and engage in thoughtful discussions. Teachers should clarify that making mistakes is a natural part of the learning process and an essential step toward growth and understanding. This approach aligns with the principles of a growth mindset, which emphasizes the value of effort and persistence over innate ability. By fostering an environment where students feel safe to experiment and fail, teachers can help them develop resilience and a love for learning.

One article emphasizes that student-centered environments, such as project- and problem-based learning, require students to engage in higher-order thinking (HOT) processes, including analysis, evaluation, and synthesis. In these environments, students collaborate on complex problems, which fosters critical thinking and the ability to apply knowledge in practical, real-world contexts. Such environments encourage deeper learning and intellectual engagement, helping students develop critical thinking skills that go beyond rote memorization and basic comprehension (Schraw & Robinson, 2011).[24]

Modeling critical thinking is another crucial component of encouraging a critical thinking mindset. Teachers must demonstrate their thought processes, showing students how to approach problems, analyze information, and draw conclusions. This can be done through think-aloud sessions, where teachers verbalize their thinking as they read a text, solve

---

[24] Loyens, S.M.M., van Meerten, J.E., Schaap, L. et al. (2023). Situating higher-order, and critical-analytic thinking in problem- and project-based learning environments: a systematic review. *Educational Psychology Review* 35 (39): https://doi.org/10.1007/s10648-023-09757-x.

a problem, or evaluate information. By sharing examples of critical thinking in various contexts, teachers can provide concrete models for students to emulate. This practice is essential in reading, which can be a very closed and solitary experience. Students must see and hear how our brains work when we read and think critically to develop their internal dialogue and analytical skills.

The study titled "Using Picture Books to Support Critical Thinking in Early Literacy Instruction" conducted in 2022 demonstrates that when teachers model critical thinking strategies, such as asking reflective and open-ended questions during literacy activities, it significantly enhances students' ability to engage critically with texts. By observing and participating in teacher-led discussions that emphasize inquiry and analysis, students were able to improve their comprehension and develop their own critical thinking skills (Wells, Morrison, & López-Robertson, 2022). This supports the idea that modeling is an essential component of fostering a critical thinking mindset in literacy instruction.[25]

Encouraging curiosity is another crucial aspect of fostering a critical thinking mindset, as emphasized in Chapter 6. When curious, students are more likely to engage deeply with the material and ask insightful questions. Teachers can nurture this curiosity by providing exciting and challenging texts, posing thought-provoking questions, and creating opportunities for students to pursue their interests and inquiries. By valuing and encouraging curiosity, teachers help students develop a lifelong love of learning and a habit of critical thinking.

Moreover, teachers should integrate discussions about the thinking process into their regular instruction. This involves explaining not just what they are thinking but why they are thinking it and how they arrived at their conclusions. For example, during a reading session, a teacher might explain how they use context clues to infer the meaning of an unfamiliar word or identify the author's purpose in a text. These insights help students understand the mechanics of critical thinking and provide them with strategies they can use independently.

Creating a supportive environment, modeling critical thinking, and encouraging curiosity are all essential strategies for fostering a critical thinking mindset in students. By linking these practices to the concepts discussed in Chapters 6 and 11, teachers can build a cohesive approach that supports students' growth as critical thinkers. Consistently modeling critical thinking processes and promoting a classroom culture that values questioning and

---

[25] Wells, M., Morrison, J., and Robertson, J. (2022). Building critical reading and critical literacy with picturebook analysis. *The Reading Teacher* 76 (2): 191–200.

exploration are key to helping students develop the skills and mindset necessary for deep, analytical engagement with texts and ideas.

\multicolumn{3}{c}{**Supporting a Critical Thinking Mindset**}
Strategy	**Description**	**Examples**
Fostering Curiosity	Encourage students to ask questions and explore topics deeply. Provide interesting and challenging texts to stimulate curiosity.	• Encourage questions • Provide inquiry projects • Use "wonder journals"
Modeling Critical Thinking	Demonstrate critical thinking processes through think-alouds and verbalizing thought processes. Show how to approach problems and evaluate information.	• Think-aloud sessions • Verbalize problem-solving • Show evaluation methods
Creating a Supportive Environment	Foster a classroom culture that values questioning and open dialogue. Encourage multiple viewpoints and create a safe space for sharing ideas.	• Value questioning • Promote open dialogue • Encourage multiple viewpoints
Encouraging Risk-Taking and Learning from Mistakes	Normalize mistakes as learning opportunities. Celebrate effort and persistence to foster a growth mindset.	• Normalize mistakes • Celebrate effort • Encourage persistence
Integrating Critical Thinking in Lessons	Use Bloom's Taxonomy to design tiered questions and include problem-solving tasks. Incorporate real-world scenarios to make lessons relevant.	• Use Bloom's Taxonomy • Design tiered questions • Include real-world scenarios
Reflective Thinking Practices	Encourage reflective thinking through journaling and think-alouds. Model how to reflect on learning experiences to improve understanding and skills.	• Encourage journaling • Use think-alouds • Model reflective thinking
Using Open-Ended Questions	Promote detailed responses and discussions through open-ended questions. Use follow-up questions to probe deeper thinking.	• Encourage detailed responses • Promote discussions • Use follow-up questions
Teaching Metacognition	Teach students to think about their thinking by using metacognitive strategies to plan, monitor, and evaluate their learning processes.	• Model self-questioning • Teach goal-setting • Encourage self-assessment and reflection

Closing

Fostering critical thinking in the classroom is not merely an academic exercise; it is a crucial life skill that prepares students for the complexities of the modern world. By equipping students with the ability to analyze, evaluate, and synthesize information, you can empower them to navigate an ever-changing landscape of knowledge and opinions. Educators create an environment that nurtures these skills through thoughtful instruction, engaging activities, and a supportive atmosphere that encourages intellectual risk-taking and curiosity.

The journey to becoming proficient critical thinkers requires consistent practice and reflection. By integrating the strategies discussed in this chapter, teachers can guide their students toward more profound understanding and more meaningful engagement with content. Remember, critical thinking is a process that develops over time, and each step forward is a valuable contribution to your students' overall intellectual growth.

As you implement these strategies, take the time to reflect on their impact and adapt them to suit the unique needs of your classroom. Encourage your students to embrace the challenges and rewards of critical thinking and celebrate their progress. Together, we can cultivate a generation of thinkers who are academically successful and equipped to make informed and thoughtful decisions in all aspects of their lives. Consider these questions as you ponder this issue more.

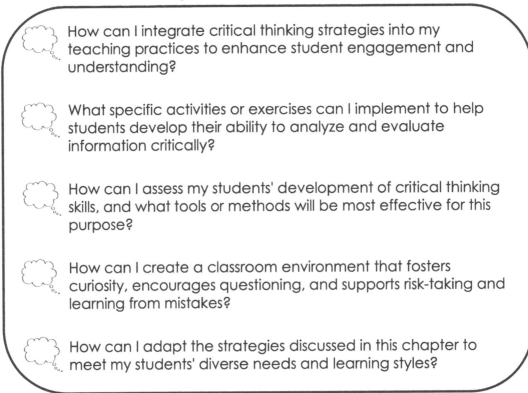

Lessons To Try

As a reminder, you can access the complete lessons for free at `http://www.cieraharristeaching.com/ttrlessons` using the passcode: `literacy for all`.

"Making Inferences" Lesson

The Making Inferences lesson focuses on helping students evaluate inferences using both text and images, solidifying their understanding of critical thinking through the lens of inferential reasoning. The lesson begins by reviewing the equation "text + schema = inference," ensuring that students comprehend how authors leave subtle clues within texts and how prior knowledge (schema) is essential to infer additional meaning. By evaluating whether an inference is accurate based on a given photo, students practice verifying claims, thus engaging in higher-order thinking. The ability to determine whether an inference is correct helps students move beyond surface-level reading to deeper comprehension.

The lesson uses visual prompts (photos) to help students make or reject inferences about the image. Students are tasked with deciding if the inferences provided about each image are correct or need to be discarded. This process enables students to scrutinize evidence, test assumptions, and arrive at a reasoned conclusion, which strengthens their critical thinking skills. The lesson transitions from whole-group activities to smaller group work, ensuring students have multiple opportunities to practice and refine their evaluation of inferences.

This lesson supports critical thinking by encouraging students to question information, use logic to interpret clues, and verify their conclusions. In doing so, they must continually assess the validity of their thoughts, a key component of critical thinking. By focusing on both textual and visual inference, students are also encouraged to apply these skills in real-world contexts, enhancing their problem-solving capabilities.

Quick Tip

When trying this lesson, start by having an open discussion about making inferences with visuals, as students might find this approach novel. Allow students to verbally explain their reasoning before writing it down—this talk-through strategy often clarifies their thinking and builds confidence in analyzing both text and images.

"Synthesizing" Lesson

This lesson focuses on helping students understand how to combine their prior knowledge with new information gained from the text. The objective is for students to grasp the concept of synthesizing while reading by practicing with simple activities. The lesson begins with a "secret word" activity where students guess a word based on limited clues, and their guesses evolve as new information is provided. This mirrors the process of synthesizing in reading, where readers continually adjust their understanding as they read further.

The lesson then progresses to three-sentence story activities, where students model how their thinking shifts after each sentence. By covering sentences as they go and encouraging students to articulate their thought process, the lesson emphasizes the importance of revising and building on initial ideas. These tasks not only foster comprehension but also encourage critical thinking by prompting students to think flexibly and integrate new knowledge.

In terms of supporting critical thinking, this lesson is essential because synthesizing requires students to engage in higher-order thinking. They must not only comprehend the text but also evaluate and transform information. The act of revising initial thoughts as new information is presented and challenges students to be open-minded, adaptable, and reflective, which are all key components of critical thinking.

Quick Tip: To enhance student engagement, consider using real-life examples for the "secret word" activity that are relevant to your students' experiences. This can make the concept of synthesizing more relatable and easier to grasp, especially for younger learners.

"Determining Importance" Lesson

This lesson focuses on teaching students how to distinguish between essential and non-essential information when reading a text. The lesson begins by introducing students to the idea that not all information in a story is equally important. Using familiar stories such as "Frozen," the teacher demonstrates how leaving out critical elements like characters, setting, and the plot prevents a story from being complete. This lesson is designed to help students practice identifying the key components that contribute to understanding both fiction and nonfiction texts. Through activities using story cards, students sort through important and interesting details to grasp the distinction between necessary and unnecessary information in storytelling.

The lesson directly supports critical thinking by encouraging students to evaluate the relevance of various details in a text. As students engage in sorting activities, they must analyze each piece of information and decide its significance in advancing the narrative or conveying essential ideas. This process develops their ability to critically assess content and make informed judgments about what truly matters in a text. By doing so, they not only enhance their comprehension but also their metacognitive abilities, as they must justify their choices based on reasoning and textual evidence.

Model the process extensively before allowing students to work in groups. By walking through a story card activity and thinking aloud, you can demonstrate how to critically assess the importance of details. Encourage students to refer to an anchor chart that differentiates between fiction and nonfiction key elements to guide their thinking as they sort through information.

CHAPTER 11

BUILDING PERSISTENCE AND CULTIVATING THE READER'S MINDSET

Building Resilience and Persistence

Provide strategies for fostering a growth mindset and teach students to overcome challenges and persist in their reading efforts.

Building persistence in readers is crucial to fostering a lifelong love of reading and enhancing academic success. Carol Dweck and many other researchers have shown that this persistence and growth mindset can have a positive effect on wanted outcomes. "Dweck has shown that people with the growth mindset tend to have greater perseverance and are more willing to take on new challenges that might stretch their abilities. Those with the fixed mindset, in contrast, often struggle to confront problems in learning. They lose motivation as soon as they have a disappointing result and tend to shy away from challenges that fall outside of their comfort zone, which means that they are less likely to improve their skills in the long term."[1] This chapter delves into the challenges students face when encountering complex texts and the strategies they can employ to overcome these hurdles. Students learn to approach reading with resilience, determination, and a proactive attitude by cultivating a reader's mindset. A reader's mindset is about improving reading skills and developing a positive and engaged approach to any text, no matter how challenging.

This chapter explores the parallels between a reader's and a growth mindset, emphasizing the importance of mental preparation, perseverance, and self-awareness. Both mindsets highlight the role of attitude and strategic thinking in overcoming obstacles. By understanding and applying these principles, students can transform their reading experience from a daunting task into an opportunity for growth and learning. This chapter provides practical steps and insights to help students build a strong reader's mindset, enabling them to navigate complex texts confidently and resiliently.

The chapter also discusses strategies to help students stay engaged with texts they find uninteresting or too complex. These strategies include identifying the purpose of the text, recognizing its benefits, defining clear goals, finding value in the content, and focusing on what is essential. By employing these techniques, students can maintain their focus and motivation, even when faced with challenging material. This proactive approach enhances comprehension, builds critical thinking skills, and fosters a lifelong love of reading.

Moreover, this chapter underscores the importance of creating a supportive reading environment. Educators can help students develop the resilience and confidence needed to tackle any reading challenge by adopting a reader's mindset. This mindset empowers students to see themselves as capable and resourceful readers, ready to engage deeply with texts and derive meaningful insights. Students can internalize these strategies through consistent practice and reinforcement, leading to continuous improvement and academic success.

---

[1] Robson, D. (2022). Perils of perfection. *RSA, The Royal Society for Arts, Manufactures and Commerce* 168 (1): 38–41.

Chapter 11 Objectives

 The readers will understand the concept of a reader's mindset and its significance in overcoming reading challenges.

 The readers will learn to identify and implement strategies for engaging with uninteresting or difficult texts.

 The readers will recognize the similarities and differences between a reader's mindset and a growth mindset.

 The readers will explore practical steps to foster a supportive reading environment in the classroom.

 The readers will develop skills to help students build resilience and confidence in their reading abilities.

A Reader's Mindset

I want you to reflect on moments when, as adults, we have to adjust our mindset to accomplish tasks. Can you recall such instances? Let me share a few examples from my own experiences.

Take exercise, for instance. I need to be in the right mindset to work out. It's all about staying motivated and thinking, "Okay, I can do this. It's just half an hour. Turn on the TV, and before you know it, it'll be over, and I'll be glad I did it." It's a mental preparation.

Another example is tackling big projects at work. When procrastination sets in, I must push myself to sit down and focus for an hour, promising a break afterward to watch TV. It's about getting into the right frame of mind.

Doing taxes is another task that requires a mental shift. It's not enjoyable, but I must mentally prepare myself to get it done. My husband suggested I add waking up in the morning to the list. I'm not a morning person and

A reader's mindset is about improving reading skills and developing a positive and engaged approach to any text, no matter how challenging.

Building Persistence and Cultivating the Reader's Mindset

detest the entire process of getting up. As I lay there, I mentally prepared myself for the day ahead.

These examples illustrate a common theme: they all require a specific mindset to achieve a goal. It's about preparing your brain and telling yourself, "Okay, brain, you ready? Here we go. We can do this."

This concept applies to reading as well. Readers encounter different situations that can make them feel frustrated or unconfident. Some readers may not be engaged or motivated yet. As a teacher, you need to empathize with this. As I don't always want to work out, kids may not always want to read. You need to make them aware that overcoming this is a mindset challenge.

Definition: A Reader's Mindset

A reader's mindset is the mental state and preparation needed to enhance focus, comprehension, and enjoyment while reading. It involves eliminating distractions, adopting a positive attitude, and preparing physically and mentally. It also includes self-awareness of one's strengths and weaknesses as a reader. This mindset helps readers tackle challenges, stay engaged, and develop a lifelong love of reading.

By teaching your students about these situations and how to face them, you can help readers see they have what it takes to push through unwanted reading situations. This chapter covers some of these scenarios and provides practical steps to help students shift their mindset and become more excited about reading. Together, we can help them recognize that with the right mindset, they can accomplish anything.

Let's start by teaching students about a reader's mindset. Think about your mindset in different situations. For example, I know my mindset when gearing up for a workout. I understand my mindset when I wake up in the morning. As an avid reader and an adult, I also know what my mindset looks like when I'm about to read. When I open a book, I consciously try to turn off my mental to-do lists. Whether it's tasks related to being a mom, a teacher, or running a business, I set those aside. I ensure I'm comfortable, my kids are settled, and the dog is cared for. This preparation is my reader's mindset, the process of getting ready to engage my reading brain.

A reader's mindset is also about employing metacognition to become an active thinker during the reading process. It involves being aware of one's thoughts and using strategies to enhance understanding and retention. This mindset encourages readers to identify themselves as capable, regardless of their challenges. One study done in 2023 by Marek Urban highlights how metacognitive strategies, such as summarizing and self-monitoring, significantly improve reading comprehension and self-efficacy. When readers engage in metacognitive practices, they become more aware of their understanding and can actively choose strategies to navigate complex texts. This proactive approach reinforces a sense of competence and resilience, contributing to their identity as capable readers.[2] Readers can navigate complex texts more effectively by recognizing when to employ specific strategies, such as summarizing, questioning, or predicting. This proactive approach improves reading skills and builds confidence and resilience, reinforcing the identity of being a competent and engaged reader.

We must teach students about their reader's mindset and how to cultivate it. How do they prepare their brains for reading, and why is this preparation necessary? Many readers encounter texts that don't engage them. They might think, "I don't like this," or "I don't care about this topic." Secondly, they might find the text too challenging, thinking, "This is too hard." This chapter covers strategies for overcoming these obstacles, helping students develop a resilient and adaptable reader mindset. By addressing these situations, you can empower your students to become more confident and engaged readers.

Growth Mindset vs. Reader's Mindset

A reader's and a growth mindset share a foundational principle: both focus on the importance of attitude and self-awareness in overcoming challenges and achieving goals. At their core, these mindsets emphasize the role of mental preparation, resilience, and proactive strategies in personal development. However, while they share several similarities, there are also distinct differences between the two.

One fundamental similarity between a reader's and a growth mindset is their emphasis on perseverance. In both mindsets, individuals are encouraged to push through difficulties

---

[2] Urban, M., Urban, K., and Nietfeld, J.L. (2023). The effect of a distributed metacognitive strategy intervention on reading comprehension. *Metacognition Learning* 18: 405–424.

and setbacks. For instance, a reader's mindset involves preparing to engage deeply with a text, even when it is uninteresting or challenging. Similarly, a growth mindset promotes the belief that abilities and intelligence can be developed through hard work and dedication, encouraging individuals to persist despite obstacles. Researcher Donna L. Miller states that "When students have a growth mindset, they understand that intelligence can be developed and doesn't depend on luck or genetics; rather, like a muscle, intelligence grows stronger through exercise. Instead of worrying about how smart they currently are, they work to improve by embracing challenges, persisting in the face of setbacks, learning from constructive criticism, and seeing effort as a path to mastery."[3]

Another commonality is the focus on self-awareness and self-regulation. A reader's mindset requires individuals to understand their strengths and weaknesses as readers and to employ strategies that enhance comprehension and engagement. This self-awareness is mirrored in a growth mindset, where individuals recognize their learning processes and actively seek improvement. Both mindsets involve a reflective component, encouraging individuals to think about their thinking and adjust their approaches accordingly.

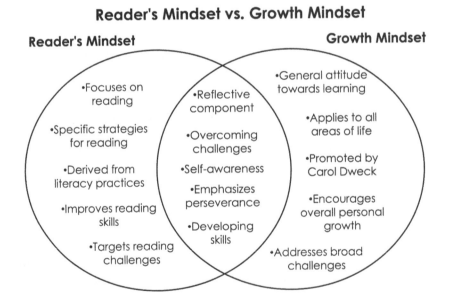

---

[3] Miller, D. (2013). Got it wrong? Think again. And again. *Phi Delta Kappa International* 94 (5): 50–52. https://www.jstor.org/stable/23611672.

Despite these similarities, the scope of each mindset differs significantly. A reader's mindset is tailored explicitly to reading, focusing on preparing the mind to engage with and understand texts. It involves specific strategies such as setting aside distractions, fostering a positive attitude toward reading, and using techniques like summarizing and questioning to enhance comprehension. In contrast, a growth mindset has a broader application, encompassing all learning and personal development areas. It is a general attitude toward one's abilities and potential, promoting the idea that skills can be developed through effort and persistence.

The origins of the two mindsets also differ. A reader's mindset is derived from educational practices and theories related to literacy and reading comprehension. It is often taught in the context of improving reading skills and fostering a love of reading. On the other hand, the concept of a growth mindset was popularized by psychologist Carol Dweck and is rooted in research on motivation and achievement. It is applied widely across educational, professional, and personal development contexts to encourage a positive approach to learning and growth.

> "I work with a struggling reader that had to learn to decode, encode and use her thinking muscles. After 18 months, she is confident and tackles new reading material with ease. She applies her strategies and is rapidly catching up to her grade level peers."
>
> -Cinthy Harner, K-12 Special Education, Mountain View Christian Academy, Virginia

Moreover, the challenges addressed by each mindset vary. A reader's mindset specifically targets reading-related issues, such as lack of interest in a text or difficulty understanding complex material. It provides strategies to overcome these specific challenges. Conversely, a growth mindset addresses a broader range of learning and personal development challenges, including fear of failure, fixed perceptions of intelligence, and lack of motivation. It offers a more general framework for approaching these issues with resilience and a willingness to learn.

While a reader's and a growth mindset share common principles of perseverance, self-awareness, and strategies to overcome challenges, they differ in scope, origins, and the specific challenges they address. Both mindsets are valuable in their respective contexts, fostering resilience and a proactive learning and personal growth approach. Understanding these similarities and differences can help individuals apply the appropriate mindset to various aspects of their lives, enhancing their ability to overcome obstacles and achieve their goals.

Why Teach About a Reader's Mindset?

Chapter 1 explored what reading is. It emphasized that students must see and identify as readers to grow and develop confidence in their reading abilities. This self-identification is crucial for them to face daily challenges related to reading. They need to recognize themselves as thinkers capable of reading or listening to a text and critically analyzing its meaning. This idea seamlessly aligns with the concept of having a reader's mindset.

A reader's mindset is essential for students as it prepares them to engage deeply with texts, setting the foundation for academic success and lifelong learning. A study done in 2016 by Susana Claro shows us that "at every socioeconomic level, those who hold more of a growth mindset consistently outperform those who do not—even after holding constant a panoply of socioeconomic and attitudinal factors."[4] By cultivating this mindset, students learn to approach reading with a positive attitude, self-awareness, and the ability to employ strategies to overcome obstacles. They become proactive, reflective thinkers who can navigate complex texts and derive meaningful insights from their reading experiences.

Teaching your students to develop a reader's mindset at the beginning of the school year has numerous benefits. First, it empowers them to see themselves as capable readers, which boosts their confidence and motivation. When students believe in their ability to read and understand texts, they are more likely to take on challenging materials and persist through difficulties. This self-belief is fundamental to their growth as critical thinkers and readers.

---

[4] Claro, S., Paunesku, D., and Dweek, C. (2016). Growth mindset tempers the effects of poverty on academic achievement. *National Academy of Sciences* 11 (31): 8664–9669.

Second, discussions about a reader's mindset help students understand the importance of mental preparation and strategy use in reading. They learn that reading is not a passive activity but an active cognitive process that requires engagement and effort. Students can adopt strategies to enhance their comprehension and retention by being aware of their strengths and weaknesses as readers. This metacognitive approach fosters resilience and adaptability, critical qualities for academic and personal success.

Moreover, establishing a reader's mindset early on creates a supportive classroom environment where reading is valued and encouraged. It sets the tone for the year, signaling to students that reading is a priority and their growth as readers is a shared goal. This collective focus on reading builds a community of learners who support and celebrate each other's progress.

Incorporating discussions about a reader's mindset aligns with the broader educational goal of developing critical thinkers. Research supports the idea that when students approach reading with a mindset that they are capable and resourceful, they are more likely to engage in higher-order thinking skills, such as analyzing, evaluating, and synthesizing information. These skills are crucial for effective reading comprehension, especially when students are faced with complex texts. A study conducted in 2018 found that self-efficacy, or the belief in one's own capabilities, plays a significant role in developing higher-order thinking during reading tasks. Students who believe they can handle challenges are more likely to apply critical thinking strategies, which leads to improved comprehension and problem-solving abilities.[5] They become adept at analyzing, synthesizing, and evaluating information, essential critical thinking skills. By recognizing themselves as critical readers, students can apply these skills across various subjects and real-life situations.

Teaching students to develop a reader's mindset is crucial for their growth as confident, capable readers and critical thinkers. By fostering this mindset, you equip your students with the tools they need to navigate the complexities of reading and learning. Starting the year with discussions about a reader's mindset enhances their reading skills and builds a foundation for academic success and lifelong intellectual engagement.

---

[5] Cho, E., Toste, J.R., and Lee, M. (2019). Motivational predictors of struggling readers' reading comprehension: the effects of mindset, achievement goals, and engagement. *Reading and Writing* 32: 1219–1242.

Do My Students Have a Reader's Mindset?

Knowing whether your students have developed a reader's mindset can significantly impact your teaching approach and their reading success. As discussed in Chapter 3, understanding your students as readers is crucial for identifying which students possess a reader's mindset and which do not. One of the first indicators, as indicated in the following table, is their attitude toward reading. Students with a reader's mindset typically exhibit a positive and enthusiastic attitude regarding reading tasks. They are curious about new texts and view reading as an opportunity for growth and learning. Conversely, students who lack this mindset may display reluctance or even dread at the prospect of reading, often seeing it as a chore rather than an engaging activity.

Aspect	Reader with a Reader's Mindset	Reader without a Reader's Mindset
Attitude Towards Reading	Positive and open attitude, sees reading as an opportunity for growth	Negative or indifferent attitude, sees reading as a chore
Preparation	Mentally and physically prepares, sets aside distractions	Does not prepare, remains distracted
Engagement with Text	Actively engages, makes connections, asks questions	Passively reads, minimal engagement, little to no questioning
Use of Strategies	Employs strategies like summarizing, predicting, and questioning	Rarely uses strategies, struggles with understanding
Response to Difficulties	Perseveres, seeks solutions, adjusts strategies as needed	Gives up easily, becomes frustrated, avoids difficult texts
Self-Perception	Sees themselves as a capable reader, confident in their abilities	Sees themselves as a poor reader, lacks confidence
Outcome	Higher comprehension, greater enjoyment, continuous improvement	Lower comprehension, less enjoyment, minimal progress

Another crucial sign is the preparation and focus students bring to their reading sessions. Those with a reader's mindset will take steps to prepare themselves mentally and physically for reading. They may find a quiet place, minimize distractions, and ensure they are comfortable before they start. This proactive preparation indicates a serious and thoughtful approach to reading. In contrast, students without this mindset may approach reading haphazardly, remaining easily distracted and unprepared, which affects their ability to engage with the text meaningfully.

Engagement with the text is a crucial difference between the two groups. Students with a reader's mindset actively engage with what they are reading. They connect to prior knowledge, ask questions, and visualize the content. This active engagement indicates that they are thinking critically about the text. Conversely, students without a reader's mindset tend to read passively, simply moving their eyes over the words without genuinely processing or interacting with the material. This leads to poor comprehension and retention.

Another important indicator is the use of reading strategies. Students with a reader's mindset will likely employ various strategies to aid their understanding. They might summarize sections, predict what will happen next, or re-read difficult passages. These strategies demonstrate their proactive approach to overcoming challenges. On the other hand, students who do not have a reader's mindset often struggle to use such strategies. They might read through confusion without attempting to clarify their understanding, resulting in frustration and disengagement.

Observing students' responses to difficulties can also reveal their mindset. Those with a reader's mindset are more likely to persevere through challenging texts. They view difficulties as opportunities to learn and grow, seeking solutions or asking for help when needed. In contrast, students without this mindset may quickly give up when faced with a complex text, expressing frustration, avoiding reading, or skipping over challenging parts. This behavior hampers their progress and development.

Self-perception is another telling factor. Students with a reader's mindset generally see themselves as capable and confident readers. They believe in their ability to tackle various texts and improve their skills, propelling them to take on new reading challenges. Conversely, students who lack this mindset often see themselves as poor readers. They doubt their abilities and may develop a fixed mindset that limits their growth and potential in reading.

It's important to note that even struggling readers can have a reader's mindset. This mindset is not about having a solid reading ability but the right attitude, preparedness, and strategies. Struggling readers with a reader's mindset will approach reading tasks with determination and use strategies to improve their comprehension and retention. They understand their reading skills can develop with effort and the right approach. Recognizing this can help teachers focus on nurturing the mindset, leading to improved reading abilities.

Knowing your students as readers is fundamental to recognizing which students have a reader's mindset. Teachers should look for indicators such as attitude toward reading, level of preparation and focus, engagement with the text, use of reading strategies, response to difficulties, and self-perception as readers. By identifying these signs, teachers can tailor their instruction to foster a reader's mindset, ultimately helping students become more confident, capable, and engaged readers. Developing this mindset not only enhances reading skills but also builds critical thinking abilities that are essential for academic success and lifelong learning.

> "Students need to connect to text to truly comprehend. Skills are a way to get there, but strategies are how readers build comprehension."
>
> -Shelly Pelletier, 4th Grade, Fort Kent Elementary School, Maine

Common Barriers and How a Reader's Mindset Can Help

Readers often encounter barriers that impede their ability to engage with and comprehend texts. These barriers can range from a lack of interest in the material to finding the content too challenging. Understanding these common obstacles is essential for developing strategies to overcome them, and adopting a reader's mindset can play a crucial role in this process.

One of the most significant barriers readers face is a lack of interest in the material. Students not engaged with a text are less likely to invest the necessary effort to understand it. This disengagement can stem from various factors, including the subject being perceived as boring or irrelevant. "Many note that a central problem for reluctant readers is that they do not use metacognitive and self-monitoring strategies. One such technique, what we call *self-talk*, is described by Marean Jordan and her colleagues as *meta-talk*. How we talk to ourselves is influential when we are trying something difficult or challenging."[6] A reader's mindset encourages students to approach every text with curiosity and an open mind. By identifying the purpose of the text and recognizing its potential benefits, students can find ways to connect with the material and stay motivated.

Another common barrier is difficulty with comprehension, mainly when the text is above the reader's current level. Complex vocabulary, intricate sentence structures, and dense information can make it challenging for students to grasp the content. A reader's mindset promotes the use of metacognitive strategies to aid comprehension. Summarizing, questioning, and predicting can help break down complex texts into more manageable parts, making it easier for students to understand and retain the information. Here are some other common barriers readers might face:

- **Lack of vocabulary:** Limited vocabulary can make it difficult for students to understand and engage with a text.
- **Decoding issues:** Struggles with phonetic decoding can slow reading and hinder comprehension.
- **Fluency problems:** Lack of reading fluency can affect the ability to read smoothly and with proper expression, impacting overall understanding.
- **Background knowledge:** Limited background knowledge on a topic can make new information harder to understand and integrate.
- **Distractions:** In today's digital age, students are surrounded by potential distractions, from smartphones to social media.
- **Pressure to perform:** The stress of needing to perform well, especially in high-stakes testing environments, can lead to anxiety and negatively impact concentration.

---

[6] Stringer, S. and Mollineaux, B. (2003). Removing the word "Reluctant Reader." *National Council of Teachers of English* 92 (4): 71–76.

The pressure to perform well is a significant barrier, particularly in high-stakes testing environments. This pressure can lead to anxiety and negatively impact a student's ability to concentrate and comprehend the text. A reader's mindset emphasizes the importance of perseverance and resilience. Students can reduce anxiety and build confidence in their reading abilities by focusing on the process rather than the outcome and reminding themselves that improvement comes with practice.

Distractions are another common obstacle that can hinder a reader's focus. A reader's mindset includes strategies for creating a conducive reading environment. This might involve finding a quiet place to read, minimizing interruptions, and setting specific reading times. Students can improve their concentration and engagement with the text by establishing a routine and distraction-free environment.

Lastly, some students struggle with a fixed mindset, believing their reading abilities are static and cannot be improved. This belief can prevent them from putting in the effort needed to develop their skills. A reader's mindset, rooted in the principles of a growth mindset, encourages students to view challenges as opportunities for growth. Understanding that their brains can form new connections and improve over time helps students stay motivated and persistent, even when the reading is challenging.

While readers face common barriers such as lack of interest, difficulty with comprehension, limited vocabulary, decoding issues, fluency problems, lack of background knowledge, distractions, and a fixed mindset, adopting a reader's mindset can help them overcome these challenges. Students can enhance their reading skills and become more confident, capable readers by fostering curiosity, utilizing metacognitive strategies, managing distractions, reducing anxiety, and embracing a growth mindset. This proactive approach improves their immediate reading experiences and equips them with the tools for lifelong learning and intellectual growth.

Building a Reader's Mindset

We don't need an entire section on how to build a reader's mindset because that has been the underlying focus of this book since Chapter 1. The goal is to cultivate readers who identify as readers and comprehend the profound impact that reading can have on their lives. Your aim is to develop individuals who recognize the immense power of reading, who can engage in critical thinking, and who understand the benefits of being active, thoughtful readers.

From the beginning, I have laid the groundwork for fostering a reader's mindset by emphasizing the importance of self-identification. Students who see themselves as capable readers are more likely to embrace reading challenges and persist through difficulties. This self-identification is crucial because it forms the foundation for all other reading skills. It instills confidence and motivates students to explore the vast world of literature with enthusiasm and curiosity.

Additionally, I have highlighted the transformative power of reading. By exposing students to diverse texts and encouraging them to connect with different perspectives, you help them understand that reading is not just a mechanical process but a gateway to new ideas, cultures, and experiences. This understanding fosters a deeper appreciation for reading and reinforces that it is a valuable, enriching activity.

Critical thinking has been another cornerstone of this approach. I have consistently emphasized the importance of thinking critically about texts, asking questions, making connections, and reflecting on the material. By teaching students to engage with texts actively and thoughtfully, you can help them develop the skills to analyze and interpret information effectively. This critical engagement is vital to a reader's mindset, transforming passive reading into an interactive, intellectually stimulating experience. Researcher John Bean argues that engaging students in critical thinking tasks—such as analyzing ideas, arguments, and points of view—helps shift them from passive learning to more dynamic interaction with the material. These activities foster deeper comprehension and reasoning, enhancing students' ability to analyze and interpret texts.[7]

Moreover, I have underscored the significance of being an active reader. This involves not just passively consuming information but interacting with the text in meaningful ways. Active readers annotate, summarize, predict, and question as they read, using strategies

---

[7] Bean, J.C. (1996). *Engaging Ideas: The Professor's Guide to Integrating Writing, Critical Thinking, and Active Learning in the Classroom.* Jossey-Bass.

that enhance comprehension and retention. By promoting these active reading strategies, you support your students in becoming more engaged and influential readers.

When these steps are consistently integrated into the reading experience, a reader's mindset is naturally and authentically created and supported. It becomes an intrinsic part of the student's approach to reading rather than an imposed set of behaviors. This organic development of a reader's mindset ensures students internalize the values and skills necessary for lifelong reading success.

This book has been dedicated to building a reader's mindset from the ground up. By fostering self-identification as readers, emphasizing the power of reading, promoting critical thinking, and encouraging active engagement with texts, you lay a comprehensive foundation for developing confident, thoughtful, and capable readers. These steps collectively nurture a reader's authentic and sustainable mindset, empowering students to thrive as readers and thinkers.

Overcoming Common Reading Challenges with a Reader's Mindset

Even the most avid readers encounter situations where they struggle to engage with a text. Two of the most common scenarios are feeling uninterested in the material, often summarized as "I don't like this," and finding the material too challenging, encapsulated by the feeling of "This is too hard." These challenges can arise in various contexts, from standardized tests to assigned readings on unappealing topics. However, by adopting a reader's mindset, students can develop strategies to overcome these hurdles and engage more effectively with any text.

"I Don't Like This"

One of the most frequent complaints from readers is encountering a text that simply doesn't engage them. This scenario is common in a variety of contexts, each presenting unique challenges:

- **Standardized tests:** Often, the content of standardized tests is dry and uninteresting, making it hard for students to stay focused and engaged. These tests require students to read passages on topics that may not interest them, and the pressure of the testing environment can exacerbate their disinterest.
- **Assigned readings:** Students may be given assignments on topics they find boring or irrelevant to their interests. When a text does not resonate with their personal experiences or passions, it can be difficult for them to invest the necessary effort to understand and appreciate it.
- **Textbooks**: Certain subjects or textbooks might not appeal to every student, leading to disinterest and lack of motivation to read. Textbooks often present information in a dense, factual manner that can seem monotonous, especially if the student does not see the immediate relevance to their lives or future goals.
- **Mandatory literature:** Classic literature or books chosen for school curriculums may not always resonate with every student's tastes or interests. While these works are selected for their educational value, they can sometimes feel disconnected from contemporary experiences and language, making it challenging for students to relate to the content.

Reader's Mindset Strategy to Battle "I Don't Like This"

Reader's Mindset Strategy to Battle 'I Don't Like It'
- **Step 1:** Identify the Purpose of the Text
- **Step 2:** Identify Some Benefits of Reading the Text
- **Step 3:** Define Your Goal
- **Step 4:** Find Value in the Text
- **Step 5:** Determine What Is Important

When students encounter a text they don't like, it's easy for them to become disengaged and frustrated. For example, research highlights that frustration in the classroom, particularly when students face difficult or uninteresting content, can create a negative emotional state. This emotional response is a significant factor in why students may disengage

---

[8] Park, D. and Ramirex, G. (2022). Frustration in the classroom: causes and strategies to help teachers cope productively. *Educational Psychology* 13: 195501983.

and lose motivation to actively participate in learning activities.[8] However, adopting a reader's mindset can teach them to persevere and push through these challenges. Here is a strategy that can help students stay focused and motivated, even when reading material that doesn't initially interest them. This approach involves identifying the purpose of the text, recognizing the benefits of reading it, understanding the goals, finding value in the content, and determining what is essential. By following these steps, students can use metacognitive strategies to stay on track and move forward.

Step 1: Identify the Purpose of the Text

The first step in tackling an uninteresting text is to understand its purpose. Why was this text assigned? What is it supposed to teach or convey? Students can see beyond their immediate disinterest by identifying the purpose and recognizing the broader educational or informational goal. For example, a passage on a standardized test might be designed to assess comprehension skills or understanding of specific literary techniques. Recognizing this can help students approach the text with a clearer sense of its importance.

Step 2: Identify Some Benefits of Reading the Text

Next, students should consider the benefits of reading the text, even if it doesn't seem appealing. What skills or knowledge can they gain? For instance, reading a dry scientific article can improve critical thinking and analytical skills, while working through a dense historical text can enhance understanding of past events and their impact on the present. By focusing on the benefits, students can find motivation to engage with the material, knowing that it contributes to their overall academic growth.

Step 3: Define Your Goal

Understanding what they are trying to accomplish with the reading can also help students stay focused. What is the specific goal of this reading assignment? Is it to prepare for a test, complete a project, or gain a deeper understanding of a subject? By clearly defining their goal, students can approach the text with a purpose, making the task more manageable. For example, if the goal is to gather information for a research paper, students can concentrate on finding and noting key facts and ideas relevant to their topic.

Step 4: Find Value in the Text

Even in the most unappealing texts, there is often something of value to be found. Students should look for aspects of the text that might be interesting or useful to them personally. This might include new vocabulary, exciting facts, or different perspectives. By finding something of value, students can make the reading experience more engaging. For instance, a student reading a textbook chapter on economics might find value in understanding how economic principles apply to real-world situations they care about, like personal finance or global markets.

Step 5: Determine What Is Important

Finally, students should focus on determining what is essential in the text. What are the key points or main ideas? What information is necessary to understand the text's purpose? Students can avoid getting bogged down by less relevant details by identifying and concentrating on the most critical aspects. This metacognitive strategy helps them stay on track and extract the necessary information to achieve their goal. For example, when reading a lengthy article, students can highlight the main arguments and supporting evidence, simplifying review and study later.

By following these steps, students can effectively navigate texts they find uninteresting. This strategy encourages them to look beyond their initial disinterest and approach the text with a purposeful and focused mindset. When students remember to identify the purpose, recognize benefits, define their goals, find value, and determine what is essential, they can focus on what matters most and push through the material. Adopting these metacognitive strategies helps them manage complex readings and builds resilience and critical thinking skills that will benefit them across all areas of study.

"This Is Too Hard"

Another common challenge is dealing with texts that seem too difficult to understand. This can be a significant barrier to reading for many students and can occur in several situations:

- **Advanced literature:** Reading complex literature above their current reading level can be daunting. Students might struggle with sophisticated vocabulary, intricate plot structures, and deep thematic content that require higher cognitive engagement and critical thinking.
- **Scientific articles:** Technical or scientific texts often contain complex vocabulary and concepts that are challenging to grasp. The specialized language and detailed explanations can be overwhelming, especially if students lack prior knowledge in the subject area.
- **Academic journals:** Scholarly articles, especially those with dense and specialized content, can be overwhelming for students unfamiliar with the field. They often assume a certain level of expertise and use jargon that can be difficult for novice readers to decode.
- **Standardized tests:** These tests often include passages that are intentionally challenging to assess higher-level reading skills. The passages might be drawn from diverse genres and disciplines, requiring students to quickly adapt to different styles and complexities of writing under time constraints.

Fostering a reader's mindset can help students develop the resilience and strategies to tackle these common reading challenges. This mindset involves approaching reading with a positive attitude, being prepared to engage deeply with the text, and having the confidence to persist through difficulties. It transforms reading from a daunting task into an opportunity for growth, enabling students to engage with and comprehend any text they encounter. Fostering a reader's mindset, where students approach reading with a positive attitude and a willingness to engage deeply, is key to building resilience and strategies to overcome reading challenges. Research shows that this mindset not only increases engagement but also builds the persistence needed to tackle difficult texts. One study highlights that resilient readers are more likely to persevere through challenges, viewing setbacks as opportunities for growth rather than obstacles. This resilience is closely tied to metacognitive strategies, where students actively monitor their understanding and apply problem-solving techniques when they encounter difficulties.[9]

When students adopt a reader's mindset, they are better equipped to navigate the complexities of standardized tests, engage with assigned readings, and tackle challenging academic material. This helps them succeed in specific tasks and builds the skills and confidence necessary for lifelong reading and learning. Cultivating a reader's mindset prepares students to be adaptable, critical thinkers who can approach any reading task with confidence and determination.

Reader's Mindset Strategy for Battling "This Is Too Hard"

> **Reader's Mindset Strategy to Battle 'This is Too Hard'**
> - **Step 1:** Check Your Thinking, Is Your Brain On?
> - **Step 2:** Remember Your YET, Things Will Get Easier
> - **Step 3:** Remember the Tools You Have To Help You
> - **Step 4:** Understand That You Are Growing Your Brain
> - **Step 5:** Use Your Vision Board To Help You With Strategies

Reading complex texts can be daunting for many students, but by adopting a reader's mindset, they can learn to persevere and push through the challenges. The following strategy provides a step-by-step approach to help students stay engaged and motivated when faced with texts that seem too difficult. This method encourages students to activate their thinking, remember the growth mindset principle of "yet," utilize their metacognitive tools, understand the cognitive growth they are experiencing, and use a vision board to guide their strategies. By following the steps described in the following sections, students can turn a seemingly impossible reading task into an achievable goal.

---

[9] McTigue, E., Washburn, E., and Liew, J. (2009). Academic resilience and reading: building successful readers. *International Literacy Association and Wiley* 62 (5): 422–432.

Step 1: Check Your Thinking, Is Your Brain On?

The first step in tackling a complex text is ensuring students are fully mentally engaged. This means actively checking their thinking and ensuring their brain is "on." Students should ask themselves if they are focused and ready to engage with the text. This mental check-in can help them recognize if they are approaching the reading with the right mindset or need to recenter their focus. Encouraging students to take a few deep breaths, clear their minds of distractions, and set an intention for the reading session can prime their brains for active engagement.

Step 2: Remember Your "Yet," Things Will Get Easier

The second step is to remind students of the power of the word "yet." This concept, rooted in the growth mindset philosophy, emphasizes that while a task might be challenging, effort and persistence make improvement possible. Students should remind themselves that they might not understand the text yet, but with practice and determination, they will improve. This mindset shift helps reduce frustration and encourages a more positive outlook on their reading capabilities, fostering resilience and a willingness to tackle challenging texts.

Step 3: Remember the Tools You Have to Help You

Next, students should recall the various metacognitive strategies they have at their disposal. These tools are designed to keep their brain activated and aid in comprehension. Strategies such as summarizing text sections, asking questions while reading, visualizing concepts, and connecting to prior knowledge can all help break down complex material. By actively using these tools, students can enhance their understanding and make the reading process more manageable. Teachers can reinforce this by providing reminders and examples of using these strategies effectively.

Step 4: Understand That You Are Growing Your Brain

It is also essential for students to understand that struggling with complex texts is part of the learning process that contributes to cognitive growth. As discussed in Chapter 4, when students engage with challenging material, their brains grow by forming new neurons and dendrites. This neuroplasticity means that each effort to understand complex texts strengthens their cognitive abilities and improves their reading skills. Highlighting this scientific perspective can motivate students to embrace the struggle as a valuable part of their educational journey.

Step 5: Use Your Vision Board to Help You with Strategies

Students can create and use a reader's vision board to support these efforts. A vision board is a visual tool encompassing different reading skills and strategies students have worked on to become better readers. Teachers can help students design their vision boards, which might include images, quotes, and reminders of the strategies they find most compelling. By referring to their vision board, students can quickly recall and apply the best strategy for them, providing a tangible reminder of their progress and the tools at their disposal.

Implementing this strategy requires consistent reinforcement and practice. Teachers should regularly encourage students to check their thinking and ensure they are mentally prepared before starting a challenging text. Reminders about the growth mindset and the power of "yet" can be incorporated into daily lessons to build resilience. Additionally, teachers can provide structured opportunities for students to practice metacognitive strategies through guided reading sessions or strategy-focused workshops.

Supporting students through their reading journey also involves celebrating their successes and reflecting on their growth. Teachers can create a classroom environment where effort is recognized, and progress is celebrated, no matter how small. Teachers can foster a community of resilient, confident readers by regularly discussing the cognitive benefits of tackling complex texts and encouraging students to share their experiences.

By following these steps and consistently applying a reader's mindset, students can effectively tackle texts that initially seem too difficult. This approach helps them succeed in their immediate reading tasks and builds the skills and confidence necessary for lifelong reading and learning. Adopting a reader's mindset transforms challenging reading experiences into growth, resilience, and cognitive development opportunities.

Reflect: Think about your students who often express frustration with difficult texts. What specific strategies can you implement to help them develop persistence? How can you adapt your instruction to foster a reader's mindset, ensuring they see challenging texts as opportunities for growth rather than obstacles?

A Reading Teacher's Mindset

Teaching is an art, filled with complexities and nuances that not everyone can master. A critical component of a strong teacher, especially a reading teacher, is their mindset. A study done by Greg Gero showed that "those who endorse more of a growth mindset valued learning over looking good or risk-free teaching. Like students who hold more of a growth mindset, they cared more about learning than about their reputation as a good teacher or their perfection as a teacher."[10] Our actions stem from our thoughts, and without the right mindset, our actions may miss the mark. So, what mindsets do reading teachers need to be successful? The following sections explore the essential mindsets for reading teachers.

The Six Parts of a Reading Teacher's Mindset	
#1	All Students Are Readers
#2	Change Is Welcome
#3	Relationships Are the Foundation
#4	Students Do Not Equal Levels
#5	Purposeful and Methodical Thinking
#6	Reading Is Thinking

---

[10] Stringer, S. and Mollineaux, B. (2003). Removing the word "Reluctant Reader." *National Council of Teachers of English* 92 (4): 71–76.

Reading Teacher Mindset #1: All Students Are Readers

There is no such thing as a person who doesn't like to read; there are only people who haven't found the right book yet. The right book can transform a nonreader into an avid reader. This mindset is crucial because it drives our mission as reading teachers. We don't just aim to teach students how to read; we aim to turn them into lifelong readers and learners.

Believing in this mindset influences our actions profoundly. If we truly believe that all students can become readers, we won't settle for students being disengaged with their reading material. We'll persist in finding the right books and strategies to ignite their passion for reading. Do you believe that all students are readers? Are you committed to doing whatever it takes to help them realize this?

Reading Teacher Mindset #2: Change Is Welcome

Adapting to change is challenging, but it's necessary. If 2020 and the pandemic taught us anything, it's that we must be prepared for and embrace change. A strong reading teacher understands that change is inevitable and welcomes it. Why? Because as the world evolves, so do our students, and new research continuously offers better instructional methods.

Resilient reading teachers don't cling to the phrase, "This has always worked." They remain open to new learning, professional development, and innovative strategies. They skillfully blend proven techniques with new insights to provide the best education for their students.

Reading Teacher Mindset #3: Relationships Are the Foundation

You've likely heard it many times, but it bears repeating: students cannot learn effectively from someone they don't know and trust. For students, reading is a vulnerable activity.

They may worry about mispronouncing words, misunderstanding the text, or how their voice sounds when reading aloud. Without a strong, trusting relationship with their reading teacher, these insecurities can become overwhelming.

Building relationships from the start establishes a foundation of trust, support, and open communication. This is especially important for reading teachers because it helps students feel secure and more willing to take risks in their reading.

Reading Teacher Mindset #4: Students Do Not Equal Levels

Guided reading levels are instructional tools, not labels for students. They illustrate the various types of thinking required as students progress through different reading stages. Students should never be identified by their reading level, as it fosters a competitive and comparative culture that can lead to feelings of inadequacy or superiority.

Adopting this mindset means focusing on supporting readers' habits and behaviors through the levels, rather than assigning levels to students. This approach should be embraced not only by individual teachers but by the entire school community, from administration to staff.

Reading Teacher Mindset #5: Purposeful and Methodical Thinking

Effective reading teachers are like CIA analysts: meticulous with data, strategic in planning and executing lessons, and organized in managing materials and knowledge. Crafting strong lesson plans requires time, effort, and thoughtful consideration, as each student has unique strengths, weaknesses, and interests.

This mindset acknowledges that teaching reading is an art. It's not enough to simply follow a curriculum; teachers must tailor their approach to meet the diverse needs of their students. This dedication to thoughtful lesson planning is a burden reading teachers proudly bear for the benefit of their students.

Reading Teacher Mindset #6: Reading Is Thinking

This mindset is my favorite and perhaps the most important. Reading isn't just about decoding words, fluency, or answering basic comprehension questions. Reading is a process of thinking, engaging with the text, and transforming it into personal knowledge. This includes employing metacognitive strategies like visualizing, making connections, and synthesizing information.

Strong reading teachers recognize that even students who struggle with reading can excel in thinking. They prioritize deep comprehension and meaningful conversations over easy-to-measure tasks. Emphasizing critical thinking in reading strengthens students' overall reading abilities and fosters a deeper engagement with texts.

Incorporating these six mindsets can transform the effectiveness of reading teachers, enabling them to inspire and educate students more profoundly.

Fostering a Reader's Mindset Culture

Building persistence in young readers is fundamental to fostering a reader's mindset culture in the classroom. A reader's mindset encompasses the belief that every student can become a proficient reader through effort, strategic thinking, and perseverance. By cultivating this mindset, teachers create an environment where students can tackle complex texts confidently and resiliently. This shift from a fixed to a growth mindset empowers students to see challenges as opportunities for growth rather than insurmountable obstacles.

Encouraging Productive Struggle

One of the key strategies to foster persistence in students is to encourage productive struggle. Research supports the claim that encouraging productive struggle is a key strategy to foster persistence in students. Productive struggle refers to the process of working through challenging tasks where students are pushed beyond their comfort zone but provided with enough support to avoid discouragement. This strategy builds not only perseverance but also resilience and problem-solving abilities.

Studies by Kapur and Bielaczyc (2012) emphasize that productive struggle helps students develop a growth mindset, which is essential for persistence. When students successfully work through difficulties, their self-efficacy grows, reinforcing their belief that effort leads to improvement. This mindset encourages them to persist even when they encounter challenges.[11]

This means designing reading activities that are challenging but achievable, ensuring that students are not overwhelmed but are sufficiently stretched to grow their skills. Teaching the necessary strategies and skills before presenting challenging texts is essential so students feel equipped to handle difficulties. Scaffolding is necessary, providing the right level of support tailored to each student's needs. For example, breaking down a complex text into manageable parts or using guided reading sessions can help students build confidence and persistence as they tackle more challenging material.

Reminding Students They Are Thinkers

Chapter 1 established that students are readers because they can think. Reminding students that they are thinkers is a powerful way to build persistence. When faced with a complex text, emphasize that thinking through challenges makes them stronger readers. Encourage them to piece things together, use their strategies, and think critically about what they do and do not understand. This reinforces the idea that struggling with a text is a natural part of the learning process. Their ability to think and analyze is a valuable tool in overcoming difficulties.

Using Metacognition Strategies

Metacognition, or thinking about one's thinking, is a crucial strategy for building persistence. When students encounter challenging reading passages, activating their

---

[11] Kapur, M. and Bielaczyc, K. (2012). Designing for productive failure. *The Journal of the Learning Sciences* 21 (1): 45–83.

metacognitive strategies is the perfect time. Encourage them to ask themselves questions like: Are you visualizing the content? Are you making connections to prior knowledge? Can you determine what's most important in the text or synthesize information as you read? Teaching students to use these strategies helps them navigate complex texts and builds their confidence and persistence as they realize they have the tools to overcome challenges. Head back to Chapter 7 for more information about metacognition!

Encouraging Goal Setting and Reflection

Setting specific, attainable goals can help students persist through complex reading tasks. Setting goals is an effective strategy to help students persist through complex reading tasks. Research shows that breaking tasks into manageable goals enhances students' motivation, persistence, and academic success. Locke and Latham's goal-setting theory emphasizes that clear, measurable goals help students stay focused and persist even when tasks become challenging.[12] Encourage students to set small, manageable goals, such as understanding a particular paragraph or identifying the main idea of a section. After achieving these goals, prompt them to reflect on their progress. Reflective practices help students recognize their growth and understand that persistence leads to improvement. This process reinforces their motivation to keep trying, even when tasks are challenging.

Creating a Safe Environment for Risk-Taking

Fostering an environment where students feel safe to take risks and make mistakes is essential for building persistence. Research consistently shows that when students perceive their learning environment as emotionally and psychologically safe, they are more likely to engage deeply with challenging tasks, take intellectual risks, and persist through difficulties. Classrooms that promote psychological safety also encourage collaborative

---

[12] Midwest Comprehensive Center. (2018). Institutes for Research Student goal settings: An evidence-based practice. https://eric.ed.gov/?id=ED589978.

problem-solving, where students feel comfortable sharing ideas and working together. This type of environment not only supports cognitive growth but also enhances students' self-awareness and emotional regulation, which are key components in developing persistence.[13]

Encourage a classroom culture that celebrates effort and learning from mistakes. Provide positive reinforcement and constructive feedback on the process rather than the outcome. When students feel their efforts are valued and it's okay to make mistakes, they are more likely to persist through challenges and develop a growth mindset.

Providing Opportunities for Peer Collaboration

Peer collaboration can be a powerful motivator for persistence. Create opportunities for students to work together on challenging reading tasks. Group discussions, peer mentoring, and collaborative projects allow students to support each other, share strategies, and build confidence. Working with peers can also help students realize that struggling with a text is a common experience and that they can learn from each other's approaches to overcoming difficulties.

Modeling Persistence

As a teacher, modeling persistence is one of the most effective ways to instill this trait in your students. Share your experiences with challenging texts and demonstrate your strategies to overcome difficulties. Show them that even experienced readers encounter rigid material, and that persistence and strategic thinking are key to comprehension. By seeing you tackle challenges with a positive attitude and effective strategies, students will be more likely to emulate these behaviors in their own reading.

---

[13] Sandler, G. & Howell, S. (2023). International Society for Technology in education 7 ways of creating psychological safety for students. https://iste.org/blog/7-ways-of-creating-psychological-safety-for-students.

By incorporating these strategies into daily instruction, teachers can build a classroom culture that not only values persistence but also views it as integral to becoming proficient readers. This culture encourages students to approach reading with a problem-solving attitude and resilience, knowing that their efforts and strategies will lead to success. Fostering a reader's mindset culture helps students develop into confident, capable readers who are prepared to tackle increasingly complex texts throughout their academic journey and beyond.

Closing

As I conclude this chapter, it is essential to recognize the profound impact that cultivating a reader's mindset can have on supporting literacy, enhancing comprehension, and developing critical thinkers. A reader's mindset equips students with the tools and strategies to approach reading with resilience and determination, transforming their reading experiences from passive consumption to active engagement. By fostering this mindset, you empower your students to navigate complex texts, overcome obstacles, and develop a lifelong love for reading.

Supporting literacy through a reader's mindset means more than just teaching students to read; it involves helping them become thoughtful and reflective readers. This mindset encourages students to employ metacognitive strategies, such as summarizing, questioning, and predicting, which enhance their comprehension and retention of information. Students can achieve more profound levels of understanding and critical engagement with texts by understanding their strengths and weaknesses as readers and actively working to improve. This process improves academic performance and builds their confidence and self-efficacy as readers.

Furthermore, developing a reader's mindset directly contributes to developing critical thinking skills. When students approach reading with an active, questioning attitude, they learn to analyze and synthesize information, make connections between different texts and ideas, and evaluate the validity and relevance of information. These skills are essential for academic success and for navigating the complex information landscape of the modern world. A reader's mindset, therefore, is a foundation for developing the higher-order thinking skills that students need to become informed and engaged citizens.

The importance of a reader's mindset cannot be overstated. It is vital in the journey toward literacy, comprehension, and critical thinking. By teaching students to adopt this mindset, you are not just helping them to read better but also to think better. This holistic approach to reading education fosters a love of learning and equips students with the skills they need to succeed in all areas of their lives. You can continue to support and encourage your students to develop a reader's mindset, knowing that you are helping shape the next generation of thoughtful, resilient, and capable readers and thinkers. Consider these questions as you ponder this issue more and try the following lessons.

End of Chapter Reflection Questions:

- What is a way to introduce a growth mindset to students if they don't already have that background knowledge?
- How can we help students identify their roadblocks to reading?
- How do we get students excited to be persistent (buy-in)?
- How can we help students identify what strategies should be on their personal "vision boards" that work for them?

Lessons to Try

Don't forget to access the complete lessons for free at `http://www.cieraharristeaching.com/ttrlessons` using the passcode: `literacy for all`.

"A Reader's Mindset" Lesson

The lesson plan, "A Reader's Mindset," focuses on teaching students the importance of adopting a positive mindset toward reading. It aims to integrate the concept of a growth mindset with reading habits, encouraging students to approach reading with confidence and resilience. The lesson begins with a review of what a mindset is and how it affects performance. Through interactive activities, such as using weighted bags to symbolize negative mindsets and their impact, students understand how their thoughts can influence their abilities. This hands-on approach helps students visualize the burden of a negative mindset and the freedom that comes with a positive one.

Teaching "A Reader's Mindset" is crucial because it addresses students' psychological barriers when approaching challenging texts. By linking the growth mindset principles to reading, students learn to persist through difficulties and view challenges as opportunities for growth. The lesson emphasizes the importance of preparation and mental readiness before engaging in reading activities. This preparation includes knowing the tools available, being ready for challenges, maintaining perseverance, staying focused, and eliminating distractions. These strategies improve reading skills and foster a lifelong positive attitude toward learning.

For teachers, this lesson offers a comprehensive framework to help students develop a constructive approach to reading. Teachers can create a supportive classroom environment that encourages positive attitudes and resilience by modeling the reader's mindset and engaging students in discussions and activities.

Quick Tip

Consistently refer back to the reader's mindset components throughout the school year. Reinforcing these concepts regularly will help students internalize the mindset and apply it not only to reading but to other areas of their academic and personal lives.

"I Don't Like This" Lesson

The lesson plan "I Don't Like This" is designed to help students develop strategies for reading and comprehending texts they find uninteresting. The core objective is to instill a growth mindset in students, encouraging them to push through challenging or tedious material by understanding how interest affects brain function and learning outcomes. Essential questions in the lesson guide students to explore the impact of interest on their cognitive processes and identify actionable steps to maintain comprehension even when faced with unengaging content.

The importance of this lesson lies in its focus on equipping students with practical tools to manage their reading experiences. The lesson underscores the significance of perseverance and strategic thinking in overcoming academic challenges by linking the concept of reading with the broader idea of a growth mindset. Students learn that while interest can enhance memory and focus, a lack of it does not have to hinder their understanding if they employ specific strategies. This lesson thus prepares students to handle various reading situations they will encounter in their academic journey and beyond, fostering resilience and adaptability.

Teaching this lesson offers multiple benefits. It enhances students' reading comprehension skills and promotes a positive attitude toward learning complex material. Students become more self-aware and better equipped to tackle similar situations independently by practicing with uninteresting texts and using the provided mindset strategies. This proactive approach to reading challenging texts can improve academic performance and instill lifelong learning habits.

Quick Tip: Model these strategies consistently with different texts and contexts. Repeated practice and discussion will reinforce the techniques and help students internalize them more effectively.

"It's Too Hard" Lesson

The "It's Too Hard" lesson plan is designed to help students develop resilience and effective strategies for tackling challenging texts. The lesson's objective is for students to recognize that not all texts will be easy to read, but they can overcome these difficulties with the right mindset and tools. The lesson starts by engaging students in a discussion about other complex tasks they've faced, such as learning to walk or ride a bike, drawing parallels to their reading challenges. This initial discussion sets the stage for students to understand that struggling with reading is a normal part of the learning process and that perseverance is critical.

The lesson introduces strategies to help students push through complex texts, including mindset shifts and practical action steps. An anchor chart is used to visually present these strategies, which include reminders about not letting a negative mindset get in the way and using specific tools like a vision board. The vision board is a crucial component of the lesson, providing students with a personalized resource they can refer to whenever they encounter a complicated text. Students create their vision boards with strategies such as asking for help, re-reading, and using text clues. These boards are designed to be ongoing projects that students can update throughout the year.

Teaching this lesson is highly beneficial as it equips students with the skills and confidence to tackle complex reading tasks independently. It promotes a growth mindset, helping students understand that struggling with reading is a natural part of learning and that they can improve with practice. Additionally, by providing concrete strategies and tools, the lesson empowers students to take control of their learning and develop problem-solving skills that are essential for academic success.

Quick Tip

When implementing this lesson, continually reinforce the strategies and use the vision boards regularly, ensuring students understand how to apply the tools effectively in various reading situations.

CLOSING

This closing section reflects on the foundational principles and strategies this book has explored. The book began with a fundamental reexamination of what reading truly is, considering its multifaceted nature. Understanding reading as personal growth, as thinking, and as power helped set the stage for a deeper engagement with texts and prepared you to foster a more profound appreciation of reading in your students.

A Quick Look Back

Emphasizing the importance of setting up for success at the beginning of the year, the book explored how laying solid groundwork can significantly impact students' reading development. This preparatory phase is crucial, as it shapes the learning environment and establishes a foundation for success. Taking the time to know your students and their reading abilities allows you to tailor your teaching strategies to effectively meet their individual needs.

Delving into the cognitive science behind reading highlighted why it's essential to understand how the brain acquires reading skills. This knowledge lays the groundwork for the strategies you implement in your classroom. I emphasized its pivotal role in comprehension and engagement by focusing on schema, perspectives, and expertise that readers bring to a text. Understanding these cognitive processes enables teachers to better support their students in their reading journeys.

The Thinking READER

Foundations of Reading

Lay the groundwork for understanding the core principles of reading and establishing a successful reading environment.

Cognitive Science of a Reader

Explore the neurological and cognitive processes behind reading, emphasizing the importance of schema.

Cultivating Metacognitive Thinkers

Focus on strategies to maintain curiosity, develop metacognitive skills, and apply effective reading techniques to engage students.

Communication & Critical Thinking

Highlight the importance of meaningful dialogue about texts and the development of critical thinking skills in reading.

Building Resilience and Persistence

Provide strategies for fostering a growth mindset and teaching students to overcome challenges and persist in their reading efforts.

Cultivating metacognitive thinkers was the next focus. I discussed the importance of maintaining student curiosity and how it is a powerful motivator for learning. Emphasizing metacognition, I highlighted the significance of students thinking about their thinking. Fostering metacognitive skills helps students become more independent and reflective readers. Practical strategies such as visualization, determining importance, and making connections were provided as essential tools for any Thinking Reader.

Exploring how to engage students in meaningful dialogues about texts underscored the importance of communication and critical thinking. These discussions not only enhance comprehension but also develop critical thinking skills. Further, fostering critical thinking in the classroom involves challenging students and encouraging deeper analysis and reflection.

Finally, addressing the inevitability of roadblocks in the reading journey, I emphasized the importance of teaching students to build resilience and persistence. By fostering a growth mindset from an early age, you help your students overcome challenges and view difficulties as opportunities for growth.

These foundational principles and strategies aim to transform how teachers approach literacy instruction, ultimately helping students become thoughtful, critical, and engaged readers. The journey to building a Thinking Reader is ongoing, and the strategies and insights shared here are meant to be revisited and adapted to fit your unique classroom dynamics.

> "I really liked the emphasis on the student getting to know themselves as a reader. Reading and comprehension become more intrinsic and students can become more self aware with the strategies that were taught. I loved thinking about the neurons in the brain and how the paths weren't there—yet!! That makes it ok for kids to struggle and work on skills, they are building those new paths. I think it will be a relief to some students to know they don't have to 'get' things right away, and there's a valid reason why!"
>
> -Charlene Churchill, 4th Grade, Spruce Mountain Elementary School, Maine

What's Missing?

While this book has focused on the art of building Thinking Readers through purpose, planning, and passion, it must acknowledge that several crucial elements of literacy education have not been covered in depth. Understanding and integrating the five components of reading—phonemic awareness, phonics, fluency, vocabulary, and comprehension—is fundamental to a student's success. Each element is an intricate puzzle piece, essential for developing strong, capable readers.

Phonemic awareness and phonics lay the groundwork for decoding words, a critical skill for early readers. Fluency, the ability to read with speed, accuracy, and proper expression, allows students to focus on understanding the text rather than decoding each word. Vocabulary development is vital as it directly impacts a student's comprehension and engagement with a text. Lastly, comprehension, the ultimate goal of reading, involves making meaning from text and requires a combination of all the other components working together seamlessly.

Another critical aspect not deeply explored in this book is the importance of diversity and inclusion in literacy education. Providing students with a diverse range of texts that reflect different cultures, experiences, and perspectives is essential. It helps students see themselves in the stories they read and broadens their understanding of the world. Inclusive teaching practices ensure that every student, regardless of background or ability, has access to quality literacy education and feels valued in the learning environment.

Proper assessment and advanced testing for students who struggle with reading are also paramount. Regular and varied assessments help teachers understand students' needs and track their progress. Advanced testing can identify specific areas where students need additional support or intervention. This personalized approach is crucial for ensuring that all students receive the help they need to succeed in literacy.

Additionally, aspects such as fostering a positive reading culture, encouraging reading for pleasure, and involving families in the literacy journey are essential components that contribute to a student's overall success in reading. While this book focuses on building Thinking Readers through metacognition, critical thinking, and resilience, it's important to remember that a comprehensive literacy program includes these elements and more.

In the beginning, I mentioned that this book is different. I hope you now see that building Thinking Readers is an art that requires purpose, planning, and passion from dedicated teachers like you. By integrating the strategies discussed in this book with a holistic approach that includes all these crucial elements, you will be well equipped to nurture a generation of students who are proficient readers and thoughtful, critical thinkers ready to engage with the world around them.

Support from Others

Creating Thinking Readers is a goal that extends beyond the classroom, requiring the involvement and support of administrators, parents, and the community. Bridging this understanding to all stakeholders is crucial for fostering an environment where students can thrive as critical thinkers and engaged readers. Each group plays a vital role in supporting and nurturing the development of Thinking Readers, and understanding what this entails can lead to a more cohesive and practical approach to literacy education.

For administrators, embracing the concept of Thinking Readers means supporting teachers with the resources, professional development, and time needed to implement these strategies effectively. Administrators should promote a school culture that values critical thinking, encourages innovative teaching methods, and provides opportunities for collaborative planning. By recognizing the importance of metacognition and critical thinking in reading, administrators can advocate for curricula beyond basic literacy skills, ensuring that students are challenged and supported to become thoughtful readers.

Parents play a fundamental role in their children's literacy development. Parents can better support their children at home by understanding what it means to be a Thinking Reader. This involves encouraging curiosity, engaging in meaningful discussions about books, and fostering a love of reading. Parents can create a home environment rich in literacy experiences by providing access to diverse reading materials and modeling good reading habits. Communication between teachers and parents about the goals and strategies for developing Thinking Readers is essential, enabling parents to reinforce these concepts at home.

How Can Stakeholders Help Support Teachers?

Stakeholder	Ways to Support Teachers
Administrators	• Provide professional development focused on metacognition and critical thinking. • Allocate resources for diverse reading materials. • Foster a school culture that values and prioritizes critical thinking.
Parents	• Encourage reading at home by providing diverse and engaging books. • Engage in meaningful discussions about books with their children. • Model good reading habits.
Policy Makers	• Advocate for policies that support comprehensive literacy programs. • Fund initiatives that provide schools with necessary resources. • Promote standards that emphasize critical thinking and metacognitive skills.
Researchers	• Conduct studies on effective strategies for developing Thinking Readers. • Share research findings with educators through publications and professional development. • Collaborate with schools to implement and test new literacy initiatives.

Community Organizations	• Partner with schools to host literacy events and programs. • Provide access to reading materials through public libraries and community centers. • Support after-school tutoring and reading clubs.
Higher Education Institutions	• Train future teachers in strategies for building Thinking Readers. • Offer continuing education courses for current teachers. • Conduct and disseminate research on literacy education.
Education Technology Providers	• Develop tools and platforms that support critical thinking and metacognitive skills. • Provide training and support for teachers on how to effectively use technology in literacy instruction. • Create interactive and engaging digital reading materials.
Literacy Coaches	• Work directly with teachers to implement best practices in literacy instruction. • Provide ongoing support and feedback. • Help teachers design and execute lesson plans that foster critical thinking.

The community, too, has a significant part to play. Libraries, local businesses, and community organizations can support literacy initiatives by providing resources, hosting reading events, and creating spaces where children can engage with texts in various ways. Community involvement can help students see the relevance of reading in real-world contexts and provide additional opportunities to practice and develop their reading skills. A community that values and supports literacy creates a network of encouragement and resources that benefits all students.

For all stakeholders, the goal is to create a unified vision of what it means to be a Thinking Reader. This vision includes recognizing the importance of critical thinking, metacognition, and resilience in reading. It involves providing teachers with the necessary support and resources, creating engaging and literacy-rich environments at home, and fostering a community that values and promotes reading. By working together, administrators, parents, and the community can ensure that students learn to read and develop the skills to think deeply and critically about what they read.

In conclusion, bridging the understanding of a Thinking Reader to all stakeholders is essential for creating a supportive and effective literacy education system. When administrators, parents, and the community are aligned in their efforts, students are more likely to succeed and thrive as engaged, thoughtful readers. This collaborative approach ensures that the development of Thinking Readers is a shared responsibility, ultimately benefiting the entire educational ecosystem and the students it serves.

Long-Term Benefits of Being a Thinking Reader

The journey to becoming a Thinking Reader, as outlined in this book, extends far beyond the elementary classroom. The skills and mindsets developed through these steps have lasting impacts that benefit students throughout their educational journey and into adulthood. By fostering critical thinking, metacognitive awareness, and resilience, we are equipping our students with tools that will serve them well in middle school, high school, higher education, and life.

In middle school, students nurtured as Thinking Readers are better prepared to tackle more complex texts and academic challenges. They approach reading assignments strategically, using metacognitive strategies to monitor their understanding and make connections. These students are likelier to engage in meaningful discussions about texts, contribute insightful perspectives, and collaborate effectively with their peers. Their ability to think critically allows them to analyze and synthesize information from various sources, an essential skill for success in all subjects.

As students transition to high school, the benefits of being a Thinking Reader become even more pronounced. High school students encounter increasingly sophisticated texts and must engage in more advanced analytical and evaluative tasks. Thinking Readers confidently approach these challenges, applying their well-developed critical thinking skills to dissect arguments, evaluate evidence, and form reasoned conclusions. They excel in written assignments, research projects, and debates, often leading in classroom discussions and group projects.

The habits and skills developed through the Thinking Reader framework are invaluable in higher education. College and university students face diverse reading materials, from academic journals to complex literature. Thinking Readers easily navigate these texts, employing advanced reading strategies and critical thinking to extract and integrate key ideas. Their metacognitive abilities allow them to adapt to various academic demands, manage their study time effectively, and approach learning as a dynamic and reflective process. These students are not just passive recipients of information but active participants in their education, capable of deep understanding and original thought.

Beyond academia, the benefits of being a Thinking Reader extend into adulthood and everyday life. As adults, Thinking Readers are equipped to navigate the vast amounts of information encountered in the digital age. They critically evaluate news, media, and other sources, discerning credible information from misinformation. Their strong reading and analytical skills enhance their professional capabilities, enabling them to excel in diverse careers. Moreover, their ability to think critically and reflectively enriches their personal lives, fostering informed decision-making, empathy, and lifelong learning.

A Thinking Reader as an adult is a well-rounded, thoughtful, and engaged individual. They can understand and interpret complex information, engage in meaningful discourse, and approach problems critically and openly. These skills are beneficial for personal and professional growth and contribute to society's betterment. By cultivating Thinking Readers, we prepare our students for a future where they can thrive, contribute positively, and continually seek knowledge and understanding. This long-term impact underscores the profound significance of the steps outlined in this book, demonstrating the transformative power of a thoughtful, strategic approach to literacy education.

Wrapping It Up

I want to leave you with excitement and optimism for the journey ahead. Your work is not just about teaching reading; it's about transforming lives. By implementing the strategies and insights shared in these pages, you are setting your students on a path to becoming proficient readers and thoughtful, critical thinkers who can navigate the complexities of the world around them.

> I hope you now see that building Thinking Readers is an art that requires purpose, planning, and passion from dedicated teachers like you.

Throughout this book, I've explored the essential components of building a Thinking Reader. You've learned how to lay the foundations of reading, understand the cognitive processes behind it, cultivate metacognitive skills, foster meaningful communication and critical thinking, and build resilience and persistence. Each of these steps is crucial to helping your students grow into confident, capable readers.

To illustrate the long-term impact of these efforts, let's consider some stories of success. Picture a student who once struggled with basic reading skills, now eagerly diving into complex texts, asking insightful questions, and making connections that showcase their deep understanding. Imagine their joy and pride as they realize their potential and embrace their identity as a reader. These stories are not just hypothetical; they are the outcomes of a dedicated and thoughtful approach to literacy instruction.

One teacher shared how their classroom transformed after implementing the strategies from this book. Students who were once disengaged and reluctant readers became excited about reading. They began to see reading as an adventure, a way to explore new worlds and ideas. Another teacher found that their students developed a newfound resilience, tackling challenging texts with determination and confidence. The critical thinking skills they cultivated helped them excel not only in reading but across all subjects.

As you continue this important work, remember that every lesson, every interaction, and every moment of encouragement contributes to your students' growth. The seeds you plant today will blossom into a lifelong love of learning and a deep, enduring capability to think critically and engage meaningfully with the world.

The journey doesn't end here. This book is a starting point, a guide to help you navigate the complexities of teaching reading in a way that truly matters. Keep exploring, questioning, and striving to be your best teacher. Your impact on your students will echo far beyond the classroom, shaping their futures and the world they will one day influence.

Thank you for committing to your students and joining me on this journey. Together, we are creating a generation of readers who think, analyze, and grow with every text they encounter. The future is bright, and I am excited for what's to come next. Keep inspiring challenge and believe in the power of reading.

Final Note from Ciera

I leave you with a choice. You can go through the motions, teach the curriculum as prescribed, and continue to see the same "bell curve" results year after year. Or, you can push the boundaries, challenge the status quo, and dedicate yourself to building your students into Thinking Readers. This path requires purpose, planning, and passion, but the rewards are immeasurable. Are you up for the challenge? The decision is yours to make. Choose to inspire, innovate, and transform your students' lives through the power of thoughtful, engaged reading. The future of your students depends on the choices you make today.

INDEX

A

Abstract ideas/relationships, understanding, 140–141
Academic conversations
 components, 280–283
 identification, 280–284
 social conversations, contrast, 279
Academic Conversations: Classroom Talk That Fosters Critical Thinking and Content Understandings (Zwiers/Crawford), 276
Academic discussions, structured format, 278
Academic journals, reading difficulty, 390
Academic language, familiarity (absence), 278
Academic performance, improvement, 96, 99
Acceptable struggle, concept (acknowledgment/discussion), 301
"Accessing My Schema" lesson, 160
Accountable talk, 297–298
Achievable goals, setting, 75
Active involvement, 23
 promotion, 25–26
Active participation, impact, 202
Active readers
 creation, 24
 inactive readers, contrast, 195
 metacognition, ability, 194
Active reading, impact, 25–27
Activities, planning, 70
Advanced literature, reading difficulty, 390
Agreements (academic conversation component), 280, 281
Amygdala, engagement, 122
Analysis
 comparative analysis, 359
 prerequisite skills, 336
Analytical skills, impact, 201
Annotation, modeling, 355
Anxiety (reduction), positive emotive connections (impact), 121
"Asking Questions" lesson, 187
Assess Plan Approach Reflect (metacognitive cycle), 236–238, 241–243
Assigned reading, issues, 387
Attention
 capture, 121
 stamina, teaching (importance), 59
Attention-focusing techniques, 73
Authentic questioning, 251

Authors
    credibility, 358
    intent, understanding, 256
    studies, 178
    visits, invitation, 180
"Author *vs.* Me" lesson, 223
Autonomous learning, 200–201
Autonomy
    increase, 45
    promotion, 87
Axons (information transmitters), 107, 108

B

Background knowledge
    absence, recognition, 263
    breadth/depth, development, 77
    building, 147
    importance, 14
    role, 136
    schema, relationship, 133
    text, connection, 135
    usage, 28–29, 44–45, 383
Beyond-the-text questions, 257
Bias, 358
Bloom's taxonomy, usage, 346
Blueprint data
    basis, 86
    collection, 79
Books
    clubs, usage, 182–183
    conversations, teacher
        questions, 81
    dynamic introductions, 178
    genre selection, creation, 82
    matching, 41
    new/old books, balance
        (maintenance), 53
    selection, 80
    showcasing, 56–57
    student immersion, 59
Book talks, usage, 83
Brain
    activation, curiosity (impact), 167
    circuitry, experiments, 113, 114
    defining, 100–111
    development, 49, 126
    diagram, 105
    education, integration, 124
    examination, reason, 97–100
    functions, 117
    growth, 392–393
    lobes, interaction process, 105–106
    malleability, 114
    physical growth, 110
    plasticity, role (emphasis), 116
    process, visualization, 106
    reading, relationship, 95
    reward system, curiosity (impact), 118, 168
    science of reading, relationship, 112–115
    teaching, 99
        benefits, 111
Brainstorming, usage, 77, 149
"Building Curiosity" lesson, 186
"Building the Library" lesson, 64
Buzz Words (interactive small group
        activity), 311

C

Cell activities, management, 107
Cell bodies (soma), 108
Challenges
    embracing, 376
    overcoming, 97
Choice boards, usage, 174

'Circle of Me' activity, 42
Clarifications (academic conversation component), 280, 282
Clarifying questions, asking, 285
Claro, Susana, 378
Classroom
   conversations, encouragement, 293–301
   critical thinking, fostering, 325–326
   culture, fostering, 30–31
   debates, 360
   discussions, 360
      expectations, defining, 296–297
   inquiry-based classrooms, 252
   schema, usage, 145–152
   seating option, flexibility, 60
   walking, 319
Classroom libraries
   building, difficulty, 52
   multi-cultural (MC) classroom library, growth, 56
   organization, importance, 54
Class, teacher question (example), 15–16
Closed questions, usage, 18–19, 302
Close reading
   implementation, effectiveness, 353
   support strategy, 352–354
   usage, 354–356
Cognitive activities, dynamic engagement, 111
Cognitive awareness, 124
   enhancement, 95, 98
Cognitive capabilities, expansion, 110
Cognitive control, 97
Cognitive demand, increase, 278
Cognitive engagement, 356
Cognitive flexibility, 118
Cognitive functions, mental processing (relationship), 73
Cognitive processes, awareness, 359
Cognitive variables, impact, 175
Collaboration
   culture, building, 316–319
   importance, 308
Collaborative learning, 203
   encouragement, 155–156
   opportunities, creation, 177
Colored Conversations strategy, 313
Communication
   skills, strengthening, 96, 99
   techniques, explicit instruction, 295
Comparative analysis, 359
Comparative questions, usage, 345–346
Complex text
   measurement data, 215
   reading, problems, 391
   term, usage, 213
   understanding, 217
Comprehension, 101
   ability, testing, 12
   deep critical comprehension, meaning, 13
   definition, 14, 15
   depth, priming, 262
   enhancement, 117, 257
   fix-up strategies, application, 196–197
   growth, 29–30
   improvement, 75
   increase, 5
   literacy component, 7
      support, 9–10
   monitoring, 196, 234
   outcomes, improvement, 8
   promotion, 17–20

Comprehension (*Continued*)
   skills, improvement, 50
   strategies, 114
   struggle, 8
   success, 116
      factors, 44–51
   text comprehension, 15
   tools, 135
Concept mapping, usage, 151
Concepts
   connection, 147
   pre-teaching, 147
   understanding, 30
Conceptual schema, 139, 140–141
Conferences, usage, 174
Confidence
   building, 318
   increase, 45
Connection-building process, 77
Connection-making, 10, 24, 26, 74, 258–269
   advice, 264–269
   comprehension tool, 135
   difficulty, 269
   metacognitive strategies, 243, 244
   skills (expectations), assessment/sharing
      (rubric usage), 265–266
   strategies, modeling (teacher role), 263
   student management, instruction, 267
Connections
   absence, 13
   examples, 268
   meaningfulness, 267
   prompting, teacher questions, 264–265
   types, 261, 262, 269
Consumption, promotion (avoidance), 17–20
Content schema, 139, 140

Content-specific vocabulary, 88
Context clues, schema support, 144
Continuous learning, usage, 51
Conversational jobs, 299
Conversational practice, modeling
      (fishbowl strategy), 289
Conversations
   components, mastery, 285–286
   encouragement, advice, 293–301
   enjoyment, 309–314
   improvement, 301–309
   skills, 294
   student ability, assumptions, 277–279
   student engagement, 300
   student knowledge, inability, 296
   surface-level conversions/
      deep conversations, 290–293
   text analysis, combination, 288–290
Craft (reading analysis), 352–353
Crawford, Marie, 276
"Creating a Book Stack" lesson, 91
"Creating a Curiosity Routine"
      lesson, 188–189
Creativity, fostering, 29
Critical thinking, 26
   analysis
      reader perspective, 335–336
      teacher perspective, 334
   components, 333–341
      levels, 340–341
   defining, 327–333
   development, 347–349
   engagement, enhancement, 348
   evaluation
      reader perspective, 336–337
      reader usage, timing/reason, 337
      teacher perspective, 336

fostering, 325–326
  importance, 303, 385
  improvement, 348
  instruction, preparation (requirement), 343–344
  integration, 364
  learner benefits, 348
  levels, 340
  mindset
    encouragement, 362–364
    support, 364
  modelling, 364
  opportunities, 342–343
    text, impact, 216
  prerequisite analysis skills, 336
  reflective questions, engagement, 345
  schema support, 144
  skill, 88
    development, strategies, 341–361
    fostering, 29
    involvement, 25
    requirement, 357–358
  strategies, teacher modeling, 363
  supportive environment, creation, 363–364
  support, questions (usefulness, determination), 344
  synthesis
    reader perspective, 338
    teacher perspective, 337–338
  tiered questioning, studies, 347–348
Cross-modal processing, 103
Cultural awareness, 142
Cultural background, impact, 78, 85, 89, 141
Cultural references, 78
Cultural responsiveness, 87
Cultural schema, 139, 141–142
Cultural understanding, 138
Culture, importance, 48–49, 78
Curiosity
  choice/autonomy, importance, 182
  defining, 164–174
  encouragement, 31, 255–256, 363
  fostering, 173–175, 178, 342, 364
  human impulse, questioning (impact), 251
  intrinsic motivation, relationship, 175–178
  journals, keeping, 174
  learning desire, 117
  motivation ability, 163–164
  nurturing, 172–173, 363
  promotion, 174
    strategies, 178–184
  provoking, 30–31
  readers, relationship, 169–171
  reading
    comprehension, link, 171–175
  reading abilities, relationship, 168–169
  scientific exploration, 166–168
  sustaining, 178
Curiosity-driven learning, impact, 121
Customized reading lists, curation, 86–87

D

Data
  application, 68
  gathering, 79–81
Decoding
  issues, 383
  parietal lobe involvement, 102
  usage, 29, 74, 101
Deep critical comprehension, meaning, 13

Deep learning, promotion, 343
Dendrites (information receivers),
    activity, 106–108
Details
    extraction, 17
    reading analysis, 352
    remembrance, 12
"Determining Importance" lesson, 368–369
Differentiated instruction techniques,
    teacher usage, 115
Digital resources, usage, 360
Disagreements (academic conversation
    component), 280, 282
Discussion
    benefits, 284–285
    collaborative nature, 316
    facilitation, 147
    usage, 50, 179
Distracting thoughts, 204
Distractions, impact, 383, 384
DOK level questions, usage, 346
Dopamine release, 118, 163–164
"Drive Your Own Reading with
    Metacognition" lesson,
    221–222
Dweck, Carol, 371

E

Elementary readers, information
    evaluation situations, 360–361
Emotional connection, 121
Emotional readiness, 76
Emotional response, 116
Empathy, fostering, 29, 315
Engagement, 74–76
    attention, relationship, 118–119
    increase, 138
    strategies, 117
Enrichment activities, supply, 147
Ethical dilemmas, usage, 344
Evaluation, prerequisite skills, 337
Explicit modeling, importance, 246
Extensions (academic conversation
    component), 280, 282

F

Facts of Five activity, 312
Facts, remembrance, 12
Figurative language, impact, 49
Firing (process), 107
Fishbowl strategy, 289, 313–314
Fluency (literacy component), 6–7
    building block, 10
    focus, avoidance, 250
    improvement, 85
    problems, 383
    support, 9
    usage, 74
From Striving to Thinking (Harvey/Ward), 46, 70
Frontal cortex, 103
Frontal lobe
    examination, 101–102
    impact, 015

G

Gelman, Bernard D., 166
Genetic information, storage, 107
Genre
    access, importance, 47
    ranges, 146
    student exposure, 53–54

Gero, Greg, 394
"Get to Know You" games, usefulness, 41
Goals
    blueprint data basis, 86
    defining, 388–389
    setting, encouragement, 399
Grapheme-phoneme teaching methods, superiority, 113
Grouping, flexibility, 85
Groups, formation, 85
Growth mindset, 371–372
    reader mindset, 375–378
Gruber, Matthias J., 166
Guest readers, invitation, 180

H

Harvey, Stephanie, 46, 70
Higher-order thinking, 167
    promotion, 180
    skills
        development, 121
        requirement, 356
    tasks, 319
    usage, 12
Hippocampus
    engagement, 122
Hippocampus, dopamine release, 118
Hot Seat (role-playing activity), 314
Hypothetical thinking, promotion, 346

I

Ideas
    identification, 141
    reading analysis, 352, 353
Identity, aspects (exploration), 92
"Identity Map" lesson, 92–93
"I Don't Like This" lesson, 404
Importance, determination (metacognitive concept), 22
Inactive readers, active readers (contrast), 195
Independent reading
    cancellation, problem, 58
    lesson, 65
    priorities, 57–59
    selections, 182
    student accountability, methods, 61–62
    success, methods, 60–61
    time, usage, 61
In-depth answers, supply, 19
Inferences
    drawing, 10
    making, 18
    reader usage, timing/usage, 340
    schema support, 144
Inference skills, enhancement, 138
Inferring, comprehension tool, 135
Information
    absorption, 13
    application, 14
    connection, 76–77
    consumption/regurgitation, student avoidance, 14
    evaluation, 342, 357–359
        elementary reader usage, 360–361
        questions, guidance, 358–359
    gathering, 82
    passive receiving, 24
    rote recitation, 12
    synthesis, 10, 291
    visual information, processing, 104
    visualization, 291

Informational texts, reading, 361
"Initial Reading Conferences" lesson, 65
Inquiry-based classrooms, 252
Inquiry-based learning, support, 180
Inquiry-based projects, usage, 174, 179
Instruction
   access, 50–51
   scaffolding, 85
Instructional activities, teacher design, 113
Instructional approaches, tailoring, 71
Intellectual engagement, promotion, 343
Interacting thoughts, 204
Interactive problem-solving tasks, usage, 73
Interactive read-alouds, usage,
      148, 156, 179
Interactive reading activities, 174
Interest
   brain, relationship, 116–123
   material engagement, 117
"Interests and the Brain" lesson, 127–128
Intrinsically motivated students, material
     relevance/interest, 74
Intrinsic motivation, 122–123
   increase, emotional engagement
     (impact), 121
"It's Too Hard" lesson, 405
I Wonder Boards, usage, 179

J

Judgment, fear (absence), 362

K

Kim, James, 133
Knowledge
   absence, 134
   acquisition, 76–77
   application, 30
   base, information (connection), 135
   integration (reading analysis), 353
Knowledge Gap, The (Wexler), 152
Know Want Learn chart (KWL chart), 77,
     149, 156, 249

L

Language
   diversities, impact, 48
   sound to letter matching, 113
Learning
   autonomous learning, 200–201
   collaborative learning, 155–156,
     177, 203
   environment
     creation, 69
     self-regulated learner
       optimization, 231
   experience, enrichment, 77
   lifelong learning
     abilities, 286
     promotion, 96
     skills, promotion, 99
   neuroplasticity, relationship, 114–115
   perseverance/resilience, building, 99
   plans, teacher creation, 114–115
   student responsibility (increase),
     questions (asking), 252
Lessons
   critical thinking, integration, 364
   delivery, improvement, 73
"Let's Talk Text" lesson, 322–323
Letters, decoding, 29
Letter-sound correspondences, 113

Library
    authors/perspectives/characters, ensuring, 82–83
    continuous student input, availability, 83
    displays, creation, 83
    importance/emphasis, 52–53
    thematic book collections, creation, 83
Lifelong learning
    abilities, 286
    promotion, 96
    skills, promotion, 99, 139
Literacy
    activities, engagement, 87
    block/routine, establishment, 97
    components, 5–7
        knowledge, accumulation, 10
    curiosity, impact, 166
    development, 85, 91
        support, 146
    discussion, 4
    education, gaps, 10
    goal, 143
    improvement, 5
    instruction, 72, 87, 111
        brain education, integration, 124
        tailoring, 92
    research, emphasis, 135
    self-reflection, 208
    skills, enhancement, 124
Literary environment, curation, 177
Literary journals, usage, 180
Literature
    advanced literature, reading difficulty, 390
    circles, impact, 182–188
    mandatory assignments, issues, 387

M

Main idea
    identification, importance, 23
    schema support, 144
"Making Connections" lesson, 273–274
"Making Inferences" lesson, 366–367
Material
    interest, assessment, 116
    long-term retention, 122
Maturity/sensitivity, 76
Meaning
    construction, 26
    making, 14–17
Medical terms/conditions, reading, 11–13
Memory
    age, relationship, 49
    aids, 73
    consolidation processes, strengthening, 118
    enhancement, 200
    exercises, student engagement, 49
    improvement, 137–138
    retention, enhancement, 117
    support, 134
Mental images (creation), connection making (impact), 259–260
Mental model, construction (difficulty), 134
Mental processing, 72–73
    interconnection, 73
Metacognition, 123, 191–192
    activities, 217–219
    adaptability, 203
    analysis, 196–198
    complex texts, relationship, 213–216
    components, 194
    defining, 192–198

Metacognition (*Continued*)
   discussion, opportunities (providing), 210–211
   efforts, long-term impact, 417
   enhancement, 138
   importance, 98, 411
   motivation, 202
   power/importance, 193
   strategies, usage, 398–399
   support, 212
   teaching, 364
     advice, 203–212
     benefits, 198–203
   usage, 15, 359, 375
Metacognitive approaches, 24
Metacognitive awareness, 98, 123
   fostering, 231
Metacognitive cycle, 234–243
   Assess Plan Approach Reflect, 236–238
   example, 239–240
     Assess Plan Approach Reflect, 241–243
Metacognitive mind map, creation, 219
Metacognitive schema, 139, 142
Metacognitive skills
   fostering, 123
   transfer, 202
Metacognitive strategies, 111, 123, 225–234, 415
   explicit teaching, 209–210, 229–231, 235
   impact, 243–269
   non-metacognitive strategies, contrast, 199
   purpose, 229
   understanding, 227–228
   usage, timing, 231–234

Metacognitive thinkers, cultivation, 408
Methodical thinking, 396
Motivation, 74–76
   curiosity, impact, 163–164
   influence, 75
   student interest, impact, 146
Motivation, importance, 45–46
Multi-cultural (MC) classroom library, growth, 56
Multimedia exploration/real-world connections, usage, 155
Multiple-meaning words, impact, 49
"Multiple Perspectives" lesson, 161
Myelin formation, stabilization function, 109

N

Narrative context, 258
Needs-based, small group reading (power), 85
Nerve fibers, insulation, 109
Neural neuroplasticity, curiosity-driven learning (impact), 121
Neural pathways, strengthening, 108
"Neuron and Dendrites" lesson, 126–127
Neurons
   activity, 106–108
   branches, 110
Neuroplasticity, 121–122
   importance, 109
   learning, relationship, 114–115
   understanding, 110–111
Neuroscience-informed education, 111
News articles, reading, 360
Non-academic goals, 85

Non-active reading, 26–27
Non-fiction articles, reading, 109
Nonfiction books, interest, 91
Nonfiction texts, exploration, 153–154
Non-metacognitive strategies, meta-
　　　cognitive strategies (contrast), 199
Nucleus, activity, 108

O

Object recognition, 104
Observations, real-time data, 79
Occipital lobe, 104–105
Occipitotemporal cortex, 103
One-on-one conferences, usage, 81
One-on-one tutoring, 115
Open-ended questions
　asking, 180–181
　chart, 304–307
　impact, 308–309, 341–342
　list, 20
　talks, involvement, 344
　usage, 19, 302–303, 364
Open questions, usage, 18
Opinions, justification
　　　(encouragement), 345
Orthographic processing, 113

P

Parietal lob, examination, 102–103
Partner metacognitive listening
　　　activity, 218–219
Peer collaboration, opportunities
　　　(providing), 400
Peer interactions, 80
Peer rejection/acceptance, navigation, 318
Performance metrics, 99
Performing, stress, 383
Perseverance, 124
　building, 99
Persistence
　building, 371–372
　fostering, 397–398
　modeling, 400–401
Personal empathy
　creation, 97–98
　fostering, 95
Personal growth (promotion), open-ended
　　　questions (impact), 308
Personal identity exploration,
　　　literacy (integration), 93
Personalized literacy instruction, 89
Personalized reading goals, 85
Personalized word lists, 88
Perspective
　diversity, encouragement, 180
　power, 129
Phonemes, dissection, 112
Phonemic awareness (literacy
　　　component), 6, 114
　building block, 10
　support, 9
Phonics (literacy component), 6
　building block, 10
　support, 9
Phonological awareness, 112–113
Phonological processing, 102
Positive emotional connections,
　　　impact, 121
Positive reinforcement, achievement, 75
Posterior superior temoral cortex, 103
Power, reading (equivalence)
　lesson, 36–37
Power, reading (relationship), 28, 30–31

Prediction
    comprehension tool, 135
    questions, facilitation, 3345
    schema support, 144
Prefrontal cortex, responsibility, 167–168
Pre-reading activities, 156–157
Print, recognition, 104
Prior knowledge, 76–77
    activation, 119–120
    assessment, 246, 249
    connection
        absence, 135–136
        inability, 8
Problem-based learning, requirements, 362
Problem-solving, effectiveness, 138, 202
Procedural schema, 139, 141
Procedures, knowledge, 141
Productive struggle, encouraging, 397–398
Progress, celebration, 75
Project-based learning
    activities, impact, 86, 183–184
    requirements, 362
Projects
    choice, 184
    providing, 147
Purposeful thinking, 396

Q

Qualitative data (text complexity measurement), 215
Quantitative data (text complexity measurement), 215
Question-driven discussions, usage, 174
Questioning, comprehension tool, 135

Questions (questioning)
    academic conversation component, 280, 282
    answering, modeling (consideration), 19
    answers, relationship, 17–18
    asking, 250–253
        encouragement, 253
        metacognitive concept, 22
        metacognitive strategy, 243, 244
        timing, 254
    authentic questioning, 251
    comparative questions, usage, 345–346
    contexts, 256–257
    discussion, connection, 295
    focus, 267–268
        student decisions, 230
    guidance, 358–359
    improvement, 301–309
    integration methods, 253–254
    parking lot implementation, 180
    prediction questions, facilitation, 345
    reader ability, 29–30
    reflection questions, usage, 209
    Socratic questioning, usage, 346
    teaching, advice, 253–255
    techniques, 341, 343–347
    thick questions, thin questions (contrast), 254
    tiered questioning, studies, 347–348
    tiered questions, usage, 19
    types, 252
    usage, 251

R

Ranganath, Charan, 166
Reacting thoughts, 204, 205

Reactions (academic conversation component), 280, 282
Reader-involved skill, 24
Reader mindsets, 373–375
   building, 384–386
   cultivation, 371–372
   culture, fostering, 397–401
   development
     student teaching, 378
   discussion, 379
   fostering, 385
   growth mindset, contrast, 375–377
   impact, 382–384
   metacognition, usage, 375
   origins, differences, 377
   scope, differences, 377
   strategy, 387–389
   student involvement, 380–382
   student teaching, 374
   teaching, reasons, 378–379
   usage, 386–393
Readers
   active readers, creation, 24
   authors, dynamic interaction, 22
   barriers, 383
   blueprint, 69–81
     data, gathering, 79–81
   blueprint, components, 71–78
   building, art, 410
   complaints, 387
   critical thinking, 335–336
   curiosity, relationship, 169–171
   engagement ability, impeding, 382–383
   inference, usage (timing/reason), 340
   interruptions/distractions, 119
   knowledge, 70
   learning, 40–42
   metacognitive strategies, usage, 229–230
   productive struggle, encouragement, 397–398
   proficiency/thoughtfulness, increase, 21
   questions, usage, 61
   reading problems, 4
   short-term small group instruction, impact, 85
   students, equivalence, 395
   task, connection, 216
"Reader's Brain" lesson, 125–126
"Reader's Mindset" lesson, 403
Read, Imagine, Describe, Evaluate, Repeat (RIDER) strategy, usage, 247–248
Reading
   ability, 15, 70
     curiosity, relationship, 168–169
   annotation, modeling, 355
   approach, transformation, 31
   assigned readings, issues, 387
   behavior, 80
   brain, relationship, 95
   challenges, 183
     overcoming, reader mindset (usage), 386–393
   changes, adaptation, 395
   choice, 60
   classroom, schema (usage), 145–152
   close reading (support strategy), 352–354
   conceptualization, 75
   connections, 260–261
   consumption, reading comprehension (contrast/confusion), 11–14
   continuation, 4
   culture, creation, 2

Reading (*Continued*)
   curiosity (promotion), open-ended questions (impact), 181
   defining, 3
   essence, 2
   focus, 256
   goals, 183
      defining, 388–389
   groups, 183
   guided reading levels, usage, 396
   identity, building, 31
   independent reading priorities, 57–59
   intellectual endeavor, 28
   interventions, analysis, 8
   journey
      roadblocks, inevitability, 408
      understanding, 67
   levels, variation (inclusion), 83
   lists, customization, 86–87
   love, curiosity (relationship), 176
   material, development differences (consideration), 49
   memory, 12
   metacognitive strategies, role, 227–228
   needs, 70
   personal experience, 28–29
   power, equivalence
      lesson, 36–37
   power, relationship, 28, 30–31
   pre-reading activities, 156–157
   reflection, 197
   safe environment, creation, 399–400
   schema, activation, 148–152
   science, 14
   sessions, student preparation/focus, 381
   stamina, issues, 59–60
   strategies, 23, 80, 352–353
      skills, contrast, 21–27
      support, 88
      usage, 381
   student support, 393
   success, 52
   tasks, goal setting/reflection (usage), 399
   teacher mindset, 394–397
      components, 394
   thinking, equivalence, 3–5, 22, 28–30
      lesson, 35
   transformative power, 385
   understanding/purpose, 354
   voices, teaching, 60
Reading comprehension, 136
   curiosity, link, 171–175
   fostering, 24, 173–175
   schema, impact, 142–145
   skills, improvement, 50
   strategies, 135
   success, 117
Reading Is Me
   lesson, 34
   relationship, 28–29
Reading skills, 23, 74, 144
   complexity, 115
   support, 88
   text-centric reading skills, 23
"Reading Uncertainties" lesson, 222
Reading with a Pencil, 355
"Read, Think, Talk" lesson, 323–324
Real reading, fake reading
   contrast, 35
   teaching, 60
Real-world experiences, connection, 74
Recall, support, 134

Recording sheets/logs, usage (avoidance), 60
Reflection
    metacognition component, 194
    questions, usage, 209
    usage, 151
Reflective questions, engagement, 345
Reflective thinking practices, 364
Relationships
    building, 69
    foundation, 395–396
    importance, 41
Repetition, usage, 112
Resilience, building, 99
Response notebooks, usage, 180
Responsibility, release, 235
Retention, improvement, 75
Risk-taking
    encouragement, 364
    environment safety, creation, 399–400
Rubric categories, explanation, 267

S

Save the Last Word strategy, 311
Scaffolded instruction, providing, 148
Schema, 129
    absence, consideration, 17
    access, 19, 134
    activation, 148–152
    background knowledge, relationship, 133
    building, 152–157
        strategies, 153–157
    defining, 131–139
    definition, 15
    example, 132
    importance, 14, 134–137, 342
    influence, 142–145
    significance, extension, 130
    student
        activation, 134
        development, 132
    types, 139
    understanding, 41, 139–145
    usage, 28–29, 44–45
        benefits, 137–139
        steps, 145–152
Science of reading, brain (relationship), 112–115
Science, social studies (integration), 154–155
Scientific articles, reading difficulty, 390
Self-assessmsent, ability (development), 201
Self-awareness (promotion), open-ended questions (impact), 308
Self-directed exploration, 162
Self-directed learning, intrinsic motivation support, 122
Self-perception, usage, 381–382
Self-reflection, encouragement, 208–209
Self-regulated learners, learning environment optimization, 231
Self-regulated learning (SRL), 122–123
    facilitation, 142
Self-regulation (metacognition component), 194, 197–198
Self-stimulation, increase, 45
Sentence
    extraction, 269
    reading, continuation, 106
    stems, providing, 297–298

Sequences, knowledge, 141
Shared interests, basis, 85
Short-term small group instruction, impact, 85
Short-term working memory, 72–73
Situation model representation, construction, 248–249
Slang, impact, 49
Small-group instruction, usage, 316
Small group work, 115
Snowball Discussion, 314
Social conversations, academic conversations (contrast), 279
Social cues/expectations, differences, 278
Socratic questioning, usage, 346
Socratic seminar, identification, 175
Source reliability, 358
Speaking/language production, 101
Speech, understanding (temporal lobe involvement), 103
Speed Dating activity, 310–311
Spelling, parietal lobe involvement, 102
Spoken-language areas, 103
Spontaneity, increase, 45
Stakeholders, unified vision creation, 414
Standardized tests
    issues, 387
    reading difficulty, 390
Status of the class routine, implementation, 61
Stoplight Discussion (visual/participatory method), 311–312
Story (stories)
    articles, comparison, 360
    cultural relevance, importance, 49

Strategies
    importance/focus, 21
    metacognitive concepts, 22
Stress reduction, 203
Structure (reading analysis), 352–353
Student-centered environments, emphasis, 362
Student-centric metacognitive strategies, text-centric metacognitive strategies (contrast), 199
Student-centric strategies, 22
Student-led book recommendations, 184
Students
    access, allowance, 51–57
    architect role, 69
    comprehension
        improvement, 73
        increase, 5
        struggle, 8
    conferencing, independent reading time (usage), 61
    confidence, increase/building, 3, 75
    connections
        assessment, 266
        consideration, questions/prompts (usage), 264–265
        encouragement, 260
        making, 265
    cultural experiences, 87
    developmental stage, consideration, 76
    differences, embracing, 317
    discussions, focus, 297
    empowerment, 87, 91
        personalized goals, impact, 85
    engagement, deepening, 19
    environment, fostering, 412–413

goals, setting, 211
grouping, 318
information, consumption/regurgitation (avoidance), 14
interests, incorporation, 86
intrinsic motivation, enhancement, 123
literacy skills, enhancement, 124
progress, monitoring, 211
questions, asking (encouragement), 253, 347
readers, equivalence, 395
reading
    blueprint, examination, 71–72
    permission, 57–62
relationships, building, 43
representation, 55–56
roles (secret missions), supply, 299
sentence stems, providing, 297–298
success, roadblocks, 3
support, 51
    in-depth answers, supply, 19
surveys/interest inventories, usage, 173
thinkers, encouragement, 398
thinking ability, 14–15
understanding, 40–42, 80
Student schema
    absence, consideration, 17
    access, 134
    building, 152–157
    derivation, 134
    development, 132
    impact, 14–15
    knowledge, 145–146
    presence/absence, 147–148
Subjects, content-rich curriculum, 133
Sub-skills, usage, 74
Success
    factors, 44–51
    metacognitive strategies, 225–226
    setup, 39
"Successful Conversations" lesson, 321
Summarization, 234
    comprehension tool, 135
    schema support, 144
    usage, 151
Surface-level activities, 89
Survey, Question, Read, Recite, Review (SQ3R), 334, 335
Synthesis, prerequisite skills, 338
Synthesizing (metacognitive concept), 22
"Synthesizing" lesson, 367–368

T

Task completion strategies, knowledge, 141
T-chart activity, usage, 35
Teachers
    critical thinking, 334
    questions
        example, 15–16
        reflection, 18–19
    stakeholder support, 412
Teachers Pay Teachers, 69
Teaching strategies, 115
Team-building activities, usefulness, 41
Technology, usage, 115
Temporal lobe, 103–104
    management, 105
Temporal/parietal areas, 103
Terminal branches, 108
Testing, usage, 12

Text(s)
    analysis, 342, 350–351, 356–358
        close reading (support strategy),
            352–354
        conversation, combination,
            288–289
    annotating, 150
    background knowledge, connection, 135
    cognitive engagement, 356
    comparative questions, usage, 345–346
    complexity, 213–214
        balancing process, 357
        data, 215
        measurement process, 214–216
    complex texts
        metacognition, relationship, 213–216
        understanding, 217
    comprehension, 15
        facilitation, 138
    connections, 259
    content, student focus, 389
    conversation, 287
    discussion, 275–277, 284–293
        benefits, 315–316
    DOK level questions, usage, 346
    engagement, 197
    ethical dilemmas, incorporation, 345
    extraction, 269
    facts/details, memory, 12
    finding, 41
    grade-level analysis, 351
    handling, challenges, 387–391
    hypothetical thinking, promotion, 346
    information, application, 14
    issue/event, perspectives
        (encouragement), 344–345
    opinions, justification
        (encouragement), 345
    parts, teaching, 286–288
    prediction questions, facilitation, 345
    pre-reading, 343
    providing, 147
    purpose, identification, 388
    range, providing, 412
    reading, 140
        ability, 15
        benefits, identification, 388
    reflection questions, usage, 209
    reflective questions, engagement, 345
    selection, 248–249, 257
    structure
        impact/definition, 48
        schema support, 144
    student choice, 87
    student relationship, 2
    teacher engagement, observations,
        350
    thinking
        annotating, 219
        matching, 218
    thoughts, differentiation, 205–206
    value, discovery, 389
Text-based discussions, 276
Text-based skill, 24
Textbooks, usage (issues), 387
Text-centric metacognitive strategies,
        student-centric metacognitive
        strategies (contrast), 199
Text-centric reading skills, 23
Text-to-self connection, 261, 262, 264
Text-to-text connection, 261, 262, 265
Text-to-world connection, 261, 262, 265

436   Index

Textual conversations
    depth levels, 292
    holding, sentence stems (usage), 298
Thematic book collections, creation, 83
Thematic units
    development, 174
    impact, 86
Theme, schema support, 144
Thick questions, thin questions (contrast), 254
Think-alouds
    demonstrations, importance, 246
    questions, 19
    usage, 150
Thinking
    ability, 14–15
    challenging, 30–31
    examination, 392
    hypothetical thinking, promotion, 346
    methodical thinking, 396
    purposeful thinking, 396
    reader awareness, 230
    reading, equivalence, 3–5, 22, 28–30
        lesson, 35
    sorting types, 218
    text, matching, 218
    types, teaching, 204–205
Thinking about thinking, 227
Thinking out loud, model, 207
Thinking readers
    building, 26
    long-term benefits, 415–416
Thought-provoking questions, posing, 363
Thoughts
    articulation, 203

text, differentiation, 205–206
    types, 204
Tiered questioning, studies, 347–348
Tiered questions, usage, 19
Top Three strategy, 312
True reading, immersion, 1
Trust, building, 318
"Types of Questions" lesson, 273

U

Understanding
    broadening, 315
    enhancement, 137

V

Verbal memory, temporal lobe involvement, 103–104
Vision board, usage, 393
Visual cortex, 109
Visual information, processing, 104
Visualization, 228
    ability, enhancement, 249
    comprehension tool, 135
    effectiveness, 246
    metacognitive concept, 22
    metacognitive strategies, impact, 200, 243, 244, 245–247
    power, display, 250
    schema support, 144
    teaching, factors/tips, 246, 249–253
"Visualization" lesson, 272
Visual processing, occipital lobe involvement, 104
Visuals, sharing, 246

Vocabulary
    absence, 383
    acquisition, improvement, 138
    building, 115, 156
    content-specific vocabulary, 88
    identification/introduction, 246
    knowledge, 74
    literacy component, 7
        building block, 10
        support, 9–10
    pre-teaching, 147
    temporal lobe involvement, 103
Voice/choice, motivators, 46

W

Ward, Annie, 46, 70
Wexler, Natalie, 152–153
What if scenarios, exploration, 346
What I Know, What I Want to Know, What I Learned, 77
"What Is Schema" lesson, 158–159
"What Would You Choose" lesson, 93–94
Within-the-text questions, 256
Wonder Walls, usage, 179
Words
    decoding, 29, 101
    identification, 249
    lists, personalization, 88
    power, 392
    processing, 102
    reading, 4–5
    recognition, temporal lobe involvement, 103
Working memory, roles, 97
Writing, learner struggle, 268
Written texts, semantic structures (handling), 102

Z

Zwiers, Jeff, 276